THE STRUCTURE OF ORGANIZATIONS

The Structure of Organizations

Peter M. Blau

Richard A. Schoenherr

BASIC BOOKS, INC., PUBLISHERS | New York, London

Library of Congress Catalog Card Number: 74–126956

SBN 465–08240–8

Manufactured in the United States of America

History tells us how in that past time
When all things happened, real,
Imaginary, and dubious, a man
Conceived the unconscionable plan

Of making an abridgement of the universe
In a single book and with infinite zest
He towered his screed up, lofty and
Strenuous, polished it, spoke the final verse.

About to offer his thanks to fortune,
He lifted up his eyes and saw a burnished
Disc in the air and realized, stunned,
That somehow he had forgotten the moon.

The story I have told, although a tale,
Can represent the witching spell
So many of us use when at our craft
Of transmuting our life into words.

The essence is always lost. This is the one
Law of every word about inspiration.
Nor will this summary of mine avoid it . . .

BORGES, "The Moon"

PREFACE

Modern organizations are complex structures for coordinating the work of many men in order to achieve specified ends. This book seeks to contribute to the theoretical understanding of the structure of formal organizations on the basis of an empirical analysis of government bureaus—all state employment security agencies in the United States and their local branches.

An organization consists of subunits that are formally differentiated along various lines. An employment security agency, for example, comprises a headquarters, which has several divisions with distinct responsibilities, and numerous local offices throughout the state, where unemployment insurance and employment services are administered to clients. Its employees occupy different positions in which they perform specialized jobs, and they are also distinguished in terms of other criteria, such as official rank, staff and line, or clerical and professional. There is vertical differentiation into hierarchical levels and horizontal differentiation into functional divisions and sections within divisions, as well as a division of labor among positions and a geographical differentiation of offices. This patterned differentiation along several dimensions defines the structure of an organization, and the extent of differentiation indicates structural complexity. Although the existence of differentiated interrelated subdivisions and individual positions is not all that is usually meant by social structure, it is its core.

Attempts to understand organizations pose two important issues, and the dilemma is that it is hardly possible to face either seriously without turning one's back on the other. On the one hand, whatever takes place in organizations is the result of decisions made and actions taken by individuals who enter into social relations and develop group practices which often depart markedly from official procedures. To study the social processes underlying the operations in an organization requires intensive interviewing and observation of its members. The time needed for this undertaking makes it necessary to limit the scope of the inquiry to one organization or to very few, and often indeed to segments within one large organization. On the other hand, an understanding of organizations depends on knowledge of the interdependence of their characteristics—for instance, how size and complexity, separately and in combination, affect various aspects of administration. The investigation of such empirical and theoretical relationships between organizational characteristics clearly requires comparable data from a considerable number of organizations.

The collection of information from many organizations, which is essential for this purpose, is almost impossible without restricting the depth of the inquiry in any one. Even if it were economically feasible to obtain intensive data on interpersonal relations and individual conduct as well as organizational characteristics from a large number of organizations, the welter of information of diverse kinds would defy systematic analysis. Hence, a choice must be made between examining sociopsychological processes within an organization, taking its basic structure as given, and investigating the interdependence among elements in the structure of organizations, while ignoring the details of daily operations and human relations. In the study to be presented we have opted for the second alternative and focus on the interrelated characteristics of organizations that shape their structure.

The assumption implicit in this approach is that formal organizations, as well as other social structures, exhibit regularities that can be analyzed in their own right, independent of any knowledge about the individual behavior of their members. To be sure, organizations cannot think or act; only the people in them can. Any characteristic of an organization is the product of decisions individuals have made; for example, how many supervisors to appoint. However, the formal structure exerts pronounced constraints on these decisions. Thus, the complexity of the organization imposes limits on a manager's freedom of choice in deciding how many supervisors to appoint. But if it is correct that the complexity and other attributes of organizations largely govern the size of the supervisory component in them, it is not necessary to investigate the social and psychological processes by which managers arrive at decisions to appoint supervisors in order to understand why some organizations have more supervisors than others. In this case, it suffices to ascertain the relationship between conditions in organizations and variations in the supervisory component; and the same holds for explaining variations in other organizational characteristics. The empirical findings will furnish a test of the assumption that much of the variation in organizational characteristics can be accounted for by differences in organizational conditions without taking into account how the individual members of these organizations make decisions.

The research on employment security agencies reported here is one of several similar studies of different types of organizations carried out at the Comparative Organization Research Program, University of Chicago, under grants GS 553 and GS 1528 from the National Science Foundation, which are gratefully acknowledged.[1] We are indebted to many officials, assistants, and colleagues for their cooperation and advice. Above all, we want to thank the directors of all state employment security agencies, who without exception extended us their cooperation, and to a number of officials in each agency who willingly devoted several hours to providing us with the needed information. We are grateful to numerous officials in the federal Bureau of Employment Security (now reorganized as part of the Manpower Administration) for advice on the study design and interpretations of preliminary findings as well as for soliciting the cooperation of the state agency directors; our particular thanks to Robert C. Goodwin, who was then the Bureau Administrator, and to H. Daniel Darling, James V. Doucet, Clayton G. Johnson, Malcolm R. Lovell, Jr., Ralph Marks, Forest L. Miller, and Charles E. Odell. The directors of the eleven regional offices of the federal bureau also were most cooperative; the late Joseph Borus and the late Edward C. Stonich of the Chicago office were especially helpful. We are obligated to Albert Aronson, Director of the Division of State Merit Systems, H. E. W., and to Lorraine Eyde and H. Hoover, members of his staff, as well as to Robert Droege and Josephine M. Meers, then at the Bureau of Employment Security, for making their data from a joint study of employment interviewers available and consulting with us.

A number of students at the University of Chicago assisted in the collection, processing, and analysis of the data, and their help is gratefully acknowledged. The data collection was carried out by Judith R. Fritz, Nathalie Funk, Alan Whitney, and the junior author. The following participated in the processing of the data and their preliminary analysis: Deborah Cohen, Anne E. Crowley, Robert E. Fay, Merilee Fritz, Jacques Gellard, Roberta Klatzky, Serena P. Laskin, James MacBeth, Michael McCaskey, Danforth R. Ross, Jay Ross, David Shaw, Kenneth P. Sowinski, and Joseph Thomas. Special credit is due to Sheila R. Klatzky for her great contributions to the statistical analysis and her many insightful suggestions for interpreting the findings. We intended to recognize her important contributions to this book by including her name as our collaborator, but a disagreement with the senior author prompted her to withdraw before the manuscript was being prepared and to refuse collaborative authorship.

We are grateful for advice on statistical problems and for helpful comments on the first draft of the manuscript to the following colleagues:

---

1. This book is C.O.R.P. report No. 12.

Terry N. Clark, James S. Coleman, James J. Fennessey, Robert W. Hodge, Nathan Keyfitz, Marshall W. Meyer, Thomas Pullum, and Peter H. Rossi. We also received valuable advice on the research design from Carol B. Stocking and Eve Weinberg, and on the computer problems from Frank Bamberger. We are indebted for the drawing of graphs and charts to Susan M. Davies and Judith A. Woods, and for an excellent job in preparing the manuscript and typing the many tables as well as the text to Ellen Slaughter. Finally, the senior author owes a debt of gratitude to Judith R. Blau [2] and Pamela L. Blau and the junior author to Judith A. Woods for their understanding and support when we were buried in work on this research.

PETER M. BLAU
RICHARD A. SCHOENHERR

Chicago
August 1970

2. He also wants to acknowledge her gift of a pedometer, which revealed that his pacing while writing the final manuscript covered 320 miles or nearly a mile per printed page.

CONTENTS

Part Four Toward a Theory of Organizations

Appendices

Tables

Figures

PART ONE

The Comparative Study of Organizations

We have only one way to demonstrate that a given phenomenon is the cause of another, viz., to compare the cases in which they are simultaneously present or absent, to see if the variations they represent in these different combinations or circumstances indicate that one depends on the other . . . Since, moreover, social phenomena evidently escape the control of the experimenter, the comparative method is the only one suited to sociology.

DURKHEIM, *The Rules of Sociological Method*

CHAPTER I

Systematic Comparison

In this book we hope to contribute to the theory of organizations on the basis of systematic research. Formal organizations have existed since ancient times. Bureaucracies in which government officials were formally organized developed in ancient Rome and Egypt. But the proliferation of large formal organizations and their penetration into nearly all phases of human existence are relatively recent phenomena. The greatest accomplishments of modern society—technological progress, superior standard of living, high level of education—would not be possible without formal organizations in which the coordinated efforts of men achieve results beyond the capacity of their separate endeavors. At the same time, organizations are also instrumental in perpetrating the worst horrors of modern times, whether they be genocide or nuclear war. For people to defend themselves against powerful organizations that threaten them they must in turn coordinate their opposition by establishing organizations of their own.

Organizations are at the roots of power in the broadest sense today, which is what makes understanding them so important for contemporary life. There are different approaches to attaining a better knowledge of organizations. The man of practical affairs might do so by acquiring more experience in administrative practices and policies. The artist provides fresh insights into the working of bureaucracy by portraying its impact on

3

the human mind, as Kafka has done. The social scientist's road to understanding organizations is to conduct research on them, and he achieves his goal of improved understanding by deducing theoretical principles that explain his research findings. We, as social scientists, will follow this procedure.

Although our aim is to advance theoretical knowledge about organizations, most of the book presents an analysis of empirical data from a study of government bureaus. For it is our conviction that systematic theory must be grounded in and derived from systematic empirical research. In Part Four, we attempt to construct a deductive theory based on the preceding empirical analysis and to justify the claim that the theoretical generalizations inferred from research on one group of organizations also apply to other kinds of organizations. In this chapter we will outline our approach and research procedures.

Approach

The study of organizations may be approached with two fundamentally different questions. One type of question that can be asked is how the various conditions in an organization affect individual conduct or human relations. Merton, for example, raises this problem and analyzes why certain bureaucratic characteristics stifle individual initiative and foster ritualistic overconformity.[1] Other studies show how pressures in formal organizations influence the daily social contacts among employees and the informal organization that develops in their work groups, thereby modifying the performance of duties.

Instead of investigating how the characteristics of organizations, taken as given, influence human behavior and informal groups, however, one can ask an entirely different question, namely, what produced these characteristics in the first place or why organizations develop some attributes rather than others. This is the problem to which Weber addressed himself in his analysis of the historical conditions and structural interrelations that give rise to the characteristics typically found in bureaucracies.[2] Though Weber largely neglects the problem on which Merton centers attention—the unanticipated consequences of bureaucratic features for individual performance—he defines as problematical what Merton accepts as given: why bureaucracies have certain features.

1. Robert K. Merton, *Social Theory and Social Structure,* 3d ed. (New York: Free Press, 1968), pp. 249–260.
2. Max Weber, *Essays in Sociology* (New York: Oxford University Press, 1946), pp. 196–244.

Weber's theoretical discussion of bureaucracy has been criticized for presenting an idealized conception of it and for examining only its formal attributes and ignoring the informal modifications that can always be observed if one looks at the ways in which empirical organizations actually operate. In response to this criticism, a number of sociologists started to investigate empirically the informal relations and unofficial patterns that emerge in bureaucracies, with special emphasis on the changes formal procedures frequently undergo in actual practice.[3] Two important traits of this research tradition are that the substantive focus is on the informal organization of work groups and that the method employed is the case study. To show the contrasting implications of this approach and Weber's, we must look at the relationship between formal and informal organization.

Whenever groups of men associate with one another their relations and conduct become socially organized, but not every collectivity has a formal organization. Social organization may either emerge in the course of social interaction without explicit design or be deliberately established by men to accomplish certain ends; the latter is referred to as a formal organization. The streetcorner groups and cliques in a neighborhood exhibit organized patterns of social relations and activities, as does the class structure of a society, although in neither case has the social structure been established deliberately. But if the members of a corner gang explicitly organize a social athletic club, or if the workers in a factory organize themselves into a union, they establish a formal organization. Work organizations are those whose members are full-time employees, such as government bureaus and private firms of all sorts, and Weber's analysis is essentially concerned with these. The distinguishing criterion of a formal organization is the existence of explicit procedures for mobilizing and coordinating the efforts of men in the pursuit of given objectives.

Not everything that goes on in formal organizations follows an explicit design, however. Within formal organizations informal organizations arise, because the daily social interaction and activities in the various work groups give rise to regularities of their own and thus manifest an implicit social structure. The study of informal organization typically seeks to explain the characteristic patterns that emerge in the work groups of formal organizations (for example, the informal norms restricting output), whereas Weber seeks to explain why formal organizations themselves de-

---

3. See, for example, Philip Selznick, *TVA and the Grass Roots* (Berkeley: University of California Press, 1949); Alvin W. Gouldner, *Patterns of Industrial Bureaucracy* (Glencoe: Free Press, 1954); and Peter M. Blau, *The Dynamics of Bureaucracy,* 2d ed. (Chicago: University of Chicago Press, 1963).

velop certain characteristics (for example, a distinctive hierarchy of authority). Although the investigations of informal organization that have been carried out have enriched our understanding of organizational life by explicating the social processes in work groups, they have simultaneously diverted attention from the fundamental problem that Weber poses. This is largely the result of the case study approach.

We shall return to Weber's problem formulation and inquire why formal organizations exhibit certain structures by analyzing the interdependence of various organizational attributes. A case study of one organization cannot do that. It must take the characteristics of the organization under observation as given and cannot investigate what conditions produced these characteristics, for it lacks the necessary comparative data about organizations with different characteristics. To be sure, the study of the influence of bureaucratic conditions on the activities of individuals and their social interaction also requires comparing activities and social interaction under different conditions. But differences in conditions that affect daily practice and informal relations usually can be found in one organization, for instance, variations in the emphasis on formal rules, in closeness of supervision, or in the use of statistical evaluation procedures. The attributes that characterize the organization itself, on the other hand, are by definition represented only once in a single organization. It has only one personnel system, only one size, only one hierarchy of authority, which makes it impossible to obtain clues about the interrelations between organizational characteristics in a case study. To answer questions such as whether the division of labor affects the number of levels in the hierarchy and under which conditions it does obviously requires observations from more than one organization at one time.

The study of the interdependence between organizational characteristics, which is the first step in building a systematic theory to explain why organizations exhibit various attributes, requires some comparison of different organizations. The comparison may take the form of tracing the development of bureaucracies at different historical periods and in different nations, which is Weber's approach; or of analyzing two contrasting types of organization, as Stinchcombe does; [4] or of examining the effects of change on organizations, which is illustrated by Burns and Stalker's study; [5] or of collecting quantitative data on many organizations and applying multivariate analysis to them. The last approach has come to be

---

4. Arthur L. Stinchcombe, "Bureaucratic and Craft Administration of Production," *Administrative Science Quarterly,* 4 (1959): 168–187.

5. Tom Burns and G. M. Stalker, *The Management of Innovation* (London: Tavistock Publications, 1961).

used only during the past decade or so by a number of research workers in England and in this country,[6] and it is the one here adopted.

The comparative approach to the study of organizations, as the term is used here, refers not to international comparisons but to systematic comparisons of a large number of organizations designed to determine how variations in some organizational conditions are associated with differences in others. For example, in what other respects do organizations that vary in size differ? If several characteristics of organizations tend to occur together, which is often the case, one wants to find out which of these associations are spurious and which reveal actual influences of one condition on another. Multivariate analysis provides the information from which such inferences about actual influences can be made, provided we make certain assumptions. The procedure used for this purpose is explicated later. We raise the issue now to point out that multivariate analysis requires comparable data on a fairly large number of organizations. This requirement precludes the possibility of obtaining detailed intensive information on individual behavior and daily operations in every organization under consideration. No data have been collected on the attitudes of individual members of organizations, their informal relations, the group structures that emerge among them, or the unofficial modifications of formal procedures in daily practice. In other words, the very problems on which case studies of organizations have concentrated attention cannot be examined in this research. By sacrificing knowledge about these problems, however, the comparative approach makes it possible to answer questions case studies cannot and contributes to knowledge about the interdependence of the basic features of formal organizations.

In short, this study follows Weber's lead in defining its problem as seeking to explain the interrelated attributes of formal organizations, rather than the informal organization of work groups within organizations. It departs from Weber in applying contemporary methods of social research to the investigation of this problem. Quantitative analysis of data collected in a survey of organizations is employed to infer, for instance, what organizational conditions influence the decentralization of authority, just as the

---

6. See, for example, Joan Woodward, *Management and Technology* (London: H.M.S.O., 1958); Stanley H. Udy, Jr., *Organization of Work* (New Haven: Human Relations Area Files Press, 1959); Theodore R. Anderson and Seymour Warkov, "Organizational Size and Functional Complexity," *American Sociological Review,* 26 (1961): 23–28; D. S. Pugh et al., "Dimensions of Organization Structure," *Administrative Science Quarterly,* 13 (1968): 65–105; and Richard H. Hall et al., "Organizational Size, Complexity, and Formalization," *American Sociological Review,* 32 (1967): 903–912.

analysis of conventional survey data on individuals is used to infer, say, which background characteristics of individuals govern their chances of occupational success. Quantitative research is often juxtaposed to exploratory studies, but the contrast is misleading. The opposite of an exploratory study, which may use more or less quantitative procedures, is one that tests hypotheses derived from a rigorous theory. Existing theoretical analyses of organizations, although they suggest some hypotheses for research, are not sufficiently rigorous to imply unequivocal hypotheses through which the theories themselves could be tested. Hence, the present research must be considered exploratory, though it employs quantitative methods. It does not test a rigorous theory of organizations by confirming or invalidating empirical predictions logically implied by the theory. Instead, it explores various problem areas with the aim of using the empirical findings as a basis for constructing a systematic theory of organizations. The conceptions of earlier theorists, notably Weber's, served as the guidelines for selecting the questions raised in the investigation, some of which may be briefly illustrated.

The differentiation in organizations is a problem of central concern. Many of the basic characteristics of formal organizations Weber outlined are manifestations of various aspects of differentiation: the allocation of responsibilities to jurisdictions, the division of labor, the hierarchy of authority, to name only the most important ones. Indeed, the fundamental conception of formally organizing complex large-scale responsibilities entails two dimensions of differentiation: the subdivision of the total responsibilities to simplify individual tasks and permit the application of expert knowledge in the performance of specialized duties, on the one hand, and a hierarchy of official authority to effect the coordination needed as the result of this subdivision, on the other. What are the major conditions in organizations that determine the extent of differentiation along various lines? How are different kinds of differentiation related? Differentiation implies structural complexity. Does such complexity raise administrative overhead, as previous studies suggest? Since there are various manifestations of differentiation and various kinds of administrative overhead, the important question is which of the former affect which of the latter.

We will also examine the differences in organizations associated with variations in their size. Is there an economy of scale even in government bureaus? Are large organizations typically more differentiated and more complex than smaller ones? Do size and complexity have parallel or opposite effects on administration, or perhaps some of each? The over-all effect of size on a given dependent variable can be dissected into direct and indirect influences, and sometimes size can be shown to exert opposite influences on the same organizational attribute—one direct and one mediated by an intervening variable, or both mediated by different intervening variables. Such findings permit inferences about the dynamics underlying the formal structure, which are of considerable theoretical interest. The implicit assumption that size is an antecedent that affects other characteristics of the organizations studied rather than vice versa will be supported with empirical evidence.

The standardization of the performance of tasks through formalized procedures is commonly considered to be a mark of bureaucratization, and so is the centralization of authority in the hands of top management. But do these two expressions of bureaucratization actually occur together? Generally, does formalization inevitably increase bureaucratic rigidity of all kinds, or do formalized procedures sometimes go together with greater exercise of discretion? Formal regulations are impersonal mechanisms of control, which raises the question whether they substitute for direct supervision by managers and thus achieve savings in personnel. Another impersonal control mechanism only very recently introduced into white-collar offices is the automation of operations through the installation of computers. How does this technological innovation, automation, influence the centralization of decision-making in the organization and the services it provides to the public?

The structure of large organizations comprises interrelated substructures that have a certain degree of autonomy. There are a number of functional divisions, and there are often also a number of branches at various distances from the headquarters. These subunits can be analyzed separately to determine whether their internal structures exhibit the same regularities as those observed for the over-all structure or different ones. For example, is the relationship between vertical and horizontal differentiation within branches and within divisions similar to that observed for the entire organization? What bearing do differences in functions among divisions have on their internal structure? A problem of special interest is to ascertain the influences exerted by the organizational context—that is, the specific larger organization of which subunits are a part—on the subunits' internal structure. To illustrate: how do an organization's size and other characteristics affect the pattern of supervision within branches?

Another social context is the broader environment in which an organization operates as well as the environment of the various communities in which its branches operate. Characteristics of the environment can be expected to affect organizations in several ways. Thus, it has been suggested that organizations adapt to more complex environments by developing more complex structures, a hypothesis that will be tested. The characteristics of the population in an organization's environment define both the potential demand for its services and the labor market that supplies its manpower. Which population groups exhibit the greatest need for, or interest in, the services the organization supplies? Which characteristics of the population in the labor market affect the organization's opportunities to fill different positions? A general question is whether the influences of the local environment on branches parallel those of the wider environment in the area of jurisdiction on the entire organization.

These illustrations suffice to give a broad overview of the topics to be discussed, although no attempt was made to cover the content of every chapter. The topics were indicated largely by concrete questions in order to emphasize that the research is not designed to test a systematic theory through the hypotheses it implies but essentially asks questions to be answered by the empirical findings. We have tried to raise problems of theoretical significance, many of which were inspired by the previous literature. The intensive analysis of the quantitative data collected to explore these problems is intended as the raw material for developing a rigorous theory of organizations. In the concluding two chapters, we start to build a systematic theory of formal organizations under which the major empirical findings can be subsumed, and the theoretical generalizations are tested with some new data.

In theory, we are interested in organizations in general. In reality, however, there are no organizations in general, only organizations of various kinds. Since it is, of course, impossible to obtain information on all organizations, a limited number must be selected for empirical research. Ideally, a theory of organizations should be based on data from a representative sample of all types of organizations, but it is not possible to specify the universe of all organizations of all types from which such a sample could be drawn. Hence, an a priori decision must circumscribe the organizations to be investigated. The two major alternatives are to select several different types—perhaps all employers of more than 100 persons in a given area—or only one major type. (In either case, data may be collected from all cases or from a sample.) The obvious advantage of the first alternative is that it draws on a wider range of organizations. Its important disadvantage is that the influences exerted by type and by other organizational characteristics become easily confounded. For example, because some types of organizations, such as steel firms, are so much larger than others, such as schools, a study including both plus other diverse types cannot readily disentangle the influence of size from that of type on other organizational characteristics. There is less danger that correlated biases of this kind distort findings in a study confined to a homogeneous category of organizations. Moreover, examining organizations of one type throughout the country rather than several types in a limited area—and the cost of studying several types in the entire country is virtually prohibitive—makes it possible to investigate the significance of variations in environment. These considerations prompted us to choose the second alternative and conduct research on one type of government bureau, collecting data from all cases rather than a sample.[7]

The organizations selected for study are the fifty-three employment security agencies in the United States, one in each state and those in the District of Columbia, Puerto Rico, and the Virgin Islands.[8] These fifty-three state agencies, which operate under federal laws and some federal supervision but are basically autonomous, are responsible for paying unemployment insurance benefits and providing public employment services. The average agency consists of a headquarters with seven major divisions and more than forty local offices. The fifty-three roof organizations (the entire agencies) are the units of analysis in Part Two, whereas the 1,201 local offices meeting minimum criteria of size and complexity, or the 387 major functional divisions, are the units of analysis in Part Three. One of this large number of local offices was the subject of a case study carried out by the senior author twenty years ago, and his acquaintance with the daily work in employment security offices stemming from that time was one of the reasons for settling on this government agency for the present research.

The empirical data pertain only to one type of government bureau. How then can we hope to derive theoretical generalizations from the findings that apply also to other organizations? The answer is that generalizing beyond the existing evidence is in the very nature of theorizing. If numerous different empirical findings can be accounted for by a single general proposition, the theorist is emboldened to advance this proposition as a theoretical generalization that is presumed to apply to other situations than the ones from which it has been derived.[9] To be sure, the data on employment

---

7. The Comparative Organization Research Program at the University of Chicago, of which Blau is director, is carrying out a number of similar projects, each devoted to one type of organization—other government agencies, hospitals, department stores, universities and colleges—in the expectations of making some systematic comparisons when the individual studies are completed.

8. The only other agency, the one on Guam, was excluded because of its very small size. It has fewer than a dozen employees, in contrast to an average size of close to 1,200. The term "state agency" will be used for the sake of brevity for all cases, although three jurisdictions are not states.

9. Our conception of theorizing is most directly derived from R. B. Braithwaite, *Scientific Explanation* (Cambridge, Eng.: University Press, 1953).

security agencies cannot establish that the generalizations derived from them also apply to other organizations. This can only be established by testing the hypotheses in other organizations. A limited test of this kind, reported in the final chapter, confirms the validity of the main generalizations for at least one other type of government bureau. Only further empirical tests will tell whether the generalizations to be advanced also apply to other types of organizations.

The many forms of organized social life differ in varying degrees, and theoretical generalizations about them vary with respect to the number of different types for which they make accurate predictions. Employment security agencies in 1966, when the data were collected, are undoubtedly quite similar to, though not identical with, the same agencies at an earlier or a later date. The differences become more pronounced as one moves to other American government bureaus; government bureaus in other countries; other work organizations, such as private firms; other formal organizations, such as unions; and social systems that are not formal organizations, such as communities. The theoretical generalizations derivable from the empirical regularities observed in any one type may be conceived of as a hierarchy, with many propositions being applicable only to the various cases of this type, and with increasingly fewer principles on successively higher levels being applicable to ever wider circles of different types. It is not known in advance how broad the scope of a given proposition is, though the use of abstract concepts in theoretical propositions—for example, "differentiation" rather than "number of local offices in the agency" —is designed to increase the likelihood that the scope will be broad. Our endeavor is, of course, to capture in the major generalizations theoretical principles of wide scope, but it would be foolhardy to hope that these propositions will make correct predictions for all kinds of organizations. The explicit statement of the major generalizations inferred from our research is intended as a step toward the development of more widely applicable theoretical propositions that modify ours on the basis of future research on other types of organizations.

Data

Initial contacts were made with senior officials in the U.S. Bureau of Employment Security to solicit their cooperation with the research in the summer of 1965. In consultation with these officials, a pilot study was arranged, consisting of personal visits by two research assistants to all eleven regional offices of the federal bureau. Inasmuch as these regional offices are in close contact with the state agencies in their regions and have much information about them, it was possible to learn a lot about the state agencies during these visits. Moreover, the pilot study provided valuable experience in the novel procedure of gathering data about organizations in short interviews with key informants.

At the end of the pilot study, a questionnaire for data collection in the state agencies was prepared and revised in consultation with officials at the regional office in Chicago and at the bureau in Washington. After being assured of the confidentiality of the information about individual agencies to be collected, the administrator of the federal bureau sent a two-page letter to every state agency director explaining our research and recommending cooperation. Another letter of recommendation was sent to the agency directors by the president of the Interstate Conference of Employment Security Administrators, an association of the state agencies entirely independent of the federal bureau.

Data collection was carried out by three experienced research assistants —sociology graduate students at the University of Chicago—in personal visits to all but two agencies during the first quarter of 1966. A letter requesting cooperation and a telephone call confirming the appointment preceded every visit. (Information from Alaska and Hawaii was collected by mail questionnaire with very detailed instructions, supplemented by telephone interviews.) The questionnaire, which had been pretested in two agencies before being put into final form, was designed to elicit mostly objective information about the organization of the agency and its personnel. Interviews with a few key executives sufficed to obtain the data required, because the factual information was either known to them (for instance, what the major divisions are) or had to be obtained from records with management's permission (for example, the number of employees in every official position), and because only senior executives could answer the few not purely objective questions (for example, whether the agency director or which of his subordinates makes various specified decisions). Interviews were conducted with the agency director or his deputy, the heads of the two major divisions, and the personnel director. In addition, all division heads were asked to complete a brief self-administered questionnaire, and a number of officials were contacted to obtain data from records or copies of various documents. The most important of these documents were a set of organizational charts for every division and every local office, rental invoices of data-processing facilities and inventories of other technical equipment, descriptions of the responsibilities of all divisions, and the form for the supervisory rating of the performance of subordinates.

Aside from information about the entire agency and its various divisions, limited data on every local office were collected at the agency headquarters. Thus, in a visit to the headquarters lasting in most cases about one working day or slightly more and only in the largest agencies two days, data were collected not only on the organization itself and its functional divisions but also on an average of about forty branches. It should be noted that three states (Arizona, North Dakota, and Wisconsin) and the District of Columbia did not have a single agency of employment security but two agencies, one responsible for unemployment insurance and the other for employment service. In these cases, appointments at both agency headquarters were made. Later, when processing the data, the problem arose how to handle these special situations. Several reasons convinced us to combine the data for the two agencies in these cases and treat them as one. A bureau merging the two agencies had already been legally established at the time of data collection in one state (North Dakota), and each of the other two states has a joint commission to which both agencies are responsible as well as some ancillary services jointly provided to both agencies, such as legal or personnel services. Besides, the unemployment insurance and the employment service function operate quite independently in some of the other states too, having separate local offices (in nine states) and different field supervisors (in twenty-one states). The only case in which the decision to combine the two agencies is somewhat arbitrary is that of the District of Columbia, though even here the fact that both agencies are housed in the same building provides much opportunity for communication. (A discussion of these four cases is presented in Appendix A.)

Whereas the interviews in the agencies provided the core of the data, additional information was extracted from a variety of sources. Statistical data on the various services performed by all employment security offices were obtained, partly in unpublished form and partly from publications of the federal bureau, and so were reports on the distribution of personnel time among various functions. The measures of services and the index of staff-line ratio were derived from those reports. The Division of State Merit Systems of the Department of Health, Education and Welfare made available to us reports on the personnel of employment security agencies as well as raw data from a recent study of interviewers in these agencies that the division had conducted jointly with the Bureau of Employment Security. (This study is described in Appendix B.) Information on civil service appointments, salaries, educational qualifications, and turnover comes from these sources. Copies of the personnel regulations and related materials were requested by mail and received from every state personnel agency. A few state administrative and political variables were taken from pertinent books. Finally, environmental characteristics were extracted from the *County and City Data Book* and the *Rand McNally Commercial Atlas*.[10] For an agency, the entire state is considered its environment; for a local office in a city with more than 25,000 people, the city is; and for a local office in a smaller place, the county in which it is located is. (Appendix C, which describes the variables used, also specifies their source.)

The fundamental problem of the research design was to translate the major concepts used in the theoretical analysis of formal organizations into quantitative variables for empirical investigation. For example, an important characteristic of formal organizations is the hierarchy of managerial authority, and Weber emphasizes its significance in his theoretical discussion, but he does not tell us in which respects hierarchies vary, let alone how to measure such variations. Four aspects of the authority structure were distinguished, and several empirical measures of each were devised: first, its differentiation, indicated by the number of hierarchical levels in the organization or in one of its subunits; second, management overhead, measured by the ratios of managerial and of staff personnel; third, the span of control of managers on different levels; and fourth, decentralization of responsibilities, manifest in the managerial level on which a variety of decisions are made. In similar ways, operational terms were constructed for other concepts in the study of organizations, such as division of labor, structural complexity, and administrative apparatus.

Many of the operational variables needed, though by no means all, could be constructed on the basis of a very detailed and accurate organizational chart. Obtaining these charts, therefore, was a crucial part of our data collection. But it soon became apparent that the organizational charts the agencies supplied were not sufficiently precise for our purpose, nor were the charts from different agencies comparable. It was necessary to set up standards for organizational charts and to revise the charts prepared by the agencies in accordance with these standards. Doing so was a major task in the interviews with key informants, who in the course of explicating the organizational charts often also pointed out inaccuracies or changes that had occurred since they were drawn up. Unfortunately, some agencies had already been visited by the time the need for improvements in the organizational charts was discovered. Besides, many of the charts that had been discussed with informants were found to be in need of further clarification when the coding of them started, which is not surprising given the

10. U.S. Bureau of the Census, *County and City Data Book 1967* (Washington, D.C.: U.S. Government Printing Office, 1967); and *Rand McNally Commercial Atlas and Marketing Guide* (Chicago: Rand McNally, 1964 and 1967).

time pressure in the interviews. It should be remembered that almost 3,000 organizational charts were collected and analyzed, one for each local office and usually one for each division as well as one for the headquarters in every agency. What needed to be clarified most often were the exact lines of authority and which officials supervised which others.

To resolve the remaining ambiguities in the charts, key informants were interviewed by telephone. When the complexity of the questionable charts made this impossible, as was often the case in the larger agencies, the charts were returned with detailed instructions for revision. In a few cases, another visit to the agency had to be made to obtain the necessary clarification. In addition, the entries on the organizational charts were compared with an official list of the agency personnel by position, typically a payroll print-out. Some of the telephone calls were made to reconcile discrepancies between the chart and the personnel list. We are convinced that the final charts accurately describe the formal structures.

The next step was to delineate the basic features of the formal structure represented by an organizational chart and construct operational measures of these features. The major dimensions of the shape of the pyramid decided on were the number of hierarchical levels as an indication of vertical differentiation, the number of major subdivisions as the main indication of horizontal differentiation, and the number of sections per division as another indication of horizontal differentiation. In measuring hierarchical levels, deputy managers or assistant supervisors were not counted. Because the number of levels is not the same throughout the headquarters, both maximum and mean number of levels were coded; the maximum number, which has the advantage of a wider range, is used in the analysis. A division is defined as a unit of at least five persons headed by a manager who reports to the agency director or his deputy, and a section is a unit of at least two persons supervised by an official who reports to a division head. Since smaller units than these or single officials often are under the direct supervision of the agency director or of division heads, the two measures of horizontal differentiation are not identical with spans of control. Therefore, a separate measure of top management's span of control was computed, counting all officials directly reporting to the director or his deputy, and so was a separate measure of the average span of control of division heads, the number of individuals reporting to division heads divided by the number of division heads.

Another measure derived from the charts is the supervisory ratio, defined as the per cent of all employees who supervise two or more subordinates, including the highest executive. (The term "manager" is used for officials whose subordinates are supervisors, but when both first-line supervisors and their superiors are referred to, as in this ratio, the terms "manager" and "supervisor" are used interchangeably.) Inasmuch as the indicators of the shape of the pyramid pertain to the agency head-quarters, the supervisory ratio was also computed for the headquarters, though another supervisory ratio for the total agency was computed as well.

Still another index based on the charts is the clerical ratio. A simple code was used to identify clerical positions, and the number of employees in these positions divided by the total number defines the clerical ratio. All these measures were also computed for every division and local office, properly transformed when necessary to make them applicable; thus, the two measures of horizontal differentiation are reduced to one for subunits: number of sections. Another index computed for all divisions and all local offices, however, can be considered a complementary measure of horizontal spread, namely, the average span of control of first-line supervisors in charge of employees on the lowest level in the hierarchy. The average span of control of middle managers, defined as managers who are neither first-line supervisors nor division heads, was also computed for divisions with four or more levels. (Appendix D presents typical organizational charts and explains how various measures are derived from them.)

The number of different job titles was decided upon as the best available indicator of division of labor. The official roster of job classifications maintained by the state's personnel agency describes in some detail the pattern of duties for all positions to be filled. Individual bureaus typically determine the distinct job classes they need but must have them authorized by the personnel bureau. Most job titles of the employment security agency are designed exclusively for it, such as claims examiner, though some are common to many state agencies, such as typist. Several job titles indicative merely of differences in grade or skill, like statistical clerk I and statistical clerk II, are counted only as one in the measure. The objection may be raised that differences in official job descriptions do not accurately reflect differences in actual tasks. This point is well taken. Employees in the same official position undoubtedly sometimes perform quite different tasks, and those in distinct official positions sometimes do similar work. On the whole, however, the job to which an employee is appointed largely governs the tasks assigned to him. Typists are not hired to do filing or interview clients, though one may occasionally be assigned to other work than typing. Moreover, the fact that an agency does not utilize a large number of different official positions but only a small number, which implies that informal variations in task assignment are more prevalent, reflects a difference in its formal structure. The number of job titles for the entire agency is taken from the official personnel roster, whereas for divisions and for local offices it is taken from the organizational charts.

The formal structure of organizations constitutes the central concern of the present study, and this is reflected in the fact that many of its basic variables are abstracted from organizational charts. It is fully recognized that important informal modifications always occur within the formally instituted patterns. This does not mean, however, that the formally established structure is of little significance. There has been much research on informal patterns in organizations during the past generation, but very little on the formal characteristics of organizations. Yet the problems of bureaucracy and "organization man," which a number of essayists have vividly portrayed, refer to the deleterious impact of the formal structure, not of informal relations, on individuals.[11] It is high time that we turn our attention to the systematic study of the formal structure of organizations, even if doing so means temporarily ignoring human relations and informal patterns, which are admittedly also important. Reducing living human beings to boxes on organizational charts and then further reducing these charts to quantitative variables may seem a strange procedure, but it is legitimate inasmuch as concern is with the formal structure in its own right rather than with the people in it.

Many variables are not based on organizational charts. There is no need to discuss most of these, because they are simple measures, such as the number of employees or the years of education of division heads, and because the operational definitions and basic statistics of all variables are presented in Appendix C. The measurement of the services to clients, however, raises some problems requiring discussion. All agencies and every local office in them maintain uniform statistical records of their activities or operations in accordance with federal requirements. The use of these statistical records of performance for evaluating individual employees or organizational units has come under considerable criticism, and they are relied on less today than formerly. An item particularly emphasized in judging the effectiveness of employment operations was the number of clients placed into jobs relative to the interviewers working on placements or the openings received or the referrals to jobs made. But it has been pointed out that placements are strongly affected by various factors outside the control of interviewers or managers, such as the labor market, seasonal fluctuations, and the nature of the job. Though differences in the time required for placements into more or less skilled jobs have been taken into account in budget allocations since 1956, critics still believe that the budget criteria encourage concentration on short-term placements of casual la-

---

11. See, for example, William H. Whyte, *The Organization Man* (New York: Simon & Schuster, 1956).

borers, contrary to the avowed policy.[12] Such criticisms indicate that the statistical data on operations must be used and interpreted with great caution.

Our concern is with the structure of employment security agencies, not with how well they perform, but it is nevertheless of great interest to determine how various aspects of the structure affect operations and the services supplied to clients. The statistical records of activities kept by the agencies provide an opportunity for doing so. Forewarned by the criticisms made against these statistical data, however, we realized that much care must be exercised in extracting reliable measures from the reported data and in analyzing them. As a first step, a factor analysis was performed, using thirty-two variables based on the quantitative data on operations made available to us, which yielded several underlying dimensions. Five variables were selected at this point, partly in terms of conceptual considerations, three of which had the highest and two of which had the second highest loading on one of the factors.

A reliability test was then performed on the four of these five variables that were based on operations during one month only, March 1966. (The fifth—personnel costs of unemployment insurance services, which was derived from a different source—was based on operations during the entire fiscal year preceding the data collection.) Were operations in March reliable indications of operations in other months? The answer to this question was obtained by computing correlations between corresponding measures for March, June, September, and December. Inasmuch as all four measures were ratios, separate correlations for their numerators and their denominators were computed as well. Though most of the correlations for different months of the raw numbers in the numerators and denominators were very high (above .97), the correlations for the four ratios were much lower. More than one-half (13) of the twenty-four correlations of the ratios were less than .80, which indicates that one month is not a reliable indicator of agency operations throughout the year. Consequently, the ratio of the two means for the four months was computed for each variable. Only two of the sixteen correlations of these ratios of means with the corresponding monthly measures were less than .80. The ratios based on four-months' means were subsequently used. (The reliability tests and the preceding factor analysis are presented in Appendix E.)

After preliminary analysis with the four measures based on four-

---

12. William Haber and Daniel H. Kruger, *The Role of the United States Employment Service in a Changing Economy* (Kalamazoo: Upjohn Institute for Employment Research, 1964), pp. 84–87, 112–114.

months' means and the fifth based on the entire fiscal year, two of the three indicators of placement operations were dropped from further consideration because they did not yield sufficiently interesting results, largely duplicating those obtained with the placement measure retained. Besides, a new measure was added, applications for jobs processed divided by number of agency employees, which is a revised version of a measure that had also been used in the preliminary analysis. Thus, three measures of employment services and one measure of unemployment insurance services are used in the analysis. First, the extent of employment service is indicated by number of applications per agency employee. Second, intensive employment service is indicated by the proportion of applicants to whom a General Aptitude Test Battery (GATB) is administered. Third, placement productivity is measured by the ratio of nonagricultural placements to job openings received. (Agricultural placements are excluded as not comparable with others.) Fourth, the index of personnel costs in the administration of unemployment insurance benefits is the ratio of employees engaged in this function to the number of insured unemployed.[13]

Efforts to make measures more reliable cannot meet criticisms directed against their validity, of course. The gist of these criticisms refers to the distorting influence of extraneous factors, such as the economic conditions in the state, the work load of the agency, and the quality of its services. To improve the validity of the measures and meet these criticisms, at least partly, suspected distorting influences are controlled in the analysis. Thus, an agency may provide intensive services and give many tests to clients simply because it has such a low client load. To take this into account, the extent of employment services is controlled when examining the influence of conditions in the organization on intensive services. Since it means little to observe high productivity in employment service without knowing the quality of this service, the intensive services provided, as indications of quality, are controlled when analyzing the factors that influence placement productivity. Finally, inasmuch as both employment and unemployment insurance services depend on economic and social conditions, it will be ascertained whether any influences on these services falsely attributed to characteristics of the organization are actually the result of various environmental conditions. It hardly needs to be stated that the possibility remains that unknown factors have distorting effects despite these precautions.

---

13. Because data on the service operations of individual local offices are available for only one month, and because measures based on one month only proved unreliable, the service measures for local offices were discarded after much preliminary work and will not be presented.

Method of Analysis

Most of the variables in this study are in continuous form, which makes it advantageous to employ regression analysis as the basic method for investigating their interrelations. Some ordinal variables are used in the regression problems, usually comprising four categories, and a dichotomous dummy variable is occasionally used, but only as an independent variable. We shall begin the analysis in Part Two by presenting some scatter diagrams, on which every agency is represented by a point in terms of its values on two variables, for example, size and number of job titles. If a straight line is fitted to these points using the least-square method, the Pearsonian correlation (r) indicates how close to this regression line the points are clustered and thus how strongly related the two variables are. The metric regression coefficient (b), on the other hand, indicates the slope of the regression line, which shows how much change in the dependent variable can be expected given a unit change in the independent variable. This metric slope depends on the scales in terms of which the variables are measured, but the standardized regression coefficient or standardized slope (b*) does not.

The zero-order correlations between all variables, which are the same as the zero-order standardized slopes, are presented in Appendix F. These are the basic data, and they, together with the statistics in Appendix C, provide all the necessary information for the reader who wants to check our results or analyze different combinations of variables from those examined in this book (except that residuals cannot be generated). Usually, we are not interested in relationships between two variables but in the relationships of several independent variables to one dependent variable. The question asked is how various conditions influence a given factor, or specifically what the influence of each condition is when all others are held constant. Multiple regression is designed to answer this question. The square of the multiple correlation (R^2) reveals the per cent of the variation in the dependent variable accounted for by all the independent variables. If R^2 were 1.00, knowledge of the independent variables would permit perfect prediction of the dependent variable. The partial regression coefficient (partial slope) and the partial correlation indicate, in the somewhat different form noted above for their zero-order counterparts, how closely a given independent variable is related to the dependent variable if all other independent variables are controlled. The partial standardized slope will be employed, because it is used in the decomposition of the zero-order relationship into its component elements, which has important theoretical implications.[14] Before explaining the procedure for decomposition, some technical problems should be discussed. (The reader not interested in statistical requirements may want to skip the next three pages.)

Regression analysis makes certain assumptions, which are not perfectly met by our data. The first is that the dependent variables be measured on interval scales, which is not true for all our variables. But this requirement has been questioned, and the use of ordinal variables appears justified.[15] The second problem is that extreme values may produce a correlation although the other cases are uncorrelated, and the agencies in California and New York are extreme in several respects, notably size. However, a comparison of four suspect correlations shows that deleting these two extreme cases does not reduce but increases two of the correlations of size (with number of levels, from .60 to .62, and with number of divisions, from .38 to .56) and reduces the other two only slightly (with number of local offices, from .94 to .90, and with number of job titles, from .78 to .76). Another assumption is that the relationship is linear, whereas several relationships with agency size are curvilinear, which is of substantive significance and will be discussed. Logarithmic transformations of size, which remove or reduce the down-bending curves observed, were performed whenever a zero-order correlation of .20 or more was improved by at least .10 by doing so.

Though regression analysis does not require normal distributions to furnish unbiased estimations, testing the significance of findings through statistical inference does. Several distributions depart markedly from normality. The most extreme case is size; the number of employees in California is 4.7 standard deviations above the mean, and the skew of the distribution is 3.3. Other variables with highly skewed distributions are extent of personnel regulations (2.4), size of computer installation, a thirteen-category ordinal variable (2.4), placements per opening (2.4), and number of job titles (1.6). Various transformations could make these distributions more nearly normal, but we were reluctant to perform different kinds of transformations on a number of variables, which would have been necessary to approximate normality in all cases, for fear of losing sight of the substantive meaning of the variables analyzed. Consequently, we made only the

---

14. The computations were performed on an IBM computer, using mostly the MESA 85 program at the University of Chicago. The assignment of N.A. cases by this program, designed to guarantee that the matrix has a positive determinant, depresses the values obtained, making them conservative estimates of the actual associations.
15. See, e.g., Richard P. Boyle, "Path Analysis and Ordinal Data," *American Journal of Sociology*, 75 (1970): 461–480.

transformations of size noted above that are necessary to meet the assumptions of linearity in regression analysis.

The lack of normality invalidates the use of statistical inference to estimate the probability that a given finding indicates a real association, which some consider a questionable procedure in any case given the fact that we have a universe of organizations of a certain kind rather than a representative sample. An unequivocal criterion is needed, however, to decide for us whether to consider a finding indicative of a possible relationship or dismiss it as revealing no relationship. The criterion selected is that the partial standardized slope (b^*) is at least one and one-half times as large as its standard error, which corresponds to a partial correlation of about .21. This is a weak criterion, necessitated by the small number of agencies, but only relationships that have a b^* at least twice its standard error or those supported by findings with several independent measures are stressed. The major conclusions are based on more pronounced associations and supported by numerous distinct findings. In the analysis of 1,201 local offices, in which very small regression coefficients considerably exceed their standard error, regression slopes are taken to reveal an association only if they are at least twice, and primarily if they are at least three times, their standard error (the latter criterion corresponds, for that sample size, to a correlation of not quite .10). The same criteria are used in the analysis of the 387 divisions.[16]

Another problem is that of multicollinearity, which refers to the fact that some of the independent variables in a multiple regression are closely correlated. In this case, the results of the regression analysis may be misleading, because insignificantly small differences may appear in exaggerated form. The problem can be highlighted by illustrating it in substantive terms. If one occupational group were composed mostly of women and another mostly of men, the conclusion whether occupation or sex influences certain attitudes would have to be based on so few and exceptional cases —the rare men taking up the first and the rare women taking up the second occupation—that one could have little confidence in it. The initial decision was not to use two independent variables that are correlated .70 or more in multiple regressions. However, a few important conditions in these

---

16. Terms such as "insignificantly small" are used for associations that do not meet the criteria level and do not refer to conventional levels of significance or the probability that a finding could have been obtained by chance. However, the difference is a technical one of primary concern to statistical purists, because the criterion that the standardized slope is twice its standard error, for example, would roughly correspond to the .05 level of significance for a normally distributed variable in a sample.

organizations exhibit a higher correlation, notably size, division of labor, and automation, and our substantive interest in tracing their relative influence won out over methodological scruples. But whenever two independent variables have a correlation of more than .82, one is eliminated (for instance, number of local offices, because of its high correlation with number of employees).

Regression analysis assumes that the independent variables do not interact in their effects on the dependent variable, for example, that the influence of a given aspect of differentiation on the supervisory span of control does not change depending on the organization's size. Three procedures were used to determine whether interaction effects exist. First, numerous three-variable contingency tables were examined, controlling size for all variables correlated with it .20 or more by substituting for the original variable the residual from its regression line on size (or the logarithmic transformation of size). Inasmuch as a number of relationships are not quite linear, this procedure does not perfectly control for size. Second, a form of covariance analysis was used to ascertain in a regression problem whether, using the same illustration, differentiation in large agencies has a different effect on the supervisory span of control than differentiation in small agencies. Third, we introduced product terms into the regression analysis, particularly when the interpretation of initial regression results implied that two independent variables combine to exert a joint effect on the dependent variable. Several hundred different combinations of variables were examined, some of them by two or all three different procedures. The majority replicated the regression results and revealed no appreciable interaction. The interesting interaction effects will be examined.

Finally, the method used for decomposing the association between an independent and a dependent variable into direct and indirect effects are discussed. It is essentially the procedure used in path analysis, but a complete path analysis will not be presented, for two reasons. First, path analysis requires inclusion of all antecedents, whereas we are often concerned with too many possible antecedents to make this feasible and drop from consideration all those that reveal no appreciable correlation with the dependent variable, unless theoretical considerations make it advisable to include particular ones. Second, the inquiry is typically conceptualized as asking, for example, how the influence of size on supervision is mediated by three other conditions, and whereas the answer to this question can be derived from a path diagram, the relative influence of several intervening variables is more easily seen if specific values for each indirect effect are directly presented.

When a variable assumed to be the antecedent, x, is correlated with another variable, *y,* two different questions should be asked to interpret the finding. The first is whether *x* actually influences *y* or whether their correlation is spurious, resulting from the influence of some other condition, *z,* on both *x* and *y.* Thus, the division of labor and the number of hierarchical levels in employment security agencies are correlated, but the correlation is spurious owing to the dependence of both factors on agency size, as indicated by the finding that the correlation drops to close to nil when agency size is controlled. The conclusion that the correlation is spurious in such a case is based on two premises. One is the assumption that the controlled variable—in the illustration, size—is antecedent to both other variables, which cannot be empirically demonstrated in the absence of longitudinal data, though indirect evidence to support it can be supplied. The other premise is the empirical finding that the association between *x* and *y* tends to disappear when *z* is statistically controlled. The conclusion follows only from both premises together—the acceptance of the sequence assumption and the empirical finding that the partial correlation is insignificantly small.

If a correlation observed is not spurious according to the existing data (though it is always possible that controlling some unknown condition would reveal it to be spurious), the second question is how *x* influences *y.* It may do so directly, or its influence may be mediated by one or more intervening variables, or it may have both direct and indirect effects. To demonstrate that an intervening variable, *u,* mediates the influence of *x* on *y* implied by their zero-order correlation, it must be shown that holding *u* constant appreciably reduces the association between *x* and *y.* But this means that the same statistical test—ascertaining whether an initial association between two variables tends to disappear when a third is held constant—may indicate either that the initial correlation is spurious or that it reflects an actual indirect influence. The choice between these two alternative interpretations must be made on the basis of assumptions or knowledge about the sequence of the variables involved, specifically, whether the third variable precedes both others or intervenes between them.[17] The assumption made in the present discussion is that the causal sequence is *z—x—u—y.* Given this sequence, if controlling *z* suppresses the association between *x* and *y,* this correlation is spurious, but if controlling *z* does not, and controlling *u* does, depress or completely suppress their association, the proper inference is that *x* exerts an influence on *y* mediated by *u.* Thus, the conclusion that *u* mediates the influence of *x* on

17. See Patricia L. Kendall and Paul F. Lazarsfeld, "Problems of Survey Analysis," in Robert K. Merton and Paul F. Lazarsfeld, eds., *Continuities in Social Research* (Glencoe: Free Press, 1950), pp. 133–196.

y also rests on two premises, an assumed sequence and an empirical finding revealing a reduced partial association, but the sequential ordering of the three variables is assumed to be different from that in testing for spuriousness. The partial association of *x* and *y* when intervening as well as preceding conditions are controlled reveals the direct effect of *x* on *y*, though any effect considered to be direct may be mediated by variables not taken into account in the analysis.

The specific procedure employed is to investigate the relationships between several independent and one dependent variable simultaneously through multiple regression analysis and decompose the zero-order correlations between each independent and the dependent variable into direct and indirect effects. The "indirect effects" obtained in the decomposition include some that are not indirect influences but reveal spurious correlations, because statistical techniques do not distinguish between the two, as noted. The direct effect of *x* on *y* with *z* and *u* controlled finds expression in the partial regression slope in standard form,

$$b^*_{yx \cdot uz}.^{[18]}$$

A given indirect effect of *x* on *y* mediated by a particular other variable in the regression problem, such as *u*, is indicated by the product of the zero-order correlation of *u* with *x* and the standardized slope of *y* on *u* under controls,

$$r_{ux} b^*_{yu \cdot xz}.$$

The same formula yields the "indirect effect" owing to *z*,

$$r_{xz} b^*_{yz \cdot ux},$$

except that in this case the value does not actually signify an indirect effect but the part of the zero-order correlation of *x* and *y* that is the spurious result of their common dependence on *z*, inasmuch as *z* is assumed to precede both of them. The sum of the direct effect and all indirect effects equals the zero-order correlation:

$$r_{yx} = b^*_{yx \cdot uz} + r_{ux} b^*_{yu \cdot xz} + r_{xz} b^*_{yz \, ux}.$$

In the regression problem with these three independent variables, the same procedure would be applied to decompose the two other zero-order correlations,

$$r_{yz} \text{ and } r_{yu}.$$

18. The equations used in decomposition are the same as those used to derive b^*'s.

Decomposition makes it possible to trace the pattern of influence exerted by various conditions on an organizational characteristic, treated as the dependent variable. It indicates which factors account for spurious correlations. (Spurious relationships between variables are not presented unless the finding that a certain condition produces a spurious association is of substantive interest.) This procedure can reveal that a characteristic of organizations influences another although there is no zero-order correlation between them, because common antecedents conceal their relationship. The results of decomposition often show that the over-all impact of a given attribute of organizations on a specific aspect of their administrative structure consists of several different influences, possibly in opposite directions. These complex configurations of diverse influences, which are largely not apparent in the zero-order associations, reflect the dynamic processes that underlie the structure of organizations.

Sequence of Variables

A prerequisite for interpreting the results of the quantitative analysis is that the variables included are ordered in a causal sequence. The interrelated elements in a social structure cannot readily be ordered in a time sequence, however, and numerous associations between elements undoubtedly result from mutual influence. Nevertheless, the analysis of systems of interdependent elements nearly always makes at least implicit assumptions about directions of influence, for example, whether economic conditions determine or are determined by religious beliefs. The requirement of the statistical procedure that such assumptions be made explicit has the advantage that any unwarranted ones are open for inspection. What must be a priori assumed is, of course, only the order of precedence among variables, not whether one in fact influences another, which is determined, given the assumptions, by the empirical findings.

The major variables used are classified into six categories in terms of their assumed sequence. Variables are also ranked within these categories. The classification scheme is based on inferences from empirical knowledge as well as conceptual and theoretical considerations. The ordering within the six categories should be considered as highly tentative; many specific rankings are actually irrelevant, because no empirical findings involving them were observed, and some will be modified as the result of the empirical analysis. Since the histories of the various agencies differ, no single set of sequence assumptions fully represents historical reality.

The first category comprises parameters, that is, conditions essentially outside the control of the organizations themselves. It includes the agency's

TABLE 1-1. *Order of Assumed Precedence among Major Variables*

State Agency	Local Office
1. Parameters	
Size	ES Function
Extent of Personnel Regulations	Specialization
Civil Service Appointments	Size
Salary of Interviewers	
2. Instrumental Conditions	
Division of Labor	Division of Labor
Automation	Mechanization
Educational Requirements	
Educational Qualifications	
Education of Division Heads	
3. Shape of Pyramid	
Levels	Levels
Divisions	Sections
Director's Span of Control	LO Manager's Span of Control
Sections per Division	
Division Heads' Span of Control	
4. Administration	
Standardized Ratings	
Clerical Ratio	Clerical Ratio
Supervisory Ratio	Supervisory Ratio
Staff Ratio	First-Line Supervisors' Span of Control
5. Decentralization	
Delegation: Personnel	
Delegation: Budget	
Decentralization: Influence	
Delegation to LO Manager	
6. Services	
Applications per Employee	
GATB's per Application	
Placements per Opening	
Employee-Client Ratio in Benefit Function	

or subunit's size, which primarily depends on the size of the population served, and various aspects of the personnel system, since these agencies do not control their own personnel procedures but operate under the state civil service system.[19] For subunits, it includes also their function and de-

---

19. States whose personnel system did not meet minimum federal requirements had to set up special personnel procedures meeting the requirements for their employment security and other grant-in-aid agencies. These personnel procedures are also not under the control of the individual agencies.

gree of specialization. Theoretical considerations led to the decisions to assume that the technology is the foundation of the formal structure and that the shape of the pyramid is the core of this structure. Thus, the second category consists of instrumental conditions, or the organization's technology in the broad sense of the term, encompassing the division of labor and personnel qualifications as well as the employment of technical equipment, and the third category is the shape of the pyramid, as defined by five aspects of it. Three administrative ratios are classified together with an index of standardization in administrative procedures under the fourth category. With the exception of the last item, the variables in the third and fourth category all refer to the formal structure in the technical sense of pertaining to subdivisions among formal positions (and so does the division of labor). The formal structure is assumed to be more basic than, and thus to exert an influence on, managerial practices or the performance of services on the operating level. Accordingly, the fifth category is composed of several indications of decentralization of responsibilities, and the four measures of services earlier discussed make up the last category which comprises agency outputs.

The order of assumed precedence among the major variables is presented in Table 1–1, the left side enumerating variables describing the entire agency or its headquarters, and the right side, those describing local offices. For any variable, those above it on either list are treated as conditions that may affect it. Additional variables are considered on occasion.[20] Essentially the same order of precedence is assumed for the attributes of divisions analyzed in Chapter 10.

---

20. The independent variables are presented in all tables in the order of assumed precedence. This order of presentation, however, does not affect the statistical analysis, which does *not* use step-wise regression procedures.

CHAPTER 2

Agency Description

Before analyzing the government agencies under consideration in detail, it is necessary to convey an over-all picture of these organizations, their responsibilities, and the system of employment security they compose. This chapter is designed to provide such an overview. (Appendix G contains a short bibliography of sources used.) After a brief history of employment security and the federal laws under which it operates, the relationship between the federal government and the state agencies as well as the administrative organization of both are described. Next, the main responsibilities of employment security agencies are discussed, and the various administrative functions performed in support of the main responsibilities are outlined. The qualitative description is supplemented by a quantitative description of a few important activities of these agencies and, particularly, their major organizational attributes, indicating their average characteristics and the ranges of variation found among them. Finally, the transition from statistical description to analysis is made by examining the most prominent simple correlations between organizational characteristics and the contrasting types of formal structure these associations imply.

Employment Security in the United States

Craft guilds furnished employment services to their members as early as the Middle Ages, but public employment services were first established by a number of cities in Europe and the United States around the middle of the nineteenth century, and it was only at the end of the century that state-wide systems developed.[1] The turn of the century also witnessed the beginning of public unemployment insurance in the form of municipal subsidies for benefits paid by trade unions and fraternal societies to members, except for one short-lived plan adopted more than a century earlier, in 1789, by Basle Town in Switzerland.[2] The first nation-wide compulsory unemployment insurance law was enacted in Great Britain in 1911. Within the next decade, bills to establish state-wide unemployment insurance systems were unsuccessfully introduced in the legislatures of Massachusetts, New York, and Wisconsin, and it was only the depression of the 1930's that gave an impetus to legislation establishing unemployment insurance throughout the United States.

The number of unemployed in this country rose from 1.5 million in 1929 to more than 12 million in 1932. The national emergency created by the depression led to the reorganization of the all but defunct U.S. Employment Service with the passage of the Wagner-Peyser Act in 1933. This law, which remains the statutory basis for public employment service today, made affiliating state agencies eligible for federal grants, thus supplying incentives to states for affiliation as well as for establishing a state employment agency if none existed already. Two years later, the passage of the Social Security Act strengthened the growing system of public employment service by making the employment offices of the states responsible for testing the eligibility of clients claiming unemployment insurance benefits.

The Social Security Act of 1935 provided for a nation-wide system of unemployment insurance administered by autonomous state agencies. This legislation, which is still in force, now levies a tax of 3.1 per cent of the first $3,000 of each employee's earnings on all employers covered by it. Coverage has been broadened over the years, and it is not the same in all states. The tax of an employer is reduced if few of his workers had been laid off and claimed unemployment insurance in the past. About nine tenths of the tax collected in a state—the exact proportion depends on the state laws—is deposited in a special trust fund of the federal treasury for that state and can be used solely for the purpose of paying unemployment

1. William Haber and Daniel H. Kruger, *The Role of the United States Employment Service in a Changing Economy* (Kalamazoo, Mich.: Upjohn Institute for Employment Research, 1964), pp. 21–22.
2. William Haber and Merrill G. Murray, *Unemployment Insurance in the American Economy* (Homewood, Ill.: Irwin, 1966), pp. 47–75. This reference and the one cited in note 1 are extensively used in the following discussion.

insurance. Wisconsin, which had enacted the first unemployment insurance law in this country in 1931, paid the first benefit check in the summer of 1936. All forty-eight states, the District of Columbia, and the two territories of Alaska and Hawaii had passed the required legislation by the middle of 1937, and all fifty-one jurisdictions had begun paying unemployment insurance benefits two years later. By that time, all fifty-one jurisdictions also had employment services affiliated with the U.S. Employment Service.

A portion of the tax collected—about one tenth but depending on state coverage laws—is reserved for administrative purposes. These administrative funds are not credited to individual states but pooled by the federal government and then redistributed. Most of the administrative budget of every agency is now allocated to it by the federal government, though some state agencies have additional sources of funds for administrative costs. The annual budget allocation is usually the subject of lengthy negotiations between state administrators and federal officials. The ratio of the budget allocated to the federal taxes collected varies considerably among states, and this ratio furnishes a rough indication of an agency's budget relative to the size of the labor force in the state because the taxes depend largely on the labor force.

Having been established during a depression with millions of men out of work, employment security grew rapidly during the early years of its existence, but most of its operations consisted of distributing unemployment insurance and placing unemployed workers on relief projects, such as PWA (Public Works Administration), WPA (Works Progress Administration), and CCC (Civil Conservation Corps). Hence, public employment offices came to be looked on as the place where people go simply to become eligible for unemployment benefits and otherwise only as a last resort for those who cannot find jobs by any other means. This unfavorable image, which haunts the public employment service to this day, is a far cry from the objective envisaged by the proponents of the Wagner-Peyser Act to set up a nation-wide labor exchange for all kinds of employees and employers. However, the advent of World War II altered conditions drastically and improved the public image of government employment agencies somewhat. Mobilization and war production reduced unemployment to an all-time low during the war years, transforming the previous labor surplus into a shortage of manpower. As a result, the emphasis in employment security shifted from unemployment insurance to employment service and specifically to improving placement operations in order to help utilize the skills of workers, or even their potential abilities, to maximum advantage. Demobilization at the end of the war further expanded the scope of employment security activities. The Servicemen's Readjustment Act entitled veterans to unemployment benefits and required that they be given preferential treatment in employment service, and a program was designed to facilitate the integration of millions of discharged servicemen into the peacetime economy.

There were few changes in the 1950's, except for those produced by economic fluctuations. Congress enacted two laws extending unemployment insurance benefits during the recessions of 1958 and 1961, and the persisting hard core of unemployment prompted it to establish federal programs that again enlarged the responsibilities of employment security agencies. The Area Redevelopment Act of 1961 and the Manpower Development and Training Act of 1962 provided for training and retraining of unemployed workers who have special difficulties finding work for some reason or other, be it skin color, age, or sheer lack of skills. Employment security agencies have been heavily involved in these programs from the beginning, notably by screening and selecting trainees for them and processing the allowances they receive during training. In an effort to deal with the serious problems that growing numbers of disadvantaged young men experience gaining a foothold in the labor market, employment security agencies set up special youth opportunity centers to service their needs, and they also participated in the youth programs of the Office of Economic Opportunity. Finally, responsibility for employment security on the federal level, which had been reorganized several times since the 1930's, was shifted once more recently. In a major change in the U.S. Department of Labor, which has taken place since the completion of our research, the Bureau of Employment Security was abolished, and its functions were assigned to the Manpower Administration.

This short review of the legal history of employment security in the United States has been essentially confined to federal legislation without attempting to deal with the different state laws that implement it; this may have conveyed an exaggerated impression of the importance of the federal government. To be sure, the major impetus for the development of employment security in this country came from the two basic federal laws of 1933 and 1935, although public employment services existed in twenty-three states and an unemployment insurance law had already been enacted in one (Wisconsin) by 1933. Besides, the federal government continues to play a crucial role in employment security by helping to coordinate activities, setting standards, and enforcing minimum standards through the purse strings it holds. However, the Social Security Act was deliberately designed to create a previously untried type of federal-state cooperation. The federal law provided compelling financial incentives for states to institute employment security and coordinate it with the federal program. But each state had to enact its own statutes, set up its own organization, and run the latter as part of the state government.

An employment security agency, therefore, is a creation of the state legislature and under the jurisdiction of the state government, but it must conform to federal laws, and it works in close connection with the U.S. Manpower Administration (formerly, the Bureau of Employment Security), which provides a variety of services, coordinates such activities as the compilation of labor-market information, and supervises compliance with federal standards. Whereas the state employment security system must conform to minimum federal requirements, there are wide variations among states in respect to the laws themselves, the administrative practices, and the organizations. For example, some state unemployment insurance laws tax all employers, whereas others cover only those with more than a certain number of employees. (The federal law originally stipulated that all firms with eight employees or more must be covered, which has since been expanded to include firms with at least four employees.) The weekly unemployment benefits paid and the number of weeks they are paid differ in the various states. Some employment security agencies concentrate on the unemployment insurance function, others on furnishing employment services. The extensive differences in the formal organizations administering employment security are described later in the chapter. Were there no such differences among state agencies and among local offices and had all been modeled after a federal formula, the analysis of the research data could not have shown, as it did, that agencies are much influenced by conditions in the state, and local offices, by those in their agency.

Thus, employment security in the United States consists of two distinct sets of organizations: the federal system and the various state systems. The basic features of these organizations may be broadly outlined (see the organizational charts in Appendix D). At the time of our survey, the top federal agency was the U.S. Bureau of Employment Security in the Department of Labor, headed by a bureau administrator. It had four services —unemployment insurance, employment, farm labor, and administration and management—and eleven regional offices throughout the country, in close liaison with the state agencies in their respective regions. The subdivisions in a regional office corresponded to those of the four services at the bureau headquarters. The recent reorganization in which this federal bureau was superseded by the U.S. Manpower Administration had little immediate bearing on the state agencies under study.

The state director of employment security usually reports to a state commissioner, though in some states he reports directly to the governor. Most state agencies have a division of employment service, a division of unemployment insurance, and several smaller divisions, such as administration, personnel, legal, research and statistics, and training. The unemployment insurance division typically includes one section responsible for benefit claims and one responsible for tax collection, and the data-processing section is often also part of it. The employment service division usually has jurisdiction over local offices as well as over the field supervisors charged with maintaining close contact with the local offices through regular visits. Local· offices differ even more widely than do state agencies. Four types can be distinguished: general offices, serving both major functions; unemployment insurance offices, which are confined to unemployment insurance; employment service offices, which provide employment services for all occupations; and specialized employment service offices, which provide employment services to selected occupations, and which are rarely found outside metropolitan areas. A recently instituted fifth type is the youth opportunity center. General local offices are smaller than the various kinds of specialized ones, and they considerably outnumber all other types combined. The internal structure of a local office depends on its function and size. General offices typically have an employment service and an unemployment insurance section, and sometimes a few others. Unemployment insurance offices are usually divided into separate sections for initial claims, continued claims, and adjustments, plus a section for office services. The sections in employment service offices generally follow industrial or occupational lines. Metropolitan area offices tend to be established in large cities to coordinate the activities of the various local offices in the urban area.

These organizations not only vary a great deal from state to state but also undergo continual change in one place or another. Lest variations in formal structure be confounded with changes over time, the organizational characteristics found at the time of the survey were "frozen" and the attempt was made to base all measures on data from the first quarter of 1966. (Other considerations sometimes made it advisable to disregard this principle; for example, reliable measures of service had to be based on data from an entire year or four months distributed throughout the year.) The distinctive federal-state relationship in employment security has some advantages for the research. Federal requirements assure that all organizations have the same basic functions and similar responsibilities, which makes their formal structure fully comparable and lessens the likelihood that differences attributed to structural conditions are actually the result of differences in function.[3] At the same time, the relative independence of

3. This identity of basic functions makes it impossible to study the relationship between function and structure in the comparative analysis of agencies. But this problem will be investigated to a limited extent when the

the various agencies under the jurisdiction of different state governments, an independence jealously guarded against undue federal infringements, produces sufficient variation to permit the analysis of the interrelations of their characteristics. At least, we initially assumed that only organizations that are not part of the same government system exhibit enough independent variation for analysis, but the considerable variations observable among divisions and among local offices within an agency revealed this assumption to be incorrect. Even the subunits within a larger organization differ markedly in structure depending on their function, their size, and the conditions under which they operate.

Responsibilities

Employment service is one of the two basic functions for which employment security agencies are responsible. On the occasion of the thirtieth anniversary of the federal-state system of public employment service, the Secretary of Labor cited President Kennedy's characterization of problems of employment and unemployment as "the number one domestic challenge of the 1960's." He went on to specify: "For the Employment Service, the basic challenge ahead is one of becoming, in a true sense, the 'Community Manpower Service Center' in every labor market area which the USES serves." [4] This ambitious goal remains to be realized in the future, but there can be no doubt about the growing significance of the public employment service for America's economy.

Placement activities constitute the core of the employment service. These activities are carried out in local offices, and they involve finding appropriate work for jobless men with various experiences and skills and simultaneously filling employers' job openings with qualified workers. All American residents are entitled to avail themselves of the public employment service, and this service is required to be furnished to them without regard to their race, creed, national origin, or sex.

Clients coming to a public employment office are routed by a receptionist to interviewers, who ascertain their work histories, skills, and preferences. The *Dictionary of Occupational Titles,*[5] which classifies 22,000 dif-

---

structures of different types of local offices and those of different types of divisions are compared. The main objective of this study, however, is to analyze the interrelations within formal structures, holding function constant.

4. W. Willard Wirtz, "New Dimensions for Labor," *Employment Security Review,* 30, no. 6 (June 1963): 1.
5. U.S. Department of Labor, *Dictionary of Occupational Titles* (Washington, D.C.: Government Printing Office, 1939, rev. ed. 1965).

ferent kinds of work under 36,000 titles, is designed to furnish uniform criteria for categorizing occupational qualifications and job requirements. The normal procedure is to prepare application forms for clients during the initial interview and place the forms into the active file. Job orders received from employers are described in detail on complementary forms, and employers are regularly contacted by telephone and personal visits to solicit job openings from them. The selection process entails matching what the job requires and what the applicant can do, ideally on the basis of the information on the two kinds of forms. But this selection procedure is often short-circuited, particularly in respect to the many requests for unskilled workers for very short periods, such as day laborers and household workers. Candidates for short-term jobs tend to be selected directly from the daily flow of incoming clients, without the use of written applications. Thus, applications are not made out for all clients, and the number of applications indicates the extent to which more than the most rudimentary employment service is provided. Prior to referral, the employer is called to make sure that the opening has not yet been filled, and another telephone call after referral verifies that the referred client was hired and a placement in fact has been made. A clearance procedure makes it possible to find candidates for job openings received in one local office among the applicants in other local offices or even among those in other states.

Placement service in agriculture differs considerably from that in other industries. In recognition of this fact, farm placements are usually handled by specialized sections. Agricultural placements are not comparable with nonagricultural ones in that the majority of them do not involve individual selection of applicants but result from referrals of entire crews or pools of farm laborers. Hence, separate records of agricultural and of nonagricultural placements are kept, and agencies rely primarily on the nonagricultural data in judging placement activities. The measure of placement service used here, which was discussed in Chapter 1, is also confined to nonagricultural jobs.[6]

The description of the official placement responsibilities ignores an important difference between two types of clients, those who do and those

---

6. Because this measure is the ratio of placements made to openings received, leaving out agricultural placements and openings reduces the case base of largely agricultural states disproportionately but does not necessarily affect the measure. As a matter of fact, agencies in highly urbanized states make slightly fewer placements per opening than others (correlation of the placement measure with per cent urban in the state, $-.16$; with per cent nonagricultural employees in the state, $-.25$). But other environmental conditions in the state overshadow the impact of urbanization on the placement measure.

who do not claim unemployment insurance. Whereas the latter come to the employment office for the sole purpose of finding work, the former must apply for a job at the public agency to be eligible for unemployment benefits, because such application is necessary to satisfy the legal requirement that recipients of unemployment benefits be "able and willing to work." Numerous clients of employment offices only apply to fulfill this requirement and are not interested in being referred to a job, perhaps because they know they can return to their former job after a seasonal layoff or because they expect to find a better job through private channels. As a result of the connection between unemployment insurance and employment service, the assignment of employment interviewers consists, in effect, partly of helping people find jobs they need and want and partly of checking up on benefit recipients.

Employment service encompasses a number of operations in addition to those directly concerned with placements. First, some counseling is provided to clients in need of advice to make vocational choices, particularly new entrants into the labor market, older workers, handicapped persons, and members of underprivileged minorities. Various tests may be given to clients to assist in their counseling, the most widely used set being the General Aptitude Test Battery (GATB), which measures a variety of occupationally relevant abilities in a two and one-half hour examination. Second, several special services, including counseling, are provided for veterans. Third, a responsibility that has been increasingly stressed in recent years is the collection and processing of information on the labor market. Data on manpower requirements and unemployment in different industries and occupations, which are collected by local offices and then combined on a state-wide and nation-wide basis, are important indicators of the state of the economy and various trends. Fourth, special services, such as job analysis, occupational classification, or job counseling programs for high schools, are sometimes furnished to employers, schools, unions, and other groups in the community. Finally, the public employment service has been made responsible for helping to establish training programs for the hardcore unemployed—particularly those set up under the Manpower Development and Training Act—by determining both which programs are needed and which men are most in need of them.

Unemployment insurance, the second of the two basic functions of all employment security agencies, involves responsibilities for the administration of benefits and responsibilities for tax collection. "Benefit payment is a right, not a charity." This sentence cited from Montana's "Operations Manual" reflects the principle that unemployed workers are entitled to unemployment benefits regardless of need provided that they meet certain conditions stipulated by the law. Though this principle applies to all jurisdictions, there are fifty-four different legal codes that specify the conditions that entitle a person to unemployment insurance. "The state laws are so complex and vary so greatly that it is hard to summarize them." [7] The discussion here is confined to the similarities underlying these differences in detailed legal provisions. Only about two thirds of the labor force in this country is covered by unemployment insurance.

A worker who has lost his job files his initial claim for benefits at the unemployment insurance office in his community. After a required waiting period, which is usually a week, he returns for an interview to establish his eligibility. The information obtained in this interview together with the claimant's wage record are the basis for the nonmonetary determination and the monetary determination of his case. The nonmonetary determination of his eligibility for benefits involves ascertaining whether the client has worked in covered employment during the preceding base period for the required number of weeks and earned the amount specified by law and whether any of the legal provisions disqualifying a claimant apply to him. There are differences among states in respect to all these factors: firms covered, base period, number of weeks worked, amount earned, and disqualifying conditions. In most agencies, thirty-two of the fifty-three in our survey, nonmonetary determinations are made in local offices; only in fifteen are they made entirely at the headquarters, whereas six agencies divide responsibility for them between local offices and headquarters. Once it has been determined that a client is entitled to unemployment insurance, he must file continued claims at regular intervals, and he may be disqualified from receiving further benefits, for example, because he has refused to accept a suitable job.

The monetary determination of the amount and duration of the claimant's weekly benefits is made by applying a complex formula, which differs in the various states, to his wage record in the base period. Hence, there are variations in the benefits provided among individuals within a state as well as among states. At the beginning of 1966, minimum weekly benefits ranged from $10 to $25, and the weekly maxima ranged, with one exception ($16 in Puerto Rico), from $30 to $65—or $75 if dependents' allowances were included. In most states, the maximum was less than one half the average wage earned in covered employment.[8] The maximum duration of benefits was twenty-six weeks in the large majority of states.[9] The pre-

---

7. Haber and Murray, *Unemployment Insurance*, p. 123.
8. Ibid., pp. 110–111.
9. Ibid., p. 202.

vailing procedure is to make monetary determinations at the headquarters, where most agencies keep a file of all wage records. Benefit payments may be made by mailing checks from the headquarters directly to clients; by sending checks from the headquarters to local offices, there to be picked up by clients; in the form of cash disbursements at the local offices; or by giving clients nonnegotiable pay orders that they can cash at the local bank. The last procedure is said to be the most economical in a statement issued by the California agency.[10] Various built-in controls are designed to protect agencies against overpayment on account of error or fraud.

Provisions are made that enable aggrieved parties to appeal the initial determinations made in their cases. Requests for administrative reconsideration may be followed, if a satisfactory settlement is not reached, by appeals to a quasijudicial referee, whose decision may in turn be appealed to a higher authority, and final recourse may be had by taking the case to the courts. Employers dissatisfied with their tax rates as well as claimants dissatisfied with the determinations in their cases have these rights of appeal.

The tax responsibilities of employment security agencies include keeping wage records of all covered employment in the state, establishing the tax rate for every employer, and collecting the taxes assessed. In 1966, employers of one or more workers had to pay unemployment insurance taxes in twenty states, whereas four states covered only employers of at least three workers and twenty-eight states covered only those with at least four employees (the federal minimum). Moreover, agricultural and domestic laborers are not covered in most jurisdictions, and neither are employees of nonprofit organizations. The tax rate of an employer is based on his "experience rating," which depends essentially on the taxes he paid in previous years and the unemployment insurance claims made by workers laid off by him, though the complex regulations determining this rating differ greatly from state to state. The taxable wage base was in most states the first $3,000 of every worker's annual earnings at the beginning of 1966, with a higher wage base in eighteen states. A maximum tax rate of 2.7 per cent of the taxable wage base for employers with the poorest experience ratings used to be considered standard, but thirty-five states had a higher maximum tax rate by 1966, with twenty-seven of them reaching 4.0 per cent or more. The minimum tax rate for employers with the best experience ratings varied in 1966 from 0 to 1.6 per cent.[11]

Maintaining the accounts necessary for tax assessment and collection

10. California Department of Employment, "California's 'Complete Cash Pay,'" *Employment Security Review*, 22, no. 8 (August 1955): 54.
11. Haber and Murray, *Unemployment Insurance*, p. 121.

can be a staggering task. An idea of the magnitude of this task is conveyed by the fact that coverage extended to 2.5 million employers and almost 50 million employees in 1966, which means that the average jurisdiction had to tax nearly 50,000 employers and covered nearly a million employees. Much of this work is nowadays carried out by computers in the majority of states and by conventional data-processing equipment in the rest.[12] Even in the most automated agencies, however, many duties pertaining to the tax function remain to be performed by human beings. Officials must decide which employers are covered under the law and which wages are taxable in a constantly changing economy characterized by the merger of some firms, the disappearance of others owing to bankruptcy or death, and the expansion of still others that makes them newly subject to taxation. Taxes must not only be collected and recorded, but action must be taken on outstanding liabilities, penalties must be assessed on delinquencies, refunds must be made on overpayments, and necessary adjustments in the tax rates must be determined. Finally, the wage records of employers are audited by field agents to assure uniform compliance with the law.

The two basic production or service functions of employment security agencies just discussed are supported by a number of maintenance or staff functions. The distinction between productive operations and administrative support for them is not fully agreed on, however, nor can it be unequivocally drawn in all cases. Thus, line management and supervision may be considered part of the basic production process or its major administrative support. But this problem is largely semantic. In this research, managers and supervisors on all levels in the agency, from the top executive at the headquarters to first-line supervisors in local offices, are all treated simply as a separate management component in charge of the administration of operations. They are distinct from the personnel engaged in maintenance or staff services, who also provide administrative support for the basic services. (Supervisors of staff services are included in the measures of both groups of officials.)

A more serious problem is raised by the distinction between line and staff services. Should data-processing, for example, be classified as part of unemployment insurance operations, on the basis of the content of the work performed, or as a special staff service? The decision in this case was twofold: first, to consider data-processing a separate function in the comparison of divisions, even for those agencies in which data-processing is not a division but a subunit of the unemployment insurance or another

---

12. Only the smallest of the fifty-three agencies in our study, that in the Virgin Islands, had no data-processing equipment.

division; and second, to exclude data-processing personnel except for computer programmers from the ratio of staff personnel, in accordance with the agency's own classification set by federal standards. The following discussion is organized in terms of the four types of supportive functions into which the large variety of auxiliary divisions in the different agencies are classified in the comparative analysis of divisions.

The first staff function is labeled "administrative services." An important part of these consists of fiscal activities pertaining to the agency's administrative budget, including processing of payrolls, purchase and rental of equipment and supplies, keeping inventories, bookkeeping and accounting, and issuing financial reports. There are also office services, which involve the work of typists, file clerks, receptionists, telephone operators, messengers, and mail clerks. Much duplicating of various documents and reports is done as well. A special time-distribution system is maintained as a tool for managerial and budgetary control. Internal audits review compliance with state and federal laws. (The building maintenance personnel has been excluded from our analysis.) It should be remembered that this classification is ours and that the various responsibilities it encompasses are not always found together in one division of administrative services. The activities included under this functional heading may be divided between two or more divisions, and there may be no separate administrative services division. The same applies to the three other categories of maintenance function, particularly the personnel and technical services.

Second, the personnel and technical services encompass a variety of staff responsibilities that require generally more skilled personnel than those categorized as administrative services. The personnel director and his subordinates are responsible for appointments, promotions, performance ratings, and other personnel matters, within the limits set by civil service, and often act largely in an advisory capacity to line managers authorized to make personnel decisions. A training unit conducts in-service training courses for new employees as well as refresher or specialized courses for others. The section often called "organization, methods, and planning" develops managerial guides and operating procedures and makes up operating manuals, bulletins, charts, and administrative forms. An information service disseminates information of public interest through various media of communication. There is usually one group that prepares reports on administrative research and on the analysis of the agency's own operations and another group that compiles the statistical data on the labor force collected in the agency, which are the basis for official publications on state and national employment and unemployment.

A third type of staff function is data-processing, which may or may not involve the use of a computer. It entails operating the mechanical equipment and, if computers are used, programming and systems analysis, but it does not include preparing the material for machine operations, which is considered a line activity and is generally not done in the data-processing unit. Data-processing constitutes a separate division in only twelve agencies, whereas it is part of another division in the rest, which is most often the unemployment insurance division.

A final type of function pertains to legal matters. Legal services encompass notably interpreting the relevant legal codes, preparing cases for the attorney general or the courts, and reviewing initial appeals. Included here also are the staff of the quasijudicial bodies hearing lower-authority and higher-authority appeals, although these officials are usually not part of the unit performing the other legal services.

Statistical Description

Before describing the characteristics of the organizations studied in quantitative form, the volume of the main activities performed by the employment security agencies in the entire country in 1966 is reviewed to indicate the large scope of these operations.[13] During 1966 10.5 million persons filed new applications for jobs at public employment offices in the United States. About one tenth of them, 1.3 million, had at least one counseling interview, and more than half of these were given the General Aptitude Test Battery. The data do not indicate how large a proportion of these applicants were placed in jobs, because more than one job placement is often made for a single applicant during the course of a year. The total number of placements made slightly exceeds the number of new applicants, being nearly 11 million. Two fifths of all placements in 1966 were in agricultural jobs and 60 per cent were nonagricultural placements, which is an exact reversal of the situation ten years earlier, when 60 per cent of all placements were in agricultural jobs. Three tenths of all nonagricultural placements in 1966 involved short-term jobs expected to last no more than three days. Thus, a considerable portion of placement operations is devoted to finding day work for casual laborers, domestic servants, and people in other itinerant service occupations.

Generally, the public employment service has penetrated the labor market of the less skilled occupations much more than that of the highly skilled occupations. The trend in recent years has been to reduce this im-

---

13. These data are taken from U.S. Department of Labor, Bureau of Employment Security, *Historical Statistics of Employment Security Activities 1938–1966* (Washington, D.C.: Government Printing Office, 1968).

balance somewhat. For example, the number of placements in professional and managerial occupations more than doubled between 1956 and 1966; that in clerical and sales occupations increased by 12 per cent; whereas that in unskilled occupations decreased slightly. Nevertheless, only 4 per cent of the nonagricultural placements in 1966 were in professional and managerial occupations, which was less than one fifth of their representation in the labor force; 15 per cent were in clerical and sales occupations, which roughly corresponds to their representation in the labor force; and 28 per cent were in unskilled occupations, which is more than four times their representation in the labor force. It is not necessarily a shortcoming of the public employment service, however, that it continues to be more heavily involved in placing the least skilled than in placing the most skilled workers. On the contrary, the proper role of a *public* employment service is precisely to concentrate on finding jobs for those who have the least resources to do so on their own.

An idea of the volume of unemployment insurance activities may be provided by two figures: more than 11 million initial claims were processed in 1966, and more than 1 million benefit checks were issued in the average week. The weekly benefit payment averaged not quite $40, and the total unemployment benefits disbursed in the year were close to $2 billion. Yet unemployment in 1966 was lower than it had been in more than a decade. The number of weeks of compensated unemployment was less than 50 million, whereas it had been more than 100 million during the peak years of 1958 and 1961.

Turning now to the organizational characteristics of employment security agencies, we note first that the mean number of employees of the fifty-three agencies is 1,195, and their size ranges from fifty employees in the Virgin Islands to more than 9,000 in California. (A full description of the basic statistics is presented in Appendix C, but the range is not shown there.) Though the mean is nearly 1,200, half the agencies have fewer than 670 employees, the median, because the distribution is highly skewed (3.2), with fewer than 1,000 employees in most agencies but several thousand in a very few. These differences correspond to differences in the population of the various states.

Three characteristics of the personnel system are examined. First, an index of the degree of formalization in personnel procedures is the extent of the official civil service regulations.[14] The approximate number of

---

14. These are the regulations of the state's system of civil service, under which the employment security agency operates. In thirty states, the civil service system covers all departments; in the rest, it covers only the employment security and other grant-in-aid agencies.

words in these regulations ranges from 3,000 to 33,000, except for the case of California, which has a much larger body of personnel regulations, consisting of about 73,000 words.[15] The mean is 18,000 words, and the median is about the same. Second, although permanent appointments are required to be competitive and based on civil service procedures, temporary or provisional employees may be hired without adhering to civil service standards. The proportion of nonpermanent appointments is not usually indicative of political patronage, we were told, but it does indicate a weak civil service system, which fails to establish sufficient lists of candidates with certified qualifications for all positions, for example, or which does not offer salaries commensurate with the skills required. The proportion of new appointments made strictly in accordance with merit standards of civil service (competitive accessions) in the three years from 1964 to 1966 averaged 60 per cent in the employment security agencies, ranging from 14 per cent in Mississippi to 96 per cent in Montana. Third, the average entry salary of employment interviewers was less than $4,800 per year during 1965–1966, with a range from $3,500 to nearly twice that.[16]

Somewhat more than half the interviewers appointed in the year preceding the survey (1965) in the average agency had college degrees, the mean and the median being virtually identical. The range in the educational qualifications of new interviewers among agencies is very wide. In several states, all entering interviewers were college graduates, whereas in one, only 6 per cent were. The mean number of years of college education of division heads is three and one-half in the average agency, which implies that most of the senior managers are college graduates. Education is probably a better measure of relevant qualifications for interviewers than for senior managers. The qualifications of the personnel help circumscribe the instrumental conditions in an organization, and so do the division of labor and the utilization of technological equipment. The mean number of job titles, indicative of the subdivision of labor among formal positions, is 106, with a median of 96 and a range from 30 to 262. The implication is that there is a separate official position for nearly every eleven employees, but some positions, such as claims taker, are occupied by many more employees than others. Computers had been installed in twenty-nine of the fifty-three agencies by the beginning of 1966, and several other agencies were in the process of automating operations.

---

15. Particular states are mentioned as examples only for variables based on publicly available sources, such as these official regulations, and not for measures based on the confidential information furnished to us.

16. Interviewers are singled out for special attention because theirs is the basic position in the daily operations of the agencies.

The shape of the pyramid in the average employment security agency can be described by stating that the number of levels at the headquarters is 6.0, the number of divisions is 6.6, and the number of sections per headquarters division is 2.5. For all three variables, the median is similar to the mean and the distribution is fairly close to normal. The ranges among agencies are from four to eight levels, from two to thirteen divisions, and from one to five sections per division. The average number of officials reporting to the agency director or his deputy, including division heads and officials in charge of units too small to be categorized as divisions, is ten, with a range from six to eighteen. The average span of control of division heads, counting single subordinates as well as section managers, is slightly more than six, and the range is between four and nine.[17]

Three administrative ratios were computed, referring respectively to the supervisory component, the staff component, and the clerical component. Between one tenth and one third of the personnel at the headquarters of the various agencies consists of managers and supervisors; the mean is 21 per cent, and the distribution is close to normal. On the average, one tenth of the personnel time is devoted to staff activities (the mean is 10.7 and the median is 10.1 per cent), ranging from 6 to 21 per cent. More than half of the headquarters personnel in the average agency are clerks (54 per cent), but the proportion is considerably lower in local offices. The mean proportion of clerical employees in the entire agency is 32 per cent, a ratio of 1:2; one agency has a ratio as low as 1:5; at the other extreme, the ratio in one agency is 1:1. The high proportion of clerks in these organizations implies that many clerks perform production functions and that the clerical ratio should not be treated as an indication of ancillary services in support of the basic production functions, except possibly in local offices.

Most measures of decentralization, as well as some others, are ordinal variables whose averages do not have substantive meaning. An exception is the proportion of division heads in the agency who, according to their own statements, can institute major changes in their divisions on their own initiative.[18] In some agencies, no division head reports he exercises such

---

17. The measure of span of control of division heads in each agency is the mean for all division heads—number of subordinates divided by number of division heads—and so are the measures of sections per division and education of division heads. The averages reported for all agencies in these cases, therefore, are means of means.

18. The number of division heads completing our questionnaire, which is the denominator in this percentage, varies between three and sixteen among agencies, and the number of division heads eligible to answer the question varies from six to eighteen. (All managers reporting to the agency director or his deputy were given the questionnaire, including those in charge of

discretion, and in one, all of them do. On the average, four out of ten division heads in an agency say that they exert major influence over changes in their divisions.

The extent of employment service provided by various agencies, as indicated by the ratio of the number of new applications filed per month to the number of agency employees, varies from eight to twenty-nine, with a mean of fifteen.[19] The proportion of new applicants to whom the General Aptitude Test Battery is administered, which is considered a measure of intensive services, varies from 3 to 23 per cent among agencies, with a mean of 8 per cent. The ratio of placements made to openings received in nonagricultural jobs varies from .54 to .90, with the exception of one extremely low score (.08), and the mean is .71. Whereas these three measures refer to employment services, a fourth is indicative of the manpower costs of unemployment benefit operations, namely, the number of employees performing unemployment benefit functions (excluding employees assigned to tax responsibilities as well as those in the employment service) per 1,000 clients claiming benefits. The mean ratio is thirteen, the minimum eight, and the maximum twenty. The median is very similar to the mean for this ratio as well as for the three measures of employment service.

The mean number of local offices in a state agency is forty-two, and the median number is thirty-two. One agency has only four such offices, whereas another has 195. There are about 2,200 local offices in the country,[20] but many of these are very small, consisting only of a supervisor with a few subordinates. For the study of the structure of local offices, all those with fewer than five employees and all those with fewer than three levels are excluded, leaving 1,201 cases for the analysis. These local offices come from fifty-one agencies, because none of those in two jurisdictions (New Hampshire and the Virgin Islands) meet the criteria. The average size of the 1,201 local offices selected (which is, of course, larger than the mean for all local offices) is twenty-seven employees. There are, on the average, 7.1 different positions or job titles in one of these local offices, 3.3 hierarchical levels, and 2.4 sections whose supervisors report to the office

units that were later not defined as divisions because of their small size.) The cases of the four agencies in which less than one half of the eligible division heads answered the questionnaire are excluded.

19. This ratio is designed to indicate extent of employment service while holding agency size constant, and it is in no sense an indication of efficiency, since it ignores the results accomplished, and since many agency employees are not engaged in employment service.

20. The exact number varies from month to month. Our count was 2,235 local offices.

manager. But the mean of the total number of subordinates of the office manager is 6.0, which is the same as the mean span of control of division heads at the headquarters. The average span of control of first-line supervisors in local offices is somewhat lower, with a mean of 5.0. The mean of the supervisory ratio in local offices is 21 per cent, which also corresponds exactly to that at the agency headquarters. As already noted, however, the clerical ratio in the average local office is much lower (1:5) than in the average agency headquarters (1:1).

Now that the characteristics of these organizations have been reviewed, the next question is which of these characteristics occur together. As a first step in answering this question, the most pronounced simple correlations between agency characteristics are examined. Eight zero-order correlations among several hundred are greater than .50.[21] Six of these eight strong associations involve only four variables, which means that the correlation between any two of the four variables is greater than .50. The other two are correlations of two different variables with one of these four, namely, size (number of employees, in logarithmic transformation).

There exists apparently a configuration of organizational characteristics that tend to vary together in employment security agencies. The core of this configuration consists of four closely interrelated elements referring to complexity and scope: the division of labor (job titles), the hierarchical differentiation of the authority structure (levels), the technology (extent of utilization of computers), and the scope of the organization (number of employees). Two other factors somewhat related to this configuration are the horizontal differentiation of functions (divisions) and the absence of a large administrative staff (staff ratio, the correlation being negative). But do these correlations reflect causal influences? And if they or some of them do not, what is the substantive significance of observing such a configuration?

It has been often noted that a correlation between two variables, *x* and *y,* does not constitute evidence that *x* causes *y*. The different reasons why this is so must be stipulated to determine under which conditions one may

---

21. The logarithmic transformation of number of employees rather than the raw number is used as the measure of size in these correlations for reasons explicated in the next chapter. The correlation between number of divisions and number of officials reporting to the agency director, though meeting the criterion, is not considered, because the latter number includes the former. Two of the correlations involving a service measure just meet the criterion for all fifty-three cases but just fall short of it when the two territories—Puerto Rico and Virgin Islands—are excluded; these two correlations are also not considered in this preliminary analysis. For the correlations, see Table F–1, Appendix F.

infer a causal nexus from a correlation. First, the correlation may be spurious, resulting from the dependence of both x and y on a common antecedent. Second, it may be that y is not influenced by x, but y actually influences x. If either is the case, the correlation, of course, does not indicate a causal influence of x on y. However, even when there are good grounds for assuming that the correlation is not spurious and that x is the antecedent, some philosophers of science hold that a causal nexus cannot be inferred. For empirical evidence can only demonstrate the concomitant variation of two variables, not that there is actually a causal connection between them. The position taken here is that although necessary causal connections cannot be empirically demonstrated, as Hume has emphasized, it is justified to infer from the concomitant variation of x and y that x influences y provided that two conditions are met: the association between the two variables is not spurious according to all available evidence, and x may be assumed to precede y.[22] Whether or not the effect of x is called a causal influence is not important. The inference always remains provisional, however, because new evidence may reveal that the correlation is spurious, after all, or that the assumptions made about sequence were fallacious.

To make inferences about the ways in which some organizational conditions influence others is the objective of the rest of the book, using the procedures and the assumptions about the sequence among variables presented in Chapter 1. Numerous zero-order correlations will be revealed to be spurious by this analysis, and these will be disregarded in the inquiry into the influences exerted. Whether spurious or not, the observed correlations between characteristics of employment security agencies are indicative of the characteristics that are actually found together in these organizations, just as long days and warm weather do in fact occur together though neither causes the other. The analysis that abstracts from empirical observations only those elements from which causal inferences may be drawn thereby ignores the typical combinations of characteristics exhibited by the organizations that exist in reality.

The significance of examining the pronounced zero-order correlations between agency characteristics is that their configuration reflects empirical types. We want to look at these empirical constellations of organizational traits now, because the refined analysis that abstracts from them obscures them from view. The more complex the technology an agency employs, as indicated by extensive automation of operations, the more complex is its structure, as indicated by the division of labor, the number of levels in the

---

22. For a discussion of this complex problem in the philosophy of science, see Richard B. Braithwaite, *Scientific Explanation* (Cambridge, Eng.: University Press, 1953), pp. 293–318.

hierarchy of authority, and, to a lesser extent, the number of functional divisions. This syndrome of structural as well as technological complexity is also associated with agency size, which, in turn, is associated with a relatively small staff component providing administrative support. To be sure, some of the correlations defining this configuration of organizational attributes will turn out to be spurious on further analysis, but this is quite irrelevant inasmuch as these characteristics are found together in the concrete employment security agencies operating in the United States in 1966. The opposite extremes of this configuration represent contrasting types of organizations.

Contrasting Types

After a brief survey of the legal history of employment security in the United States, this chapter presented a description of the responsibilities of employment security agencies in both qualitative and quantitative terms, and it indicated the major characteristics of these organizations to be analyzed. The strongest zero-order correlations between these characteristics manifest a configuration of elements that tend to occur together and the polar extremes of which reflect contrasting empirical types of the organization of government bureaus. In conclusion, these polar types of organization and their implications are reviewed.

Machine technology has played a major role in many organizations for a long time, be they manufacturing concerns or armies, but its significance in government bureaus and other white-collar offices has been minor until quite recently. The invention and production of computers changed the situation drastically, though conventional data-processing equipment had already brought about some lesser changes earlier. Even if computers are essentially used only for routine accounting and record-keeping functions, as is the case in these agencies, automation basically alters many operations.[23] The introduction of extensive automated facilities in an agency is part of a constellation of characteristics, which include also a complex structure, with much occupational, hierarchical, and functional differentiation, large size, and a proportionately small administrative staff. It is rather surprising that the type of organization characterized by a high de-

---

23. Though the concept of technology does not refer to the hardware itself but to the procedures and skills employed in performing tasks, the size of the computer installation and whether computers are used at all are convenient indications of important differences in technology. For a conceptual analysis of technology in organizations, see Charles Perrow, "A Framework for the Comparative Analysis of Organizations," *American Sociological Review*, 32 (1967): 194–208.

gree of structural and technological complexity as well as large size tends to have a comparatively small administrative staff.[24] To be sure, one may suspect that the various complexities do not actually produce a reduction in the staff ratio (and the analysis in the following chapters will ascertain whether the suspicion that these correlations are spurious is correct), but the fact remains that large and complex agencies typically have a relatively small administrative staff.

The opposite type is a small organization with a simple structure—little division of labor, few hierarchical levels, and few functional divisions—in which operations are not automated and which has a high ratio of staff personnel. In these organizations, top management may well exercise more direct control over operations than in the first type, not only because the organization is smaller, but also because management is less far removed from the operating level, is not dependent on computer specialists, and has a relatively larger staff to assist it in administration. It might even be that top management's reluctance to relinquish more or less direct control over operations unless the pressure of large size forces it to do so plays a role in this configuration of organizational characteristics. Of course, most agencies do not represent one of the two extreme types, which are merely used to illustrate the polar opposites of the configuration of organizational characteristics found in varying degrees in these agencies.[25]

Which one of the two polar types expresses a bureaucratic form of organization? The answer is by no means obvious. On the one hand, the large size and structural complexity of the first type seem to mark it as the more bureaucratic. On the other hand, the only distinctly bureaucratic trait among the variables included, a large administrative staff, is characteristic of the second type, in which authority may also be more centralized in the hands of top management than in the first, if our conjectures are correct. It does not appear warranted to classify either extreme as the typical bureaucracy. As a matter of fact, the view taken here is that the search for the typical bureaucracy is a chimera. There are various bureaucratic characteristics, such as formalized procedures or centralized authority, but they do not necessarily occur together, and when one empirically investigates their interrelation and effects they are often not what the prevailing conception of bureaucracy would lead one to expect.

---

24. Whereas only the staff ratio's zero-order correlation with size meets the criterion ($-.60$), its zero-order correlations with the other four variables in the configuration are also considerable, ranging from $-.42$ to $-.31$.

25. Jerald Hage derives contrasting types with some similar features from an axiomatic theory: "An Axiomatic Theory of Organizations," *Administrative Science Quarterly,* 10 (1965): 289–320, esp. 304–305.

PART TWO

Formal Structure

The present study begins by examining . . . the bearing
the mere *number* of sociated individuals has upon
[the] forms of social life. It will be immediately
conceded on the basis of everyday experience, that a
group upon reaching a certain size must develop forms
and organs which serve its maintenance and promotion,
but which a smaller group does not need. . . . They are
the abstract form of group cohesion whose concrete form
can no longer exist after the group has reached a
certain size. Their utility, which ramifies into a thousand
social characteristics, ultimately depends on numerical
premises. They are the embodiment of group forces and
thus have a superpersonal and objective character with
which they confront the individual.

SIMMEL, *Sociology*

CHAPTER 3

Differentiation

The scope of an organization's responsibilities is not the same as the complexity of these responsibilities. The scope or volume of responsibilities of the employment security agency in California is, of course, much larger than that of the agency in the Virgin Islands, although both are legally responsible for the same basic functions, which means that their official responsibilities are quite similar in complexity. To be sure, variations in state laws and in administrative policies create certain differences in responsibilities among agencies, because some emphasize intensive employment services, for example, whereas others stress primarily the simpler unemployment insurance activities. But such differences in complexity are obviously something else than differences in the scope of operations.

A parallel distinction can be drawn between the scope and the complexity of an organization's formal structure. A straightforward indication of the scope of the organization is the number of its employees, or members, whose interrelated positions define the structure.[1] The complexity of the formal structure is indicated by the number of different positions and dif-

1. The number of positions rather than the number of persons occupying them might be considered a better measure of the scope of the structure, but we prefer to treat the distinct positions as an expression of differentiation.

ferent subunits of various sorts in the organization to which employees are allocated. There is an extremely close relationship between the scope of responsibilities of employment security agencies and the scope of their structures as manifest in the number of their employees. Two measures of scope of responsibilities are the number of clients claiming unemployment benefits and the number of applicants for employment services. The former's correlation with number of agency employees is .98, and the latter's is .96. Hence, the scope of responsibilities and the personnel size of any agency can virtually not be distinguished. Size defined by number of employees is used as the over-all indicator of the scope of an organization. These very high correlations also reveal that an agency's size depends essentially on the demands for its services, which are largely outside of its own control,[2] and they therefore constitute supportive evidence for the decision to treat size as the antecedent of the internal structure in the analysis.

This chapter is concerned with the influences exerted by the size of employment security agencies on their other organizational characteristics, with primary emphasis on the implications of size for the differentiation of positions and subunits along various lines. In other words, the impact of the scope of an organization on the complexity of its formal structure is analyzed. Structural complexity is assumed to have its source in differentiation, and the operational definition of differentiation in any one dimension is the number of different subunits or positions observed along this dimension, be it local offices, job assignments, or hierarchical levels. The effects of size on some aspects of internal administration and the services administered will be examined in the next chapter.

Pervasive Effects of Size

The size of employment security agencies has pervasive effects on their organizational characteristics. The most prominent influence of large size is that it gives rise to the differentiation of the formal structure in various respects. The larger an agency is, the greater the number of local offices under its jurisdictions, the number of official job titles indicative of the division of labor, the number of hierarchical levels in the authority structure, the number of major divisions under top management, and the number of sections per division. All these associations are pronounced, and the consistency of the pattern is impressive. Larger agencies not only are differen-

---

2. Anticipating a later discussion, it might also be noted that the correlation between the state's population and the size of its employment security agency is .95.

tiated into more subunits along various lines than smaller ones, but their subunits also contain a larger number of persons. As agency size increases, so does the number of employees per local office, the number of officials directly reporting to top management, the average number reporting to each division head,[3] and even the average number of operating employees at the bottom level reporting to each first-line supervisor, both in local offices and in headquarters divisions. These associations imply that size affects the supervisory ratio, but this effect as well as that of size on the staff ratio and on the clerical ratio are reserved for discussion in Chapter 4.

Other conditions are associated with agency size as well. Larger agencies have more formalized personnel procedures than smaller ones, as indicated by extent of regulations, and they pay better salaries. One of the relatively few factors unrelated to size is the proportion of appointments made strictly on the basis of merit criteria of civil service, and another is the education of the interviewers recently appointed. In contrast, size has much bearing on whether an agency has automated operations and on the scope of its computer installation. Partly directly and partly through the other influences it exerts, agency size also affects evaluation procedures, decentralization of responsibilities, the services the agency provides and the personnel costs of providing them, and even the supervisory patterns in local offices.

This quick review of findings, preliminary to their full analysis, is merely intended to convey an over-all impression of the penetrating impact of size in these organizations. The conclusion to which our data point, that size is the most important condition affecting the structure of organizations, differs from that reached by some other investigators. For example, Woodward states that size in the ninety-two British manufacturing firms she studied "did not appear to affect organization as much as might have been expected."[4] Her data show that size is unrelated to the technical complexity of the production systems employed by these firms and that technical complexity exerts considerable influence on various measures of the administrative structure, but she does not present data on the relationships between size and these measures.[5] On the other hand, the more care-

---

3. Whereas the total number of officials reporting to top management is closely related to the number of divisions (.69), the average number reporting to division heads is not closely related to sections per division (.18). The main reason for this is that division heads, notably in small divisions, have many subordinates who are not section managers.

4. Joan Woodward, *Industrial Organization* (London: Oxford University Press, 1965), p. 31.

5. Ibid., pp. 35–67. The only relevant data presented indicate that the span of control of supervisors becomes wider with increasing size; ibid., pp. 31–32.

fully designed study by Hickson and his colleagues of a random sample of forty-six British firms and other organizations in the Birmingham area finds that size exerts much, and technology considerably less, influence on structure as defined by their complicated scale "structuring of activities," which includes several concepts used by us to designate structural complexity, such as division of labor and hierarchical levels, as well as some others, such as standardization and formalization.[6] To cite one more case, Hall and his colleagues conclude from their research on a group of seventy-five miscellaneous organizations that "size and organizational structure are not closely related." [7] However, most of their indications of structure comparable to ours are in fact shown to be related to size. Specifically, although size is unrelated to number of divisions in their data, it is directly related to number of sections per division, hierarchical levels, and dispersed locations.[8] Associations between size and various aspects of differentiation in the formal structure, as here defined, are observable also in other organizations than employment security agencies, but some investigators appear to be reluctant to credit size with exerting these influences.

Two conditions correlated with size should be examined before turning to the analysis of size and differentiation because they precede all or most of the variables pertaining to differentiation in the assumed sequence. The first of these is the degree of formalization of personnel procedures, as indicated by the extent of written regulations in the state's civil service system under which the employment security agency operates. Its correlation with agency size is .58.[9] But agency size is really not the appropriate independent variable in this instance, since the personnel procedures are part of the state government and not of its component, the employment security agency. Hence, the correlation between number of state employees, indicative of size of state government, and the extent of formalized personnel

6. David J. Hickson et al., "Operations Technology and Organization Structure," *Administrative Science Quarterly,* 14 (1969): 378–397. Size, in logarithmic transformation, has a correlation of .69 with the scale and one of .67 with levels (the only comparable structural variable separately shown), which is very close to the corresponding correlation in employment security agencies.

7. Richard H. Hall et al., "Organizational Size, Complexity, and Formalization," *American Sociological Review,* 32 (1967): 912.

8. Ibid., pp. 908–911.

9. This correlation was not included in the analysis of the most pronounced ones in the last chapter, not only for the technical reason that the correlation of the logarithm of size, the variable used there, with extent of regulations (.44) does not meet the criterion set (.50), but also because agency size is not the proper antecedent and because an extreme case makes this correlation misleadingly large, as noted below in the text.

regulations was computed (.54); it is nearly as large as the original one.[10] Inasmuch as the state merit system covers nearly all state employees in some states, but primarily those in grant-in-aid agencies—including the employment security agency—in others there is the possibility that the body of merit regulations is related to number of state employees only if most of them are under the merit system and not if only those in a few agencies are.

The multiple regression in Table 3–1 reveals that the association be-

TABLE 3-1. *Multiple Regression of* **Extent of Personnel Regulations** *on State Government Conditions*[a]

Independent Variable	Standardized Regression Coefficient	Zero-Order Correlation
Size of Government	.49**	.54
Merit System Coverage	.21*	.33

Multiple R = .58; $n = 51$.

*Greater than one-and-a-half times its standard error.

**Greater than twice its standard error.

[a]Dependent variable is set in bold face.

tween size of state government and extent of personnel regulations in the merit system is only slightly reduced when one controls whether the employees in all or only in some state bureaus are covered, but the fact that all state employees are covered exerts some additional influence on the amount of these regulations. The suspicion that the association prevails mostly in states with full coverage is not justified. Indeed, inspection of the scatter diagram (not presented) reveals that the extent of merit regulations increases more consistently with increasing numbers of state employees if only some of them, rather than if all, are covered. The scatter diagram indicates another problem, however. The extent of regulations in the largest state government (that of California, which has also the largest employment security agency) is five standard deviations above the mean, which produces a misleadingly large correlation. When this extreme case is elimi-

---

10. It should be noted that the regulations of state merit systems deal only with the principles determining appointments, promotions, separations, and other personnel matters. They do not include descriptions or requirements of specific positions or even a list of positions. Hence, the association between size of state government and extent of these regulations is not simply the result of a larger number of positions being described in the regulations of larger governments.

nated, the correlation between size of state government and extent of merit regulations is much reduced though not entirely erased (.24).

The elaboration of formalized personnel procedures appears to be a typical case of the growth of bureaucratic red tape in large government organizations, but this first impression may well oversimplify matters. Personnel practices that are governed by explicit standards of civil service have several advantages. They maintain uniformity in making appointments, provide that these be based not on political patronage but, at least partly, on merit, and protect candidates against personal bias. But they also have the disadvantage, particularly in a large organization, that a great variety of personnel decisions are determined by a limited set of rules that are not fully appropriate for all situations. A way to reduce this disadvantage of explicit personnel standards without foregoing their advantages is, paradoxically, to elaborate these standards and establish appropriate ones for what were before exceptional cases, for example, by stipulating procedures for appointment when the list of certified candidates has been exhausted. However, a large body of rules is unwieldy and difficult to administer. Whether the new administrative problems created by elaborate personnel regulations outweigh the problems they are designed to meet must be judged on the basis of their influences on operations and managerial practice, which will be examined in subsequent chapters.[11]

A second condition strongly influenced by size that is assumed to be antecedent to most aspects of the formal structure (all but the division of labor) is the automation of operations. The measure is a thirteen-category score of the scope of the computer installation, based on the number of computers and the number of input-output units. The correlation between this measure and number of employees is high (.82). It is hardly surprising that larger agencies, with their larger volume of activities, have more extensive computer facilities once they institute automation than smaller ones. Though this fact accounts for the strength of the correlation, it does not account for all of it. Large agencies are also more likely than small ones to introduce automation. Whether or not an agency has any computer of whatever capacity, coded as a dummy variable, is correlated with agency size .30.

The size of an employment security agency exerts the dominant influence on the extent of automation, but another condition reveals also a slight association with it that persists when size is controlled, namely, the

---

11. Inasmuch as the personnel regulations are the states', not the agencys' own, this variable and agency size are both assumed to be antecedents of all other organizational characteristics and neither will be considered as an antecedent of the other in the analysis.

salary of interviewers (see Table 3–2). These findings suggest that the volume of work largely governs whether automated equipment is being introduced and the scale on which it is introduced in these organizations, but that the cost of labor exerts some additional influence on the tendency to install such equipment. For the higher the cost of labor, the lower is the volume of work necessary to make it economical to substitute machines for manpower.[12] The salaries of interviewers tend to be indicative of the salary levels of other employees, that is, of the agency's labor costs. The rental of computers is economically advisable only if the cost it entails is less than the potential manpower savings it can realize. The volume of

TABLE 3-2.   *Multiple Regression of* **Automation** *on Agency Conditions*

Independent Variable	Standardized Regression Coefficient	Zero-Order Correlation
Agency Size	.65**	.82
Salary of Interviewers	.13*	.39
Division of Labor	.16	.71

Multiple R = .84; $n = 53$
 *Greater than one-and-a-half times its standard error.
 **Greater than twice its standard error.

work at which this occurs is lower if the salaries paid to employees are high than if they are low. Besides, as the cost of labor increases more rapidly over time than that of mechanical equipment, it becomes economical for smaller and smaller organizations to introduce mechanical equipment,[13] which is reflected in the tendency of larger agencies to have instituted automation earlier and of increasingly smaller ones to do so now.

Thus, the decision to install and enlarge computer facilities seems to depend primarily on the volume of work and, to a much lesser extent, on the cost of labor in employment security agencies. The interpretation advanced implies that the managerial decisions concerning mechanization are governed by essentially the same economic considerations in these government agencies as in the private firms Melman studied, though labor costs may exert more influence in private firms than in these public agencies. To be sure, factors other than the volume of work and the cost of labor affect the extent of automation in employment security agencies. The division of labor is not one of them, however. Despite its pronounced zero-order cor-

12. Seymour Melman, *Dynamic Factors in Industrial Productivity* (Oxford: Blackwell, 1956), pp. 35–66.
13. Ibid.

relation with automation (.71), no appreciable association between the two remains when size and salary are controlled (Table 3–2). The division of labor does not promote automation, and the high zero-order correlation between the two noted in Chapter 2 is the result of the influence of size on both of them.

Number and Size of Structural Components

The technology of an organization, including notably the skills of the personnel utilized to perform operations as well as the machines used, is designed to meet the problems posed by its responsibilities. We just saw that a large volume of responsibilities encourages automation, which affects both the skills and the machines needed, and we shall see later that the performance of complex activities, such as those involved in intensive services, is associated with an agency's skill requirements for personnel appointments. Technological differences of this sort can be observed whether one compares the work of individuals or the operations of organizations. The technology is not the sole means employed by organizations to manage their responsibilities, however. Another means for this end is distinctly organizational, that is, characteristic only of the operations of organizations and not of the work of individuals.

A fundamental method by which organizations discharge their responsibilities is to subdivide them along several lines into components and to assign these components to different groups of employees. Indeed, the implementation of objectives by subdividing tasks constitutes the very nature of a work organization. The subdivision of tasks is what makes it possible for organizations to accomplish missions of staggering magnitude and complexity. No manager could coordinate, let alone perform, the diverse activities entailed by the mass production of cars were it not for the organization of the manufacturing concern. No general could command an army if responsibilities were not organized through subdivision within it. No official, nor any number of them without an organization, could process weekly unemployment checks for 100,000 individuals. The most complex executive duties have been simplified by the subdivision of responsibilities in organizations, without which subdivision they would not be humanly manageable.

Subdivision produces differentiation in the structure. The important point is that the subdivision of responsibilities in organizations occurs along several intersecting dimensions. Responsibilities for clients in various places or with varying needs are divided among branch offices; those for different tasks are distributed among occupational positions; those for various functions are assigned to different divisions or sections; and those for managerial supervision and coordination are divided among hierarchical levels. Consequently, organizations are differentiated not only vertically into authority levels but also horizontally in several distinct ways, for example, by function, by occupational specialty, and by location. These intersecting dimensions delineate the formal structure and its complexity. The subdivision of responsibilities along various lines simplifies the tasks of individuals and simultaneously makes the structure more complex. Pronounced differentiation in organizations, which intensifies problems of communication and coordination, may be said to substitute greater structural complexity for lesser complexity of individual tasks.

Let us start the analysis of the influence of size on various aspects of differentiation in employment security agencies by examining the relationship between number of employees and number of local offices.[14] These two variables are very highly correlated (.94). Since the size of local offices varies from fewer than five employees to more than 200, such a high correlation is by no means inevitable. One might consider the number of local offices as the antecedent condition that determines the complement of employees an agency needs.[15] An alternative interpretation is that the scope of an organization and its operations, as indicated by number of employees, affects the number of different branch offices that are established, just as it affects other aspects of differentiation. In any case, the very high correlation makes it virtually impossible to distinguish between the influence of number of employees and that of number of local offices, given the previously mentioned problem of multicollinearity. The number of local offices may best be thought of simply as an alternative measure of agency size. Because number of employees is the preferred measure of size, number of local offices is excluded from further analysis. But one more point should be noted. The rate of increase in the number of local offices with increasing agency size slightly declines among larger agencies, that is, the regression line of number of local offices on number of employees reveals a somewhat declining slope.

The larger an agency is, the more pronounced is the division of labor within it. The correlation between size and number of job titles is .78, which means that size accounts for 60 per cent of the variance in this measure of division of labor.[16] The scatter diagram of the relationship between

14. The variable is the total number of local offices in every agency, of course, not only those selected for further analysis.
15. See Hall et al., "Organizational Size, Complexity, and Formalization," p. 909.
16. This association could be conceptualized as indicating that the number of positions determines the number of employees hired to fill them, but we think it is more accurate and meaningful to consider size the independent variable and occupational differentiation the dependent one.

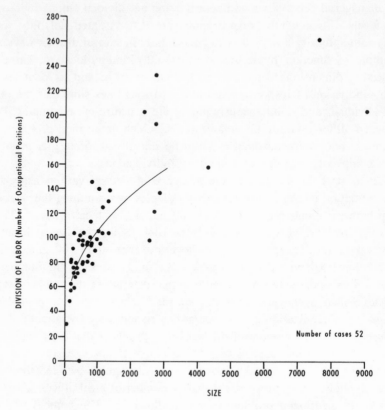

FIGURE 3–1   Scatter Diagram of Division of Labor and Size

these two variables (Figure 3–1) shows that the expansion of job titles with increasing agency size is quite rapid at first but tapers off for agencies with more than 1,000 employees. Thus, the regression line of division of labor on size reveals that the distribution of observations is not a straight line but a curve that becomes less steep as size increases, just as is the case for the (not shown) regression curve of local offices on size.[17] The shape of this curve suggests that a logarithmic transformation of size might

17. The points used to produce rough estimates for regression curves were obtained by averaging values within groups based on the variable size. Three points were calculated for the total agency, one each for the following size categories: less than 500, 500–999, 1,000 or more. Seven points were calculated for the scatter diagrams of local offices in Part Two, one each for the following size categories: less than 13, 13–24, 25–37, 38–49, 50–67, 68–99, and 100 or above. For each graph the points plotted are the averages within each category of both the size and the y variable, and a smooth curve has been drawn between these points.

straighten it out, but such a transformation actually produces a slope in the opposite direction, bending upward, as Figure 3–2 indicates.

The pattern observed implies that increasing agency size fosters occupational differentiation at a declining rate. In other words, the impact of size on the division of labor declines with increasing size. As Figure 3–1 shows, a difference in size of, say, 500 employees has more effect on the division of labor among agencies with fewer than 1,000 employees than among those with several thousand employees. Although the power of size to expand the division of labor declines with increasing size, this decline is not very pronounced. It is not so pronounced that one could say that it is the rate at which size increases that governs the expanding division of labor, for were it that pronounced the logarithmic transformation of size would produce a straight regression line and not one curved upward. Yet, small though it is, this declining slope of the curve has important substantive implications.

Not only the number of different occupation specialties (job titles) but

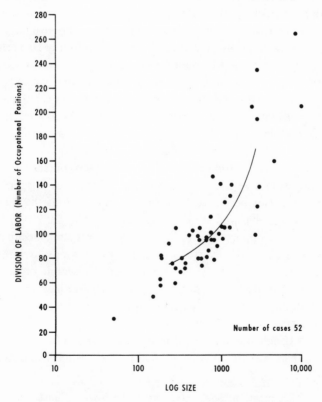

FIGURE 3–2 Scatter Diagram of Division of Labor and the Logarithm of Size

also the average number of persons in each specialty is greater in large than in small agencies. This conclusion can be directly derived from the shape of the regression line of number of job titles on number of employees, and it can also be confirmed independently. If two coordinates are drawn from any point on this curve, the ratio of the horizontal to the vertical coordinate represents the ratio of number of employees to number of job titles. Because the curve rises steeply at first and then more gradually, the number of job titles in the denominator of this ratio increases less than proportionately as the number of employees in the numerator increases, which means that the ratio of employees per job title must increase with increasing size. One might suspect that this association between employees per job title and total number of employees is not very strong, inasmuch as the declining slope of the curve is not pronounced. But when the correlation between these two variables is computed, it turns out to be no less than .94. The average number of employees in the various occupational positions of an employment agency is very closely related to its size.

The men and women in an organization who share the same occupational position may be considered an ingroup of colleagues, who have common problems and interests, and who supply a homogeneous occupational environment for one another. The existence of a great variety of occupational specialties in an organization creates a heterogeneous occupational environment for employees, in which they have much opportunity for social contacts with others outside their own specialty. Since the average number of employees in an occupational specialty as well as the number of different specialties is greater in large than in small agencies, large organizations provide a more homogeneous as well as a more heterogeneous occupational environment for their employees, paradoxical as it may seem. (This is the case notwithstanding the geographical dispersion of the personnel of employment security agencies, inasmuch as the same pattern of relationships is observed in local offices, as we shall see.)

There is more opportunity for social contacts within occupational ingroups as well as with diverse occupational outgroups in large than in small organizations. A study of a government research organization by Pelz suggests that those individuals perform best who have extensive social contacts with both ingroup colleagues, from whom they receive social support, and outsiders with different viewpoints, whose discussions stimulate them.[18] This conclusion implies, if it may be extended to other government employees than research workers, that larger agencies constitute better

18. Donald C. Pelz, "Some Social Factors Related to Performance in a Research Organization," *Administrative Science Quarterly,* 1 (1956): 310–325.

working environments than smaller ones, because they make either type of social contact more readily available. The existence of much opportunity for diverse social contacts, however, does not assure that these contacts will actually occur. Members of large organizations are often said to confine their social contacts more to their colleague ingroups than those of small ones. If this impression is correct, the reason cannot be that there is less opportunity in large than in small organizations for contacts with others in a variety of speciàlties. The likely reason is rather that ingroup contacts are so seductive that they tend to preempt most of the time, with the result that workers engage in extensive outgroup contacts primarily if forced to do so by the fact that they have few ingroup colleagues in a small organization.

Size then has two effects on the occupational structure of employment security agencies, both reflected in the shape of the regression curve of number of job titles on number of employees, that is, its somewhat concave shape from above. The larger an agency is, the greater is the number of occupational positions that have become formally differentiated, and the larger is also the average size of the personnel component in a single occupational position. The large volume of operations in large agencies requires more employment interviewers and more claims examiners and more typists than are needed in small agencies, as one would expect. At the same time, the larger volume of tasks in larger agencies makes it possible to subdivide responsibilities more into narrower specialties than can be done in smaller agencies, which do not have enough work to occupy, for instance, several specialists in their in-service training program or their administrative research. The occupational differentiation within an agency that large size promotes segregates simpler from more complex duties, and it consequently finds expression in the routinization of some jobs and the specialization of others. The routine jobs can then be filled with less skilled personnel and the specialized tasks can be performed by specialists with expert training. But larger agencies need more personnel per position than smaller ones, particularly because they have more local offices among which their employees are distributed, and the expansion of the personnel in most positions with increasing agency size limits the impact of size on the differentiation of positions.

Although the regression line of number of local offices on number of employees exhibits only a very slight tendency to be concave from above, this curvature is sufficient to reflect a parallel twofold connection between size and local offices. The local offices in larger agencies are not only more numerous but also larger on the average than those in smaller agencies. In other words, as agency size increases, so does the mean size of local offices as well as their number. (The correlation between agency size and mean size of local offices is .65.) The regression lines of other structural components on agency size have a similar shape, with still more pronounced curvatures, which indicates that size has the same kind of double effect on all these aspects of the formal structure.

Large agency size generates hierarchical differentiation of the authority structure into many managerial levels. The correlation between size and the maximum number of hierarchical levels in any segment of the headquarters is .60. The scatter diagram (Figure 3–3) shows that the number of levels increases sharply and rather consistently first but that the regression curve ultimately becomes quite flat, as all four largest agencies have the same number of levels in their hierarchy. A multilevel hierarchy increases the distance between management and the operating level and creates problems of communication and managerial control, which seem to set limits to hierarchical differentiation. The decline in the slope of the regression line is more pronounced in this instance than in those of local offices and of job titles. Logarithmic transformation of size produces a regression curve that is much closer to linear than the original curve, as can be seen in Figure 3–4, and it improves the correlation from .60 to .73. This trans-

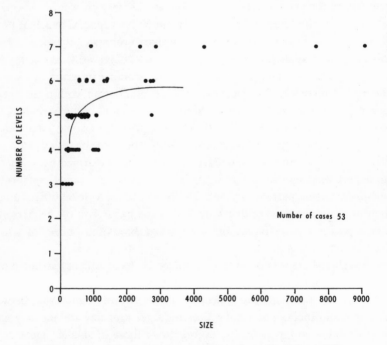

FIGURE 3–3   Scatter Diagram of Number of Levels and Size

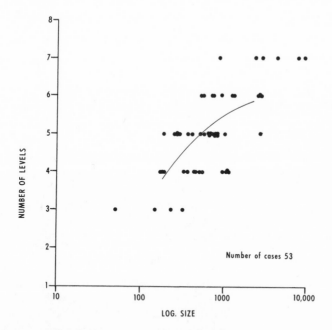

FIGURE 3–4   Scatter Diagram of Number of Levels and the Logarithm of Size

formation is therefore employed when the number of levels is the dependent variable. The substantive implications of the considerable decline in the slope of the original regression curve are that the impact of size on hierarchical differentiation declines with increasing size and that the personnel complement per level as well as the number of levels increases with growing size.

Large size also promotes functional differentiation of the agency headquarters into divisions at a declining rate. The scatter diagram of size and number of divisions (Figure 3–5) shows that the two largest agencies have fewer divisions than four of the six next largest. It would be hardly worthwhile to mention this drop at the extreme end based on only two cases were it not for the fact that the interrelations within the formal structure, to be examined presently, furnish good grounds for expecting the largest agencies not to have the largest number of divisions. Logarithmic transformation of size is clearly indicated in this case by the great improvement it produces (Figure 3–6). Whereas the correlation of number of divisions with raw size is .38, its correlation with the logarithm of size is .54. Inasmuch as increases in agency size increase the number of divisions much at

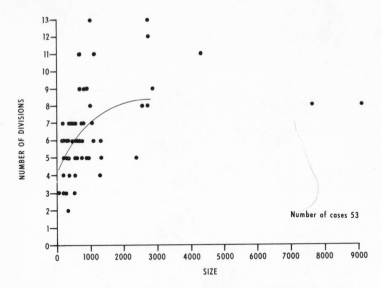

FIGURE 3–5   Scatter Diagram of Number of Divisions and Size

first but not at all ultimately, the average division consists of many more employees in large than in small agencies. In fact, the correlation between the size of an agency and the average size of its divisions is .96.

The same pattern is observed again, in more extreme form, when one examines the relationship between size and number of sections per division, as an indication of horizontal differentiation on the next level in the headquarters hierarchy. The scatter diagram reveals much dispersion and a decline in number of sections per division for the three largest agencies (Figure 3–7). Logarithmic transformation of size increases the correlation from a mere .16 to .43 and straightens the curve, though it brings the downward trend of the very largest agencies into still sharper focus (Figure 3–8). Divisions become differentiated into more sections as agency size increases to about the mean, but additional increases in size do not produce further differentiation within divisions. The conclusion is once more parallel to those reached earlier. The larger an agency is, the larger are both the number of sections per division and the average size of these sections.

These effects of the size of employment security agencies on their formal structure are pronounced and amazingly consistent. Whether local offices, occupational positions, hierarchical levels, functional divisions, or sections per division are considered, size has a double effect. It simultaneously increases the number of any of these structural components and their average size. These two effects are not independent, however.[19] The growth in the average size of structural components with increasing agency size dampens the effect of agency size on the number of components, that is, on differentiation. Consequently, the size of the organization promotes structural differentiation at declining rates.

Agency size is most closely related to the number of different local offices (.94), and the extent of its impact on other aspects of differentiation is in the following order: division of labor (.78), hierarchical levels (.73), functional divisions (.54), and sections per division (.43). Though size has been logarithmically transformed to compute the last three correlations (because doing so met the criterion), this rank order of decreasing associations corresponds to the degree of curvature of the regression lines of the various measures of differentiation on raw size. The regression curve of

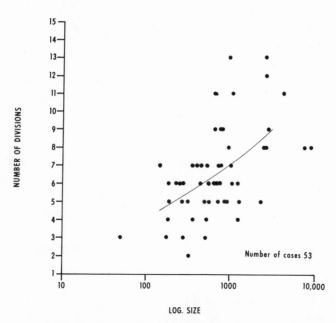

FIGURE 3–6   Scatter Diagram of Number of Divisions and the Logarithm of Size

19. In the case of occupational positions, the product of number of positions and average number of employees in each equals the total size of the agency. In the case of local offices, the corresponding product equals the personnel outside the agency headquarters, and in the case of the other three variables, it equals the personnel in the agency headquarters. The correlation between the number of employees at the headquarters and the total number of agency employees, both in logarithmic transformation, is .98.

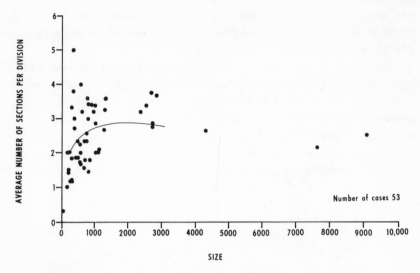

FIGURE 3–7   Scatter Diagram of Number of Sections
per Division and Size

local offices on size declines only very little; that of job titles declines some; that of levels flattens out; and those of divisions and sections per division even turn down with the most extreme cases. The increases in the correlations resulting from the logarithmic transformation of size, which provide a more rigorous criterion of degree of curvature, or decline in slope, exhibit the same rank order. This pattern suggests that the over-all impact of size on various forms of structural differentiation depends in good part on the limits set by the growing size of the structural components themselves that accompanies increases in agency size; these limits are reflected by the degree of decline in the slope of the curve of number of components on agency size.

Shape of the Pyramid

The shape of the pyramid is defined by three variables and their relationships: the number of hierarchical levels, the number of functional divisions, and the number of sections per division at the agency headquarters. The questions raised now are what antecedent conditions in addition to size influence these three variables, and how are the three interdependent. Two related factors are examined in the same connection. The number of divisions is indicative of the scope of major supervisory responsibilities of top management, and it is supplemented by a measure of the agency director's total span of control, including not only division heads but also supervisors of smaller units and individual specialists directly reporting to him or his deputy. Similarly, the number of sections per division, which may be said to circumscribe the major responsibilities of division heads, is supplemented by a measure of total average span of control of division heads, including single officials as well as section managers who report to them.[20]

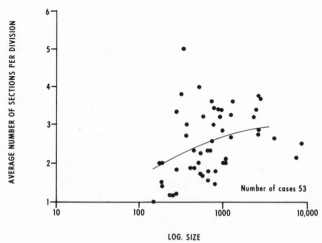

FIGURE 3–8 Scatter Diagram of Number of Sections
per Division and the Logarithm of Size

Agency size exerts the dominant influence on the differentiation of the authority structure into multiple levels, accounting for more than one-half of the variance in number of levels, but another condition also exerts a slight influence on hierarchical differentiation, namely, whether agency operations are automated (see Table 3–3).[21] It has been noted in the last

───────────

20. Because it makes little sense to consider the total span of control of an official as either the antecedent or the consequence of the number of his major responsibilities that are included in the measure of total span, the regression analysis treats neither variable as antecedent of the other, whether reference is to top management or to division heads.

21. Whether or not automation has been instituted affects levels. Extent of computer installation does not have an observable effect on levels (possibly because of the serious problem of multicollinearity created by three very highly correlated independent variables in the same regression problem if the thirteen-category variable of extent of automation is substituted for the dummy variable).

TABLE 3-3. *Multiple Regression of* **Hierarchical Levels** *on Agency Conditions*

Independent Variable	Standardized Regression Coefficient	Zero-Order Correlation
Agency Size (Log)	.75**	.73
Division of Labor	−.11	.58
Automation (Dummy)[a]	.16*	.44

Multiple R = .75; n = 53
 *Greater than one-and-a-half times its standard error.
 **Greater than twice its standard error.
 [a]Dichotomous dummy variable: whether or not any computer exists. Unless indicated, "automation" refers to thirteen-category variable of extent of computer facilities.

chapter that a multilevel hierarchy tends to be found together with a pronounced division of labor as well as large size and automation. Despite the high zero-order correlation between division of labor and levels, however, their association vanishes when other conditions are controlled or, for that matter, when size alone is controlled. The division of labor, though correlated with hierarchical levels, apparently does not exert an independent influence on them inasmuch as the correlation between the two factors is the result of the influence of size on both of them.[22]

The number of headquarters divisions as well as that of hierarchical levels is strongly influenced by size, which would lead one to expect divisions and levels to be correlated. Though a positive zero-order correlation is indeed observed between number of levels and number of divisions, it is less than the association expected on the basis of their common dependence on size. The theoretically expected correlation is .40 (the product of the two correlations of the variables with size in logarithmic transformation), whereas the observed correlation is only .19. This discrepancy suggests that a negative force operates to counteract the influence of size and to depress the correlation between the two dimensions of structural differentiation below that expected on the basis of this influence. The direct influence of one of these structural dimensions on the other seems to constitute this negative force.

The more pronounced the vertical differentiation into a multilevel hierarchy is at the headquarters of an employment security agency, the less pronounced is the horizontal differentiation into many divisions (Table 3–4). The strong negative effect of levels on divisions ($b^* = -.45$) is only

22. The correlations of the division of labor with automation and with levels are the only two that turned out to be spurious of the eight in the configuration discussed in Chapter 2.

evident when size is controlled in a multiple regression analysis. At the same time, the multiple regression reveals that the direct positive effect of size on divisions is much stronger ($b^* = .88$) than the zero-order correlation implies (.55), because part of it is concealed in the simple correlation by the fact that the many levels typically found in large agencies tend to reduce the number of divisions. How can these findings be interpreted?

The initial response of a growing organization to the expanding volume of its responsibilities may often be to establish additional divisions specialized in various functions under the direct supervision of top management. The proliferation of divisions widens the span of control of the top executive, and his consequent time-consuming administrative burdens impinge on his major executive functions, such as long-range planning and maintaining external communication. Appointing a deputy improves the situation, but only temporarily if the number of divisions continues to increase.

TABLE 3-4. *Multiple Regression of* **Number of Divisions** *on Agency Conditions*

Independent Variable	Standardized Regression Coefficient	Zero-Order Correlation
Agency Size (Log)	.88**	.55
Levels	−.45**	.19

Multiple R = .63; n = 53
**Greater than twice its standard error.

A reorganization, not just a new appointment, is needed to effectively relieve the agency director of excessive administrative burdens and free his time for major executive responsibilities. The reorganization frequently takes the form of creating a small number of superdivisions, whose chiefs alone now report directly to top management, whereas the former division heads (who would be termed section managers after the change by our criterion) report to them. The changes instituted during the Lindsay administration in the departmental organization of the city of New York took this form. Other illustrations are the establishment of the Department of Defense and the Department of Health, Education and Welfare in the federal government. These changes made officials previously directly responsible to the mayor of New York or to the President of the United States subordinates of city commissioners or U.S. Secretaries.

Instituting such an intervening level of managers, and thereby inevitably increasing the number of levels, is intended to reduce the number of divisions directly under top management. The sequence of historical events does not have to be the same as the one here reconstructed and illustrated, however, for the basic principle to be valid. Managerial training or experience may enable top executives to anticipate the administrative problems a proliferation of divisions would create. An experienced executive might forestall these problems by maintaining a small number of divisions, creating subunits within these divisions rather than new divisions for specialized functions, and establishing the necessary additional managerial levels at lower tiers in the hierarchy. Whether there is a reorganization or the problem had been anticipated, the end result is the same: additional managerial levels are added to keep the number of divisions small.

The interpretation advanced is that hierarchical differentiation into multiple levels tends to occur in large organizations because it relieves management of excessive supervisory burdens that interfere with its executive responsibilities. Another measure of the supervisory duties of the top executive is the total number of officials reporting directly to him and his deputy. Table 3–5 shows that the effect of size on the agency director's

TABLE 3-5. *Multiple Regression of* **Director's Span of Control** *on Agency Conditions*

Independent Variable	Standardized Regression Coefficient	Zero-Order Correlation
Agency Size (Log)	.59**	.39
Levels	−.27	.16

Multiple R = .43; *n* = 53
**Greater than twice its standard error.

total span of control is parallel to, though not so pronounced as, its effect on number of divisions, but hierarchical levels exert no significant influence on the measure that includes minor as well as major supervisory duties. Top management's major responsibilities for divisions are more sensitive as an indicator of the administrative load than is the total span of control; the total span is less affected by the pressure of large size than the number of divisions, and hardly at all by the counterpressure of multiple levels.

The inverse association between vertical differentiation into multiple levels and horizontal differentiation into many divisions suggests that organizations have a tendency to develop either a squat pyramid or a tall one, though large organizations are typically both taller and wider at the top than small organizations. Only one of the conditions that affect in which one of these two directions an employment security agency is likely to expand could be identified. The automation of operations slightly encourages the development of tall pyramids, as Table 3–3 has shown, quite possibly because it minimizes their disadvantages. A tall hierarchy has the advantage of reducing top management's administrative load but at the same time the disadvantage of increasing its distance from the operating level. How serious this disadvantage is depends on the form of management. Many hierarchical levels engender problems of communication that seriously impede top management's control over operations if it is primarily exercised by issuing directives through channels. The more top management relies on impersonal mechanisms of control, on the other hand, the less of a liability is a tall hierarchy.

Automation serves as an impersonal mechanism of control. It mechanizes some tasks and routinizes others that continue to be performed by employees, thus lessening the need for managerial guidance. Moreover, automation enables top management to control operations by having the decisive voice in determining, in consultation with its staff, the computer set-up and how it is used. The automated set-up, once designed, exerts constraints over the performance of employees, who must adapt their work to the requirements of the computer and the programs used. Consequently, automation obviates the need for many of the directives management otherwise communicates through channels in order to guide daily operations. Since automation makes management less dependent on hierarchical channels of communication, it reduces the disadvantage of multiple levels and fosters their development. Although this conclusion is based only on weak evidence of a direct influence of automation on levels in employment security agencies, confidence in it is strengthened by parallel results obtained in research on other organizations. Thus, Woodward finds that the most automated of eighty British manufacturing firms have the largest number of levels;[23] a case study of the introduction of automation in an American white-collar office shows that it resulted in the addition of a managerial level;[24] and a study of 254 government finance departments in this country also finds a positive association between automation and hierarchical levels.[25]

Three conditions besides agency size influence the number of sections per division (Table 3–6). The most pronounced of these influences is that

---

23. Woodward, *Industrial Organization,* pp. 51–52.
24. Floyd C. Mann and Lawrence K. Williams, "Observations on the Dynamics of a Change to Electric Data-Processing Equipment," *Administrative Science Quarterly,* 5 (1960): 221.
25. Peter M. Blau, "The Hierarchy of Authority in Organizations," *American Journal of Sociology,* 73 (1968): 463–464.

TABLE 3-6. *Multiple Regression of* **Sections per Division** *on Agency Conditions*

Independent Variable	Standardized Regression Coefficient	Zero-Order Correlation
Agency Size (Log)	.47**	.43
Automation (Dummy)[a]	.29**	.43
Education of Division Heads	.20*	.31
Divisions	−.43**	−.11

Multiple R = 66; n = 53

*Greater than one-and-a-half times its standard error.

**Greater than twice its standard error.

[a]Dichotomous dummy variable: whether or not any computer exists.

of number of divisions. Whereas both number of divisions and number of sections per division increase with increasing size, controlling size makes it apparent that the larger the number of divisions the smaller is the average number of sections in each. This finding supports the earlier conjectures that forestalling the proliferation of divisions requires establishing more functional subunits within them and that reducing the number of divisions once it has become too large entails establishing a few superdivisions that probably contain more subunits than the earlier divisions did. The smaller the number of divisions in agencies of a given size, the more encompassing are these divisions and the wider is the scope of major responsibilities of their heads, as indicated by the average number of sections in each.

The total span of control of the average division head is similarly affected by agency size and number of divisions, as Table 3–7 shows.[26] The span of control of division heads is on the average wider the larger an agency is and the fewer divisions it has, given its size. But the total span of control is less responsive to antecedent conditions than the scope of major responsibilities in the case of division heads, just as in that of top management. Comparison of the data in Tables 3–6 and 3–7 reveals that size and, particularly, number of divisions affect the number of section managers under the average division head more than the total number of officials directly reporting to him. Besides, two other factors influence the

26. This pattern is observable only if size is logarithmically transformed, as has been done in Table 3–7, although the transformation does not meet the criterion established that it be performed only if doing so improves the correlation by at least .10; the correlation of mean span of control of division heads is .21 with raw size and .30 with its logarithm. If raw size is substituted for its logarithm in Table 3–7, its b* is .25 (less than two standard errors) and the b* of divisions is − .12 (less than one standard error).

number of section managers but not that of total immediate subordinates per division head. Conditions in the agency apparently make more difference for the responsibilities over whole sections assigned to a division head than for the number of individual officials placed under his direct supervision.

Agencies in which operations are automated tend to have more sections per division than those without computers (Table 3–6).[27] Automation

TABLE 3-7. *Multiple Regression of* Division Heads' Mean Span of Control *on Agency Conditions*

Independent Variable	Standardized Regression Coefficient	Zero-Order Correlation
Agency Size (Log)	.44**	.30
Divisions	−.26*	−.02

Multiple R = 37; n = 53
*Greater than one-and-a-half times its standard error.
**Greater than twice its standard error.

therefore exerts some influence on horizontal as well as on vertical differentiation, but its influence on horizontal differentiation is reflected in an increase of sections within divisions rather than the addition of more divisions. The reason may well be that the multilevel hierarchies in most automated agencies, which reduce the number of divisions, as we have seen, prevent the influence of automation on horizontal differentiation from finding expression in number of divisions and permit it to find expression only on the next level in the organization. An advanced technology seems to be more compatible than a simple one with a complex structure differentiated both vertically into multiple levels and horizontally into many sections though not into a large number of divisions.

Finally, the higher the average education of the division heads in an agency, the larger is the average number of sections under each of them. There is no corresponding association between average education and total span of control of division heads. One might be tempted to interpret these

---

27. However, the extent of automated facilities is not associated with number of sections per division, which is the reason why the dummy variable of whether or not an agency has a computer is used. The elimination of the twelve data-processing divisions does not alter the association between the existence of a computer and the number of sections per division. In other words, the observed association is not owing to the number of sections in data-processing divisions but to that in other divisions.

findings by saying that the educational qualifications of division heads determine the scope of their major responsibilities, as indicated by the number of sections assigned to them, whereas the minor additional responsibilities over single subordinates manifest in the span of control do not depend on these qualifications. Although this conclusion seems plausible enough, what makes it questionable is the fact that it is based on an "ecological correlation" between education and sections—the averages for all division heads in an agency, not the specific values for individual division heads. Indeed, the education of individual division heads is neither correlated with the total size of their division ($-.05$) nor with the number of sections controlling size ($-.04$).

An alternative interpretation rests on the assumption that the average education of these senior managers in an agency reflects the utilization of technological knowledge in administration, just as automation reflects the use of modern technology. An advanced technology appears to foster the development of tall pyramids that are horizontally differentiated not so much on the level of divisions as on the next level of sections within divisions. A possible explanation, though it is mere conjecture, is that pyramids are unlikely to assume this shape unless the administrative efficiency attainable with an advanced technology overrides top management's concern with keeping in close touch with operations by having many division heads directly report to it. Some data will later be presented in support of the contention that the pressures of large size and the advantages of an efficient technology are the main conditions under which top executives let go of close direct control over subordinates.

Conclusions

The size of an employment security agency exerts a predominant influence on its formal structure, its technology, and its administrative overhead. Partly directly and partly indirectly through these other factors, agency size also influences administrative practices, such as decentralization and the services rendered to the public. Attention in this chapter centered on the differentiation in the structure generated by size and the interrelations of structural elements that delineate the shape of the pyramid.

Large size promotes differentiation within organizations along various lines. In employment security agencies, large size is associated with spatial differentiation into many local offices; a pronounced division of labor; vertical differentiation into multilevel hierarchies; and horizontal differentiation into numerous functional divisions and sections within divisions. The strong impact of size on most aspects of differentiation is illustrated by the findings that differences in agency size account for more than one half of the variance in the division of labor and in hierarchical differentiation. The operational definition of differentiation is the number of structural components in a given dimension, such as the number of occupational positions or the number of hierarchical levels. Large agency size increases not only the number of structural components in each dimension, and thereby differentiation, but also the average size of these components. For example, the average size of local offices as well as their number increases with increasing agency size, so does the average size of the personnel component in each position as well as the number of positions, and the same is true for all dimensions of structure examined. Hence, size has a double effect on each aspect of the formal structure. The increase in the average size of structural components affected by size, however, dampens the effect of increasing size on the number of components. As a result, size generates structural differentiation at declining rates.

The structural complexity to which large size gives rise by producing differentiation often exerts influences in the organization that are the opposite of those of large size itself. Thus, the multilevel hierarchies that typically develop in large agencies tend to reduce the number of divisions, whereas large size usually increases the number of divisions. Similarly, many divisions, which are prevalent in most large agencies, reduce the number of sections per division and the average span of control of division heads, but large size increases both. Although the formal structure expands in all directions with increasing size, the interrelations between various elements of the structure produce tall pyramids in some cases and squat ones in others. Specifically, a multilevel hierarchy tends to reduce the number of divisions, and few divisions in turn tend to be accompanied by many sections in each. Squat pyramids, in contrast, have few levels, many divisions, and few sections per division.

The indirect effect of size mediated by one facet of the formal structure sometimes counteracts its direct effect on another facet. But in the cases so far examined, the direct influence of size is so strong that its counteracting indirect influence only lessens its over-all impact without obliterating the direct influence. The zero-order correlation reveals a pronounced over-all effect of size on divisions, despite the counteracting effect mediated by levels, and there is a considerable zero-order correlation between size and sections per division, despite the counteracting effect mediated by divisions. In other cases, however, the indirect effects of size neutralize or even outweigh its direct effects. A number of opposite influences of size and of the structural complexity it produces will be analyzed in Chapter 4, and other direct and indirect effects of size will be discussed in subsequent chapters.

CHAPTER 4

Administration

Data on two different implications of the term "administration" are analyzed in this chapter. On the one hand, "administration" refers to the management of an organization's internal affairs, as distinguished from the activities involved in the production of the goods or the rendering of the services that constitute the organization's output. In manufacturing concerns, for example, management, accounting, and clerical services are part of administration, in contrast to production departments. On the other hand, in the case of government bureaus, we refer to the output or services provided also as administrative activities. One bureau administers the revenue statutes of the state, another its health program, and the one under consideration here its unemployment insurance and employment services. The second meaning of the term is not completely unrelated to the first because administrative agencies of a government constitute its executive branch and are responsible for managing the internal affairs of state. (A nation's military forces and diplomatic corps, of course, have responsibilities for external rather than internal affairs, and they are, accordingly, not generally thought of as administrative agencies.) This chapter deals with some aspects of the internal administration of employment security agencies and with several of the services they administer.

The influence of size on two administrative ratios is examined first, followed by an analysis of other conditions affecting these ratios. The indicators of the relative size of two different administrative components are the managerial ratio, or per cent of supervisory personnel, and the staff ratio, or per cent of total personnel time devoted to staff and technical activities. The next topic is the investigation of the contrasting influences on internal administration exerted by size and by the structural complexity it produces. The clerical ratio is affected by these contrasting influences, and so is the degree of standardization in supervisory ratings, the only measure of administrative procedures available. The clerical ratio, or per cent of clerical personnel,[1] was initially intended as an index of the relative size of a third component of the administrative machinery, which is the way it has been used in a number of studies of other organizations. In employment security agencies, however, the clerical ratio is not indicative of the proportionate size of the administrative apparatus, for many clerks are directly engaged in providing unemployment insurance or, to a lesser extent, employment services rather than in furnishing administrative support for these services.[2] What the clerical ratio is indicative of here is the extent to which an agency relies on personnel with low skills. Finally, the third section of the chapter presents an analysis of the ways in which various organizational characteristics affect the services administered by employment security agencies.

Administrative Ratios

The relationship between size and administrative ratio has probably been examined more frequently in comparative studies of organizations than any other. The bulk of the evidence indicates that the administrative ratio declines with the increasing size of an organization. Research results are sufficiently ambiguous, however, to prompt Starbuck to conclude a review of numerous quantitative studies on the subject by stating that the administrative ratio for "organizations with more than 100 employees . . . is essentially independent of organizational size."[3] A possible reason for the

---

1. The terms "ratio" and "proportion" are used synonymously in these three cases; the actual measure employed in the analysis in every case is the per cent of the total in the given category.
2. Officials from the former Bureau of Employment Security (now the Manpower Administration) confirmed the inference from our data that many clerks in these agencies perform production functions and not administrative support for them. However, the distribution of clerks in these two categories is not known, and it varies much among agencies according to our informants.
3. William H. Starbuck, "Organizational Growth and Development," in James G. March, ed., *Handbook of Organizations* (Chicago: Rand McNally, 1965), p. 509.

inconsistency of findings is the variety of measures of administrative ratio used. As a matter of fact, Rushing's analysis of census data for thirty to thirty-four industries at two time periods shows that the relationship between average size of firm and ratio of administrative to production personnel in an industry depends entirely on the operational definition of the administrative component. An inverse correlation is observed if the administrative component includes only men in managerial and related occupations but not if it includes all categories of white-collar occupations.[4] Though the correlations in this investigation are based on averages for industries, not on values for individual firms, similar discrepancies are likely to be found if different measures of administrative ratio are used in comparisons of individual organizations. Methodological shortcomings notwithstanding, however, a growing body of empirical results indicates that the administrative ratio declines with expanding size in organizations of various kinds.

An early study by Melman concludes that the size of American manufacturing firms and the ratio of administrative to production personnel are inversely related, though he used the crude measure of administrative ratio criticized by Rushing.[5] Bendix observes the same tendency among German industrial concerns.[6] Haire's comparison of four industrial firms in this country shows that the larger the company, the larger are the ratio of supervisory and the ratio of higher managerial personnel to production workers, though the reverse is the case for the clerical ratio.[7] This pattern is not confined to industrial organizations. The study of forty-nine hospitals of the U.S. Veterans' Administration by Anderson and Warkov indicates that the ratio of administrative personnel decreases with the hospital's size but increases with its complexity.[8] It is of special interest that they

---

4. William A. Rushing, "Organizational Size and Administration," *Pacific Sociological Review,* 9 (1966): 100–108. If only persons in clerical occupations or only those in professional occupations are included in the administrative component, positive correlations with mean size of firm are observed.

5. Seymour Melman, "The Rise of Administrative Overhead in the Manufacturing Industries of the United States, 1899–1947," *Oxford Economic Papers,* 3 (1951): 61–112. For manufacturing, the crude measure is probably satisfactory.

6. Reinhard Bendix, *Work and Authority in Industry* (New York: Wiley, 1956), pp. 221–222.

7. Mason Haire, *Modern Organization Theory* (New York: Wiley, 1959), pp. 296–297.

8. Theodore R. Anderson and Seymour Warkov, "Organizational Size and Functional Complexity," *American Sociological Review,* 26 (1961): 23–28.

were able to observe these opposite effects without refined research procedures; for example, their only indication of complexity is whether a hospital is a general rather than a tuberculosis hospital. Hawley and his colleagues also find that the ratio of administrators to faculty in ninety-seven public universities and colleges is inversely related to size, but its positive correlation with complexity disappears when other conditions are controlled in their data.[9] A last illustration to be cited is research on five sets of different types of organizations by Indik that shows not only that the supervisory ratio declines with size in all types but also that this decline occurs at decreasing rates to which logarithmic curves can be fitted.[10]

The data on employment security agencies confirm the principle that the larger the size of an organization the lower is the ratio of supervisors in it. Though this is not unexpected, it is rather surprising that the inverse correlation between number of personnel and supervisory ratio is by no means less pronounced for the agency headquarters alone ($-.42$) than for the total agency ($-.34$), given the known increase in the number of levels at the headquarters with size and the fact that an increase in supervisory levels must necessarily raise the proportion of supervisors, *ceteris paribus*. Other things are apparently not equal. Specifically, the disproportionate number of managerial levels in larger agencies is more than compensated for by the disproportionate wide span of control of the agency director, of division heads, and, as we shall see, of supervisors on lower levels; otherwise, the ratio of supervisors at the headquarters could not decline with increasing size. The scatter diagram (Figure 4–1) reveals a negative regression line with a convex curve, which shows that the decline in the proportion of supervisors with size occurs at a decreasing rate, and which replicates the findings of Indik. The per cent of supervisors at the headquarters declines rapidly as agency size increases up to about 1,000 employees, but much more gradually as it increases further. Logarithmic transformation produces a fairly linear regression curve, as Figure 4–2 indicates, but it improves the correlation little, raising it only from $-.42$ to $-.45$, undoubtedly because several of the smallest agencies have an exceedingly low proportion of supervisors.

There is an economy of scale with respect to managerial personnel in employment security agencies, and such an economy of scale seems to be typical also of other kinds of organizations. Larger agencies require pro-

9. Amos H. Hawley et al., "Population Size and Administration in Institutions of Higher Education," *American Sociological Review,* 30 (1965): 252–255.
10. Bernard P. Indik, "The Relationship between Organization Size and Supervision Ratio," *Administrative Science Quarterly,* 9 (1964): 301–312.

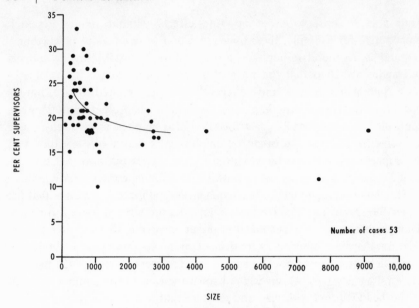

FIGURE 4–1   Scatter Diagram of Supervisory Ratio at the
Headquarters and Size

portionately fewer managers than smaller ones for administering their headquarters as well as for supervising operations throughout the organization. Inasmuch as all agencies but one have more than 100 employees and sixteen have more than 1,000, the data do not support Starbuck's conclusion that the administrative ratio is independent of size among organizations with more than 100 employees. It is true, however, that the managerial ratio varies much less with size among larger than among smaller agencies. Hence, the economy of scale in managerial overhead decreases with increasing agency size. Putting the matter in terms of growth, which means making longitudinal inferences from cross-sectional data, the implication is that organizational growth among small agencies achieves more savings in managerial manpower than corresponding growth among large ones. Increasing organizational size effects savings in manpower at a declining rate, just as it effects differentiation and structural complexity at declining rates. It may well be that the great complexity of large organizations is what counteracts the influence of further expanding size on savings in managerial manpower and that the increased need for managerial personnel created by structural differentiation in turn limits the impact of size on further differentiation.

The staff ratio also declines with the increasing size of employment security agencies. The measure is the proportion of the total personnel time in the agency devoted to staff and technical services (that is, not directly to unemployment insurance or employment services), which encompass essentially the responsibilities described under the four types of supportive functions (Chapter 2, pp. 41–43), whether these duties are carried out at the agency headquarters or at local offices, though most of them are performed at the headquarters.[11] One tenth of the man-hours in the average agency is taken up by staff activities. As the proportion of personnel time required for staff work declines with increasing size, the proportion remaining for work on the basic services to the public increases with size. A large scope of operations makes it possible to use staff personnel more efficiently in support of line operations, because the marginal cost of processing the salaries of an additional 500 employees, for example, is less than the cost of processing those of the first 500. The result is that a larger portion of the personnel budget in large than in small agencies is available

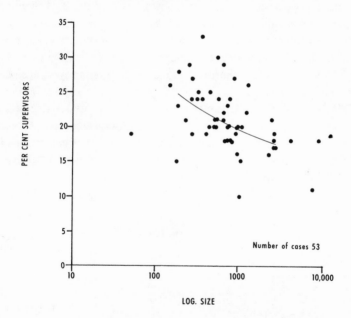

FIGURE 4–2   Scatter Diagram of Supervisory Ratio at the Headquarters and the Logarithm of Size

11. The time distribution reports kept by all personnel include sixteen categories defined as "administrative, staff, and technical" activities. The four of these referring to managerial or other nonstaff responsibilities (such as building maintenance) were excluded, on the advice of federal officials, to leave a fairly pure measure of supportive staff functions in terms of full-time equivalents.

for filling line positions in unemployment insurance or employment services.

The rate of decline in the staff ratio decreases considerably with increasing size, as the convex curve of the negatively sloped regression line in Figure 4–3 shows. The smallest agencies devote up to one fifth of their manpower to staff activities, with an average of about 15 per cent; this average declines rapidly to less than one tenth for agencies of 1,000 employees, but it declines little with further increases of size, though it does drop to 6 per cent for the largest agency with more than 9,000 employees. Figure 4–4 shows that logarithmic transformation of size reduces the curvature of the regression line, without entirely eliminating it, and produces a pronounced increase in the correlation. The negative correlation of the staff ratio with raw size is $-.44$; its correlation with the logarithm of size is $-.65$.

The manpower costs of staff functions as well as those of management and supervision exhibit an economy of scale in employment security agencies, but this economy of scale diminishes in both instances with increasing size. The cost of the administrative overhead indicated by the two administrative ratios declines first sharply and then more gradually as agencies become larger. The same difference in size that greatly reduces administrative overhead among smaller agencies reduces it to a lesser degree among larger ones. The economy of scale has the consequence that the share of manpower needed for internal administration in larger organizations is not so big as it is in smaller ones. However, the savings in administrative manpower effected by expanding size diminish with expanding size. A possible explanation of the lesser economy of scale among larger than among

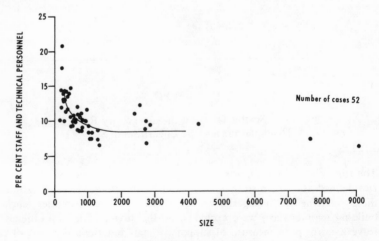

FIGURE 4–3   Scatter Diagram of Staff Ratio and Size

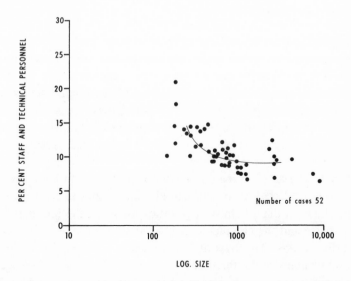

FIGURE 4–4   Scatter Diagram of Staff Ratio and the Logarithm of Size

smaller organizations is the counteracting force of the growth in structural complexity that tends to accompany increases in size, because complexity may be expected to increase the need for administrative personnel. But an alternative reason in regard to the staff ratio is simply that its initial decline with size is so sharp (as Figure 4–3 shows) that it could not conceivably continue at the same rate, for if it did the proportion of staff would become negative for agencies that have more than 2,000 employees, which is obviously impossible.

Not only these government bureaus but also private firms and other work organizations probably exhibit an economy of scale in administrative overhead. Results of some empirical studies that support this proposition have been cited above, though the evidence is clearly not conclusive. Should it turn out that administrative overhead does not decline with size in private firms, however, it would mean that large private firms administer their internal affairs less efficiently than these government bureaus, without taking advantage of the economies large scale makes possible. Given the economic pressures in private industry, this seems unlikely. On the other hand, the rate of administrative savings may not decline with increasing size in private firms, whereas it does in employment security agencies. But this too seems unlikely, because basic structural conditions appear to account for this decline.

Size and Complexity

The complex structure in large agencies creates special problems of coordination and communication that require the attention of administrative officials. The decrease in the rate with which administrative overhead declines as size increases has been attributed to the counteracting force of these administrative problems. Three related hypotheses are implied by this interpretation: (1) the direct negative effect of organizational size, independent of complexity, on the administrative ratios is greater than that manifest in the zero-order correlations; (2) the structural complexities generated by large size raise the administrative ratios; and (3) the indirect effects of size mediated by the structural complexities it creates reduce its over-all effect on the administrative ratios. In short, the interpretation implies that size and the complexity it produces have opposite effects on administrative ratios. The hypotheses are tested by using as indicators of structural complexity the three measures of differentiation discussed in the last chapter: number of levels, number of divisions, and number of sections per division at the agency headquarters.

Size and structural differentiation affect the ratio of supervisors at the agency headquarters exactly as hypothesized (see Table 4–1).[12] The direct effect of large size drastically reduces the supervisory ratio. All three aspects of structural complexity—multiple levels, many divisions, and many sections per division—increase the proportion of supervisory personnel at the headquarters considerably. Large size, by giving rise to differentiation in the structure, indirectly raises the managerial ratio and thereby counteracts its own direct effect of reducing it. As a result, the over-all influence of size on the supervisory ratio is far less ($r = -.45$) than its direct effect ($b^* = -1.13$), with the mediating influence of levels accounting for most of the difference (.34), that of divisions for less (.20), and that of sections per division for least (.14).[13]

---

12. Size has been logarithmically transformed in Table 4–1, although doing so does not meet the criterion of raising the correlation at least .10, because the scatter diagrams in Figures 4–1 and 4–2 show that such a transformation makes the regression slope more linear and does by no means produce a curve in the opposite direction. If raw size is used instead, the same results are not obtained, undoubtedly because the regression lines of the other three independent variables and of the dependent variable on raw size all reveal logarithmic curves, thus producing spurious positive relationships that counteract the direct negative effect.

13. The sum of the direct and all indirect effects, preserving signs, equals the over-all effect represented by the zero-order correlation. The formula for decomposition was presented in Chapter 1.

TABLE 4-1. *Multiple Regression of* **Supervisory Ratio at Headquarters** *on Agency Conditions*

Independent Variable	Standardized Regression Coefficient	Zero-Order Correlation
Agency Size (Log)	−1.13**	−.45
Levels	.47**	−.18
Divisions	.36**	−.20
Sections per Division	.33**	−.04

Multiple R = .58; n = 53
**Greater than twice its standard error.

The more differentiated is the formal structure of the agency headquarters, the more managerial personnel is needed to administer it. Large size, by promoting differentiation, has the indirect effect of enlarging the managerial component, but the savings in managerial manpower resulting from a large scale of operations outweigh these indirect effects, so that the overall effect of large size is a reduction in the managerial component. These data lend considerable support to the argument that the indirect effects of expanding size mediated by the growing structural complexity it produces impinge increasingly on its direct effect on the managerial ratio, which may well be the reason why the savings in managerial manpower realized by expanding size diminish with expanding size. The influences of the complexity of the headquarters on the managerial ratio in the entire agency reveal a similar but less consistent pattern,[14] which is not surprising since one would expect the proportion of supervisors outside the headquarters to be governed primarily by the structure of local offices, not that of the headquarters. The supervisory ratio in local offices will be analyzed separately.

The staff ratio is not as much affected by structural complexity as the managerial ratio. Table 4–2 shows that multiple levels in the headquarters hierarchy increase the administrative staff, but neither number of divisions nor number of sections per division have an appreciable effect on it. Nev-

14. The standardized regression coefficient of per cent supervisors in the total agency on one of the three measures of structural differentiation—levels—does not quite meet the criterion (b* = .29, with a standard error of .20). The rest of the values in the table with per cent supervisors in the total agency as the dependent variable, and the same independent variables, parallel the pattern in Table 4–1. If number of local offices is added as a fourth measure of differentiation to the other three and size to the regression problem with supervisory ratio in total agency as the dependent variable (ignoring problems of multicollinearity), it has no effect (b* = −.01), and it does not alter any other b* by as much as .02.

TABLE 4-2. *Multiple Regression of* **Staff Ratio** *on Agency Conditions*

Independent Variable	Standardized Regression Coefficient	Zero-Order Correlation
Agency Size (Log)	−1.04**	−.60
Levels	.33*	−.33
Divisions	.21	−.31
Sections per Division	.18	−.18

Multiple R = .65; n = 52

*Greater than one-and-a-half times its standard error.

**Greater than twice its standard error.

ertheless, the direct effect of size (b^* = − 1.04) considerably exceeds its over-all effect (r = − .45) on the staff ratio. Large size reduces the proportion of staff personnel less than it would if the differentiation it fosters did not increase the staff component. But it is primarily vertical and not horizontal differentiation that enlarges the administrative staff, perhaps because a multilevel hierarchy, which hampers communication through line channels, makes a relatively large staff complement especially important for management to maintain alternative channels of communication. Although structural complexity offsets the impact of size on the staff ratio less than its impact on the managerial ratio, the decrease in the rate of decline with increasing size is more pronounced for the staff ratio. The reason probably is that the steeper initial decline of the staff ratio, compared to that of the supervisory ratio, is more affected by the floor effect, that is, by the fact that the ratio cannot drop below zero.

Another factor on which size exerts opposite influences is the clerical ratio, which represents the proportion of agency personnel with low skills rather than an administrative component, as previously noted.[15] The pattern of influence is different, however. There is hardly any zero-order association between an agency's size and the proportion of clerks among its personnel (.09). The negligible zero-order correlation in this case may be considered the reverse of a substantial spurious correlation. For this lack of an appreciable zero-order correlation conceals two indirect effects of size in opposite directions, whereas a spurious correlation gives the appearance of an effect when none exists.

The regression coefficients in Table 4–3 reveal that two conditions have a direct effect on the proportion of clerical jobs in an employment security agency. The division of labor increases the proportion of clerical

15. The measure is the per cent of clerks in the entire agency.

personnel, whereas the extent to which operations are automated reduces it.[16] Neither of these influences is fully evident in the zero-order correlation, because the positive correlation between division of labor and automation and their positive correlations with size obscure some of their opposite influences on the clerical ratio unless the other variables are statistically held constant through multiple regression analysis to ascertain the distinctive effect of each. The number of headquarters divisions, though correlated with the clerical ratio, is seen to exert no appreciable influence on it once conditions assumed to be antecedents of both are controlled. Let us interpret the two direct effects on the clerical ratio observed before turning to the analysis of the indirect effects of size on it.

TABLE 4-3. *Multiple Regression of* **Clerical Ratio** *on Agency Conditions*

Independent Variable	Standardized Regression Coefficient	Zero-Order Correlation
Agency Size	.22	.09
Division of Labor	.48**	.25
Automation	−.70**	−.13
Divisions	.19	.31

Multiple R = .54; $n = 53$
**Greater than twice its standard error.

The extensive subdivision of labor among many different official positions segregates the more routine from the more complex tasks. Whereas positions that include some complex and some routine duties must be filled by personnel qualified to perform the complex ones, an advanced subdivision of labor separating these duties makes it possible to fill the routine positions with clerks and thus raises the proportion of clerical employees. The influence of automation on the clerical ratio, on the other hand, probably results not so much from a change in the proportion of positions filled by clerks as from a change in the absolute number of clerks in the agency.

A question of general interest is whether the introduction of automation in an organization effects savings in manpower. Cross-sectional data cannot give a direct answer to this question. Thus, the positive correlation be-

---

16. Despite problems of multicollinearity created by three closely related independent variables, it was not possible to substitute the dummy variable of whether or not automation has been instituted for the thirteen-category automation variable, because doing so fails to reveal the influence of automation.

tween automation and agency size surely does not imply that automation increases manpower needs but that large-scale operations influence the likelihood that computer facilities are installed. An indirect answer to the question posed can be inferred, however, from the cross-sectional data that indicate that automation reduces the clerical ratio. The employment of computer specialists when automation is instituted undoubtedly is responsible for a slight decrease in the proportion of clerks among the total personnel. But extensive automation is likely to reduce the proportion of clerks far more for another reason, namely, that many routine tasks otherwise performed by clerks are carried out by computers. The implication is that automation does help realize savings in manpower. It should be noted that the assumption underlying this interpretation differs from that made interpreting the effect of the division of labor. The increase in the proportion of clerks produced by the division of labor is assumed to reflect a shift from nonclerical to clerical employees without any necessary change in the total personnel. The decrease in the proportion of clerks produced by automation, in contrast, is assumed to reflect a decrease in the number of clerks and in the total personnel. Longitudinal data would be required to test the validity of these assumptions.

Decomposition reveals that agency size exerts two indirect influences on the clerical ratio, although neither the zero-order correlation nor the regression coefficient of these two variables indicates an appreciable effect according to the criterion established, as Table 4–3 shows. By promoting an intensive division of labor in the agency, large size indirectly increases the proportion of clerks (.37). At the same time, large size, by encouraging extensive automation of operations, indirectly reduces the proportion of clerks (− .57).[17] Because size has no substantial direct effect on the clerical ratio (.22), and because its indirect effects are in opposite directions, its gross effect on the clerical ratio indicated by the zero-order correlation is negligible (.09). Nevertheless, if the interpretations advanced for the effect of the division of labor and that of automation on the clerical ratio are correct, large size achieves through its two indirect effects on the clerical ratio a reduction in manpower costs. This can be shown by applying the interpretations to the indirect effects of size on the proportion of clerks.

Large size intensifies the subdivision of labor, which raises the number of positions with routine duties that can be filled by clerks, thereby reducing personnel costs; and it fosters extensive automation of operations, which substitutes the work of machines for that performed by clerks, thus further reducing personnel costs. These conjectures are readily testable,

---

17. The inconsequential indirect effect mediated by divisions is .07.

since they imply two specific hypotheses: the division of labor increases the proportion of clerks without increasing the total number of employees, whereas automation decreases the proportion of clerks and simultaneously decreases the total number of employees. Evidence confirming these two hypotheses would suffice to demonstrate that the two indirect effects of size on the clerical ratio, notwithstanding their being in opposite directions, both reduce the agency's costs for personnel. Although the longitudinal data needed to perform these tests are not available in our research, some indirect evidence that large size and the automation it promotes achieve manpower economies is provided by the findings that large size reduces administrative overhead and by other findings to be presented shortly.

Size and the division of labor also seem to have opposite effects on the standardization of the administrative procedure governing the supervisory ratings of the performance of subordinates. The measure is an ordinal variable based on the form used in an agency for the periodic evaluation of every official by his immediate superior. These forms were coded in terms of degree of standardization into four categories, ranging from procedures asking for a descriptive paragraph on the performance of each subordinate to those requiring a quantitative rating on a list of factors without any verbal explanation. Table 4–4 indicates that the division of labor discourages

TABLE 4-4. *Multiple Regression of* **Standardized Ratings** *on Agency Conditions*

Independent Variable	Standardized Regression Coefficient	Zero-Order Correlation
Agency Size	.40*	−.18
Division of Labor	−.53**	−.36
Automation	−.22	−.26

Multiple R = .42; n = 49

*Greater than one-and-a-half times its standard error.

**Greater than twice its standard error.

resort to standardized rating procedures, large size directly somewhat encourages such standardization, though its opposite indirect effect mediated by the division of labor outweighs its direct effect, and automation exerts no substantial influence on the rating procedure.[18]

18. The finding that size has a direct effect under controls must be treated as merely suggestive, given the problem of multicollinearity in this regression analysis. The regression coefficient does not quite exceed one and one-half

The principle mentioned in Chapter 3 that differentiation in organizations simplifies the duties of individuals but at the same time enhances structural complexity finds expression in the influences of the division of labor on the clerical ratio and on rating procedures, respectively. A pronounced subdivision of responsibilities into many different official duties allocated to various positions makes the tasks encompassed by a given position in most instances more homogeneous and in the very process increases the heterogeneity among positions. Inasmuch as the division of labor simplifies and routinizes the tasks of numerous positions, it raises the proportion of employees in the organization of whom only clerical skills are required. One would expect that such simple jobs can be more easily evaluated on the basis of standardized procedures than more complex duties. Another factor, however, apparently overrides this one in importance in affecting the standardization of evaluation procedures. Inasmuch as the division of labor increases the number of formal positions to which different responsibilities are assigned, it discourages the use of a single standard for rating the performance of officials in all positions. There is some indication, though it is not conclusive, that a large number of employees to be rated promotes the standardization of rating procedures, but the negative indirect effect of large size on standardization owing to the division of labor it engenders overshadows this direct effect.

In sum, the occupational differentiation through which large size standardizes the duties of many positions discourages the use of standard procedures in evaluating the performance in all positions, though large size itself would otherwise probably encourage standardized ratings. The finding that large size has no positive zero-order correlation with rating standards contrasts with the finding earlier reported that it does have a positive zero-order correlation with formalized personnel standards. This difference may reflect different stages in the development of formal procedures. What the structural complexity typical of large organizations discourages is the application of a single standard throughout the organization. Differentiation in the organization creates pressures either to abandon the application of standardized procedures or to elaborate the formal standards in order for them to take into account the variety of situations to which they must be applied. The first alternative is illustrated by the inverse association between occupational differentiation and standardized ratings in employment security agencies, and the second by the positive correlation between the size of state governments and the elaboration of formalized personnel stand-

---

times its standard error if automation is deleted from the regression, but it does if automation is deleted and environment conditions are controlled instead, as will be seen in Chapter 6.

ards in their civil service systems. The development of formalized standards appears to have advanced further in the personnel procedures of state governments than in the rating procedures of employment security agencies.

Services

How do the organizational characteristics of employment security agencies affect the services they administer? To answer this question, the relationships between organizational characteristics and four indications of the services performed are analyzed: (1) the extent of employment services provided, measured by the ratio of new applications for jobs processed to number of agency employees; (2) how intensive the employment services rendered to clients are, as indicated by the ratio of General Aptitude Test Batteries administered to new applicants for jobs; (3) placement productivity, which is the ratio of nonagricultural placements made to job openings received; and (4) the economy in man-hours of unemployment insurance activities, the index being the ratio of the number of employees in positions administering unemployment benefits to the number of clients claiming such benefits.

The construction of these four measures of services was discussed in Chapter 1 (a fuller discussion is in Appendix E), and so were the problems posed by the use of quantitative measures of this kind to assess operations and estimate the influences exerted on them by different conditions. One difficulty is that many placements per opening, for instance, may not signify effective but on the contrary superficial employment service, because high placement productivity can be achieved by concentrating on short-term placements and neglecting to provide more thorough employment services to clients. To mitigate this problem, a rough indication of the quality of employment service—the measure of intensive service—is controlled when analyzing the influences of agency attributes on placement productivity. Similarly, since the client load affects the time that can be devoted to each applicant, the volume of applications (per agency employee) is controlled when analyzing the organizational conditions that affect how much intensive employment services are furnished to clients. (Controlling placement productivity in the regression problem with man-hour economy as the dependent variable was revealed to make no difference in the preliminary analysis, and this control variable therefore is not included in the final tabulation presented.) Despite these cautions, it must be acknowledged that we are largely measuring quantitative and not subtle qualitative variations in performance.

Another problem is that unemployment insurance and employment services are affected by economic conditions outside the control of the agency. Differences in services that actually result from variations in social and economic conditions among states may falsely be attributed to differences in agency characteristics. This problem is ignored for the time being, but we shall return to it in Chapter 6, in which influences of the external situation on employment security agencies and their services are analyzed. This analysis will provide an opportunity to determine to what extent controlling several socioeconomic conditions in the state modifies the relationships between the characteristics of employment security agencies and the services they provide. It will be seen that only a few of the conclusions derived from the present analysis have to be revised when environmental influences are taken into account.[19]

The number of applications for jobs processed in an agency relative to its size is indicative of the degree to which it assumes responsibilities beyond the minimum legally required. Whereas the volume of unemployment insurance activities is essentially determined by the number of persons in the state entitled to unemployment benefits, the extent to which employment services are furnished to the people in the state depends comparatively more on the initiative of the agency itself. Besides, inasmuch as written applications are generally not taken for short-term and other routine placements, the number of these applications reveals how many clients receive more than merely superficial employment services. More than one third of the variance in this measure of extent of employment service is accounted for by differences in five internal conditions of employment security agencies (see Table 4–5).

The automation of operations in an agency exerts most influence on the volume of its employment services relative to its size.[20] This is of special interest because automation in these agencies at the time of the survey was essentially confined to unemployment insurance operations and was not used for employment service operations. Hence, automation expands employment services even though the computer is not involved in the tasks comprising these services, which means that its influence on them must be entirely indirect. The automation of routine unemployment insurance oper-

---

19. We deliberately refrain from anticipating the later findings and present even those results that the later analysis will prove to be incorrect. For doing so serves as a useful reminder that in nonexperimental research, relationships accepted as genuine on the basis of existing evidence may turn out to be spurious when additional evidence is brought to bear on them.

20. Whether or not automation has been instituted rather than the extent of the computer installation is the significant factor here.

TABLE 4-5. *Multiple Regression of* Applications per Employee *on Agency Conditions*

Independent Variable	Standardized Regression Coefficient	Zero-Order Correlation
Salary of Interviewers	−.32**	−.28
Automation (Dummy)[a]	.38**	.29
Clerical Ratio	−.24**	−.28
Staff Ratio	−.20*	−.38
Delegation to Local Office Manager	.20*	.27

Multiple R = .63; n = 53

*Greater than one-and-a-half times its standard error.

**Greater than twice its standard error.

[a]Dichotomous dummy variable: whether or not any computer exists.

ations frees manpower, or budgetary resources to hire different personnel, and thereby makes it possible to expand other services that cannot yet be done by machines.

Two factors that are inversely related to the number of applications per agency employee are the salaries of employment interviewers and the clerical ratio. A plausible interpretation of the latter relationship is that clerks are more widely used for unemployment insurance than for employment services, and the processing of applications for jobs in particular is done by nonclerical personnel, so that concentration on applicant services requires that an agency employ disproportionate numbers of nonclerical personnel. The negative relationship between interviewers' salaries and volume of employment services, on the other hand, is puzzling. Why should lower earnings be accompanied by a larger volume of work? We shall come back to this anomalous association in Chapter 6.

The two other agency conditions that exert some influence on the extent of its applicant services suggest that a decentralized management is better suited than a centralized one for the duties involved in rendering employment services to clients. The more responsibilities are delegated to the managers of local offices, the more extensive are the applicant services provided by an agency. Although the relationship observed is slight, the conclusion derived from it is indirectly supported by another slight relationship in Table 4–5, namely, the inverse one between the staff ratio and extent of employment services. For this relationship also may be interpreted as implying that extensive applicant services are more likely if management does not seek to centralize authority in its own hands, on the assumption that a disproportionately large administrative staff is a means for management to maintain centralized authority. A bit of evidence in support of this assumption will be presented in the next chapter; nevertheless, the interpretation remains admittedly highly speculative.[21] But granting for the moment that there is a connection between decentralization of responsibilities to local offices and extensive employment service, this connection does not necessarily indicate that decentralization produces greater concentration on services to applicants for jobs. A more plausible reason for this connection is that employment services, which are largely carried out in local offices and are less routine, require more decentralization of responsibilities than unemployment insurance activities, a good part of which are performed at the agency headquarters and are routine.

The likelihood that intensive employment services are provided to applicants depends to a considerable degree on a small volume of work in the agency. Table 4–6 shows that the proportion of new applicants who

TABLE 4-6. *Multiple Regression of* **GATB's** *per* **Application** *on Agency Conditions*

Independent Variable	Standardized Regression Coefficient	Zero-Order Correlation
Agency Size (Log)	−.67**	−.55
Educational Requirements	.18*	.22
Staff Ratio	−.31**	.22
Applications per Employee	−.22*	−.21

Multiple R = .62; n = 53
*Greater than one-and-a-half times its standard error.
**Greater than twice its standard error.

receive intensive services (General Aptitude Test Batteries) is inversely related to their number relative to the agency's size (applications per employee). Even when this measure of applicant load is controlled, the chances that an applicant is given a GATB decrease rapidly as the size of an agency and thus its scope of operations increase. The decline in the proportion of applicants to whom GATB's are administered with increasing size reveals a logarithmic curve; hence, size is logarithmically transformed in the regression analysis. The two influences—that of applicants per employee and that of number of employees—show that the absolute

---

21. It should also be noted that extent of applicant services is only affected by decentralization to local offices and not by the measures of decentralization within the agency headquarters to be discussed in Chapter 5.

volume of applicants in the organization is the main factor depressing intensive services.

Specialized services to applicants are not the major responsibility of employment security agencies and consequently tend to become residual activities performed when other work is not pressing. Seasonal variations (shown in Table E–2, Appendix E) bear this out. The number of GATB's given in the average agency is lowest in June, when the average number of applications for jobs is highest, and nearly the reverse is the case in December. (The mean ratio of GATB's per applicant for the various seasons in all agencies is .08.) The primary responsibilities of these agencies of administering unemployment insurance and furnishing simple placement services, particularly for those with the fewest skills and resources, preempt the attention of management and the time of operating officials, which relegates intensive services to applicants to a minor role. The greater the sheer volume of these primary responsibilities, the more concentrated is the focus of administrative attention on them, with the result that few intensive vocational services are provided to clients.[22]

The proportionate size of the administrative staff is inversely related to intensive services to applicants. Although the zero-order correlation between staff ratio and GATB's per applicant is positive, as Table 4–6 shows, this is largely the result of a spurious correlation between the two produced by the negative influence of size on both of them, and the regression coefficient under controls reveals a negative relationship. A large administrative staff seems to be most appropriate for unemployment insurance operations, less appropriate for the administration of extensive employment services, as we saw in Table 4–5,[23] and least suitable for provid-

---

22. The balance of employment services relative to unemployment insurance operations also declines as the size of agencies increases. The correlation between size and the ratio of applicants for jobs to claimants for unemployment benefits is $-.32$. But the sheer volume of operations is more important than concentration on unemployment insurance activities for reducing intensive services to clients. The standardized regression coefficient of GATB's per applicant on applications per claims when size (in logarithmic transformation) is controlled is not significant ($b^* = .15$), whereas that of GATB's per application on size (log) when applications per claim are controlled is substantial ($b^* = -.49$). The decision to use the variable applications/size rather than the variable applications/claims as the major indicator of concentration on employment services was made because the independent variations in the numerator and the denominator of the variable applications/claims make it less stable and often difficult to interpret.

23. The relative emphasis on employment service rather than unemployment insurance operations, as indicated by the ratio of applicants to claimants, declines too with increase in the staff ratio when size (in logarithmic transformation) is controlled ($b^* = -.47$).

ing intensive employment services to clients, as the present finding indicates. Intensive vocational services are the most professional activities in these agencies, whereas unemployment insurance operations are the most administrative, involving much routine work on lower levels and problems of coordination on higher ones. The findings imply that the management of an organization with the aid of a large staff component is better suited for dealing with largely administrative problems than for professional work. A related finding is that the higher the educational requirements for interviewers are in an agency, the more intensive are its services to applicants. Higher educational requirements may encourage more professional work, though it is more likely that agencies in which intensive services are emphasized adopt higher requirements than others.

Only two agency characteristics that influence placement productivity could be identified (Table 4–7). In order to keep quality roughly constant

TABLE 4-7.   *Multiple Regression of* **Placements per Opening** *on Agency Conditions*

Independent Variable	Standardized Regression Coefficient	Zero-Order Correlation
Agency Size	−.18	−.00
Sections per Division	.42**	.48
Standardized Ratings	−.25**	−.32
GATB's per Application	−.19	−.28

Multiple R = .58; *n* = 53
**Greater than twice its standard error.

when examining the influences on production quantity, the measure of intensive service is controlled in the multiple regression analysis, but doing so turns out to make little difference. Though there is an inverse relationship between intensive services and placement productivity, little of this relationship remains once other conditions are controlled. The size of an agency also has no bearing on the placements per opening made in it; the zero-order correlation is nil, and the regression coefficient is too small to be considered meaningful. The number of sections per division at the agency headquarters, on the other hand, exhibits a substantial positive association with the productivity of the placement operations in the agency's local offices. Many sections per division are indicative of a complex formal structure and of a wide scope of major responsibilities of division heads. But why do these characteristics of the organization of the headquarters raise placement productivity in local offices? Chapter 8 will provide a clue for answering this question.

Standardized procedures that supervisors must follow in evaluating the performance of subordinates impede placement productivity. Rigid standards for rating the performance of all officials, regardless of the nature of their work or the conditions under which it is performed, apparently do not constitute an effective incentive system. A flexible procedure that gives supervisors discretion to take varying conditions into account in the rating of the work of their subordinates seems to strengthen the effectiveness of these ratings as incentives for placing many clients in jobs. The finding suggests that the bureaucratic standardization of rating procedures engenders rigidities that are detrimental for placement operation. But we shall see that bureaucratic formalization sometimes has the very opposite effects.

Turning attention now to unemployment insurance operations, Table 4–8 presents five organizational characteristics that affect the cost in

TABLE 4-8. *Multiple Regression of* **Employee-Client Ratio in Benefit Function** *on Agency Conditions.*

Independent Variable	Standardized Regression Coefficient	Zero-Order Correlation
Agency Size	−.05	−.14
Extent of Personnel Regulations	−.25*	−.31
Division of Labor	.41*	−.01
Automation (Dummy)[a]	−.27*	−.19
Staff Ratio	.42**	.39

Multiple R = .54; n = 52

*Greater than one-and-a-half times its standard error.

**Greater than twice its standard error.

[a]Dichotomous dummy variable: whether or not any computer exists.

man-hours of these operations, that is, the ratio of the number of employees in the benefit function to the number of clients claiming unemployment benefits. A proportionately large administrative staff raises these man-hour costs.[24] Of course, one would expect a large administrative overhead to increase the ratio of personnel to clients, but in fact not all aspects of admin-

---

24. Such terms as "man-hour cost" or "manpower economy" are used loosely here to refer to cost in man-hours, not in actual dollars. The earlier interpretation of the indirect effects of size on the clerical ratio, however, referred to assumed reductions in actual salary costs.

istrative overhead do so.[25] Neither the proportion of supervisors at the headquarters (.03) nor that in the entire agency (.06) is related to the manpower ratio in the benefit function; only the proportion of staff personnel is. This finding supports the earlier conclusion that staff personnel is used most extensively for unemployment insurance operations. It also indicates that a large staff overhead raises manpower requirements, whereas a large managerial overhead appears not to do so, which implies that a large managerial component is more likely than a large staff component to achieve compensating manpower economies that make up for the administrative overhead.

The automation of operations reduces the manpower required to administer unemployment insurance to a given number of claimants.[26] Here we see that automation reduces not only the proportion of clerks but also, as was surmised, the total personnel relative to the volume of work in one of the two functions directly affected by the use of computers. (The other is the tax function, the personnel of which is not included in the ratio of benefit personnel.) Whether the savings in personnel cost resulting from automation exceed the cost of the computer facilities is not known. A pronounced division of labor, on the other hand, increases the manpower needed to process unemployment benefits. This influence is only apparent when other conditions are controlled and not in the zero-order correlation, because other conditions associated with a pronounced division of labor, notably a small staff and automation, reduce the personnel ratio in the benefit function. One might suspect that the disproportionate number of clerks in agencies with a pronounced division of labor is what raises this personnel ratio, but actually the proportion of clerks exerts no appreciable influence on it.[27] Hence, it seems to be the complexity entailed by much occupational differentiation that increases manpower requirements.

The formalization of personnel procedures manifest in an extensive body of written regulations lowers the man-hour costs of benefit operations. In this case, a factor generally considered to be an expression of bureaucratization—an extensive system of rules standardizing personnel decisions—improves rather than impairs operations. The standardization

25. It should be noted that the measures of the component of benefit personnel and of the component of staff personnel are independent.

26. The influential factor is again the fact that automation has been instituted, not the size of the computer installation.

27. The clerical ratio is therefore not included in Table 4–8. An earlier regression analysis of the same dependent variable with four independent variables showed the following values for the clerical ratio, with size, the division of labor, and automation (dummy) controlled: $r = .18$; $b^* = .14$, with a standard error of .14.

of personnel procedures in a merit system probably has the advantages that it simplifies recruitment and assures that all permanent appointments meet minimum qualifications by excluding extraneous considerations from influencing appointment decisions. Besides, the elaboration of personnel standards into an extensive body of regulations is likely to have the further advantage that it can take variations in conditions into account, whereas a simple set of standards cannot, as pointed out in Chapter 3. The question raised there was whether the problems created by such an unwieldy system of elaborate personnel regulations do not outweigh its advantages. A negative answer is supplied by the finding that extensive personnel regulations promote manpower economy.

Finally, the man-hour cost of processing unemployment benefits exhibits an economy of scale, but the latter is hidden by the greater manpower requirements resulting from the complexity of large agencies. The size of an agency exerts indirect effects in the opposite direction on the employee-client ratio in the benefit function, which nearly cancel each other out. Hence, size has little over-all effect on this ratio, and neither does it have any direct effect, as Table 4–8 indicates. The subdivision of labor and the consequent complex occupational structure to which large size gives rise increase manpower requirements, as we have seen. This indirect effect of size, owing to structural differentiation, on the man-hour expenditure in benefit operations is sufficiently great (.32) to conceal the economy of scale. Decomposition indicates not only that the man-hour cost of benefit operations decreases with increasing agency size once occupational differentiation is controlled but also what accounts for this economy of scale. The main intervening variable responsible for the reduction in the personnel-client ratio with increasing size is the comparatively small administrative staff in larger agencies ($-.28$). Two other factors that contribute to the economy of scale are the more extensive personnel regulations ($-.14$) and the automation of operations ($-.08$) typically found in larger agencies.[28]

Let us briefly review the findings discussed in this section by looking at them somewhat differently, from the perspective of each organizational characteristic and the influences on various services it exerts, starting with size. Although large agencies have a more differentiated structure than small ones, which would lead one to expect that they can more readily cope with a variety of responsibilities, a large scope of operations seems to produce a single-minded focus on the major responsibilities of these agen-

---

28. Number of levels, number of divisions, and number of sections per division exert no influence on the ratio of benefit personnel to clients.

cies and a consequent neglect of supplementary responsibilities. The larger an agency is, the less likely it is to furnish special vocational services to applicants, notwithstanding the fact that the largest agencies are in such cosmopolitan states as New York and California, where one would anticipate a greater interest in professional vocational services. The administrative problems engendered by a large volume of basic services apparently override all other factors and suppress much concern with specialized services. Whereas large size discourages intensive employment services to clients, it improves the man-hour economy of benefit operations, notably because of the decline in staff overhead with increasing size, though this economy of scale is counteracted by the greater need for manpower created by the complex structure of large organizations.

Several of the conditions to which large size gives rise improve services in various respects. Automation not only reduces the man-hour cost of unemployment benefit operations but also expands the volume of employment services in an agency, despite the fact that employment services are not automated. By substituting machines for manpower in the unemployment functions, automation makes more personnel resources available for employment services. The use of a relatively large staff component in the management of an agency finds expression in both a lesser volume of employment services and less intensive services to job applicants. Though this would imply that a large staff is best suited for the administration of unemployment insurance, it actually raises the costs in man-hours of unemployment benefit operations. The proportionately smaller administrative staff in large than in small organizations therefore is more conducive to providing intensive as well as extensive employment services, and it promotes manpower economy in benefit operations to boot. (Because the size of an agency and the proportionate size of its staff are inversely related, their influences on intensive services counteract each other.) A large number of sections per division, another condition associated with large size, raises placement productivity. But not all conditions that are prevalent in large organizations improve services. One that does not is the division of labor. Though the subdivision of responsibilities among specialized positions undoubtedly has some advantages for operations, excessive fragmentation of duties seems to increase the man-hour cost of administering benefits to clients.

Formalized standards, which one might consider manifestations of bureaucratized procedures, have conflicting implications for effective services. The standardization of the supervisory ratings of the performance of subordinates apparently makes these ratings weaker incentives for placing many clients in jobs than are less standardized, more qualitative evaluations. On the other hand, an elaborate body of formalized personnel regulations improves the man-hour economy of benefit operations. Why do formalized standards have detrimental consequences for operations in the first case but beneficial ones in the second? The difference in the content of the standards may be responsible, whether reference is to formalized personnel or to formalized operating procedures. Explicit personnel regulations are undoubtedly of special importance for government bureaus to prevent political patronage from interfering with appointments based on merit. Moreover, standardized personnel procedures, in contrast to standardized operating procedures, do not restrict the exercise of discretion in actual operations or their supervision, only in recruitment and making promotions. Strong restraints on the exercise of discretion in decisions directly pertaining to the performance of tasks may well be greater impediments to effective operations than such restraints on personnel decisions, thus nullifying the advantages of uniform procedures in the former but not in the latter instance. Another possible reason for the difference in consequences, which is the one previously mentioned, is that a single standard makes unreasonable decisions unavoidable in the numerous cases in which it does not fit, whereas an elaborate system of standards can take varying situations better into account.

Some of the relationships between organizational characteristics and services are probably the result of feedback influences of the type of services rendered on organizational arrangements. Concentration on extensive employment services appears to promote delegation of responsibilities to local offices, where these services are offered. A strong emphasis on serving the needs of applicants looking for jobs also tends to discourage the use of a proportionately large administrative staff in the management of agency affairs, which is perhaps another reflection of greater decentralization in agencies stressing employment services than in those predominantly concerned with unemployment insurance activities. Agencies that furnish considerable intensive vocational services to clients, which constitute the most professional services offered, adopt higher educational requirements for employment interviewers than other agencies. A large volume of employment services depresses the frequency with which intensive applicant services are provided. In sum, the greater the emphasis on employment services and even intensive vocational services rather than primarily unemployment insurance in an agency is, the more decentralized are responsibilities to local offices, the smaller is the administrative staff, the higher are the educational qualifications required of interviewers, and the smaller is the agency likely to be.

Conclusions

Large size and the differentiation in the formal structure it generates have several opposite consequences for the internal administration in employment security agencies, which means that the indirect effects of size mediated by structural complexity counteract its direct effects. Thus, the managerial ratio declines with increasing size but increases with increasing complexity. In this case, the indirect effects of large size owing to the structural complexity associated with it only weaken its direct effect, and its over-all effect is a reduction in the managerial ratio. The balance of the direct and indirect effects of size on the administrative procedure governing performance ratings is different. A large scope of operations seems to promote standardization of the rating procedure, whereas a pronounced division of labor strongly discourages such standardization, and the indirect negative effect of size mediated by the division of labor it engenders outweighs its positive direct effect on the standardization of ratings. The influences of size on the proportion of clerks in the agency reveal still another pattern. Size has neither a direct net effect nor a gross effect on the clerical ratio, inasmuch as its two indirect effects in opposite directions neutralize each other. By promoting the division of labor, large size raises the proportion of clerks, but by promoting automation as well, it lowers this proportion again, because much subdivision of labor makes it possible to fill many positions with clerical personnel, and automation substitutes the work of machines for that of some of these clerks.

Large size and the organizational conditions to which it gives rise also have opposite consequences for the services administered by employment security agencies. Large agencies, preoccupied with the difficult administrative problems of managing a large volume of unemployment insurance activities, devote a lesser share of their resources than small agencies to providing extensive employment services [29] and especially to offering intensive vocational services to job applicants. But automation, which is most prevalent in larger agencies, expands the volume of employment services provided, in all likelihood because it makes manpower available for these services by reducing the manpower needs of the automated unemployment insurance functions. Besides, both employment services generally and intensive ones particularly are furnished on a wider scale in agencies with a comparatively small administrative staff, and a relatively small staff is most likely to be found in larger agencies.

---

29. As mentioned in note 22, the correlation between size and the ratio of applications to claims is $-.32$.

An economy of scale can be observed in employment security agencies, though it is measured in this research in terms of manpower rather than actual dollars. Two aspects of administrative overhead exhibit an economy of scale. The proportion of managerial personnel in an organization declines with increasing size, and so does the proportion of staff personnel. The economies of scale in administrative overhead outweigh the diseconomies resulting from the administrative problems created by the structural complexity of large organizations, as indicated by the finding that the over-all effect of large size reduces administrative overhead despite the counteracting effects of structural complexity. Another measure of man-hour economy is the ratio of personnel to clients in the unemployment benefit function. In the case of this measure, the economies effected by large size are nearly nullified by the opposite effects of the differentiation large size generates.

Two organizational characteristics improve the man-hour economy in the benefit function, namely, the automation of operations and an extensive body of personnel regulations. The propitious influence of an elaborate system of formalized personnel procedures on operating economy belies the stereotype that bureaucratic procedures necessarily engender inefficiency. The inverse relationship between automation and the proportion of clerks in an agency has been interpreted to indicate that automation reduces personnel needs, and the finding that automation decreases the employee-client ratio in one of the two functions directly affected by it supports this interpretation. Two other agency characteristics, in contrast, have adverse effects on the measure of man-hour economy. A large administrative staff relative to an agency's size raises man-hour costs, and so does a pronounced division of labor. The administrative overhead created by a large staff component increases the manpower required to serve a given number of benefit clients, but the administrative overhead created by a large managerial component does not. This implies that a large management component tends to achieve efficiencies that compensate for its cost, at least in man-hours, whereas a large staff does not. Large agency size indirectly reduces the ratio of personnel to clients in the benefit function primarily because the proportionate size of the staff decreases with increasing organizational size, though the more extensive personnel regulations and the greater prevalence of automation in larger agencies also play a role in this reduction. The manpower economies indirectly effected by large size more than outweigh the extra manpower needed to cope with the complexity of large organizations.

The decline in administrative ratios with increasing organizational size may be considered expressions of the dynamics of feedback adjustments. The differentiation in large agencies raises requirements for administrative personnel, which would make operations in large agencies excessively costly were it not for the compensating reductions in administrative manpower owing to the economy of scale. The need to keep manpower requirements at a reasonable level in the face of the demands for administrative personnel created by a complex structure constrains organizations to reduce the relative size of their administrative components as their own size, and with it their complexity, increase.

Do the formalization of personnel procedures and the mechanization of operations through computers in large organizations, which achieve manpower economies, do so at the cost of greater centralization of authority and less flexible decision-making? The next chapter presents some data to answer this question.

CHAPTER 5

Decentralization

The authority structure may rightfully be considered the core of a formal organization. Most studies of authority, however, do not analyze it in terms of structure but in terms of the underlying processes that legitimate the authority of management or that describe the functions of executives. This inquiry, in contrast, has centered attention on the dimensions of the formal structure of authority in organizations, notably the number of levels of authority positions and the differentiation of positions on the two levels below the top, the number of divisions and the number of sections per division. We have noted that large size promotes the differentiation of authority positions in all dimensions, but vertical differentiation into many managerial levels tends to reduce the number of division heads, and few division heads typically are in charge of many sections each. One of the factors likely to transform a squat pyramid, in which there are many division heads each having a comparatively narrow range of authority, into a tall pyramid is the automation of operations. We have also seen that all three dimensions of differentiation in the authority structure raise the ratio of managers, but that the negative effect of size on this ratio exceeds all these three positive effects combined.

Yet a fundamental question about the authority in organizations still to be answered is to what extent is it centralized in the hands of top management or delegated to middle managers. We want to know, for example, not

111

only that size and automation affect the number of authority levels but also how they affect the degree of centralization of authority. In order to be able to investigate how various organizational conditions influence the decentralization of responsibilities in employment security agencies, several senior officials in each were asked who made decisions on a number of specific matters, such as hiring a supervisor at the headquarters. Whereas most other information used in the study is based on facts that could be looked up in records, the answers to these questions are subjective estimates. To make these estimates fairly realistic, inasmuch as the informants were limited to the top executive or his deputy and the division heads, we asked only about decisions they made themselves or delegated to officials below them at the headquarters or to the managers of local offices, and not about delegation from first-line supervisors to operating officials, about which our informants would have no firsthand knowledge. Hence, decentralization here does not refer to decision-making by officials on the lowest levels in the organization but to decisions made by middle managers, either those at the headquarters or those in charge of local offices.

Decentralization does not appear to be a unidimensional factor in these government bureaus. Numerous correlations between different measures of decentralization were low, and some were negative. Although these results may be partly the result of the lack of reliability of some of the measures, which were, after all, subjective judgments, it seems unlikely that they are entirely the result of that. Decentralization may in fact consist of several unrelated components. Thus, delegation of responsibilities to the managers of local offices is apparently not related to delegation within the agency headquarters. An arbitrary score of delegation of responsibilities to managers of local offices was constructed, based on whether or not they were authorized to make decisions in five areas.[1] A factor analysis guided us in selecting three of seven items pertaining to decentralization within the agency headquarters, though substantive considerations led to the selection of the item with the second highest rather than the highest loading in two cases.[2] The three items refer to delegation of personnel author-

1. Two of the five responsibilities were delegated to local managers in close to one half of the agencies, namely, hiring of personnel and approving overtime. The three other responsibilities, which were delegated more rarely, pertained to establishing substations ("itinerant points"), changing the physical plant, and negotiating building leases. The interrelations between the five dichotomous items are low; the mean value for the ten zero-order correlations, which in this case are phi coefficients, is only .11.

2. Inasmuch as the factor analysis was used merely as a general guide for selecting items representative of different dimensions of decentralization at the headquarters, it is not presented. A fourth factor seems to be indicative of the fact that minor duties have been relegated to subordinate managers

ity, delegation of responsibilities for preparing the budget, and decentralization of influence over making major structural changes in divisions, as reported by the division heads. The three differ not only in respect to subject matter but also in the degree to which decentralization is the result of explicit delegation of authority. The assignment of personnel responsibilities to division heads or lower managers is a clear case of explicit delegation of official authority, whereas the division heads' self-reported influence over major changes indicates decentralization without formal delegation of authority, and the participation of middle managers in the preparation of the budget can be considered to represent an intermediate degree of official authority.

Thus, this chapter deals with the effects of conditions in employment security agencies on decentralization, with special emphasis on the implications of the formalization and standardization of procedures and of the automation of operations for centralized decision-making. Four nearly orthogonal components of decentralization are analyzed for this purpose, none of which has as high a correlation as .17 with any of the others. Three of the four measures are ordinal variables coded in four or five categories (the fourth is the proportion of division heads stating that they can institute major changes in their divisions), and all four are based on personal judgments about decisions. The findings obtained with these measures are consequently not so reliable as other findings. To mitigate this problem somewhat, the discussion stresses mostly those influences of organizational conditions that are manifest in relationships with two of the four relatively independent measures of decentralization. To repeat, the four components of decentralization analyzed are (1) delegation of personnel authority within the headquarters, (2) delegation of budget responsibilities within the headquarters, (3) the influence the heads of divisions at the headquarters exercise over major structural changes in their divisions, and (4) delegation of responsibilities to managers of local offices.

Standardization and Formalization

The standardization of decision-making in organizations on the basis of a detailed system of formalized procedures is generally considered to be an expression of bureaucratization, whether reference is to the popular notion

rather than that significant responsibilities have been delegated to them, as indicated by the inverse correlation between this factor and the education of division heads. Assigning responsibilities to a subordinate entails both investing authority in him and requiring him to perform a chore, and one of the four orthogonal dimensions yielded by the factor analysis apparently singled out the latter.

of bureaucratic red tape or to Weber's theoretical analysis of bureaucracy. In Weber's words, "The reduction of modern office management to rules is deeply embedded in its very nature." [3] And again, "Bureaucratization . . . primarily means a discharge of business according to *calculable rules* and 'without regard for persons.' " [4] Another distinctive feature of bureaucracy emphasized by Weber is that the "organization of offices follows the principle of hierarchy; that is, each lower office is under the control and supervision of a higher one." [5] The inclusion of both these factors among the defining characteristics of a typical bureaucracy implies that the standardization of decisions through formalized regulations and centralization of authority generally occur together in organizations. However, Weber qualifies this conclusion by stating also that the impersonal system of formal rules restricts the arbitrary exercise of authority by the superior, who is no less bound by the formal standards than his subordinates are.[6] Though the domination of subjects by a chief is more pronounced in some other social systems than in bureaucracies, according to Weber, his analysis does imply that responsibilities for decisions pertaining to the work performed are more centralized through the hierarchy of offices in those social systems that have developed highly formalized and standardized operations than in those with less bureaucratized procedures.

Merton is critical of the prominence Weber gives to the contributions to efficiency made by bureaucratic formalization and standardization, and he calls attention to the unanticipated consequences of bureaucratization that impede efficiency. Strong pressures to conform with formalized procedures, designed to assure reliable and disciplined performance, engender rigidities that interfere with effective performance in varying and changing situations.

Adherence to the rules, originally conceived as a means, becomes transformed into an end-in-itself; there occurs the familiar process of *displacement of goals* whereby . . . conformance with regulations, whatever the situation, is seen not as a measure designed for specific purposes but becomes an immediate value in the life-organization of the bureaucrat. This emphasis, resulting from the displacement of the original goals, develops into rigidities and an inability to adjust readily.[7]

---

3. Max Weber, *Essays in Sociology* (New York: Oxford University Press, 1946), p. 198.
4. Ibid., p. 215 (italics in original).
5. Max Weber, *The Theory of Social and Economic Organization* (New York: Oxford University Press, 1947), p. 331.
6. Ibid., p. 330.
7. Robert K. Merton, *Social Theory and Social Structure*, 3d ed. (New York: Free Press, 1968), p. 253 (italics in original).

Despite the contrast between Merton's and Weber's analysis in regard to the significance of adherence to formalized standards for efficiency, the two discussions seem to have parallel implications for the relationship between standardized performance in conformity with formal rules and centralization of authority. To be sure, Merton does not explicitly examine centralized authority and its relationship to the displacement of goals, but the plausible inference from his analysis is that the two are positively related. The concept of displacement of goals does not mean merely that effective pressures to comply strictly with a given formal standard of performance reduce discretion with respect to this particular performance, which is true by definition and is hence tautological, but it implies that a prevailing emphasis on strict conformity with formalized standards leads to greater rigidity generally, which is manifest in other respects as well. For example, one would expect greater resistance to change in organizations in which formalized procedures are heavily stressed than in others. One would also anticipate that a high degree of formalization and standardization finds expression in a comparatively rigid structure of decision-making, in which decisions are centralized and officials on middle and lower levels exercise little discretion. Thus, the hypothesis derived from Merton's analysis—though it should be noted that it is our inference and not his conclusion—is the same as that derived from Weber's ideal type: formalization and standardization of procedures should be positively associated with centralization of authority in organizations.

One test of this hypothesis is provided by ascertaining whether decentralization of responsibilities in an employment security agency is adversely affected by the existence of an extensive body of personnel regulations in the civil service system under which the agency operates. The sheer existence of an elaborate body of civil service regulations, however, does not indicate how closely these regulations are followed in actual practice. An indication of the degree of compliance with these personnel standards is the proportion of new appointments that conform to civil service procedures. (The index is based on data from three years, 1964, 1965, and 1966.) Whatever the reasons are for making many temporary and provisional appointments, which are not required to meet civil service criteria, doing so reflects weak adherence to civil service standards. A second test of the hypothesis is, therefore, whether a high proportion of regular appointments made in strict compliance with established personnel standards is associated with centralized decision-making. The only available measure of standardization of operating procedures, as distinct from personnel procedures, is the use of objective criteria in the supervisory ratings of the performance of subordinates, which furnishes a third test of the hypothesis.

Strict conformity with personnel standards in making appointments does not promote centralization of authority in the hands of top management in employment security agencies; neither does the elaboration of these standards into an extensive system of formalized personnel regulations; nor does the standardization of the procedure governing the supervisory ratings of subordinates. On the contrary, all three manifestations of bureaucratized procedures foster decentralization. The proportion of regular appointments made in accordance with civil service standards is positively related to two of the four independent measures of decentralization (see Tables 5–1 and 5–2). The extent of formalized personnel regulations is also positively related to two of the four decentralization measures (see Tables 5–1 and 5–3). (It is noteworthy that the two measures of personnel regulations foster decentralization not of personnel but of other decisions.) And standardized ratings are positively related to one of them (Table 5–1). These findings clearly negate the hypothesis that the standardization of procedures and the elaboration of formalized standards give rise to a more rigid structure of decision-making in which authority is highly centralized. In these government bureaus, at least, the opposite is the case. Why is this so?

Compliance with civil service standards restricts, of course, the exercise of discretion in making appointments, and this may prevent adjustments that are called for. Some officials told us, for instance, that civil service requirements make it impossible to help implement programs to employ more underprivileged groups, such as blacks, inasmuch as large numbers of these cannot meet the requirements. There are undoubtedly also many instances in which the judgment of the appointing officer concerning the qualifications of various candidates provides far superior grounds for selection than the score that determines their ranks on the civil service register. However, though appointments made unhampered by civil service standards would improve the selection process in some cases, they would result in inferior selection in others, because political considerations would be given weight, or simply because the appointing official would not be very skilled in judging qualifications. Conformity with merit standards of civil service assures that all employees do have appropriate minimum qualifications, which is important for large-scale administration. It must be remembered that the management of a large organization has little direct control over the qualifications of the personnel, because many were employed under a previous management and most of the rest are in effect appointed by junior managers, often distributed in widely dispersed branches.

The top executive is held responsible for effective operations in an organization, which can hardly fail to make him reluctant to decentralize ad-

TABLE 5-1. *Multiple Regression of* **Delegation of Responsibilities to Local Office Managers** *on Agency Conditions*

Independent Variable	Standardized Regression Coefficient	Zero-Order Correlation
Extent of Personnel Regulations	.21*	.19
Civil Service Appointments	.32**	.33
Standardized Ratings	.23*	.28

Multiple R = .46; *n* = 53
*Greater than one-and-a-half times its standard error.
**Greater than twice its standard error.

TABLE 5-2. *Multiple Regression of* **Decentralization of Influence to Division Heads** *on Agency Conditions*

Independent Variable	Standardized Regression Coefficient	Zero-Order Correlation
Agency Size	.34**	.33
Civil Service Appointments	.21*	.18

Multiple R = .39; *n* = 49
*Greater than one-and-a-half times its standard error.
**Greater than twice its standard error.

TABLE 5-3. *Multiple Regression of* **Delegation of Budget Responsibilities at Headquarters** *on Agency Conditions*

Independent Variable	Standardized Regression Coefficient	Zero-Order Correlation
Extent of Personnel Regulations	.31**	.34
Automation (Dummy)[a]	.28**	.31

Multiple R = .43; *n* = 46
**Greater than twice its standard error.
[a]Dichotomous dummy variable: whether or not any computer exists.

ministrative decisions if doing so entails much risk. Institutionalized compliance with civil service standards of appointment is his best guarantee that employees meet at least minimum qualifications, regardless of the personal preferences or skills in judging candidates of his predecessors and subordinates. The adequate qualifications of most operating employees—though fewer may have outstanding qualities than under another system of personnel selection—supply the basis for consistent performance of duties and reliable operations. Decentralization inevitably increases the variability of managerial decisions and thus the chances that some administrative decisions rest on poor judgment, since not all middle managers can be expected to be equally good administrators. The more reliable the performance of operating employees, the less dependent it is on supervisory guidance, which makes somewhat more variable managerial judgments less of an impediment to effective operations. As strict adherence to civil service standards improves the reliability of operations, according to the reasoning advanced, it lessens the risk that decentralization involves for top management and therefore encourages decentralization.

The interpretation suggested is that centralized decision-making in an organization reduces the variability of managerial judgments and thus compensates, so to speak, for the greater variability in the qualifications and performance of operating employees resulting from frequent departures from merit standards of civil service in making appointments. Conformity with civil service requirements, correspondingly, diminishes the risk of decentralization by increasing the reliability of operations. The implication of this interpretation is that other conditions that make operations more reliable also foster decentralization. The qualifications of interviewers are a condition that affects the performance of a basic service of employment security agencies. Indeed, superior educational qualifications of recently appointed interviewers slightly encourage delegation of responsibilities, though only one measure of it (see Table 5–5 below, p. 128).[8] The indirect nature of the underlying process of influence should be noted. The point is not simply that the delegation of responsibilities to officials depends on the qualifications of these officials.[9] The interpretation implied by the findings is rather that the reliability of the performance of nonsu-

---

8. The only reason for using the educational qualifications of *recently appointed* interviewers is that no educational data on all interviewers are available, which undoubtedly depresses the relationship observed.
9. As a matter of fact, the education of division heads is not related to decentralization of influence to them (the zero-order correlation vanishes when size is controlled), quite likely because education is not a good indication of the relevant managerial qualifications.

pervisory employees promotes decentralization of decisions to middle managers several levels above them in the hierarchy because reliable operations by qualified employees can tolerate variable managerial judgments. Whereas the slight influence of the qualifications of interviewers on delegation of responsibilities provides only weak support for the interpretation,[10] another condition that improves the reliability of operations exerts a pronounced influence on decentralization, as will be seen shortly.

Civil service requirements not only assure minimum qualifications, however, but also may become a straitjacket into which a large variety of cases must be forced, to the detriment of good personnel selection. A civil service regulation designed for the recruitment of clerks is unlikely to make suitable provisions for that of professionals; one appropriate for personnel selection in metropolitan labor markets is likely to be inappropriate in small towns; and similar considerations apply to other differences in situations, such as that between periods of labor surplus and of labor shortage. The more extensive the body of formalized personnel regulations is, as previously noted, the greater is the variety of conditions that it can take into account. As a result, managers making appointment or promotion decisions are less likely to be caught on the horns of the dilemma of having to choose between following inappropriate requirements and disregarding civil service requirements (for example, by making provisional instead of permanent appointments). An elaborate system of civil service regulations improves personnel selection by lessening the likelihood of either rigid adherence to inappropriate standards or idiosyncratic departures from merit standards. This contribution of extensive civil service regulations to personnel selection on the basis of merit is probably the reason why more extensive regulations promote delegation of responsibilities to middle managers in the local offices as well as at the headquarters of employment security agencies (Tables 5–1 and 5–3). A question raised at the end of Chapter 4 was whether the improvement in operating economy effected by extensive personnel regulations results from their furthering centralization of authority, thereby helping top management to keep closer watch on expenditures. The present findings clearly give a negative answer to this question; far from leading to centralization, extensive personnel regulations promote decentralization of authority.

Rigidity in some respects, strangely enough, may breed flexibility in others. Not all aspects of bureaucratization are concomitant. The bureau-

---

10. Jerald Hage and Michael Aiken report a parallel positive correlation between college education and decentralized decision-making in sixteen health and welfare organizations: "Relationship of Centralization to Other Structure Properties," *Administrative Science Quarterly,* 12 (1967): 83–84.

cratic elaboration of formalized personnel procedures and rigid conformity with these standards do not necessarily occur together,[11] and neither of the two manifestations of bureaucratized personnel practice gives rise to a more rigid structure of decision-making with authority centralized at the top, at least not in employment security agencies. On the contrary, both strict conformity with personnel standards and the elaboration of these formalized standards encourage decentralization of responsibilities. Standardized personnel procedures are not so much a source of centralized authority as an alternative to it. The greater the reliability of operations resulting from standards of personnel selection, the less need is there for centralized authority.

Insufficient rather than excessive standardization of personnel practice seems to foster the development of a rigid authority structure with responsibilities centralized in the hands of top management. This inference is analogous to the psychoanalytical principle that the anxieties and insecurities rooted in excessive freedom from meaningful standards lead to authoritarian and rigidly conforming behavior.[12] Unambiguous standards apparently make the authority structure of organizations less rigid, just as they make the personality structure of individuals less rigid. The parallel is no more than an analogy, however. The social processes assumed to underlie the nexus in organizations differ from the psychological processes through which meaningful standards, by relieving anxieties, enable individuals to be more spontaneous and less rigid in their behavior. The interpretation does not assume that extensive reliance on merit standards makes executives feel less anxious and for this reason less rigid and more inclined to delegate decisions. Instead, it assumes that standardization actually improves the reliability of operations, thus furnishing objective grounds for delegating responsibilities. The reduction of objective risks resulting from reliable operations rather than the reduction of subjective anxiety is the mechanism through which standardization promotes decentralization in organizations. Changes in the objective situation in which top executives find themselves that were brought about by standardization, not changes in their subjective experience of this situation, are the factors assumed to prompt them officially to delegate responsibilities and to encourage informal decentralization as well.

Formalized standards exert a stronger influence on delegation of respon-

---

11. There is no correlation between extent of civil service regulations and proportion of appointments conforming to these regulations in employment security agencies (− .09).

12. See, for example, Erich Fromm, *Escape from Freedom* (New York: Farrar & Rinehart, 1941), pp. 40–207.

sibilities to the managers of local offices than on any of the aspects of decentralization within the agency headquarters. Table 5–1 shows that delegation of decisions to local offices is affected by all three manifestations of formalized standards for which indicators are available—compliance with civil service regulations, extent of these regulations, and standardization of the supervisory rating procedure. Formalized standards that restrict the scope of discretion make decentralized decisions less precarious for effective management and coordination, which diminishes the reluctance of executives to delegate responsibilities way down the line to local managers far removed in space as well as in social distance from top management at the headquarters. Inasmuch as delegating responsibilities to many local managers in geographically dispersed branches implies more flexible decision-making than delegating them within the headquarters alone, these findings strengthen confidence in the conclusion that the restraints imposed by formalized procedures encourage the development of a less centralized authority structure that permits more flexible decision-making.

Nevertheless, the inference that rigid procedures promote a flexible authority structure clearly is a generalization that goes far beyond the existing evidence. One question that arises is whether the relationships observed are confined to government bureaus, in which merit standards of civil service would be expected to play a particularly important role. Do standardization and formalization also further decentralization in private firms? Some empirical evidence that they probably do, though it is equivocal, is provided by the study of Pugh and his colleagues of forty-six British organizations, the large majority of which are private firms.[13] Their measures of standardization and formalization are complicated scales and quite different from the ones used here, though the underlying concepts are similar, except that most items refer to operating rather than personnel procedures. Despite these differences, Pugh and his colleagues also observe that standardization reduces centralization ($r = -.27$), and so does formalization, though only slightly ($r = -.20$), using their over-all scales for the variables. They present data on two subscales; that for formalization is negatively correlated with centralization ($-.27$); however, the subscale for standardization of personnel selection is positively correlated with centralization ($.30$), in contrast to our finding. It may be that standardized personnel practices only promote decentralization in government agencies, where merit standards stem political influence, but the standardization of other

13. D. S. Pugh et al., "Dimensions of Organization Structure," *Administrative Science Quarterly,* 13 (1968): 65–105; the matrix of correlation coefficients is on page 83.

procedures and formalization generally appear to promote decentralization in other organizations as well.

Another question raised by the paradoxical conclusion that more rigid procedures lead to a less rigid authority structure in employment security agencies, and quite possibly in other organizations too, is whether decentralized responsibilities are really indicative of a flexible authority structure.[14] In part, this is a matter of definition. If the concept of flexible authority structure refers to the fact that operations in various parts of an organization can be adapted by administrative decisions to differences in conditions, decentralized responsibilities undoubtedly are indicative of a relatively high degree of flexibility in this sense of the term. But if the concept of flexibility is meant to imply that an organization readily changes and adapts to new situations, decentralization is not an indication of flexibility in this second sense. Hence, the findings show only that formalized standards tend to make administrative decisions less rigidly controlled by a central authority, not that these standards make an organization less resistant to change. Whether or not decentralization furthers innovations and adaptation to new conditions is an empirical question not answered by these data. It can be argued that centralized authority facilitates instituting change in organizations, because it makes innovation primarily dependent on the decision of top management and less dependent on overcoming the resistance to it of large numbers of persons. Some indirect support for this argument is provided by the finding of a quantitative study of another type of government bureau that the most important influence on the chances of organizational change is exerted by the fact that the chief executive is a recent successor to his post rather than an oldtimer.[15] But centralization is not related to change in that study, and another study finds, contrary to this argument, a positive relationship between *decentralization* and change in health and welfare organizations.[16] The evidence on the subject is clearly inconclusive. No reliable data on change are available for employment security agencies, though automation, as a recent innovation, has bearing on the problem of the relationship between decentralization and change.

---

14. Alan P. Bates raised this question in his insightful comments on an earlier version of this chapter published in Mayer N. Zald, ed., *Power in Organizations* (Nashville: Vanderbilt University Press, 1970), pp. 175–176.

15. Jacques Gellard, "Determinants and Consequences of Executive Succession in Governmental Finance Agencies," M.A. thesis, University of Chicago, 1967.

16. Jerald Hage and Michael Aiken, "Program Change and Organizational Properties," *American Journal of Sociology,* 72 (1967): 503–519.

Automation

Computers have proliferated tremendously since the first one became operative shortly after the end of World War II. Twenty years later, more than half of the employment security agencies (twenty-nine) utilized computers in their work, and of the remaining, all but the smallest one utilized conventional data-processing equipment. Agencies use computers mostly for large-scale bookkeeping functions, such as processing unemployment compensation claims, maintaining wage and tax records, statistical reporting, and processing the agency's payroll. According to the estimate of senior executives in the U.S. Bureau of Employment Security, nearly 90 per cent of the use of computers involves unemployment insurance activities, most of the remaining time entails administrative activities, and hardly any, employment services.

The number of employees in the data-processing unit of the average agency is forty-nine, nearly as large as the mean for all headquarters divisions (fifty-six), although data-processing constitutes an independent division rather than a subunit of one in only twelve agencies. The routine nature of data-processing is indicated by the high proportion of clerks: 83 per cent of the personnel in the data-processing unit is clerical, compared to only about one half in the rest of the headquarters and one fifth in the average local office. The structure of the data-processing unit is simpler than that of other headquarters divisions, corresponding to the simpler duties, though possibly also affected by the fact that most of these units are not divisions in their own right. Relative to the size of the data-processing unit, for example, its division of labor is least pronounced, it is least hierarchically differentiated into supervisory levels, its managerial ratio is lowest, and the mean span of control of its first-line supervisors is widest in the average agency.[17] The main reason for the wide supervisory span of control is that the average span of control of the supervisors of keypunchers is 12.3, more than twice that of other first-line supervisors either at the headquarters or at local offices.

Automation raises the skill level of the data-processing component, as indicated by a decrease in the proportion of clerical personnel from 89 per cent in the absence of computers to 78 per cent in their presence. Most of the difference is the result of the employment of computer programmers, systems analysts, and computer operators when automation is instituted, who then make up one seventh of the personnel. The supervisory span of

---

17. The data are presented in Appendix H.

control over these skilled employees is only one third of that over key-punchers, who continue to constitute two fifths of the data-processing component. Automation reduces the number of operators of tabulating machines, and it makes their work more difficult, which is reflected in a narrower span of control of their supervisors (the mean span being 9.0 with, and 4.6 without, computers). Hence, the average first-line supervisor is in charge of fewer subordinates in automated (6.9) than in other data-processing units (9.6).[18]

How does the automation of operations through computers affect the degree of centralization of responsibilities in the hands of top management? There has been considerable discussion of this subject in the literature. In a paper written when computers were still rare, more than ten years ago, Leavitt and Whisler predicted that automation would lead to greater centralization, or "recentralization," of authority on the level of top management and a decline in the importance of middle managers.[19] Authors of a number of subsequent papers arrive at the same conclusion. For example, Mann and Williams's case study of the introduction of automation in a white-collar division of an electric power company infers that the increased need for coordination concentrates the exercise of control in the hands of fewer executives on higher levels.[20] And Hoos's study of nineteen business firms also concludes, without presenting quantitative data, that the introduction of automation leads to greater centralization.[21] The general reasoning is that the computer speeds the feedback of information to top executives and thus enables them to exercise as much centralized control over a large administrative organization as was possible without the computer in a small concern. But the argument that the use of computers for managerial decision-making recentralizes administrative au-

---

18. Less skilled operating employees, such as keypunchers, whose supervisors have a wider span of control, are located on lower levels, further removed from the unit chief, than more skilled employees, such as computer programmers, whose supervisors have a narrower span of control. To isolate other influences of the span of control of first-line supervisors from those of location in the hierarchy, the analysis of the span of control of first-line supervisors will be confined to those whose operating employees are on the bottom level, thus controlling location in the hierarchy.

19. Harold J. Leavitt and Thomas L. Whisler, "Management in the 1980's," *Harvard Business Review,* 36, no. 6 (1958): 41–48.

20. Floyd C. Mann and Lawrence K. Williams, "Observations on the Dynamics of a Change to Electric Data Processing Equipment," *Administrative Science Quarterly,* 5 (1960): 217–256.

21. Ida R. Hoos, "When the Computer Takes Over the Office," *Harvard Business Review,* 38, no. 4 (1960): 102–112.

thority in large organizations is mostly a prognosis of future affairs rather than a diagnosis of existing conditions. Today, computers in administrative organizations are still primarily used for routine tasks and little for complex managerial coordination and planning, even in the very organizations whose members have the most scientific knowledge about advanced computer usage. Rourke and Brooks find that universities employ computers *in administration* largely for such routine tasks as registration and keeping records of grades, though they too anticipate the danger that automation will centralize authority at universities in the hands of top administrators.[22]

Whatever the implications for centralized management of the extensive use of computers in arriving at managerial decisions may be in the future, the little systematic evidence that exists on the subject indicates that automation does not foster centralization at present. Mann and Hoffman compare the influence of foremen in an automated and a nonautomated power plant on the basis of survey data.[23] The influence of foremen relative to that of top management is greater in the automated than in the other firm. Foremen in the automated firm are more likely to be considered part of management by themselves and by the men under them. They are also more satisfied with the amount of influence they exercise than foremen in the firm that is not automated. Hickson and his colleagues report as well an inverse zero-order correlation (− .30) between their factor "work-flow integration," which is a technology measure extracted by factor analysis on which the automation scale is most heavily loaded, and their factor of "concentration of authority" among forty-six British organizations.[24]

Automation in employment security agencies clearly promotes decen-

---

22. Francis E. Rourke and Glenn E. Brooks, "Computers and University Administration," *Administrative Science Quarterly*, 11 (1967): 575–600.
23. Floyd C. Mann and L. Richard Hoffman, *Automation and the Worker* (New York: Holt, 1960), pp. 31, 57, 170.
24. David J. Hickson, et al., "Operations Technology and Organization Structure," *Administrative Science Quarterly*, 14 (1969): 378–397. Although the measure of centralization these authors use in their 1968 paper (see reference note 13) is most heavily loaded on the factor "concentration of authority," which they use in this paper, the correlation of the centralization measure with the technology factor is only − .16. They report separate correlations for the thirty-one of the forty-six organizations that are manufacturing concerns; among these, the correlation between technology and concentration of authority is nil, which implies that it must be very high among the rest, the fifteen private and public service organizations that are most similar to the bureaus under study here.

tralization. It is inversely related to two independent measures of delegation of responsibilities within the headquarters, delegation of budget and delegation of personnel decisions to division heads or managers below them (Table 5–3, pp. 117 and Table 5–5, p. 128). Automation standardizes operations, not only directly by mechanizing some tasks but also indirectly by imposing restraints on others that are performed by employees, inasmuch as their performance must conform to the computer set-up. The design of the computer installation serves as an impersonal mechanism of control, which makes operations partly self-regulating and less dependent on supervisory intervention. Inasmuch as automation consequently increases the reliability of operations, just as superior qualifications of employees and formalized standards of appointment do, it encourages decentralization of responsibilities by reducing its risk for top management, just as they do. The influence of automation on decentralization and its influence on multilevel hierarchies (noted in Chapter 3) both probably reflect the tendency of top executives to be less reluctant to give up personal control over operations if a computer puts an impersonal mechanism of control at their disposal.

The positive relationship between automation and decentralization has been interpreted to signify that automation fosters delegation of responsibilities by reducing the risk of such delegation. Though this is the preferred interpretation, because it is in accordance with the assumptions made about causal sequence, a complementary or alternative interpretation is possible if one assumes that the causal nexus is partly in the opposite direction. Computers were introduced in employment security agencies during the last decade or so. Perhaps those agencies that have instituted automation were already more decentralized before they did than the others. If this is so, it would answer the question raised earlier whether centralized or decentralized organizations are more flexible and ready to change in response to new developments. It would imply that decentralized agencies have a more flexible authority structure than others not only in the sense of permitting different adaptations among various segments but also in the sense of being less resistant to change and more ready to adopt innovations.

Automation is positively related to both measures of official delegation of responsibilities within the headquarters but not the measure of official delegation to local levels. The implication is that automation only fosters delegation of authority within the headquarters, where the computer is located, and not delegation of decisions to the managers of branches in other locations. Actually, however, this seems to be the case only for small agencies and not for large ones. Cross-tabulation indicates that size and auto-

TABLE 5-4. **Per Cent of Agencies with Much Delegation of Responsibilities to Local Office Managers,** *as Affected by Size and Automation*

	Agency Size	
Automation	50-670	671-9,078
No Computer	47	14
	(17)	(7)
Computer	20	47
	(10)	(19)

mation interact in their effects on delegation to local offices (Table 5–4).[25] In small agencies automation reduces the likelihood that responsibilities are delegated to local managers, but in agencies above median size it increases this likelihood.

Thus, automation appears to lead to the concentration of responsibilities on the level of middle managers at the headquarters in small agencies, with authority being delegated to them but not further down to local levels, whereas it seems to encourage delegation of responsibilities to local offices as well as within the headquarters in large agencies. The pattern in small agencies is what one would expect. On the one hand, the greater reliability of operations and the greater dependence on technical specialists resulting from automation foster delegation of responsibilities by top management. On the other hand, the location of the computer at the headquarters and the lesser familiarity of local managers with how to utilize computers, compared to the greater familiarity of headquarters managers (not merely the computer specialists), are conducive to concentration of administrative responsibilities at the headquarters rather than delegation of them to outlying branches. Why then is this pattern not found in large agencies?

If the interpretation is correct that a computer at the agency headquarters leads to the concentration of administrative responsibilities in the hands of headquarters middle managers, the finding that the expected pattern is not observed in large agencies implies that a large scope of opera-

25. This finding, as well as the others in the contingency tables discussed later in this chapter, should be treated as only suggestive, not merely because of the small number of cases, but also because we were not able to duplicate the pattern with regression procedures. The scatter diagram of the data in Table 5–4 shows that there is much scatter within each cell of the table. It should be noted, however, that one of the variables is a genuine dichotomy —whether or not the agency has a computer—and the other two are dichotomized as close to the median as possible, not in a way that would maximize the relationship observed. The continuous and ordinal variables in all contingency tables are dichotomized at the median or as close to it as possible.

tions exerts a force in its own right on the decentralization of responsibilities. Specifically, it implies that large size creates pressures to delegate administrative decisions to lower levels and that these pressures overcome the otherwise existing tendency in automated agencies not to decentralize responsibilities beyond the headquarters. Indeed, this impact of large size on decentralization is observable within the headquarters as well.

Pressures and Risks

Four conditions could be identified that are related to at least two of the four independent measures of decentralization: agency size as well as the three already discussed—proportion of appointments adhering to civil service standards, extent of formalized civil service standards, and automation. The influence of size on delegation of responsibilities to local managers interacts with that of automation, as just noted, and its influences on decentralization of responsibilities within the headquarters are not straightforward either. Before turning to the analysis of these influences, the weaker ones exerted by two other agency characteristics, which are reflected in only one of the measures of decentralization, are briefly examined.

Table 5–5 shows that multiple levels in the hierarchy of authority promote the delegation of personnel responsibilities by top executives to middle managers in the agency headquarters. The further removed top executives are from operating employees and first-line supervisors, the more difficult it undoubtedly is for them to acquire sufficient knowledge about these jobs to make intelligent personnel decisions on how to fill them. A multilevel hierarchy that removes top executives far from the lowest levels

TABLE 5-5. *Multiple Regression of* **Delegation of Personnel Responsibilities at Headquarters** *on Agency Conditions*

Independent Variable	Standardized Regression Coefficient	Correlation Zero-Order
Agency Size	−.45*	.22
Automation	.48**	.34
Educational Qualifications	.20*	.16
Levels	.29*	.36
Staff Ratio	−.23*	−.28

Multiple R = .51; $n = 53$

*Greater than one-and-a-half times its standard error.

**Greater than twice its standard error.

of supervisors and operating employees consequently creates pressures to delegate personnel decisions to middle managers in closer contact with the skills needed in the positions to be filled. Two other comparative studies of organizations also find that many hierarchical levels discourage centralization of authority.[26]

A proportionately large administrative staff, on the other hand, disinclines top management to delegate personnel responsibilities to division heads or their subordinates. The finding gives some support to the interpretation previously suggested that a large staff is an instrument that helps top executives to exercise control and maintain centralized authority in the face of other pressures to decentralize responsibilities.[27] A relatively small staff component to assist the top executive in administration puts pressure on him to lighten his administrative burden by delegating some responsibilities, such as those over personnel matters, to subordinate managers at the headquarters. Once again, the study of forty-six British organizations reports a parallel inverse relationship between the proportion of "nonworkflow personnel," which is essentially equivalent to our staff ratio, and centralization ($-.40$).[28]

Large size as such discourages delegation of personnel authority, but it gives rise to other conditions in employment security agencies that encourage such delegation, and its consequent indirect positive effect on personnel delegation outweighs its direct negative effect. The negative standardized regression coefficient ($-.45$) and the positive zero-order correlation (.22) in Table 5–5 reveal that the pronounced negative direct effect of large size on personnel delegation is overshadowed by a positive indirect effect. Decomposition indicates that automation is the intervening variable responsible for most of this indirect effect of size on personnel responsibilities (.39), and hierarchical levels (.17) and the staff ratio (.10) play some

---

26. Pugh et al., "Dimensions of Organization Structure," p. 83, report a zero-order correlation of $-.28$ between levels and centralization among their forty-six British organizations. Marshall W. Meyer finds a parallel relationship between levels and the top executive's policy to decentralize most decisions in 208 American government finance departments; "Two Authority Structures of Bureaucratic Organization," *Administrative Science Quarterly*, 13 (1968): 221.

27. Cases in which the personnel director, a staff officer, makes personnel decisions are coded as delegated responsibilities. Hence, the finding does not merely indicate that personnel decisions are more likely to be made by staff than by line managers if the staff is large, but it indicates that personnel responsibilities are less likely to be delegated either to staff or to line middle managers if the staff is large.

28. Pugh et al., "Dimensions of Organization Structure," p. 83.

role as intervening variables. Thus, the positive indirect effect of large size on decentralization of personnel authority, which exceeds its negative direct effect, is mediated primarily by the automation of operations to which large size gives rise and to a lesser extent by the multilevel hierarchies and the relatively small staff components that prevail in large organizations.

The larger the scope of operations, the wider is the significance of managerial decisions, and the greater therefore is the risk top executives incur by delegating responsibilities and losing personal control over them. Independent of other conditions, according to these considerations, one would expect large size to discourage delegation of authority, and the data reveal such a direct effect with respect to personnel authority. However, the large size of an agency not only enhances the import of managerial decisions and the risk entailed by poor administrative decisions, which affect hundreds of employees and thousands of clients, but it also increases the amount of work involved in the management of the organization. The pressures created in large agencies by the heavy work load generally and by the great administrative burdens on top management particularly are probably responsible for the greater likelihood of large than of small agencies to institute automation. For automation, in addition to reducing the work load of operating employees, lessens the risk of delegating responsibilities and consequently permits the top management in a large organization to delegate authority without incurring the risk doing so would otherwise involve.

In short, the large size of an agency produces conflicting pressures on top management, as it heightens the importance of managerial decisions, which discourages delegating them, and simultaneously expands the volume of managerial responsibilities, which exerts pressures to delegate some of them. The implications of these conflicting forces can be clarified by examining the effects of size on decentralization of influence and on delegation of official authority together. Table 5–2 (p. 117) shows that size exerts a considerable impact on the proportion of division heads in an agency who state that they can make major organizational changes in their divisions on their own initiative. This proportion is considered an indication of decentralization of influence without formal delegation of authority. The finding indicates that large size promotes decentralization of influence, and no factor mediating this effect of size could be discovered.[29]

---

29. Thus, size affects three of the four measures of decentralization. It is also correlated with the fourth, budget delegation (.24), but because this zero-order correlation disappears under controls ($b* = -.04$), owing to the influence of extent of personnel regulations, size is considered to exert no effect on the delegation of budget responsibilities, in accordance with the

The cross pressures on top management in large organizations engendered by the greater risk of, and the greater need for, decentralization of responsibilities find expression in a complex pattern of effects of size on decentralization. One manifestation of these conflicting pressures is that they make top executives reluctant officially to delegate authority but simultaneously lead to inadvertent decentralization of influence that accrues to division heads despite this reluctance. This inference is drawn from the findings that large size has a negative direct effect on formal delegation of personnel authority and a positive effect on decentralization of influence. Another manifestation of the same conflicting forces is that the large size of an organization creates resistance against official delegation of responsibilities and at the same time gives rise to conditions, such as automation, that help overcome this resistance by making delegation less risky. The direct and indirect effects of size on personnel delegation suggest this inference. Still another expression of these dual forces is that increasing size fosters delegation to local levels only if operations are automated. Table 5–5 implies this. The pressure of a large volume of managerial responsibilities brings about the decentralization of some administrative decisions, even without their being formally delegated, and the development of conditions that facilitate the formal delegation of others.

The findings in this chapter can be subsumed under two principles that appear to govern decentralization in these organizations: (1) the push exerted by administrative pressures and (2) the pull of the lesser risk of administrative decisions produced by conditions that improve the reliability of operations. To be sure, there are at least two other factors that also affect the likelihood that decisions will be decentralized. One of these is the content of the decision, inasmuch as those that require highly technical knowledge must be delegated to professional specialists, whose expert recommendations are likely to become influential even when executives reserve final authority to themselves.[30] The other is the personality of the executive. Differences among executives in abilities, political ambition, and sheer lust for power undoubtedly affect their tendencies to delegate responsibilities or refrain from doing so. The present study has no information on these personality traits, however, and could therefore not ascertain what influences they exert. The assumption is that within the limits imposed by personality differences executives strive to discharge their responsibilities by finding rational solutions to administrative problems,

---

assumption made (Chapter 3, note 11) that extent of personnel regulations is a concomitant and not a consequence of size.

30. See Michel Crozier, *The Bureaucratic Phenomenon* (Chicago: University of Chicago Press, 1964), pp. 112–174.

which makes the delegation of responsibilities by them subject to the structural constraints of the conditions in the organization here under investigation. Not to delegate very risky decisions is such a rational criterion, and to delegate sufficient responsibilities so as not to be inundated with administrative detail is another. Conditions in the organization govern the pressure of administrative responsibilities on top management as well as the risks entailed in delegating them.

The sheer size of an organization creates pressures on top management to decentralize responsibilities. A large number of clients to be served and employees to serve them, reinforced by the structural complexity that typically accompanies large size, expand the volume of responsibilities of top management beyond capacity, constraining managerial decisions to spill down to subordinate managers, as it were, whether or not top executives formally delegate them. A large administrative staff may enable top management to maintain centralized control in the face of these pressures. The strong inverse relationship between agency size and the staff ratio implies, however, that large agencies do not need so large an administrative staff, proportionately, as small agencies and that it would be uneconomical for them to maintain one. Most large agencies have a comparatively small staff, which constitutes another pressure on top management to delegate responsibilities. The multilevel hierarchies that prevail in large organizations further constrain top executives to delegate responsibilities to middle managers less far removed from operations. In brief, pressures to decentralize are generated by a small administrative staff, by a multilevel hierarchy, and particularly by a large scope of operations. But the pressures to delegate responsibilities tend to be resisted, although not always successfully, until they give rise to conditions that facilitate delegation by lessening its risk.

The delegation of responsibilities to different managers in various divisions and possibly also dispersed local branches entails risks from the perspective of top management, simply because it enhances the variability of administrative decisions. This greater variability increases the chances of some poor managerial decisions, and though it also increases the chances of some excellent ones, the latter are less of an asset than the former are a liability to sound administration. For great reliability and the absence of unpredictable variations are essential for effective administration on a large scale. Excellent performance in some cases by no means makes up for poor performance in others. It is as if lesser reliability and more idiosyncratic variation on the operating level have to be compensated for by centralization of managerial responsibilities; a more centralized authority structure diminishes the variability of managerial decisions, and thereby keeps down the risk of unpredictable performance that interferes with management's plans.

Several of the conditions that foster decentralization of responsibilities in employment security agencies can be considered to do so by contributing to the reliability of performance on the operating level and thus diminishing the risk of variability in managerial decisions. An outstanding example is the introduction of computers, which literally makes some operations automatic. Others are conformity with civil service standards, which assures that all employees meet appropriate minimum qualifications; the elaboration of these formalized standards to take different situations into account; and the actual qualifications of employees. Standardized rating procedures limit the discretion of supervisors and thus the variability of their criteria in evaluating subordinates. Generally, imposed impersonal controls on operations—though those of recruitment procedures are very indirect—make it less important to retain centralized control in order to maintain uniformity and reliability. Standardized ratings seem to foster delegation of responsibilities by giving the appearance of greater reliability while simultaneously impeding effective operations, according to the findings in Chapter 4. But three of the other four conditions that promote delegation by enhancing the reliability of operations also improve services (automation, extent of personnel regulations, and qualifications; see Tables 4–5 through 4–8; the fifth, civil service appointments, is unrelated to the four available measures of services).

The two principles that decentralization results from the need for it produced by administrative pressures, on the one hand, and from the facilitation of it created by reliable operations, on the other, can account for all the characteristics that have been found to influence decentralization in employment security agencies. The interpretation advanced implies that decentralization, although affected by either force, is most strongly affected by the combination of the two. Specifically, it has been assumed that the pressure to delegate decisions exerted by the large size of an organization tends to be resisted, owing to the greater risk of delegating decisions encompassing a wide scope, unless this pressure is accompanied by conditions that facilitate decentralization by reducing its risk. Contingency tables provide some indication that such interaction effects occur. Table 5–6 shows that the chances that personnel responsibilities are delegated are greater in large than in small agencies only if extensive civil service regulations exist and not if there are comparatively few such regulations.[31] Size

---

31. All variables in contingency tables that have a zero-order correlation of .20 or more with size are transformed into their residuals from their regression

TABLE 5-6. **Per Cent of Agencies with Much Delegation of Personnel Responsibilities within Headquarters,** *as Affected by Size and Regulations*

Extent of Personnel Regulations[a]	Agency Size			
	50-670		671-9,078	
Few	50		42	
		(14)		(12)
Many	36		77	
		(11)		(13)

[a]Residual from its regression line on size.

and the proportion of civil service appointments exhibit a similar interaction effect on the likelihood that influence is decentralized in an agency.[32] The effect of size on decentralization of responsibilities is contingent on automation as well as on formalized personnel procedures. The data in Table 5–4 (p. 127), already discussed from a different viewpoint, show that responsibilities are delegated to local managers more often in large than in small agencies if operations are automated but less often in large than in small ones if they are not. These findings support the interpretation that the greater importance of managerial decisions in large organizations

TABLE 5-7. **Per Cent of Agencies with Many Placements per Opening,** *as Affected by Size and Local Delegation*

Delegation of Responsibilities to Local Office Managers	Agency Size			
	50-670		671-9,078	
Little	65		38	
		(17)		(16)
Much	20		70	
		(10)		(10)

lines on size, to control size. (If the logarithmic transformation of size improves its correlation with a variable by at least .10, it rather than raw size is used in computing the residuals.)
32. The proportion of agencies with much decentralized influence increases with size from 54 per cent (6 of 11) to 77 per cent (10 of 13) if most appointments are based on civil service, but it decreases with size from 38 per cent (5 of 13) to 20 per cent (2 of 10) if fewer than three fifths of appointments conform to civil service standards.

discourages their delegation, notwithstanding the greater pressure to delegate in large organizations, unless such conditions as automation or formalized personnel standards facilitate delegation by improving the reliability of operations.

Given the conflicting pressures on delegation of responsibilities engendered by large size, the questions arise how delegation in large agencies affects the services rendered and whether these effects differ from those in small agencies. Of particular interest are the effects of delegation of responsibilities to local offices, where the direct contacts with clients involved in furnishing services take place. It has been noted in Chapter 4 that the positive relationship between delegation to managers of local offices and the extent of employment services in an agency is probably due to the influence that extensive employment services at local offices have on delegation of responsibilities to these offices. What influence does such delegation have on the effectiveness of the employment services provided, as indicated by the ratio of placements to openings? Table 5–7 indicates that this influence depends on the agency's size. In large agencies, delegation of responsibilities to local managers raises placement productivity, whereas in small agencies, delegation lowers it. Effective placement operations suffer in large agencies if responsibilities are not delegated to local levels, but they suffer in small agencies if they are delegated. The joint effect of these two conditions on unemployment benefit operations is similar, though not exactly parallel. Delegation of responsibilities to local offices improves the economy of benefit operations (in man-hours) substantially in large agencies but has virtually no effect on it in small ones.[33] In small agencies with their few local offices, decentralization of decisions to the managers of these offices is not required for effective operations; indeed, centralized direction from the headquarters may even improve productivity. In contrast, effective operations in large agencies, which have typically many local offices, seem to require decentralization of responsibilities to the local managers.

These findings supply an interesting illustration of feedback adjustments. As we just saw, effective operations in large agencies, though not in small ones, depend on delegation of responsibilities to managers of local offices. The data discussed just before indicate that large agencies are more likely

---

33. The proportion of *large* agencies with a high ratio of personnel to clients, indicative of uneconomical operations, drops from 62 per cent (10 of 16) if few responsibilities are delegated to local managers to 10 per cent (1 of 10) if many are, but the proportion of *small* agencies with a high ratio is no larger if few (56 per cent, or 9 of 16) than if many (60 per cent, or 6 of 10) responsibilities are delegated to local levels.

than small ones to delegate responsibilities only if conditions such as automation exist that facilitate delegation (Table 5–4). Finally, data presented earlier have shown that large size promotes automation (as well as other conditions that foster delegation, such as extensive personnel regulations, multilevel hierarchies, and small staff ratios). It seems that the need for delegation to local offices in large agencies, without which effective operations suffer, has feedback effects that encourage large agencies in disproportionate numbers to institute automation, which in turn is essential in order for many of the large agencies to meet this need and to delegate responsibilities to local levels. Whereas the chain of reasoning is inferential, the data do show that large size tends to bring about the very conditions on which delegation and effective operations in large agencies depend.

Conclusions

Two principles have been suggested to account for the conditions in employment security agencies that affect decentralization of responsibilities. The first is that the administrative pressures engendered by a large volume of managerial duties and a complex structure exert constraints to decentralize decisions, whether top executives will it or not. The influences of three conditions on decentralization—size, hierarchical levels, and small administrative staff—reflect this force. The second principle is that top management seeks to minimize the risk excessive variability poses for large-scale administration by delegating responsibilities to middle managers (which increases the variability of managerial decisions) only if conditions in the organization make operations highly reliable and reduce unpredictable variations in the performance on lower levels. This second force is manifest in the influences of five factors on the decentralization of responsibilities—compliance with civil service standards, elaboration of these standards, automation, standardized ratings, and qualifications of interviewers.

The broader the administrative task of management, the more important are reliable operations and the stronger is the reluctance to tolerate the greater variability of decisions resulting from decentralization. The reluctance can be overcome by conditions that lessen unforeseeable variability on the operating level to compensate for more variability on the managerial level. This interpretation implies that the pressure created by large size to delegate responsibilities tends to be resisted and that large size must be complemented by conditions that improve the reliability of operations in order to effect official delegation of authority. Both these implications are supported by empirical findings. Another implication of the interpretation is that large organizations are not hospitable to specialized professional activities that have no direct bearing on their major responsibilities, which may well account for the finding in Chapter 4 that the large size of an employment security agency exerts a strong negative influence on the likelihood that intensive vocational services are furnished to clients. There are other implications that go beyond the empirical findings. One of them is that the emphasis on reliable performance and the low tolerance for variability engendered by large-scale administration (not merely by the whims of stupid bureaucrats) make very large organizations not ideally suited for professional and scientific work, at least, not unless special arrangements succeed in combining tolerance for ambiguity with effective administration. This is, of course, the problem faced by large universities.

The significance of reliability and certainty for administration has received considerable attention in the literature. Weber stresses the superior reliability of bureaucratic administration that "makes possible a particularly high degree of calculability of results for the heads of the organization," without laying equal stress on the problems created by the need for disciplined and reliable performance.[34] Others have not ignored these problems. Thompson states that a fundamental paradox in administration is posed by "the dual searches for certainty and flexibility," adding that certainty tends to be more important on lower levels and flexibility on higher ones.[35] The findings of this study that the greater reliability of performance on lower levels leads to decentralization of decision-making on higher ones are in general agreement with Thompson's conclusion. The correspondence is misleading, however. According to our interpretation, it is the greater certainty of top executives (not of operating employees) resulting from reliable operations that encourages them to relax centralized authority, thereby giving rise to a more flexible authority structure with decentralized managerial responsibilities. Rigid procedures limit the uncertainty of administrative management sufficiently to permit the development of a more flexible structure of decision-making. A thesis suggested by Crozier and further explicated by Hickson and his colleagues is that an executive's ability to cope with uncertainty is at the roots of his power in an organization, whereas routinization of responsibilities eliminates uncertainty and consequently the basis of this power.[36] Our data bear only tangentially on this problem. To be sure, the conclusion that conditions that

34. Weber, *The Theory of Social and Economic Organization*, p. 337.
35. James D. Thompson, *Organizations in Action* (New York: McGraw-Hill, 1967), p. 150.
36. Crozier, *The Bureaucratic Phenomenon*, pp. 112–174; D. J. Hickson et al., "Uncertainty and Power in Organizations," unpublished.

lessen top management's uncertainty by making operations more predictable tend to lead to decentralization might be interpreted to indicate that routinization weakens top management's power. However, to equate delegation of responsibilities with a loss of power is questionable. As a matter of fact, this raises an important issue.

A paradox has been implicit in the analysis of this chapter, which should be made explicit. With slight exaggeration, one could say that managerial decisions in employment security agencies are either significant, in which case they are not delegated, or delegated, in which case they are not significant. There is an element of truth in this caricature. Given the top executive's responsibility for operations, he is likely to reserve the most important administrative decisions to himself, though his final decisions may be much influenced by the counsel of subordinate managers and the advice of staff experts whose professional knowledge he lacks. Yet if top executives delegate only those decisions they deem relatively insignificant, what difference does decentralization of responsibilities make?

To put the question bluntly: Is the over-all managerial power within the organization really more widely distributed in agencies in which responsibilities are decentralized than in those in which they are not? [37] This question cannot be answered unequivocally on the basis of empirical evidence without an index of over-all power, and it is not clear how such an index of total power would be constructed. The approach in our research was to ascertain whether decisions in several important administrative areas, such as personnel, budget, and change in structure, are made by top management or by middle managers. The data show that division heads in larger employment security agencies, for instance, exercise undoubtedly more important administrative responsibilities than their counterparts in small agencies and probably even more important ones than top executives exercise in small agencies, considering the wider implications of a given managerial decision in a larger organization. But the data also show that the conditions most likely to lead to delegation of responsibilities to middle managers are impersonal mechanisms of control that simultaneously strengthen the exercise of control by top management.

New forms of power appear to have emerged in modern organizations, which have their source in impersonal mechanisms of control. It is essential to realize both that these are forms of power, despite their difference from the old-fashioned kind typified by the power of the drill sergeant over the recruit, and that they are new, despite some similarity with pre-

37. I am grateful to Richard H. Hall and Alan P. Bates for comments that called attention to this issue; see Mayer N. Zald, ed., *Power in Organizations*, pp. 175–180.

cursors in earlier organizations. An illustration is automation, which empowers top executives to control operations by having the final voice in determining the design of the computer set-up, thereby obviating the need for many of the centralized directives through which executives otherwise control operations. Recruitment standards that govern the qualifications of employees supply a still more extreme example of these tendencies. Insofar as the selection procedure effectively screens candidates and assures that only those with proper qualifications are hired or promoted, top management can give employees complete discretion in the performance of their work and confine its own decisions to establishing general policies and to stipulating which subdivisions of employees, and hence which functions, to expand, contract, or create anew. These decisions suffice to give top management the power to determine what the organization does and in which direction it is moving, even though everybody within the organization is virtually free to exercise full discretion in his own sphere. Although this is not a description of the actual situation in employment security agencies but a speculative forecast, it is inferred from some tendencies observable there.

The new forms of power visualized do not depend on commands that subordinates must obey. They are more compatible with democratic values than the power of command. But perhaps for this very reason, the new forms of power are more elusive and probably also less easy to restrain than the older forms. As Auden says in "The Managers":

> The last word on how we may live or die
> Rests today with such quiet
> Men, working too hard in rooms that are too big,
> Reducing to figures
> What is the matter, what is to be done.[38]

There is no tyrant whose possible overthrow provides a rallying ground for opposition, only specialists in executive positions on various levels making decisions in their sphere of jurisdiction. Yet the tremendous power that the new forms put at the disposal of top executives of large organizations does call for the imposition of appropriate restraints in a democratic society.

---

38. W. H. Auden, *Collected Shorter Poems 1927–1957* (New York: Random House, 1966), p. 301. (Copyright 1949 by W. H. Auden.)

CHAPTER 6

External Situation

Organizations do not exist in a vacuum but in the context of a social environment that supplies their manpower, budget, and technology, and the demands of which govern their services. The social context in which organizations are embedded undoubtedly affects their characteristics and their operations. Research on organizations is often criticized for treating them as if they exist in a glass cage and for ignoring the influences of the external situation. The analysis presented so far is subject to this criticism. Employment security agencies not only operate under the different social and economic conditions in the various sections of the United States, but they are also part of different systems of political administration—the various state governments. This chapter examines some of these influences of the external situation on agencies.

In order to investigate how differences in the external environment influence the organizational characteristics and services of employment security agencies, a variety of environmental conditions in the fifty states and the District of Columbia was coded from census monographs and other published sources.[1] (The variables are described and the sources supplied

---

1. No environmental data on the two territories (Puerto Rico and the Virgin Islands) are available. The correlation between the organizational characteristics for the fifty-one cases, excluding the two territories, are not exactly the same as those for all fifty-three cases. Both sets of correlations are presented in Appendix F.

in Appendix C.) The inquiry is therefore confined to data on state environments and governments that were available in existing sources. Information on several environmental conditions is only available for the year of the last census, 1960, more than five years before the date of the survey. The frequently great variations in social or economic conditions within states are necessarily ignored when describing the entire state by its average, but most of these variations will be taken into account later, in the investigation of the influence of local environments on the organization of local offices. Considerable exploratory analysis was carried out to select those external characteristics that reveal persisting associations with agency attributes when other environmental characteristics are controlled. A few indirect influences of one environmental factor mediated by another are discussed because of their substantive interest, but generally environmental variables were deleted from further analysis if they have no relationships with agency characteristics when other environmental conditions are controlled. Some aspects of the environment we had expected to have considerable bearing on employment security agencies, such as the proportion of blacks in the state and several political variables, were found to exert no influence when other socioeconomic conditions are controlled.

The characteristics of the external situation selected for investigation can be grouped into four categories. The first comprises some basic conditions in the ecosystem: the geographical region, the size of the state's population, and the degree of urbanization of the state. The second category refers to economic and related conditions reflected in the population composition: wealth, as indicated by median family income; industrialization, as indicated by proportion of manufacturing workers; education, as indicated by median years of schooling; and ethnic heterogeneity, as indicated by the proportion of foreign stock (which includes natives with foreign-born parents as well as the foreign born). Third, three characteristics of the state government are examined: its relative size, represented by the ratio of state employees to population; expenditures per capita for state and local government; and the governor's appointive power, that is, his authority to appoint the heads of the major executive agencies in the state.[2]

---

2. As noted, we did not detect any appreciable influences on employment security agencies of strictly political variable, such as the proportion of democratic votes or urban underrepresentation, because the influences of socioeconomic conditions override those of political ones. Thomas R. Dye similarly finds in his analysis of the fifty states that political factors have little bearing on various public policies once socioeconomic conditions are controlled; *Politics, Economics, and the Public* (Chicago: Rand McNally, 1966), esp. pp. 293–296.

The last group pertains to external conditions of direct relevance for the administration of employment security: the proportion of insured unemployed, the duration of weekly benefits, and the ratio of operating funds received by the agency to unemployment insurance taxes collected.

The analysis of the influences of these variations in the external situation on employment security agencies also provides an opportunity for checking whether controlling differences in environment reveals spurious correlations between agency characteristics. A few of the previous conclusions will have to be revised, inasmuch as a relationship between two conditions in agencies earlier attributed to the influence of one on the other turns out to be actually the result of the influence of an environmental condition on both of them, that is, the relationship disappears when the environment condition is controlled. The fact that some conclusions prove to be incorrect when new conditions are controlled in the analysis calls attention to the tentative nature of all conclusions, as other conclusions might prove to be incorrect if still further conditions were controlled. At the same time, the fact that few major findings are altered when numerous environmental conditions are controlled strengthens confidence in these findings. The assumptions about causal sequence made in the analysis are that all environmental variables precede all agency variables; that the environmental conditions within each of the four categories are concomitant; and that the sequence among the four environmental categories with respect to their influence on employment security agencies is roughly in the order presented above. (Environmental variables are presented in the tables above organizational characteristics, in accordance with the assumptions about sequence.)

Adaptation to Environment

Were one to take Parkinson's famous law seriously rather than as the tongue-in-cheek caricature that it is,[3] one would have to assume that the personnel in an employment security agency increases as the population it serves decreases. This is, of course, not the case. On the contrary, the dominant influence on the size of an agency is exerted by the size of the state's population it serves, as Table 6–1 shows. Population differences in their jurisdiction account for fully nine tenths of the variance in the number of employees of these agencies. The *proportion* of insured unemployed among the population has some additional effect on agency size. These two

---

3. C. Northcote Parkinson, *Parkinson's Law* (Boston: Houghton Mifflin, 1957).

TABLE 6-1. *Multiple Regression of Agency Size on Agency and Environmental Conditions*

Independent Variable	Standardized Regression Coefficient	Zero-Order Correlation
State Environment		
Population	.93**	.95
% Urban	.02	.48
% Foreign Stock	.11**	.32
% Manufacturing Employees	−.07*	.32
Median Family Income	−.07	.33
% Insured Unemployed	.18**	.33

Multiple R = .97; *n* = 51

*Greater than one-and-a-half times its standard error.

**Greater than twice its standard error.

influences together indicate that the *number* of insured unemployed in a state essentially governs the size of its employment security agency. Indeed, the number of insured unemployed in the state and the number of employees in the agency exhibit a zero-order correlation of no less than .98. One would expect a positive correlation, of course, because the number of insured unemployed largely determines the volume of unemployment benefit operations and partly that of employment services. But we did not expect the correlation to be quite so high, inasmuch as we assumed it would be reduced by fluctuations in unemployment over the years as well as by the demands made on the public employment service by unemployed persons who do not or no longer receive unemployment insurance benefits. Apparently, these factors are of minor significance compared to the impact the load of clients who receive unemployment insurance benefits has on agency size.

Two characteristics of the state's population exert some further influence on the size of its employment security agency. A large proportion of men and women of foreign stock increases agency size, and a large proportion who are employed in manufacturing slightly decreases agency size (as is evident in the slight negative regression coefficient in Table 6–1, the positive zero-order correlation resulting largely from the correlation of proportion of manufacturing employees with both the state's population and the agency's size). Inasmuch as these influences are independent of the volume of insured unemployment, they appear to imply that persons of foreign stock use the public employment service more than others, possibly because of discrimination in private agencies, and that industrial workers use the public employment service less than other types of workers. The analysis of environmental influences on the services provided, to be presented later in this chapter, shows that the second inference is correct but the first is not. It seems to be true that disproportionately few unemployed workers in manufacturing industries find jobs through the public employment service, but it is not true that disproportionately many men and women of foreign stock come to these public agencies to look for jobs.

Highly urbanized states tend to have larger employment security agencies than others, and so do more affluent states compared to poorer ones. However, Table 6–1 shows that the positive relationships of urbanization and of family income with agency size disappear under controls, mostly owing to the influence of the state's population. The more populous states, which have large employment security agencies, are more urbanized and tend to be more affluent than the less populous ones, but urbanization and affluence of the population exert no direct influence on the size of these agencies. The high zero-order correlation between the size of the state's population and agency size makes it inadvisable to enter both of them as independent variables into a regression analysis. Consequently, state's population is not controlled in any regression analysis in which agency size is an independent variable,[4] though given their high correlation it is justified to assume that most agency characteristics that are substantially influenced by its size are indirectly influenced by the size of the state's population.

Data on three aspects of the personnel system are available. It has already been noted that the extent of formalized regulations in the state's civil service system under which the employment security agency operates is affected by the size of the state's government and by whether all or only some of the state agencies are covered by this merit system (Table 3–1). Because the state's population is highly related to the size of its government, as defined by the number of state employees (.96), state population and extent of personnel regulations also exhibit a positive zero-order correlation (.48). No other environmental condition that affects the extent of civil service regulations could be identified. Neither is the proportion of appointments in the agency made in accordance with civil service standards much affected by any of the environmental variables examined. Its strongest zero-order correlation is with the agency's location in the West rather than one of the three other regions in the United States (.26). Per-

---

4. A methodological implication of this decision is that the influences of urbanization on agency characteristics and services, which otherwise might be overwhelmed by that of population size, are free to express themselves. This is substantively legitimate, because it is the significance of urbanization rather than that of sheer population size that is of interest, except in the case of the size of the agency.

haps the constitutional changes in the Western states resulting from the populist movements there at the turn of the century are responsible for stricter adherence to civil service in these states. A third characteristic of the personnel system, however, is strongly influenced by one environmental condition and through it indirectly by several others.

Table 6–2 shows that the entry salary of interviewers in employment security agencies depends greatly on government expenditures per capita in

TABLE 6-2. *Multiple Regression of* **Salary of Interviewers** *on Agency and Environmental Conditions*

Independent Variable	Standardized Regression Coefficient	Zero-Order Correlation
State Environment		
Southern Region	.01	−.35
Western Region	.09	.46
Median Family Income	.05	.53
Population Increase	−.01	.41
Expenditures per Capita	.66**	.68
% Insured Unemployed	−.11	.50
Agency		
Size	.33**	.33

Multiple R = .75; n = 50
**Greater than twice its standard error.

the state. Though the operating budget of the employment security agency does not directly come from the state but from funds distributed by the federal government, the federal policy of allocating these administrative funds is to match agency salaries with those paid in the state for comparable government positions. The greater the expenditures in a state for government services, the better are the salaries in the state's employment security agency, as well as undoubtedly in other bureaus. In addition, the salaries of interviewers are affected by the size of the agency, which suggests that the managements of larger agencies are more successful in obtaining funds for higher salaries from the federal government than those of smaller agencies. An alternative interpretation of the finding might be that the larger and wealthier states pay higher salaries, producing a spurious correlation between agency size and salaries, but the data do not support this alternative reasoning. Interviewers' salary exhibits a less strong zero-order correlation with state's population (.24) than with agency size (.33), and the latter relationship persists when income level and government expenditures in the state are controlled. Larger agencies apparently are more influential than smaller ones in getting funds for higher salaries approved.

A number of other environmental conditions are associated with interviewers' salary, but all these relationships vanish under controls, and government expenditures are responsible in every case. The only reason that employment interviewers in wealthier states receive higher salaries than those in states with lower incomes is that wealthier states spend more per capita on their governments. Government expenditures are higher in Western states and lower in Southern states than in the rest of the country, and salaries vary in parallel manner. The influence of income level and of region on salaries may be considered to be mediated by government expenditures. But is government expenditure also the intervening variable that mediates the influence of the proportion of unemployed in the state's population on interviewers' salary? There are indications that another interpretation is more plausible than this one.

Whereas one might at first assume that a high proportion of insured unemployed is an expression of poor economic conditions in a state, it seems on the contrary to be an indication of a state's affluence and its resulting ability to pay unemployment insurance to large numbers for long periods. The zero-order correlation between median family income and per cent insured unemployed in a state is .55, and it is not, or only slightly, reduced when controlling a number of environmental conditions, such as urbanization ($b^* = .68$), proportion of agricultural employment ($b^* = .47$), or the dummy variable Western region ($b^* = .44$).[5] It is most unlikely that such a high correlation could be the spurious product of some unknown common antecedent. A high income level in a state makes it possible to pay benefits to more of its unemployed for longer periods, and it also makes it possible to spend more on government services and pay higher salaries to government employees, and these consequences of affluence produce a spurious correlation between the proportion of insured unemployed in the state and the salary of interviewers. The correlation between population expansion and interviewers' salaries in Table 6–2 is probably the spurious result of the same forces, for differences in income levels among states account for a good part of the differences in population expansion ($r = .48$).

Let us turn now to an examination of the influences the external situation exerts on differentiation in the formal structure of employment secu-

---

5. Controlling government expenditures in the state reduces the relationship between income level and per cent insured unemployed considerably ($b^* = .22$), which indicates that the influence of socioeconomic level on providing unemployment insurance benefits, just as its influence on government salaries, is in large part mediated by the government expenditures the state's population is willing to incur.

rity agencies. Lawrence and Lorsch suggest that organizations adapt to a diverse environment by developing a more differentiated internal structure.[6] If the degree of urbanization in a state is taken as an indication of the diversity of the employment security agency's environment, the data support this hypothesis. Table 6–3 shows that an agency's division of

TABLE 6-3. *Multiple · Regression of* **Division of Labor** *on Agency and Environmental Conditions*

Independent Variable	Standardized Regression Coefficient	Zero-Order Correlation
State Environment		
% Urban	.19*	.52
Agency		
Size	.69**	.78

Multiple R = .80; n = 50

*Greater than one-and-a-half times its standard error.

**Greater than twice its standard error.

labor, which is most strongly affected by its size, is more pronounced the more urbanized the state is in which it is located. The diversified labor markets in highly urbanized communities make complex demands on employment security agencies, and they apparently adjust to these more varied demands by developing a more differentiated occupational structure.

Other forms of structural differentiation as well as the division of labor are fostered by the heterogeneous environment in urbanized states. Tables 6–4 and 6–5 indicate that urbanization promotes both vertical differentiation into multilevel hierarchies and horizontal differentiation into many divisions. Part of the reason that agencies in highly urbanized states have a more complex structure is that they tend to be larger than those in less urban states, but urbanization also exerts some direct influence on structural differentiation.[7] Urbanization exerts no similar influence on the number of sections per division. (The zero-order correlation between these

6. Paul R. Lawrence and Jay W. Lorsch, *Organization and Environment* (Boston: Graduate School of Business Administration, Harvard University, 1967), esp. pp. 156–158.

7. The direct influence of urbanization on either levels or divisions is only apparent when the other one of these two variables is controlled. To make Tables 6–4 and 6–5 comparable, the same independent variables are used in both, although this means that the two tables are not quite parallel to the corresponding ones without environmental variables, Tables 3–3 and 3–4.

TABLE 6-4. *Multiple Regression of* **Hierarchical Levels** *on Agency and Environmental Conditions*

Independent Variable	Standardized Regression Coefficient	Zero-Order Correlation
State Environment		
% Urban	.18*	.47
Agency		
Size (Log)	.79**	.71
Divisions	−.34**	.15

Multiple R = .77; n = 51
*Greater than one-and-a-half times its standard error.
**Greater than twice its standard error.

TABLE 6-5. *Multiple Regression of* **Number of Divisions** *on Agency and Environmental Conditions*

Independent Variable	Standardized Regression Coefficient	Zero-Order Correlation
State Environment		
% Urban	.24*	.41
Agency		
Size (Log)	.74**	.52
Levels	−.49**	.15

Multiple R = .64; n = 51
*Greater than one-and-a-half times its standard error.
**Greater than twice its standard error.

two variables is only .16, and controlling size reduces the regression coefficient to − .04.) Subdivisions deeply inside the structure, like those within a division, are not affected by the diversity of the environment. But the diverse environment in urbanized states encourages all three other manifestations of differentiation in the agency structure, as Lawrence and Lorsch predict. A complex structure probably helps an agency to meet the heterogeneous demands made by the variety of organizations and groups in highly urbanized states, for example, big business, strong unions, large government bureaus, and various ethnic groups in need of jobs.

The diversified demands made by an urbanized environment on the performance in employment security agencies also discourage the use of standardized rating procedures for the supervisory evaluation of performance. This negative effect of degree of urbanization in the state on standardized ratings is mostly mediated by the division of labor.[8] The greater variety of demands made on these agencies in highly urbanized states leads to the development of a greater number of different occupational positions and consequently decreases the likelihood of standardized procedures in rating the performance of employees in these positions.

In sum, the findings reflect a number of adaptations of employment security agencies to differences in their external situation. Variations in the client load produce closely parallel variations in the number of agency employees. Lower government expenditures require reduced salaries for employment interviewers. To adjust to the diverse demands of an urbanized environment, the formal structure of agencies becomes more differentiated in several respects, and less standardized rating procedures appropriate for a differentiated occupational structure tend to be adopted. The automation of operations has also further progressed in agencies in more urbanized states than in others, but the influence of urbanization on automation is entirely owing to the larger size of agencies in urbanized states and the more extensive computer systems in larger agencies.[9] The next question to be raised is how the environment affects the personnel in these government agencies.

Labor Market and Resources

The proportion of clerks in an employment security agency depends not only on the need for clerical duties to be performed but also on the supply of clerks in the labor market. Two main internal conditions affecting the need were discussed in Chapter 4, which indicated that the division of labor, by simplifying the duties of some positions, raises the clerical ratio, whereas automation, by reducing the personnel required for routine tasks, lowers the clerical ratio. Large size, which promotes both the division of

8. The gross effect of urbanization on standardized ratings, represented by the zero-order correlation, is $-.32$. If urbanization is added as a third independent variable to the two shown in Table 4–4 (size and division of labor) in a multiple regression analysis, decomposition shows that the division of labor mediates most of the influence of urbanization on standardized ratings ($-.27$), size has some counteracting effect (.15), and the standardized regression coefficient ($-.21$) is less than one and one-half times its standard error (.15).

9. The zero-order correlation between urbanization and automation of .40 is reduced to a standardized regression coefficient of .00 if size is controlled.

labor and the automation of operations, has little over-all effect on the proportion of clerks, because its indirect effects in opposite directions roughly cancel one another (see Table 4–3). Controlling environmental conditions alters these effects of agency conditions little, as Table 6–6

TABLE 6-6.   *Multiple Regression of* **Clerical Ratio** *on Agency and Environmental Conditions*

Independent Variable	Standardized Regression Coefficient	Zero-Order Correlation
State Environment		
% Urban	.03	.28
% Foreign Stock	.25*	.37
Benefit Duration	.24*	.38
Agency		
Size	−.05	.10
Division of Labor	.59**	.28
Automation	−.53**	−.13

Multiple R = .64; n = 51
  *Greater than one-and-a-half times its standard error.
**Greater than twice its standard error.

shows, except that it produces a more even balance of the effects of the division of labor and of the automation of operations on the clerical ratio, and thus a nearly perfect balance of the opposite indirect effects of size mediated by them.[10] The table also includes three external factors, two of which have direct effects on the clerical ratio.

The longer the period stipulated by state law during which unemployed persons are entitled to draw benefits, the larger is the proportion of clerks in the employment security agency. When unemployed men and women file initial claims for benefits at the agency, the determination of their eligibility for these benefits entails some work of skilled personnel. But processing continuing benefits once eligibility has been established involves primarily clerical tasks. A greater number of weeks during which unemployed persons are entitled to receive benefits consequently increases mostly the need for clerical personnel and hence the ratio of clerks in the agency. An expanded volume of routine duties imposed by state law on the agency raises the proportion of clerks among its personnel. This influ-

10. Decomposition of the data in Table 6–6 shows that the indirect effect of size mediated by the division of labor raising the clerical ratio is .46, and its indirect effect mediated by automation lowering the ratio is − .43.

ence, just as those of agency characteristics, operates by changing the need for clerks, but another environmental condition affects their supply.

A large proportion of men and women of foreign stock in a state increases the proportion of clerks in its employment security agency. The interpetation this finding in Table 6–6 suggests is that the agency's ability to employ many clerks depends on their availability in the labor market and that an ethnically mixed population with many persons of foreign stock constitutes a labor market with a disproportionate supply of clerks. Most men and women of foreign stock today are not foreign born but second generation, that is, native-born children of immigrants. These are largely men and women who have been raised in poor immigrant homes in cities and many of whom have strong ambitions to improve themselves, but their limited resources often prevent them from acquiring the educational qualifications necessary to achieve high managerial or professional positions. The assumption is that such urban young workers from lower income homes with a strong drive to be upwardly mobile and with insufficient resources to attain a higher education provide a ready-made pool of clerical labor for government bureaus or private employers. Men and women from poor homes who are less eager to rise to white-collar levels are not likely to acquire the competence necessary for clerical positions, and persons with higher educational qualifications are not interested in clerical jobs.

But are the assumptions warranted that the second generation exhibits disproportionate strivings for upward mobility and disproportionate tendencies to occupy clerical jobs? There is empirical evidence to support these assumptions. A recent study shows that men with immigrant parents are more likely to be upwardly mobile than any other group; more than three tenths of them achieve a substantial amount of upward mobility, as much as is achieved by only one quarter of white native-born Northerners of native parentage, the majority group.[11] Furthermore, data from the 1960 U.S. Census indicate that the second generation is considerably overrepresented in clerical occupations.[12] Whereas 6.9 per cent of all men in the labor force are clerks, 8.2 per cent of the American-born sons of foreign-born parents are. Among all women in the labor force, similarly,

---

11. Peter M. Blau and Otis Dudley Duncan, *The American Occupational Structure* (New York: Wiley, 1967), p. 232.
12. U.S. Bureau of the Census, "Nativity and Parentage," Subject Report PC(2)–1A, *U.S. Census of Population: 1960* (Washington, D.C.: Government Printing Office, 1965). For data indicating the same tendency at earlier periods, see E. P. Hutchinson, *Immigrants and Their Children* (New York: Wiley, 1956), p. 202.

fewer are clerks (29.7 per cent) than among second-generation women (35.5 per cent). If 100 signifies an equal distribution, the index for the native born of foreign parentage in clerical jobs would be 119. As a matter of fact, second-generation men are overrepresented in all nonmanual occupational groups, and they are underrepresented in all groups of farm and manual occupations except craftsmen, and the pattern for second-generation women is the same for eight of the ten major occupational groups (the two exceptions are that women are not overrepresented in the professions and not underrepresented among operatives). However, the proportion of second-generation men and women is higher among clerks than in all but one of the nine other major occupational groups (it is still higher among managers, proprietors, and officials).

These data support the interpretation that an ethnically mixed population with many persons of foreign stock increases the supply of clerks in the labor market and for this reason enables employment security agencies to fill large proportions of positions with clerks. Some additional support is provided by our own data. If the large-scale employment of clerks in an agency depends on both the supply of clerical labor provided by an ethnically mixed population and an advanced division of labor, one would expect the division of labor to reinforce the influence of an ethnically mixed population on the clerical ratio. The empirical evidence confirms this inference. The proportion of persons of foreign stock in the state is correlated with the agency's division of labor (.27), though not so much as with the clerical ratio (.37), and decomposition reveals that its direct influence on the proportion of clerks (.25) is supplemented by an indirect influence mediated by the division of labor (.16). A further test of the interpretation is whether the clerical ratio in local offices is similarly affected by the ethnic composition of the population in the places in which the offices are located. The results of this test will be presented in Chapter 8.

The clerical ratio of an agency is also larger in highly urbanized states than in less urbanized ones. However, Table 6–6 indicates that the influence of urbanization on the proportion of clerks is entirely indirect. Decomposition reveals that the more pronounced division of labor of agencies operating in highly urbanized environments is largely responsible for the higher proportion of clerks in them (.31), though this mediating influence of the division of labor is counteracted by that of automation (−.21) and slightly reinforced by that of the proportion of foreign stock in the population (.13). In other words, an urbanized environment increases an agency's clerical ratio primarily because it promotes occupational differentiation and thus the need for clerks, and secondarily because its ethnically mixed population increases the supply of clerks. But the greater likelihood of automation in agencies in urbanized states, which reduces the need for clerks, depresses the over-all impact of urbanization on the clerical ratio below what its two indirect effects would otherwise produce.

Does the managerial component in an agency depend in similar fashion on the supply of educated persons in the labor market? There is a shred of evidence in Table 6–7 that it does. Median years of education in the state

TABLE 6-7. *Multiple Regression of* **Supervisory Ratio at Headquarters** *on Agency and Environmental Conditions*

Independent Variable	Standardized Regression Coefficient	Zero-Order Correlation
State Environment		
Median Education	.15	.24
Governor's Appointive Power	−.23*	−.35
Agency		
Size (Log)	−.97**	−.51
Levels	.42**	−.21
Divisions	.32*	−.21
Sections per Division	.25*	−.07

Multiple R = .66; n = 51

*Greater than one-and-a-half times its standard error.

**Greater than twice its standard error.

and proportion of supervisory personnel in its employment security agency exhibit a small positive correlation (.24). Although neither the direct effect of education in the state (.15) nor its indirect effects on the supervisory ratio mediated by size (.08) and levels (.06) are substantial, they add up to a gross effect that is not pronounced but not entirely inconsequential either. Another environmental condition exerts more influence on the managerial ratio, namely, the governor's appointive power, which depresses it. The appointment of most senior executives in the state government by the governor, in contrast to their election or appointment by a board, probably reflects a management orientation to state government as distinguished from a political orientation.[13] An emphasis on management efficiency on

13. The governor's appointive power similarly is somewhat inversely correlated with the frequency with which the agency director communicates with the governor or with the commissioner under him (−.24). This correlation also indicates that appointive power implies a less political government, on the assumption that a politically oriented government would entail frequent communication. The measure of the governor's appointive power is taken

the top level of state government may constrain state bureaus generally, including those whose funds do not come out of the general state treasury, to economize by maintaining sparser managerial components. Table 6–7 also shows that the previously discussed positive effect of agency size and the negative effects of three dimensions of structural differentiation on the managerial ratio persist when these environmental conditions are controlled.

One might expect the educational level in the state to exert more influence on the educational attainments of employment security personnel than on the proportion of them that achieve, usually through promotion, supervisory positions. But this is not the case. The median level of education in the state does not exhibit an appreciable positive zero-order correlation with the educational attainments of interviewers (.15). Why is the superior education of the state's population not reflected to a significant degree in superior education of the agency personnel? Possibly because the people in a state are most likely to acquire much education if there are many job opportunities requiring such training, which in turn implies that the competition among employers for highly trained manpower increases as the population's education increases. Though this is mere conjecture, there is some indirect indication that competition among government bureaus for managerial personnel makes it more difficult to retain managers with superior educational qualifications. The environmental condition most strongly associated with the average education of division heads in an agency is the ratio of government employees to population in the state, and when it is controlled no other environmental variable reveals an appreciable persisting relationship with the education of division heads. The greater the number of government employees relative to the size of a state, the lower are the educational attainments of the division heads in the employment security agency ($r = -.47$).

The finding suggests that stiffer competition among government bureaus in a state for highly trained managerial personnel makes it more difficult for an agency to keep its best-educated managers or to attract well-educated substitutes for them. One assumption underlying this interpretation is that the most likely alternative jobs for managerial officials in the employment security agency are those in other government bureaus in the state, because their seniority rights are preserved. Another underlying as-

from Joseph A. Schlesinger, "The Politics of the Executive," in Herbert Jacob and Kenneth N. Vines, eds., *Politics in the American States* (Boston: Little Brown, 1965), pp. 222–223, who states that the value "for each state is based on the governor's power of appointment in sixteen major functions and offices" (p. 223).

sumption is that college training is indicative of managerial qualifications (though probably not the best indication of them), which is supported by the finding earlier reported that the education of division heads is positively related to the scope of their major responsibilities, as indicated by sections per division (Table 3–6). Moreover, this measure of scope of major responsibilities of division heads is inversely related to the ratio of government employees to population in the state (r = −.38), just as the education of division heads is. The influence of many government employees in a state on the scope of major responsibilities of division heads is largely indirect, mediated by agency size (− .17) and the education of these division heads (− .10).[14]

The relative size of the staff component in an employment security agency is profoundly affected by environmental conditions, which together with two organizational characteristics account for more than three quarters of its variation among agencies, as can be seen in Table 6–8. The strongest influence on the proportionate size of the administrative staff is exerted by the ratio of the agency's operating funds to the unemployment insurance taxes collected in the state. As mentioned in Chapter 2, the part

TABLE 6-8. *Multiple Regression of Staff Ratio on Agency and Environmental Conditions*

Independent Variable	Standardized Regression Coefficient	Zero-Order Correlation
State Environment		
Southern Region	−.31**	−.37
Western Region	−.37**	.32
% Government Employees	.21*	.65
Expenditures per Capita	−.10	.55
% Insured Unemployed	.19*	.34
Funds/Taxes	.54**	.74
Agency		
Size (Log)	−.49**	−.65
Levels	.14	−.34

Multiple R = .90; n = 51

*Greater than one-and-a-half times its standard error.

**Greater than twice its standard error.

14. These values are obtained from the decomposition carried out after per cent state government employees is added as a fifth independent variable to the four organizational characteristics shown in Table 3–6. The standardized regression coefficient is − .18, with a standard error of .16.

of the taxes collected in various states that is set aside for administrative purposes is put into a national pool of funds, and federal officials—formerly, from the Bureau of Employment Security, now, from the Manpower Administration—draw on this pool to allocate the funds needed for internal operations (not including the unemployment benefits themselves) to the various agencies. Bureau officials at Hearings of a Subcommittee of the Committee on Appropriations, U.S. House of Representatives, in 1964 stated that the following are the major considerations governing the allocations of these funds: the higher operating costs in more sparsely settled areas; variations in work load; differences in salary rates; differences in rent; the complexity of the state law; the existence of intensive programs of employment service for special groups, such as youth or minority groups.[15] The total funds of an agency vary too closely with variations in size to provide a useful measure without being first standardized. The ratio of funds allocated to taxes collected may be considered an indicator of an agency's comparative affluence, that is, its operating budget relative to the size of the labor force it serves (which is the main determinant of the amount of taxes collected).

Generous administrative funds greatly expand the proportionate size of the staff component in an agency. Of course, more personnel can be employed with an ample operating budget than with a tight one, but the finding indicates more specifically that differences in operating funds have their major impact, not on line personnel, but on the staff. An adequate budget enables an agency to enlarge its staff services and consequently provide on its own needed auxiliary services for which other agencies presumably have to depend on outside help from other government bureaus. For example, an agency with an insufficient personnel staff is more likely to have to rely extensively on the state personnel department than one that has a personnel staff commensurate with its needs. As a matter of fact, the relative size of the staff component in an agency reduces the extent of regular contacts it has with other state agencies ($r = -.24$), which may be an indication of lesser dependence on other agencies. Though a large ratio of staff personnel seems to make an agency more autonomous, the question remains whether the use of abundant funds to enlarge the staff personnel is not an expression of bureaucratic tendencies on the part of management to build a relatively independent empire as well as to centralize internal control in its own hands.

There are some indications that a disproportionately large administra-

---

15. Cited in William Haber and Merrill G. Murray, *Unemployment Insurance in the American Economy* (Homewood, Ill.: Irwin, 1966), pp. 413–414.

tive staff may be a tool for empire building, though they are not conclusive. If a large staff were needed to substitute for the auxiliary services the state government fails to provide, one would expect the staff ratio to increase as the relative size of the state government decreases, on the assumption that a relatively small state government furnishes few auxiliary services. Actually, however, Table 6–8 shows that the staff ratio in agencies is positively related to the comparative size (employees) of the state government.[16] The greater the inclination in the state to invest in government administration, the greater is the inclination in the agency to invest in administrative overhead. Is this indicative of a willingness to make investments in administration in order to improve services, or rather of a general tendency toward bureaucratic centralization? As far as our data reveal, the latter is the more plausible inference. For a large staff ratio by no means improves services to clients (at least as far as our measures show), it raises the man-hour cost of benefit operations, and it encourages centralization of authority. Whereas these findings do not demonstrate it, they invite the conjecture that a disproportionately large administrative staff serves little function besides that of helping build bureaucratic empires.

Three other environmental conditions directly influence the size of the administrative staff. The agency's staff ratio is lower in Southern and Western states than in states in the other two regions of the country, but in the case of Western states other conditions, notably high administrative funds, counteract the negative net effect and produce a positive gross effect of region on the staff ratio. One might speculate whether a tradition of dominant political machines, such as those in New York, Boston, Chicago, and Kansas City, has fostered empire building in many agencies in Northeastern and Northcentral states.[17] A large proportion of insured unemployed in the state increases the proportionate size of the administrative

---

16. The positive effect of relative size of state government on the agency's staff ratio is partly direct (.21) and partly indirect, mediated mostly by fund ratio (.32) and agency size (.33). These positive effects are counteracted by some negative "indirect effects," the most important being that of the Western region (− .21), which is not an indirect effect but an indication of how much larger the correlation would be were it not for the influence of location in the West. The gross effect indicated by the zero-order correlation is .65.

17. The influence of regions was analyzed by using three dummy variables and considering the fourth region—Northeast—as the residual. Although only two of these dummy variables (South and West) have a substantial negative association with staff ratio, the third (Northcentral) also is negatively correlated with it (−.14), which implies that administrative staffs are particularly large in states in the Northeastern region.

staff, the direct positive effect being reinforced by an indirect one mediated by the fund ratio. A large volume of unemployment insurance activities in the agency implies that administrative problems are of foremost importance, and the tighter managerial controls a large administrative component makes possible are more appropriate for dealing with these problems than with the more professional ones entailed by employment services.

The government expenditure per capita in the state is a final environmental condition greatly increasing the proportionate size of the administrative staff, but Table 6–8 indicates that this positive effect is entirely indirect. The most important intervening variable responsible for this effect is the ratio of funds allocated to taxes collected (.37), with three other intervening variables playing a lesser part (state employees, unemployment, and agency size). Whereas state government expenditures directly influence interviewers' salary, as we saw earlier, and agency funds exert no independent influence on it,[18] the situation is reversed in respect to the staff ratio. The finding that the fund ratio exerts no independent influence on salaries when one controls government expenditures, which also very roughly controls the level of government salaries in the state, indicates that the federal bureau is successful in its policy of providing the right amount of funds for agency salaries to match those of comparable government employees elsewhere in the state. At the same time, the finding that the funds allocated to the agency exert the most pronounced influence on its staff ratio, whereas the general level of government expenditures influences the staff only indirectly, reveals that the federal government provides some agencies with the extra funds needed to establish a particularly large administrative staff. Such a large staff may enable these agencies to provide specialized services to clients that our data did not take into account. But there are indications that a disproportionately large staff does not improve regular services, to say the least, and one might even surmise that its main function is to maintain centralized authority through an oversized bureaucracy.

At last, let us briefly examine how controlling environmental conditions modifies the influence of organizational characteristics on the staff ratio. Agency size continues to have a strong negative impact on the relative size of the staff component, though it is not so strong as appeared when differ-

---

18. The correlation of salary with government expenditures of .68 remains a standardized regression coefficient of .64 if funds are controlled, but its correlation with funds of .49 vanishes if government expenditures are controlled ($b^* = .05$). Because government expenditures in the state are considered antecedent to agency funds, the latter variable has not been included in the regression problem in Table 6–2.

ences in the external situation were not controlled (compare Tables 6–8 and 4–2). The regression coefficient of hierarchical levels becomes too small when environmental conditions are controlled, however, to attribute any independent influence on staff ratio to levels. The reason for the differences between the two tables is that the predominant influence of funds on the staff ratio absorbs some of the influence formerly attributed to size and thereby also diminishes the significance that controlling size has for revealing a positive net effect of levels.[19] The substantive conclusion is that organizational size exerts a strong negative influence on the ratio of staff personnel, but that differentiation in the hierarchy of authority has no appreciable influence on it, inasmuch as its apparent influence is no longer evident once differences in the financial situation among agencies are taken into account. Even stronger than the negative influence of agency size on the proportionate size of the staff component is the positive influence exerted on it by ample budgetary resources.

External Influences on Services

External conditions over which employment security agencies have no control affect the services they administer as well as their size, their formal structure, and the composition of their personnel. The most relevant aspects of the environment are not the same in all these cases, however. The volume of insured unemployment in a state, which in turn is closely related to the size of its population, and the degree of urbanization, which also is related to population size, are the external conditions that affect the size and formal structure of the agency. The composition of the personnel, on the other hand, is most influenced by the conditions in the labor market and the financial resources allocated to the agency. And the environmental factors that have most bearing on service operations are the socioeconomic and ethnic characteristics of the state's population.

The extent of public employment services administered by the employment security agency declines sharply with rising income levels in the

---

19. The gross effect of size (log) on staff ratio of $-.65$ is composed of a direct effect of $-.49$ and the following indirect effects: funds, $-.25$; South, $.00$; West, $.08$; unemployed, $.02$; state employees, $-.13$; levels, $.10$; government expenditures, $.03$ (the rounding error is $.01$). The gross effect of levels on staff ratio of $-.34$ can be decomposed into an insignificant net effect of $.14$ and the following "indirect effects," which are actually reflections of spuriousness: funds, $-.16$; South, $.07$; West, $.00$; size, $-.35$; unemployed, $.02$; state employees, $-.08$; government expenditures, $.00$ (the rounding error is $-.02$).

state, as Table 6–9 shows. This finding might seem entirely obvious were it not for the curious fact previously noted that average family income is positively related to the proportion of insured unemployed in a state. Hence, the finding does not merely reflect either the lower rates of unemployment in richer states or the greater reluctance of affluent people to seek free services at public agencies. As a matter of fact, richer states not only insure more of their unemployed but actually have a larger proportion of unemployed people than poorer ones. Average family income exhibits a slight positive correlation with the proportion of *all* unemployed in a state (.21), though not so strong a correlation as with the proportion of *insured* unemployed (.55). Economic circumstances tend to be bifurcated in our society, with the prosperity of some occurring side by side with the indigence of others. Besides, more persons in affluent than in poor populations are legally entitled to and actually do claim unemployment benefits. A high income level does not make people generally disinclined to take advantage of the services of the public employment security agency when they become unemployed, but it makes them specifically less interested in the job placement services it has to offer. The likely reason is that most of the skilled jobs that are of interest to higher socioeconomic strata are not available at the public employment agency and must be obtained primarily through private channels.

An ethnically mixed population, as manifest in a high proportion of persons of foreign stock in the state, also reduces the volume of applicants for jobs relative to the size of an agency. Whereas part of the strong negative zero-order correlation is owing to income, which is positively associated with foreign stock, the regression coefficient that remains in Table 6–9 when income and other conditions are controlled is not entirely inconsequential, indicating some net effect of foreign stock reducing the extent of employment services. The finding suggests that the job opportunities at these public agencies are less appealing to men and women of foreign stock than to others. The disproportionate striving for upward mobility among persons of foreign stock that makes them good candidates for clerical and other white-collar jobs, as has been mentioned, also inhibits their interest in the predominantly low-skilled jobs the public employment agency has to offer. Besides, immigrant subcultures may make it easier for young people to obtain jobs through a *paisano* than at impersonal agencies.[20] The extent of employment services is also greater in Southern states

20. It should be noted that the negative ecological correlation for states between proportion of foreign stock and proportion of applicants for jobs at the public agency does not demonstrate that it is actually the persons of foreign stock who are less likely to apply for jobs than others. It could be

TABLE 6-9. *Multiple Regression of* **Applications per Employee** *on Agency and Environmental Conditions*

Independent Variable	Standardized Regression Coefficient	Zero-Order Correlation
State Environment		
Median Family Income	−.53**	−.67
% Foreign Stock	−.20*	−.59
Agency		
Salary of Interviewers	.05	−.28
Automation (Dummy)[a]	.32**	.29
Clerical Ratio	−.01	−.27
Staff Ratio	−.18*	−.41
Delegation to Local Managers	.14*	.24

Multiple R = .81; n = 51

*Greater than one-and-a-half times its standard error.

**Greater than twice its standard error.

[a]Dichotomous dummy variable: whether or not any computer exists.

than in those in the three other regions (r = .45), but this difference is entirely due to the lower incomes and the lower proportions of foreign stock in the South and disappears when these two variables are controlled.[21]

When environmental conditions are taken into account, it becomes apparent that two of the conditions to which an influence on the extent of employment services was previously attributed actually do not exert any influence. We were originally puzzled by the inverse correlation between interviewers' salary and volume of applicant services observed in Chapter 4. Why should paying lower salaries to interviewers increase the amount of work they perform? The results in Table 6–9 help solve the puzzle by showing that the negative zero-order correlation between salaries and applications per employee (−.28) does not persist when environmental conditions are controlled, and decomposition reveals that the median income in the state is responsible for the spurious correlation (−.27). Higher sala-

that an ethnically mixed population in the state discourages people generally, those of native parentage as well as the second generation, from applying for jobs at the public employment agency. (Similar considerations apply to the negative correlation between income level and applicants for jobs in a state.)

21. Because the Southern region has no direct effect, it is not included in the regression analysis in Table 6–9.

ries do not depress the volume of employment services rendered, but a higher economic level in the state results in both higher salaries for interviewers and a lower demand for public employment services.

Whereas in this case the fact that the initial correlation seemed puzzling provided a clue that it might be spurious, another correlation for which an interpretation readily came to mind also turns out to be spurious. The interpretation suggested in Chapter 4 that a low proportion of clerical, and thus a high proportion of nonclerical, personnel is required for an agency to furnish extensive employment services is incorrect. Table 6–9 indicates that the negative zero-order correlation between clerical ratio and applications per employee (− .27) disappears under controls, largely owing to the income level (− .15) and proportion of foreign stock (− .07) in the state, both of which are positively associated with the clerical ratio and have a negative influence on the volume of applicant services.[22] The relationships of three other organizational characteristics with extent of employment services are little altered by controlling environmental conditions (compare Tables 4–5 and 6–9). Automation frees more manpower to engage in extensive applicant services, and a centralized management relying heavily on an administrative staff and delegating few responsibilities to local levels is not well suited for concentration on employment services.

Not a single environmental factor was discovered that influences the degree to which intensive vocational services are furnished to job applicants, except those that do so through their influence on agency size. The outstanding example of the latter is the size of the state's population, which is inversely correlated with intensive services (− .40), simply because large states have large agencies, and intensive services are rarer in large than in small agencies.

Two elements of the population composition of a state affect the ratio of placements made to job openings received in the employment security agency. Table 6–10 shows that the proportion of men and women of foreign stock and the proportion working in manufacturing industries both reduce the effectiveness of placement operations as indicated by this ratio. Manufacturing is characterized by strong unions and big firms with their own employment offices, which probably reduces the importance of the public agencies as a labor exchange in manufacturing industries. Persons of foreign stock are less likely to utilize the public employment agency, perhaps owing to their disproportionate achievement orientation, as has

---

22. Since the positive relationship between income level and clerical ratio disappears when other environmental conditions are controlled, largely owing to the influence of proportion of foreign stock, income level is not used in the regression problem in Table 6–6.

TABLE 6-10. *Multiple Regression of* **Placements per Opening** *on Agency and Environmental Conditions*

Independent Variable	Standardized Regression Coefficient	Zero-Order Correlation
State Environment		
% Foreign Stock	−.33**	−.46
% Manufacturing Employees	−.27**	−.35
Agency		
Sections per Division	.36**	.40
Standardized Rating	−.27**	−.37

Multiple R = .70; n = 51
**Greater than twice its standard error.

been inferred above from the findings in Table 6–9 and some other data. Two processes may reinforce each other here. Public agencies have fewer jobs in manufacturing and fewer of the kind in which most people of foreign stock are interested, discouraging these two groups from applying for jobs at the public agencies. The few applicants in these categories, in turn, make it more difficult to find suitable candidates for the job openings that do exist, discouraging employers from using the public agencies for these types of jobs. To ask which is cause and which is effect is like trying to solve the chicken-and-egg problem. A high income level in the state also reduces placements per opening ($r = -.35$), but this influence is essentially produced by the larger proportions of persons of foreign stock in more affluent states.[23]

Many manufacturing employees in a state reduce the importance of the public employment agency as a labor exchange, and this is reflected in its size. Table 6–1 has shown that a large proportion of workers in manufacturing slightly reduces agency size. However, many men and women of foreign stock in a state also reduce the significance of the public agency as a labor exchange, yet this variable is positively related to agency size. A possible reason for the discrepancy might be that a large proportion of persons with immigrant parents raises the volume of unemployment insurance work of the agency, whereas a large proportion of manufacturing workers does not. Indeed, the proportion of insured unemployed in the state is positively correlated with the proportion of foreign stock (.42) but

23. The standardized regression coefficient of placements per opening on income level, controlling foreign stock, is only −.09. Given its lack of direct effect on placements, median income is not included in the regression problem in Table 6–10.

not with that of manufacturing employees (.00). Nevertheless, the explanation is not satisfactory, because Table 6–1 indicates that the proportion of foreign stock exerts a small positive influence on agency size independent of that of the proportion of unemployed. It may be that the more abundant supply of candidates for clerical positions provided by a large proportion of foreign stock in the population actually enlarges the personnel of the agency. In the absence of an adequate supply of clerks in the labor market, an agency must be staffed by fewer but better-paid employees, whereas a sufficient supply of clerks makes it possible to hire for many functions a larger number of lower-paid employees instead.

The earlier conclusion concerning the effects of two organizational characteristics on placement productivity (Table 4–7) does not need to be modified on the basis of the multiple regression analysis in which environmental conditions are controlled (Table 6–10). A large number of sections per division has a substantial positive effect on placement operations. This finding implies that effective employment services benefit from an agency structure that is functionally differentiated particularly on the second level below top management (within divisions) rather than on the highest levels of the divisions themselves, which also means that division heads have a broad scope of responsibilities. Another indication that broader responsibilities of managers improve placement service is that the supervisory evaluation of performance is less likely to encourage a high rate of placements if governed by standardized rating procedures than if left to the discretion of supervisors.

Turning now to unemployment benefit operations, Table 6–11 presents data on the only one of the environmental conditions examined that affects the cost in man-hours of these operations. The higher the income level in the state, the higher is the personnel cost of providing benefit services to clients. The better salaries paid in wealthier states cannot be responsible for this finding, because costs are reckoned in man-hours, not in dollars. (The zero-order correlation between interviewers' salary and the employee-client ratio is an inconsequential .09.) Agencies in affluent states apparently devote more effort to serving recipients of unemployment benefits than those in poorer ones. One reason for this is that the former can afford to do so, but a second reason may well be that they are constrained to do so by the expectations of their clients. The style of life and former standard of living of individuals who have become unemployed undoubtedly continue to govern their demeanor and expectations when they come to the public agency to claim unemployment benefits, and the reactions of officials toward them can hardly help being affected by these differences. Men and women of higher socioeconomic strata, though now unemployed, are

TABLE 6-11. *Multiple Regression of* **Employee-Client Ratio in Benefit Function**
on Agency and Environmental Conditions

Independent Variable	Standardized Regression Coefficient	Zero-Order Correlation
State Environment		
Median Family Income	.29**	.34
Agency		
Size	−.10	−.15
Extent of Personnel Regulations	−.30**	−.33
Division of Labor	.30	−.03
Automation (Dummy)[a]	−.29**	−.23
Staff Ratio	.28*	.40

Multiple R = .62; *n* = 51

*Greater than one-and-a-half times its standard error.

**Greater than twice its standard error.

[a]Dichotomous dummy variable: whether or not any computer exists.

more likely than those with long experiences of deprivation to exhibit self-assurance and express in their behavior the expectation of being treated with polite consideration. It is quite possible that agency employees treat clients from higher socioeconomic strata with more consideration and less curtly than those from lower ones, with the result that a superior socioeconomic level of the population raises the time per client required to provide benefit services.

Controlling the median income in the state changes the pattern of influences of organizational characteristics on this employee-client ratio only in minor ways, with one exception, as can be seen by comparing Tables 4–8 and 6–11. The regression coefficient of this ratio on the division of labor is now not quite one and one-half times its standard error, which makes the former conclusion that occupational differentiation impedes operating economy questionable. But the other conclusions stand: automation, extensive personnel regulations, and a small administrative staff improve operating economy in terms of man-hours, and so does large size indirectly through its association with these three conditions.[24]

---

24. The influence of size is less clear than when environmental conditions are not controlled, although controlling income does not change the pattern much, because the slight changes it does produce create ambiguities. The direct negative effect of size on the employee-client ratio is inconsequential (−.10), but together with the three negative indirect effects mediated by automation (−.08), regulations (−.17), and staff ratio (−.12) it would

The services employment security agencies administer are considerably affected by the external situation. Its personnel components and particularly its total personnel complement are still more strongly dependent on external conditions. The environment appears to have a less strong impact on the internal structure of these agencies and none at all that we could discover on such administrative practices as the decentralization of decision-making.[25] This pattern of findings suggests that the boundaries of personnel input and service output are where the organization is most subject to the influences of the external situation, whereas the formal structure and the administrative practices constitute an internal core somewhat shielded by these boundaries from external stimuli.

Conclusions

The external situation exerts much influence on employment security agencies, but the focus of attention on these external influences may have given the misleading impression that they are more important than the internal influences of antecedent organizational conditions on agency characteristics and operations. The empirical findings do not warrant this conclusion; indeed, they suggest the opposite, namely, that in most cases internal influences predominate over external ones. To be sure, the size of an agency is largely a function of external conditions determining the demand for its services, and the salary of interviewers depends more on externally supplied resources than on internal antecedents (though these results are

---

make up a substantial negative effect of $-.47$, which is reduced by only .10 when income is controlled. The division of labor exerts no appreciable influence of its own on the ratio, but its mediating influence reduces the negative effect of size on it sufficiently (.23) to make the total effect too small to be accepted as meaningful ($-.15$). The point is simply that several effects each of which is inconsequential may add up to a substantial one, and this sometimes makes substantive interpretation awkward.

25. The slight association of delegation of personnel authority with agency funds vanishes when the staff ratio is controlled, and its only other substantial correlation is with population, which vanishes when agency size is controlled. The strongest correlations of budget delegation and of decentralization of influence are also with population; the former has no other appreciable association; decentralization of influence also has a positive correlation with governor's appointive power (.29), but it becomes insignificantly small when size is controlled. Delegation to local offices is not substantially correlated with any of the major environmental variables considered, but it is correlated .29 with the per cent of agricultural employees in the state, which suggests that the wide dispersion of local offices in more thinly populated rural areas promotes delegation of responsibilities to them.

only partly empirical and partly owing to the sequence assumptions, which do not permit any or most other internal variables to be considered antecedents of these two). As far as the other dependent variables investigated are concerned, however, the amount of variation accounted for by internal organizational antecedents alone is in all cases greater than the additional amount of variation accounted for by adding environmental conditions to the regression problem,[26] and it is in most cases also greater than would be the amount of variation accounted for by the environmental conditions alone. Thus, though the external environment has substantial effects on employment security agencies, particularly on their size, salaries, staff ratio, and services, other organizational conditions typically have the strongest direct effects, notably on various aspects of structural differentiation and managerial practices, such as decentralization.

The often intricate analysis of direct and indirect effects of the external situation in this chapter makes it desirable to recapitulate the main findings. Because the various environmental and organizational conditions that influence each dependent variable can be reviewed at a glance by looking at the tables in this chapter, the findings are summarized from a different perspective here in the conclusion, namely, by examining for each environmental condition the various influences on employment security agencies it exerts. To round out the concluding discussion in this last chapter on entire agencies before we turn to the analysis of their components, the interrelations between agency characteristics are also briefly summarized, again from the perspective of each independent variable and its various influences on dependent variables.

There are some regional differences among employment security agencies. Adherence to civil service standards is most prevalent in the West, and salaries are highest in the West and lowest in the South, as a result of

26. Adding environmental independent variables to the organizational ones examined in Chapters 3 and 4 increases the amount of variation explained in the nine dependent variables in Tables 6–3 through 6–11 as follows: division of labor, from 61 to 62 per cent; levels (not fully comparable), from 53 to 57 per cent; divisions, from 37 to 37 per cent; clerical ratio, from 23 to 34 per cent; supervisory ratio, from 28 to 36 per cent; staff ratio, from 37 to 77 per cent; applications/employee, from 34 to 60 per cent; placements/opening, from 27 to 45 per cent; benefit employees/client, from 21 to 30 per cent. Both sets of antecedents account thus for between 30 and 77 per cent of the variance in these nine organizational characteristics. To correct for degrees of freedom eliminated, the formula $\bar{R}^2 = 1 - (1 - R^2) \frac{n - 1}{n - k - 1}$ is used, where n is sample size and k number of variables.

corresponding differences in government expenditures and in income levels. Agencies in both the West and the South maintain disproportionately small administrative staffs, whereas those in Northeastern states maintain large ones. The size of a state's population is the major condition determining agency size, and it therefore affects indirectly the internal conditions in the agency strongly influenced by its size, such as division of labor, automation, structural differentiation, and, inversely, administrative overhead, that is, both the staff and the supervisory ratio. A high degree of urbanization in the state promotes, directly as well as owing to its association with agency size, differentiation of occupational positions, hierarchical levels, and functional divisions, which supports the hypothesis suggested in the literature that organizations adjust to a diverse environment by developing a complex structure. Through its influence on occupational differentiation, urbanization also indirectly raises the clerical ratio and discourages the use of standardized rating procedures.

Socioeconomic conditions in the state, as well as related factors reflected in the population composition, influence the demand for the services of employment security agencies and the supply of their personnel. A high income level reduces the demand for public employment services, though not that for unemployment insurance, inasmuch as the proportionate volume of applications for jobs is lower but that of claimants for unemployment benefits is higher in affluent than in poorer states. Besides, higher socioeconomic strata may expect and receive more attentive and less curt treatment at the unemployment insurance office; this has been surmised from the positive relationship between income level and man-hours per client required for benefit services. Income level also indirectly affects agency salaries through its influence on government expenditures.

Much manufacturing and many persons of foreign stock in the state depress placement operations, which implies that manufacturing workers and individuals of foreign stock are less likely than other people to find jobs at the public employment agency. The lesser significance of the public agency as a labor exchange for these groups has been interpreted as resulting from the unions and company employment offices in manufacturing industries, on the one hand, and the prevalent striving to move up into white-collar positions among younger workers raised in poor immigrant homes, on the other. Because the second generation contains a disproportionate number of young men and women ambitious to obtain white-collar jobs but with insufficient resources to acquire a higher education, according to this interpretation, their presence increases the supply of clerical labor, which may explain why the proportion of foreign stock in the population raises the proportion of clerks in the agency. Though a large share of manufacturing workers in the state reduces the size of the employment security agency, as one would expect from their lesser utilization of public employment services, a large share of persons of foreign stock increases it, possibly because their availability as clerks enables an agency to substitute a larger number of low-salaried clerks for a smaller number of better-paid employees. A high educational level of the population increases in parallel fashion the supply of labor for superior white-collar positions, which is reflected in a slight positive relationship between median education in the state and proportion of supervisors in the agency.

A large state government with many employees relative to the state's population appears to increase the occupational opportunities of highly qualified senior officials and the competition for their services among state agencies, making it more difficult for a given agency to keep its best educated managers. In any case, this inference is suggested by the finding that the relative size of the state government is inversely related to the education of division heads in the employment security agency, and indirectly also to the scope of major responsibilities assigned to them. Two other effects of the size of the state government have been observed. The larger the state government, the more extensive is the body of civil service regulations governing its personnel procedures. A large state government also seems to foster the development of a large administrative staff in the agency. Thus, the greater the general inclination in the state to invest in government services, the greater is the inclination in the particular agency under consideration to invest in staff services. A large government machinery in the state may reflect superior services of various kinds to the people, but its association with the proliferation of staff overhead in at least one agency raises the suspicion whether it may not reflect a tendency toward bureaucratization and empire building.

Government expenditures per capita in the state have a direct effect on the salary of agency interviewers and an indirect one on the size of the administrative staff, mediated by the agency's operating funds. These funds allocated to the agency by the federal government from a national pool exert the strongest impact on the proportionate size of its staff component. A large volume of unemployment insurance claims also increases the relative size of the administrative staff, as well as the total personnel of the agency, which suggests that a large staff component is more appropriate for unemployment insurance than for employment services. The rate of insured unemployment in the state exhibits a spurious correlation with interviewers' salary, because more affluent states not only can incur the government expenditures to pay higher salaries but also can afford to insure more of their unemployed—and, strangely enough, actually have a larger total proportion of unemployed—than poorer ones. An administrative rather than a political orientation on the top level of state government, as indicated by the governor's appointive power, reduces the proportion of supervisors in the agency, possibly in response to pressures to economize. Finally, the longer the period during which unemployed persons are entitled by law to receive benefits, the larger is the proportion of clerks, because processing continuing benefits primarily entails clerical work.

We start now the quick review of the interdependence between agency characteristics with an examination of the many influences exerted by agency size. The scope of its impact is indicated by realizing that size has a direct influence, when other conditions are controlled, on fifteen of the twenty-five other basic agency characteristics listed in Table 1–1, not including the conflicting indirect and the interaction effects it has on several other variables. Moreover, in most cases the influence of size is pronounced. To enumerate: large size is associated with extensive personnel regulations, a high salary of interviewers, and the automation of operations; it promotes differentiation of occupational positions, hierarchical levels, functional divisions, and sections per division; it widens the agency director's and the average division head's span of control; it reduces the ratio of supervisory and the ratio of staff personnel; it slightly fosters standardized rating procedures; it engenders reluctance to delegate official authority, and it simultaneously creates pressures to decentralize decisions despite this reluctance; and it produces administrative constraints that discourage intensive vocational services to clients. Through these direct effects, large size exerts indirect effects in opposite directions on the clerical ratio and on the operating economy of benefit operations (in terms of man-hours), and it also exerts indirect effects counteracting its own direct ones on the number of divisions, the managerial ratio, the standardization of ratings, and the delegation of authority. In addition, large size combines with the automation it promotes to give rise to delegation of responsibilities to local offices, and it interacts with such delegation to improve placement productivity and operating economy.

The formalization of personnel procedures effected by an extensive body of civil service regulations fosters decentralization of responsibilities, both within the agency headquarters and to local offices, and so does strict compliance with these civil service standards. Extensive personnel regulations also reduce the man-hours required for benefit operations, thus furthering operating economy. Conformity with civil service standards raises the qualifications of interviewers, and high salaries, too, attract better qualified interviewers.[27] There is some indication that the greater personnel

---

27. These two effects on qualifications of interviewers will be discussed in Chapter 9.

cost entailed by higher salaries encourages the installation of computers, which makes it possible to substitute machines for some of the personnel.

Indeed, automation probably decreases the manpower needs of the agency, as suggested by the findings that it is inversely related to both the proportion of clerks and the ratio of employees to clients in the benefit function. By substituting machines for some men in unemployment insurance operations, automation frees manpower to engage in more extensive employment services. As an impersonal mechanism of control, moreover, automation makes it less important for top management to maintain direct control over operations. This is reflected in the pronounced influence of automation on delegation of responsibilities, its slight influence on the development of a multilevel hierarchy, and its substantial influence on the scope of major responsibilities of division heads, as indicated by the number of sections per division.

The differentiation of occupational positions simplifies the duties of many positions but simultaneously increases the diversity among them. As a result of the former, the division of labor raises the proportion of clerks in an agency, and as the result of the latter, it discourages the use of standardized procedures for rating performance. The three major dimensions of structural differentiation are interrelated. A multilevel hierarchy tends to reduce the number of divisions, and few divisions in turn increase the number of sections per division as well as the span of control of division heads. All three aspects of structural differentiation—levels, divisions, and sections per division—raise the supervisory ratio, thereby diminishing without completely suppressing the reduction in the supervisory ratio realized by large size. A multilevel hierarchy slightly encourages delegation of responsibilities by top management. Many sections per division seem to represent an advantageous form of functional differentiation, inasmuch as they further placement productivity.

Standardized rating procedures, which reduce discretion in the evaluation of performance, thereby encourage delegation of responsibilities to local offices but also impede placement productivity. In large organizations, at least, decentralization of responsibilities to local levels seems to improve operations. Whatever effects the managerial ratio and the clerical ratio have on operations were not discovered in our research, but it is of interest that managerial overheard does not raise manpower requirements, whereas staff overhead does.

As far as our data are able to tell, a large administrative staff relative to the size of the agency has little to recommend it. A large staff discourages delegation of responsibilities. It is inversely related to the extent of employment services and the likelihood that intensive vocational services are offered to applicants. Whereas these two findings imply that a large staff is more appropriate for unemployment insurance than for employment service operations, it raises the cost in man-hours of unemployment services to boot. To be sure, a large staff may make contributions that we were unable to detect. It is unquestionably not always merely a tool for building a bureaucratic empire. Yet its detrimental effects on operations suggest that it sometimes may have little function beyond that. If this conjecture has any validity, it leads to the rather surprising conclusion that the tendency to build bureaucratic empires is less prevalent in large than in small organizations. As a matter of fact, the large size of an organization may well be a bulwark against the despotism of little kings.

PART THREE

Substructures

Once it is fully established, bureaucracy is among those social structures which are the hardest to destroy. . . . The individual bureaucrat cannot squirm out of the apparatus in which he is harnessed. . . . In the great majority of cases, he is only a single cog in an ever-moving mechanism which prescribes to him an essentially fixed route of march. The official is entrusted with specialized tasks and normally the mechanism cannot be put into motion or arrested by him. . . .

WEBER, *Essays in Sociology*

CHAPTER 7

Local Conditions

The public's contact with employment security agencies takes place at the more than 2,000 local offices that are dispersed throughout the United States. All employment services of these agencies are provided in local offices, and a substantial part of unemployment insurance services is administered there. An agency's local offices are its component substructures, which, together with its headquarters, compose its formal structure. We turn now to the analysis of the interdependence of various conditions in these local substructures, treating for this purpose the individual branch office rather than the entire agency as the unit of analysis.

Not all local offices are included in the investigation, although data were collected on all of them. Many local offices are extremely small and uncomplicated, consisting merely of two or three operating employees and their supervisor, who is also the local office manager. It hardly makes sense to analyze the formal structure of such a simple office. Hence, all local offices that do not have at least five employees and at least one supervisor between the manager and the operating level are excluded, which leaves 1,201 cases for analysis. On the average, 54 per cent of a state agency's local offices are included, though the proportion varies from a maximum of 91 per cent for Pennsylvania's agency to a minimum of zero for two agencies that had no single local office meeting the criteria (those in New Hampshire and the Virgin Islands). The data are not representative of all employment security offices in the country, because they exclude the smallest and simplest ones.

The basic objectives of this chapter are to analyze the interrelated characteristics that define these small substructures and determine in which respects they parallel the interrelations observed in the much larger structures of entire agencies. For example, are vertical and horizontal differentiation inversely related to each other though both depend on size in local offices, as is the case for state agencies? In addition, the chapter devotes particular attention to the question of how organizational conditions influence the span of control of supervisors whose subordinates are at the bottom of the hierarchy in direct contact with clients. Here concern is with the characteristics of the local organization that govern the man-hour costs of supervising daily operations.

The design of the inquiry corresponds to that in the study of entire agencies. The assumptions made concerning the causal sequence of variables are analogous, as Table 1–1 shows. The same criterion for deciding whether to use logarithmic transformations of size is used, namely, that the improvement in the correlation of a variable with size realized by such transformation is .10 or more. A stricter criterion is used for accepting a relationship as valid, however, because standard errors are small with so many cases, which makes very low regression coefficients exceed their standard error considerably. Regression coefficients that are less than twice their standard error will be considered to indicate no relationship, and only those that are at least three times their standard error will be emphasized, which corresponds to a partial correlation of not quite .10 for 1,201 cases.[1] (Organizational charts of typical local offices are discussed in Appendix D; the variables are described in Appendix C; and the matrix of their zero-order correlations is presented in Table F–2, Appendix F.)

Inasmuch as local offices are obviously not autonomous units but com-

---

1. The criteria used for accepting a relationship as meaningful are a compromise solution for the dilemma posed by the large difference in the number of local offices and of agencies. Using the same weak criterion of one and one-half standard errors for local offices that has been used for agencies would mean accepting extremely small relationships. Using only relationships that are as strong as those accepted as consequential in agencies would entail committing many Type II errors, specifically, rejecting relationships though the regression coefficients are more than five times their standard error. Whereas quite small relationships are interpreted as meaningful in the analysis of local offices, it should be remembered that these are based on a large number of cases. A condition that heightens the pyramid by only an average of one tenth of one level in 1,201 offices, for example, heightens it by one or two levels in about 100 offices.

ponents of state agencies, is it justified to treat them as independent cases in the statistical analysis? The important question is not whether they are entirely independent, which they are clearly not, just as the individuals in a sampling survey are not entirely independent but interrelated and part of the communities in which they live. The important question is rather whether the variations in the characteristics of local offices under investigation are largely accounted for by differences between agencies or whether a substantial amount of these variations are the result of within-agency differences. Inspection of the data convinced us that the variations within agencies are greater than those between agencies. The following illustrates a procedure used to test this impression: each local office was classified by its own clerical ratio and by that of the agency to which it belongs; the correlation between these two variables is .59. Thus, only 35 per cent of the variance in the clerical ratio in local offices is accounted for by the clerical ratio of the entire agency to which they belong, and 65 per cent is produced by other factors. This is the highest correlation observed between a characteristic of a local office and the corresponding characteristic of its agency. All others are below .40,[2] except that for education of interviewers, which is available only for a subsample, and which is .44. To be sure, these correlations do not show whether various characteristics of local offices are not influenced by *different* characteristics of the agencies to which they belong. This is a problem of great substantive interest, to which much of Chapter 8 is devoted. But first the various types of local offices are described and their internal structure is analyzed in this chapter.

Differences among Local Offices

Local offices can be classified into five types: (1) general local offices (General LO's), which provide both employment and unemployment insurance services; (2) employment service offices (ES LO's), which furnish services to job applicants in all occupations; (3) specialized employment offices (Specialized ES LO's), which provide employment services only for certain occupations; (4) unemployment insurance offices (UI LO's); and (5) youth opportunity centers (YOC's), which have been set up in recent years to deal with the special employment problems of disadvantaged young people. More than one half of all local offices are General LO's.

Table 7–1 shows that General LO's are smaller than others, with a mean number of employees of only twenty-two, whereas Specialized ES

2. The zero-order correlations between local office and corresponding agency characteristics can be found in the second matrix in Appendix F.

TABLE 7-1. *Mean Characteristics of Five Types of Local Offices*

	1 General LO	2 ES LO	3 Specialized ES LO	4 UI LO	5 YOC
Size	22.12	27.31	42.61	28.38	29.45
Occupational Positions					
(Division of Labor)	7.11	7.22	7.68	6.25	7.64
Electric Typewriters[a]	.68	.80	1.02	.37	1.08
Levels	3.25	3.30	3.48	3.32	3.26
Sections	2.10	2.43	3.17	2.34	2.90
Employees/Occupational					
Positions	3.11	3.78	5.55	4.55	3.85
Employees/Levels	6.71	8.28	12.25	8.54	9.02
Employees/Sections	10.55	11.11	13.43	12.15	10.15
Manager's Span of Control	5.60	7.00	7.62	4.99	6.74
Clerical Ratio	.19	.18	.20	.31	.15
Supervisory Ratio	.21	.24	.19	.22	.20
Mean Span of Control of					
First-Line Supervisors	4.82	4.09	5.44	5.99	5.32
Number of Cases[b]	632	121	138	170	121

[a]The number of cases for this variable is slightly lower; it is, in order, 631, 121, 130, 168, and 119.

[b]The few offices that combine Specialized ES and UI functions, and the few Specialized UI LO's are not included.

LO's are by far the largest, with an average of forty-three employees. These differences imply that General LO's are mostly found in small cities, because they tend to be subdivided into more specialized offices when the size of the community permits it, but Specialized ES LO's tend to grow larger instead of being further subdivided. Indeed, the average size of the community in which General LO's are found is 200,000, while that in which Specialized ES LO's are found is 2 million and Specialized ES LO's vary more in size than any other type (the standard deviation of their number of employees is thirty-two, that for General LO's is nineteen, and that for all LO's is twenty-four). Electric typewriters, the only measure of mechanization available for local offices, are most prevalent in Specialized ES LO's and YOC's.

The numbers of occupational positions, of hierarchical levels, and of sections under the office manager are all largest in Specialized ES LO's, and the two latter are smallest in General LO's, whereas the number of oc-cupational positions is smallest in UI LO's. Thus, these three aspects of differentiation vary by type as size varies, except that the division of labor is particularly rudimentary in those local offices that are exclusively responsible for the simpler unemployment insurance function. The table shows that the number of employees per occupational position assumes roughly the same rank order, and so does the number of employees per level and that per section. In other words, the number of different structural components as well as the average size of these components in local offices varies with variations in office size, just as is the case for entire agencies. Whether this conclusion based merely on the crude comparison of five types is borne out by the systematic analysis of variations in the 1,201 local offices remains to be seen.

The high clerical ratio of nearly 1:2 in UI LO's, compared to one of 1:5 or less in all other types, indicates that clerks are used considerably more in unemployment insurance than in employment services, because they have line as well as staff duties in UI LO's. The relatively routine nature of the tasks in UI LO's is reflected not only in a high proportion of clerical employees but also in a wide span of control of first-line supervisors, as Table 7–1 shows, although the ratio of supervisors in these offices is not particularly low and the span of control of the manager is narrow.

To summarize the outstanding characteristics of each of the five types: (1) General LO's are small and located in small cities. (2) ES LO's, also mostly found in small cities, have largely average characteristics, except for a high ratio of supervisors. (3) Specialized ES LO's, in contrast, are established only in large cities and have many extreme characteristics; they are large; they are subdivided into many formal positions, sections, and levels, yet nevertheless have a large complement of employees per position, per section, and per level; their manager has a wide span of control; and their ratio of supervisors is low. (4) UI LO's, which too are most prevalent in large cities, use few electric typewriters, have a simple division of labor, and include many routine jobs filled by clerks, which permits their first-line supervisors to have a wide span of control, though that of the office manager is narrow. (The joint occurrence of a rudimentary division of labor and many clerks in these offices, which conflicts with the finding that the division of labor and the clerical ratio are positively related in agencies, raises a problem to which we shall have to return later.) (5) The new YOC's, which are appropriately established in localities with high rates of unemployment, have few clerks, few employees per section, and many electric typewriters.

Because organizational conditions differ considerably in the five types of local offices, it is important to ascertain whether the relationships between these conditions also differ in the five types before proceeding to the regression analysis in which all types of local offices are combined and such interaction effects are therefore ignored. To determine interaction effects, many cross-tabulations of three variables, controlling size whenever necessary, were examined, a large proportion of which included type of local office as one of the three variables. Most interaction effects observed in the contingency tables are sufficiently small not to invalidate the assumptions of regression analysis. But three interaction effects involving type are pronounced and require examination now, and several strong interaction effects not involving type that are of substantive interest will be discussed later.

Operations in local offices are not highly mechanized, and one of the few differences in the extent of mechanization is the use of electrical rather than conventional typewriters, superficial though this indicator of mechanization is. Table 7–2 shows that electric typewriters are more likely

TABLE 7-2. **Per Cent of Local Offices with At Least One Electric Typewriter,** *as Affected by Type and Size*

LO Size	General LO		ES LO		Specialized ES LO		UI LO		YOC	
5-19	27		30		26		23		48	
		(378)		(67)		(31)		(82)		(44)
20-225	67		76		42		19		49	
		(253)		(54)		(99)		(86)		(75)

to be available in large than in small local offices of all three types that are responsible for regular employment services, but not in the type responsible for unemployment insurance services only (where they are rare regardless of size), and neither in the type responsible for intensive services to young people (where they are fairly frequent regardless of size).[3] A reason why offices responsible for employment services are more likely than UI LO's to have electric typewriters is that they need these machines for testing clients who apply for jobs as typists as well as for their own clerical work. Is the independent influence of size also owing to this factor, that is, to the greater likelihood of larger than smaller employment service offices to have numerous clients applying for typing jobs? It may be, but it may also reflect other differences in conditions between small and large offices, as we shall see.

Local offices engaged in employment services have a more pronounced

---

3. The table indicates that the likelihood that *any* electric typewriter exists is affected by size in three types of local offices. This finding shows that the correlation between *number* of electric typewriters and size later to be reported is not simply owing to the fact that larger offices have more typewriters of whatever kind than smaller ones.

division of labor than UI LO's, and they have a proportionately smaller clerical component, regardless of either their size or their division of labor.[4] However, there is a positive relationship between the division of labor and the clerical ratio that is contingent on type, specifically, on the fact that a local office engages in some unemployment insurance activities, in which clerks are used as production personnel. Table 7–3 shows that

TABLE 7-3. **Per Cent of Local Offices with High Clerical Ratio,** *as Affected by Type and Division of Labor*

Division of Labor[a]	General LO		ES LO		Specialized ES LO		UI LO		YOC	
Low	18		33		29		45		12	
		(283)		(54)		(89)		(127)		(59)
High	42		18		26		65		10	
		(349)		(67)		(49)		(43)		(62)

[a]Residual from its regression line on the logarithm of size.

the division of labor increases the proportion of clerks in UI LO's and in General LO's but not in the three other types.[5]

Although the division of labor is least pronounced and the clerical ratio is highest in UI LO's, the two are *positively* related in this type of local office, and they are not so related in the other types, except in the one that is also responsible for unemployment insurance services, namely, General LO's. The simpler unemployment insurance services require less occupational specialization and can be performed to a larger extent by clerks than the more complex employment services. Whereas the division of labor is most advanced in employment services, however, it has no impact on the proportion of clerks in offices confined to these services, in which clerks are mostly used for administrative support and not for production functions. It is probably only if a considerable number of basic tasks are sufficiently simple to be performed by clerks that the division of labor can achieve a reallocation of tasks among positions that permits more of them to be filled by clerks. A substantial proportion of tasks in unemployment

---

4. Data to be presented in Chapter 9 indicate that the higher clerical ratio in UI LO's is contingent on the qualification of interviewers.

5. Parallel findings are obtained using covariance analysis in this case as well as in those of the data presented in Tables 7–2 and 7–4. To illustrate: the partial correlations between number of occupational positions and per cent clerks, controlling size, are .44 in UI LO's and .25 in General LO's, and they are .20 in Specialized ES LO's, .16 in ES LO's, and .12 in YOC's.

insurance operations are that simple, but few in employment services are.

A high proportion of clerks, in turn, widens the average span of control of first-line supervisors primarily in those offices engaged in unemployment insurance activities, where clerks are used in production functions, and where the division of labor affects the clerical ratio. Table 7–4 indi-

TABLE 7-4. **Per Cent of Local Offices with a Wide Supervisory Span of Control**[a], *as Affected by Type and Clerical Ratio*

Clerical Ratio[b]	General LO	ES LO	Specialized ES LO	UI LO	YOC
Low	44	26	32	39	45
	(431)	(91)	(99)	(85)	(108)
High	59	33	23	76	15
	(201)	(30)	(39)	(85)	(13)

[a]Average span of control of first-line supervisors at the bottom; residual from its regression line on the logarithm of size.

[b]The division was made at 23 per cent clerks.

cates that the mean span of control of first-line supervisors becomes wider with an increasing proportion of clerks in General LO's and UI LO's, though not in two and hardly in the third of the three other types. The more routine the work is, the greater is the number of subordinates whose performance a supervisor can guide and review. But if clerks are largely used for auxiliary activities, such as typing, manning the switchboard, or reception, there are not likely to be enough of them to permit extensive aggregation under a supervisor, whereas if they are used in the basic operations, more clerks with highly similar simple duties can be assigned to a supervisor. In local offices where an extensive division of labor results in the large-scale utilization of clerks, the span of control of first-line supervisors tends to be wider than in others. This is even evident when type of local office is not taken into account and one examines merely the joint effects of division of labor and clerical ratio on mean span of control of first-line supervisors. The supervisory span of control exceeds that expected on the basis of size in three fifths of the local offices with a pronounced division of labor and a high clerical ratio but only in two fifths of those in which either the division of labor or the clerical ratio or both are low.[6]

Contingency tables like those presented can reveal interaction effects

6. Specifically, the proportion of such offices are: 64 per cent of 200 cases if both the division of labor and the clerical ratio are high; 41 per cent of 336 if only the division of labor is high; 44 per cent of 73 if only the clerical ratio is high; and 38 per cent of 492 if neither is high.

that are concealed in the regression analysis.[7] On the other hand, regression analysis makes it possible to trace the direct and indirect effects of half a dozen conditions or more on a dependent variable, which hardly is feasible on the basis of cross-tabulation, even with a case base of more than 1,000. As a matter of fact, the main problem is not merely the large number of cases used up by cross-classifications but the intellectual one that it is utterly impossible to comprehend the pattern exhibited by values in several dozens of cells without some systematic procedure for transforming the data into a simpler form. Regression analysis is essentially such a procedure. Although interaction effects are not taken into account by the regression analysis, except in the special cases when product terms are used, the influences of type of local office are considered. For this purpose, the two dimensions underlying the five types are converted into two three-category ordinal variables.

The degree of specialization of a local office is an attribute of substantive interest that is expressed in the five types. General LO's are the least specialized ones. ES LO's and UI LO's exhibit an intermediate degree of specialization, and so do the few offices in the country that combine specialized employment services with unemployment insurance functions. Specialized ES LO's and YOC's are classified into the most specialized category, together with the handful of specialized UI LO's. The data presented above show, however, that for some characteristics of local offices the degree of specialization is less important than whether the function is employment service or unemployment insurance. Hence, a second classification of function is used: UI LO's (including specialized ones) constitute the low extreme; General LO's (together with those combining specialized ES and UI services) are in the intermediate category; and ES LO's, Specialized ES LO's, and YOC's represent pure employment services. One or the other of these two variables is controlled in every regression problem.

Internal Structure

The size of a local office has a strong impact on its internal structure. For one, large size promotes the subdivision of labor. The larger the number of employees in a local office, the larger is the number of distinct occupational positions. But occupational differentiation does not proceed at a constant rate with increasing size. Figure 7–1 reveals the by now famil-

---

7. An alternative procedure would be to use product terms in regression analysis, but we confine use of this technique to testing specific interpretations implying such interaction effects. Two hypotheses of this kind are tested later in this chapter.

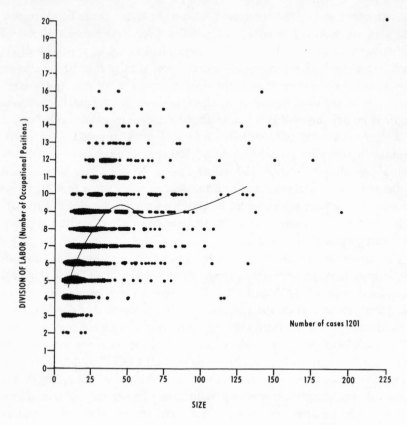

FIGURE 7–1 Scatter Diagram of Division of Labor and
Size in Local Offices

iar logarithmic curve (though with a hump), which indicates that even in these small organizational segments the number of formal positions expands at first rapidly and then more gradually as size expands. The logarithmic transformation of size produces a straighter regression line, though one slightly curved in the opposite direction, and it improves the correlation from .51 to .62. (Controlling either classification of type of local office does not reduce this correlation.) The substantive implication is that the growing size of local offices increases both the number of occupational positions and the average size of the personnel complement in each, which was surmised from the comparison of the five types, and which replicates the finding for entire agencies. The larger a local office, the more colleagues in their own specialty and the more fellow workers in a variety of other specialties most employees can find. These data confirm the earlier conjecture, based on agency data, that large organizational size creates paradoxically a more homogeneous as well as a more heterogeneous occupational environment.

Not all interrelations in local offices parallel those in entire agencies, however. Occupational differentiation plays a more prominent role in these substructures than in the larger structures of which they are a part. It reinforces the influence exerted by size on several characteristics of local offices. The complexity of the structure that emerges in a local office appears to depend not only on the number of its employees but also on the number of different formal positions among which they are distributed. And modern office equipment exhibits the same double dependence on size and the subdivision of labor.

Occupational differentiation exerts most influence on the likelihood that electric typewriters are used in a local office, as Table 7–5 shows, much more influence than that directly exerted by the office's size or its function

TABLE 7-5. *Multiple Regression of* **Electric Typewriters** *on Local Office Conditions*

Independent Variable	Standardized Regression Coefficient	Zero-Order Correlation
ES Function	.09**	.15
LO Size	.07*	.25
Division of Labor	.32**	.37

Multiple R = .38; n = 1,188
*Greater than twice its standard error.
**Greater than three times its standard error.

(the predominance of employment services). Electric typewriters are indicative of the degree of mechanization and of the manager's success in getting old-fashioned office machines replaced by modern ones. (The variable is the number of electric typewriters; it is highly skewed [2.9], because more than one half of the local offices have no electric typewriter.) Though the influence of function—and possibly also partly that of size, which we know from Table 7–2 to be confined to offices performing employment services—may result from the need for electric typewriters in order to test the skills of clients applying for typing jobs, it is not plausible to attribute the substantial independent influence of the division of labor, or the influence of size that it mediates, entirely to this factor. Occupational differentiation and large size may constrain the manager to adopt a more universalistic orientation in terms of abstract categories of administrative efficiency than the kind of managerial approach appropriate for undifferentiated small offices, where supervision can more readily be exercised in paternalistic and informal ways. Such a universalistic orientation toward technical efficiency is likely to induce the manager to devote much effort to obtaining modern office equipment. Data to be presented in Chapter 8 provide a bit of support for this speculation.

The large size of local offices promotes internal differentiation. Whereas the influence of size on mechanical equipment is mostly mediated by the division of labor, most of its influence on structural differentiation is direct. The two main measures of structural differentiation in local offices are identical with two used for agency headquarters: the number of hierarchical levels and the number of sections whose chiefs report directly to the top manager. A third measure is the span of control of the local office manager, which corresponds to the span of control of the agency director. No measures are used for local offices that are parallel to those of sections per division and mean span of control of division heads at the headquarters, because most of the section chiefs in local offices are first-line supervisors, whose span of control is analyzed separately. The span of control of the office manager is widest if there is only one section, because in this case many operating employees report directly to him; it is narrowest if there are two sections; and it increases again for offices with three or more sections.[8] Despite this curvilinear relationship, there is a positive zero-order correlation between number of sections and manager's span of control (.27), but it vanishes when other conditions are controlled, mostly owing to the influence of size, complemented by that of the division of labor. The three regression lines of levels and size, sections and size, and manager's span of control and size all exhibit slight logarithmic curves, but logarithmic transformation of size produces curves in the opposite direction and improves the correlations by less than .10. Hence, the raw number of employees is used as the measure of size with these three dependent variables.

The strong influences of office size on vertical differentiation into hierarchical levels and horizontal differentiation into many sections are complemented by weaker influences of the division of labor on both dimensions of structural differentiation, as Tables 7–6 and 7–7 show, and the influence of size on the manager's span of control is similarly complemented by that of the division of labor (Table 7–8). The impact of the

---

8. In offices with fewer than twenty employees, the manager has a span of control of six or more in 45 per cent of the 252 cases with one section, 22 per cent of the 295 cases with two, and 33 per cent of the 64 cases with three or more sections. In those with twenty or more employees, he has that large a span of control in 95 per cent of the 20 cases with one, 48 per cent of the 86 cases with two, and 68 per cent of the 390 cases with three or more sections.

TABLE 7-6. *Multiple Regression of* **Hierarchical Levels** *on Local Office Conditions*

Independent Variable	Standardized Regression Coefficient	Zero-Order Correlation
Specialization	−.06*	.11
LO Size	.65**	.68
Division of Labor	.10**	.42

Multiple R = .69; n = 1,201

*Greater than twice its standard error.
**Greater than three times its standard error.

TABLE 7-7. *Multiple Regression of* **Sections** *on Local Office Conditions*

Independent Variable	Standardized Regression Coefficient	Zero-Order Correlation
Specialization	.17**	.31
LO Size	.56**	.61
Division of Labor	.22**	.46
Electric Typewriters	.05	.24
Levels	−.17**	.33

Multiple R = .67; n = 1,201

**Greater than three times its standard error.

TABLE 7-8. *Multiple Regression of* **Manager's Span of Control** *on Local Office Conditions*

Independent Variable	Standardized Regression Coefficient	Zero-Order Correlation
Specialization	.12**	.20
LO Size	.32**	.31
Division of Labor	.19**	.30
Electric Typewriters	.12**	.23
Levels	−.25**	.09
Sections	.01	.27

Multiple R = .44; n = 1,201

**Greater than three times its standard error.

number of employees on structural differentiation is reinforced in local offices by that of the number of distinct formal positions entailing different duties. It has been suggested that organizations cope with the problems posed by a large scope of operations by subdividing responsibilities for operations among various sections and subdividing responsibilities for administrative coordination among managers on several hierarchical levels. The pressure to create such subdivisions engendered by the volume of responsibilities in an office is apparently less if most employees perform the same duties than if their official duties are highly differentiated. A large number of occupational specialties also tend to widen the span of control of the office manager, because single specialists are likely to report directly to him, which keeps the work within sections more homogeneous and gives the manager better access to specialists.

To be sure, the number of formal positions manifest in the division of labor does not perfectly mirror the variety of tasks or functions performed in a local office. However, if a given number of different tasks are all assigned to the same employees, the problem of how to deal with diverse duties must largely be solved by each employee, whereas the problem of coping with diverse duties becomes primarily the organization's if the various tasks are assigned to different positions. The allocation of different tasks to differentiated positions intensifies the problem of coordination in an organization, and with it structural complexity, because part of this problem would be otherwise absorbed, as it were, by the efforts individual employees must devote to managing diverse task assignments.[9]

The number of major functions for which a local office is responsible has some independent effects on structural differentiation. The measure is the classification of local offices by degree of specialization. A high degree of specialization of the local office, which means that it has a narrow range of functions, encourages horizontal differentiation, as reflected in both number of sections and manager's span of control (Tables 7–7 and 7–8), but slightly discourages vertical differentiation of hierarchical levels (Table 7–6). Diversity of main functions, which one might have expected to enlarge the number of sections, promotes on the contrary the development of a slim pyramid with fewer sections and more levels. A high degree of differentiation of local offices into specialized ones seems to have

---

9. The process inferred here is analogous to that described by James S. Coleman when he suggests that conflict over issues in communities becomes less severe if some of it is dissipated by the cross pressures experienced by individuals with allegiance to both sides or the internal dissent in organizations containing partisans of both sides; *Community Conflict* (Glencoe: Free Press, 1957), pp. 21–23.

an avalanche effect that fosters functional differentiation of sections within them. However, the specialization of an office does not further occupational differentiation within it; indeed, when size (in logarithmic transformation) is controlled, office specialization is seen to reduce internal occupational differentiation ($b^* = -.12$). In short, specialized local offices organize the fewer occupational specialties needed in them into a larger number of more homogeneous sections, producing a squat pyramid, which is also manifest in the manager's wider span of control and his lesser hierarchical distance from the operating level.[10]

The pyramids exhibited by the structure of local offices tend to expand primarily either in height or in width, not simultaneously in both directions, just as those of the structure at agency headquarters do. Although both the number of sections and the number of levels depend in similar manner on the size of the office and the division of labor in it, levels and sections are inversely related when these antecedent conditions are controlled. As the number of hierarchical levels increases, the number of sections decreases (Table 7–7), and so does the office manager's span of control, even when number of sections is held constant (Table 7–8). An expanding scope of operations generates differentiation along all dimensions and widens in the process the office manager's span of control. However, hierarchical differentiation relieves the top manager in a large local office of excessive supervisory burdens by reducing the number of sections under his direct supervision and particularly his total span of control.

What other conditions influence the tendency of a squat pyramid to become transformed into a tall one? For entire agencies, mechanization in the form of computers does so, but for local offices, mechanization does not, quite possibly because electric typewriters are a superficial indication of mechanization. The one factor identified that reduces both sections and manager's span of control, and simultaneously raises levels slightly, is the multifunction character of the local office (the opposite of specialization in the tables). Specialized responsibilities appear to make the top manager particularly reluctant to become further removed from the operating level by appointing middle managers that would relieve him of supervisory burdens. A plausible reason is that effective management requires closer contact with the more professional work in specialized employment offices

---

10. Mechanization in the form of electric typewriters exerts no influence on either hierarchical levels or functional sections, but it is positively related to the office manager's span of control (Table 7–8). Because its lack of relationship with levels did, but with sections did not, become apparent in the preliminary analysis, the variable, electric typewriters, has been deleted from the regression problem in Table 7–6 but not from that in Table 7–7.

than with the less specialized operations in general offices. The underlying principle may well be that the core problems of management are largely professional in a single-function office and become increasingly adminis-trative as the sheer number of functions increases. Thus, the advantages of multilevel hierarchies outweigh their disadvantages for management if it is less concerned with professional than with administrative problems, and a variety of specialties tend to redirect management's attention from profes-sional to administrative issues.

Large size promotes both vertical and horizontal differentiation, but the negative relationship between the two when size is controlled suggests that it does not do both at the same time, that is, in the same local offices. In other words, the pattern of findings can be interpreted to indicate that large size gives rise to multilevel hierarchies in some local offices and to many sections in others. This interpretation implies that once size has produced multiple levels it combines with them to counteract its positive influence on the differentiation of sections, or in statistical terms that size and levels have a negative interaction effect on sections.[11] To test this in-terpretation, the product term "size times levels" is introduced as an addi-tional independent variable into the regression problem with sections as the dependent variable in Table 7–9.[12] The findings conform to expecta-

TABLE 7-9. *Multiple Regression of **Sections** on Local Office Conditions*

Independent Variable	Standardized Regression Coefficient	Zero-Order Correlation	Metric Regression Coefficient
Specialization	.12**	.31	.1728**
LO Size	2.52**	.61	.1266**
Division of Labor	.16**	.46	.0725**
Levels	.12**	.33	.2972**
LO Size X Levels	−2.14**	.54	−.0244**

Multiple R = .72; n = 1,201
**Greater than three times its standard error.

tions: size and levels have a pronounced interaction effect depressing the number of sections, as indicated by the negative regression coefficient of the product term. Size as such has a strong positive effect on sections, which is counteracted by its combined effect with levels, and levels as such

---

11. We are grateful to Robert W. Hodge for pointing out this statistical impli-cation of the interpretation.
12. The independent variable that exerts no influence—electric typewriters—has been deleted from this table.

also have a positive effect on sections, but it is overshadowed by the strong negative effect that levels jointly with size have on sections. How much the joint effect overrides the direct effect of levels, and whether it also counteracts completely the strong direct effect of size, can be deduced from the metric regression coefficients.

What the negative regression coefficient for the product term, in conjunction with the positive ones for each direct effect, shows is that the joint negative effect of size and levels increasingly counteracts their individual positive effects and sooner or later outweighs them. The ratio of the metric regression coefficient of one of the terms to that of the product term (b_i/b_{ixj}) indicates the value of the second term (j) at which the joint negative effect starts to predominate over the first variable's (i's) positive effect. For example, the positive effect of levels on sections is evident only in smaller local offices and is overpowered by its joint negative effect with size in larger ones. The specific size of the local office at which this tends to occur is supplied by the ratio of the metric regression coefficient of levels (.2972) to that of the product term ($-$.0243). This ratio is 12.2, which means that the addition of a fourth level (three being the minimum) leads to the addition of a section only in the very smallest offices, where four levels are extremely rare, whereas in the large majority of the 1,201 offices under consideration—all those with more than twelve employees— hierarchical differentiation into levels reduces horizontal differentiation into sections.[13] The very opposite is the case for the influence of size. The ratio of the metric regression coefficient of size (.1266) to that of the product term is 5.2, which indicates that the positive effect of size on sections is diminished but never turned into a negative effect by its joint effect with levels, for it would turn into a negative effect only in local offices with more than five levels, of which there are none. One might infer, however, that large size jointly with more than five levels would reduce horizontal subdivisions, and the data for the largest agencies in Figures 3–5 and 3–7 support this inference.

In sum, large size frequently generates multilevel hierarchies in local offices and then combines with these tall hierarchies to reduce the number of sections, increasingly counteracting its direct effect of raising the number of sections. Multiple levels reduce the number of sections, except in offices with no more than a dozen employees, but hardly any offices that small have more than three levels. There is a similar negative joint effect of size and levels on the span of control of the local office manager. The only dif-

---

13. The scatter diagram indicates that only about three local offices with fewer than thirteen employees have four levels. Overprinting at the same point makes it impossible to determine the exact number from this plotting.

ferences are that this joint negative effect completely neutralizes the direct positive effect of size itself in offices with five levels (the turning point is 4.9 levels) and that the direct effect of levels by themselves is inconsequential.[14] The decrease in the office manager's span of control that occurs as levels are added with increasing size tends to fully counteract the influence of size on widening the manager's span of control when office hierarchies reach five levels. Thus, the expansion of both the manager's span of control and the number of sections with increasing size occurs primarily in those local offices in which increasing size does not raise the number of hierarchical levels. These findings support the interpretation that hierarchical differentiation serves to lessen management's load of supervisory responsibilities in large offices by stemming the impact of growing size on section's and manager's span of control.

The clerical ratio is affected by three conditions in local offices. Data in contingency tables have already indicated that clerks are used for basic services as well as administrative support more extensively in unemployment insurance than in employment offices. The same result is manifest in the negative zero-order correlation between the three-category variable of function, the extreme of which refers to offices without any unemployment insurance responsibilities, and the proportion of clerks ($-.27$). The subdivision of labor increases the number of jobs that are sufficiently simple to be performed by clerks, which is indicated by its positive zero-order correlation with the clerical ratio (.20). However, the contingency tables have shown that this effect of the division of labor is restricted to local offices that use considerable numbers of clerks in production functions and is not observable in offices exclusively responsible for employment services. The conclusion that the influence of occupational differentiation on the proportion of clerks is the result of job routinization rather than of a greater need for a clerical administrative apparatus in differentiated structures is supported by the findings that the clerical ratio is uncorrelated with differentiation of either levels ($-.02$) or sections ($-.02$). Finally, the size of the office exerts some direct influence on the proportion of clerks in it, as well as an indirect one through the division of labor, but the former influence is only apparent when environmental conditions are controlled, and its discussion is therefore reserved for the next chapter.

---

14. If the product term, size times levels, is added to the independent variables in Table 7–8, with office manager's span of control as dependent variable, deleting sections, the standardized regression coefficients are: specialization, .08 *; size, 1.81 **; division of labor, .14 **; electric typewriters, .12 **; levels, $-.04$; size times levels, -1.62 **. (Two asterisks indicate a value of more than three times, and one asterisk a value of at least two times, the standard error.)

Supervision

Two measures of supervision in local offices are available: the supervisory ratio and the average span of control of lowest-level supervisors. The two are not the exact reverse of each other. The ratio is the proportion of supervisory personnel on all levels in the local office. The span-of-control measure includes only first-line supervisors and is restricted to those whose subordinates are at the bottom level of the office. For example, if two of three section chiefs in a four-level office are in charge of supervisors but the third is in charge of operating employees, the latter and his subordinates are excluded from the computation of the span-of-control index, which is operationally defined as the number of employees at the *bottom* level per supervisor in charge of them. It is advantageous to control the level in the structure in this manner, because the intensive analysis of the data-processing unit earlier mentioned revealed that operating employees on higher levels tend to have more complex duties and their supervisors tend to have narrower spans of control than those on lower levels. Although the two measures are not precisely complementary, the influences exerted on them by conditions in local offices are essentially alike. The reason is that most supervisors in these small offices are first-line supervisors. The case base for the span-of-control measure is 3,127 first-line supervisors, 2.6 per local office.

A number of studies cited in Chapter 4 indicate that the ratio of supervisory to production personnel declines with size, and some of them also suggest that this ratio increases with complexity, though the evidence is not consistent. Our own data presented there show that the supervisory ratio at the agency headquarters is reduced by size and raised by complexity, as manifest in three aspects of structural differentiation at the agency headquarters (Table 4–1). It is of interest to ascertain whether the same conditions affect the supervisory ratio in local offices and whether they are also manifest in the span of control of first-line supervisors at the bottom of the hierarchy. Another question is raised by the findings of two studies that the supervisory span of control becomes narrower the more complex responsibilities are, with complexity being measured directly in one case and inferred from the qualifications of the personnel in another.[15] Is the span of control of first-line supervisors narrower in offices responsible for the more complex employment services than in unemployment insurance offices?

The supervisory ratio in local offices declines with increasing size, just

---

15. Gerald D. Bell, "Determinants of Span of Control," *American Journal of Sociology,* 73 (1967): 102–105, and Marshall W. Meyer, "Expertness and the Span of Control," *American Sociological Review,* 33 (1968): 947–950.

as the supervisory ratio at the agency headquarters does. Figure 7–2 shows that this decline occurs at a decreasing rate, which is more conspicuous than that at the agency headquarters (Figure 4–1). Logarithmic transformation of office size reduces the curve, though some convex curvature remains, and it improves the correlation from −.46 to −.64. There is an economy of scale with respect to supervisory personnel in local offices as well as at agency headquarters. Given the decreasing rate of this economy

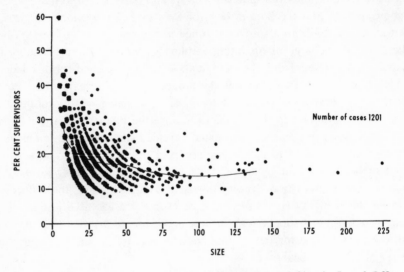

FIGURE 7–2   Scatter Diagram of Supervisory Ratio and Size in Local Offices

of scale with increasing size of local offices, it is rather surprising that such an economy of scale is still observable among the considerably larger agency headquarters. The scatter diagram of span of control of first-line supervisors and office size reveals a complementary curve, in which the negative slope at a declining rate is replaced by a positive slope at a declining rate. Logarithmic transformation of size produces a slight curve in the opposite direction, and it raises the correlation from .55 to .66. Because the influences of other conditions on the supervisory span of control also largely correspond, in reverse, to their influences on the supervisory ratio, there is little point in discussing both sets of data. The span-of-control measure has the great advantage over the ratio that it has no mathematical nexus with number of levels and of sections, whereas the ratio of supervisors does, and that it, but not the ratio, consequently makes it possible to investigate the empirical influences of structural differentiation on supervision independent of this mathematical connection. Hence, the span of control of first-line supervisors is the measure presented.

The data in Table 7–10 indicate that conditions in local offices account for nearly two thirds of the variation in the mean span of control of first-line supervisors. The most important influence on it is exerted by the size of the local office. The standardized regression coefficient of 1.36 signifies that the slope is about 60°, which is exceptionally steep. A small number of employees in one location wastes supervisory manpower by making it impossible to aggregate sufficient numbers with similar duties in a work group under a supervisor. To be sure, supervisors in very small offices undoubtedly are in charge of employees with a variety of duties. The very fact that they must provide guidance for a heterogeneous group of subordinates, however, makes it more difficult to supervise as many as they could were their duties more homogeneous. The consolidation of a greater number of operating employees with similar duties under each first-line supervisor that large size permits is the main factor that produces the pronounced economy of scale in supervisory personnel, which is indicated by the negative relationship between size and supervisory ratio.

TABLE 7-10. *Multiple Regression of* **Mean Span of Control of First-Line Supervisors** *on Local Office Conditions*

Independent Variable	Standardized Regression Coefficient	Zero-Order Correlation
ES Function	−.12**	−.08
LO Size (Log)	1.36**	.66
Division of Labor	−.11**	.32
Levels	−.49**	.25
Sections	−.42**	.25
Clerical Ratio	.04*	.19

Multiple $R = .81$; $n = 1,201$

*Greater than twice its standard error.
**Greater than three times its standard error.

The structural complexity resulting from either vertical differentiation or horizontal differentiation, in contrast, sharply narrows the span of control of first-line supervisors. Table 7–10 indicates that both multiple levels and many sections in local offices have a strong negative net effect on the span of control, their positive zero-order correlations with it being the spurious result of the influence of size. Inasmuch as an increase in the number of hierarchical levels in an office of a given size necessarily raises the supervisory ratio (and an increase in the number of section chiefs may too), one might have expected this greater proportion of middle managers to reduce the need for first-line supervisors and increase the number of subordinates assigned to each. Actually, however, the opposite is the case and the larger number of middle managers in differentiated offices than in others is complemented by a larger number of first-line supervisors, relative to the number of their subordinates. This twofold expansion of supervisory personnel that multilevel hierarchies produce—mathematically by adding middle levels and empirically by narrowing the span of control of supervisors—is manifest in a strong dependence of the supervisory ratio on hierarchical differentiation.[16]

Structural differentiation greatly intensifies problems of communication and coordination, many of which are not apparent in undifferentiated small offices at all as they are taken care of without formal design by individual officials and the informal contacts among them. Differentiation develops in response to the pressures created by a large volume of work and a large number of employees. Hierarchical differentiation, particularly, entails the appointment of middle managers to relieve the top manager of excessive administrative burdens. Though the middle managers contribute to administrative coordination and communication, the very presence of many of them, which reflects a highly differentiated structure, simultaneously engenders new problems of coordination and communication. This is the paradox of administrative complexity. Far from relieving first-line supervisors of some of their duties of guidance and review, the existence of many middle managers in highly differentiated structures imposes additional duties on first-line supervisors, because the much enhanced problems of coordination and communication impinge on the other duties of first-line supervisors. The duties of supervisors can be analytically divided into two categories, guiding and reviewing the performance of subordinates and coordinating their work with that of the rest of the organization, although actually many supervisory tasks entail elements of both. The more complex the structure, the more does the work that supervisors have to perform as communication links infringe on the time they have left for guiding and checking on subordinates, which finds expression in a reduced number of subordinates per supervisor in highly differentiated offices.

The dramatic direct effect of large office size widening the span of control of supervisors is much diminished by its indirect effects that result from the differentiation in large offices. The over-all effect of the size of the local office on the average span of control of first-line supervisors is .66, whereas its net effect independent of other conditions in the office as-

16. The net effects (standardized regression coefficient) on supervisory ratio of levels (.59) and that of sections (.59) are greater than their respective net effects on the span of control of first-line supervisors ($-.49$, $-.42$; see Table 7–10).

sociated with it is 1.36. Decomposition indicates that the counteracting indirect effects of size on span of control are largely mediated by structural differentiation of both hierarchical levels ($-.34$) and functional sections ($-.28$), with occupational differentiation playing a minor part as another intervening variable ($-.07$). The influences of size on the *supervisory ratio* exhibit a complementary pattern, except that occupational differentiation plays no role. The strong over-all effect of large size reducing the supervisory ratio ($r = -.64$) is produced by a powerful negative direct effect ($b^* = -1.43$) that is partly counteracted by positive indirect effects mediated by levels (.41) and sections (.40). These findings parallel those obtained for agency headquarters (Table 4–1).[17] In both the local offices and the headquarters of employment security agencies, the tremendous savings in supervisory manpower realized in large-scale operations far outweigh the greater requirements for supervisory manpower created by the structural complexity of large organizational units.

Occupational differentiation in local offices tends to narrow the span of control of supervisors, just as other aspects of differentiation do, but the pattern of its direct and indirect influences suggests that two different processes are involved, one rooted in structural complexity and the other in heterogeneity of duties. The negative effect of the division of labor on the supervisory span of control is not evident in the zero-order correlation in Table 7–10, which is positive (.32), because the strong positive effects of size on both division of labor and span of control produce a pronounced spurious positive relationship between them, which is revealed by decomposition (.84). However, the division of labor promotes structural differentiation of both levels and sections in local offices, as we have seen, and through them it indirectly narrows the supervisory span of control (via levels, $-.21$; via sections, $-.19$). Thus, the subdivision of labor reduces the number of employees per first-line supervisor in part because it gives rise to a more complex structure. But occupational differentiation has also some negative direct effect on the span of control of supervisors even when the two indicators of structural complexity are controlled ($b^* = -.11$). This negative net effect may well be the result of heterogeneity. The more pronounced the division of labor, the more likely it is that some or all supervisors are in charge of employees in several different occu-

---

17. To permit comparison with Table 4–1, the standardized regression coefficients obtained in the multiple regression of supervisory ratio in local offices on antecedent conditions are presented: specialization, .10**; size, -1.43**; division of labor, .01; levels, .59**; sections, .59**; manager's span of control, $-.09$**. The zero-order correlations, in the same order, are: $-.07$, $-.64$, $-.37$, $-.19$, $-.16$, $-.42$.

pational positions, and not so many employees with heterogeneous as with homogeneous duties can be supervised by one man.[18]

The difficulty as well as the heterogeneity of the duties of subordinates increase the demands made on the supervisor's time, which is reflected in his span of control. The duties in offices solely responsible for employment services are more complex than those in offices partly or entirely responsible for the simpler unemployment insurance activities, and the supervisory span of control is narrower the more an office's work concentrates on employment services (Table 7–10). Clerks have simpler duties than nonclerical personnel, and the clerical ratio slightly widens the supervisory span of control in expected fashion. It is hardly surprising that the influence of the clerical ratio on the average span of control of supervisors in all offices is so slight, inasmuch as we know from material earlier presented that this influence is confined to offices engaged in some unemployment insurance operations and that even there clerks constitute less than one third of the personnel. Both the complexity of responsibilities and the complexity of the structure in local offices make claims on supervisors that delimit the number of subordinates that can be assigned to each.

The effects of structural complexity on supervision can be further clarified. Multiple levels narrow the supervisory span of control in local offices, and so do many sections. But previous analysis has indicated that levels and sections are inversely related and that the greater the increase in levels with expanding size the less likely is the increase in sections (an inference confirmed by the data in Table 7–9). If multilevel hierarchies and many sections are not usually found in the same local office, it follows that, although both reduce the supervisory span of control, they do so in different local offices, not in the same ones, which means that their effects are not cumulative. The implication is that the more a multilevel hierarchy narrows the span of control of supervisors, the less are the chances that many sections do so, and vice versa. In more precise language, the negative effect of either levels or sections on span of control is counteracted by their joint or interaction effect. To test this hypothesis, the product term, levels times sections, is introduced into the multiple regression of span of control on its antecedents in local offices in Table 7–11. The positive regression coefficient of the product term confirms the hypothesis.

Both vertical and horizontal differentiation narrow the span of control of supervisors, but the more the one does so the less likely is the other to

---

18. Jon G. Udell observes also that dissimilarity of jobs supervised is inversely related to the span of control of marketing executives; "An Empirical Test of Hypotheses Relating to Span of Control," *Administrative Science Quarterly,* 12 (1967): 435–437.

TABLE 7-11. *Multiple Regression of* **Mean Span of Control of First-Line Supervisors** *on Local Office Conditions*

Independent Variable	Standardized Regression Coefficient	Zero-Order Correlation	Metric Regression Coefficient
ES Function	−.12**	−.08	−.5534**
LO Size (Log)	1.36**	.66	12.9038**
Division of Labor	−.10**	.32	−.1192**
Levels	−.61**	.25	−3.6509**
Sections	−.75**	.25	−1.8812**
Levels X Sections	.39*	.29	.2492*
Clerical Ratio	.04*	.19	.8387*

Multiple R = .81; n = 1,201
*Greater than twice its standard error.
**Greater than three times its standard error.

do so, because these two dimensions of structural differentiation do not typically prevail in the same local offices. Does the positive joint effect imply that in those offices that have both multiple levels and many sections, few though they be, the span of control of supervisors becomes wider again? The ratio of the metric regression coefficient of either term to that of the product term, as explained above, gives a negative answer. Computation of these ratios indicates that the negative effect of levels on supervisory span of control would turn into a positive one in local offices with more than fourteen sections, and the negative effect of sections on span would turn into a positive one in offices with more than seven levels. But this is beyond the range of variation of the 1,201 local offices, which have a maximum of nine sections and five levels. The pattern in Table 7–11 shows not that much differentiation has less effect than little on the supervisory span of control but that the strong negative effects on it of the two dimensions of differentiation are not cumulative, for they rarely are observed together.[19]

In sum, the size of local offices and the complexity of their structure have the greatest impact on the span of control of supervisors, and the complexity of their responsibilities has some additional influence on it. A differentiated structure creates problems of communication and coordination that demand the attention of supervisors. Structural complexity requires not only middle managers but also first-line supervisors to devote special effort to maintain channels of communication and coordinate

---

19. While adding the product term hardly raises the amount of variation explained (from 65 to 66 per cent), it clarifies the pattern of influence.

the work of their subordinates with that of the rest of the organization. The extra time supervisors must spend serving as communication links in highly differentiated offices leaves them less time for supervising their subordinates, which finds expression in the reduced number of subordinates assigned to each of them. Both vertical differentiation into multiple levels and horizontal differentiation into many sections reduce the span of control of first-line supervisors, but they typically do so in different local offices, because levels and sections rarely expand together in the same office. Occupational differentiation also tends to narrow the span of control of supervisors, in part owing to the structural complexity it produces, and in part, perhaps, to the greater heterogeneity of positions it entails. Finally, the complexity of responsibilities narrows the supervisor's span of control, because difficult duties require the supervisor to consult more extensively with every subordinate. The inverse relationship of employment service and the direct relationship of clerical ratio with supervisory span of control are indicative of this influence of task complexity.

By far the most important determinant of the supervisor's span of control is the size of the office. The larger the local office, the larger is the number of employees in each position, and the easier it is to utilize the capacity of every supervisor to the full and assign subordinates with homogeneous duties to each. In small offices, this is not possible, and some supervisors probably spend a considerable part of their time in the role of operating official providing services rather than in that of supervisor. A limited amount of such work may have the advantage that it keeps supervisors in closer touch with operating problems, but if it takes up too much time it entails a wasteful use of costly supervisory manpower.

The profound direct impact size has on the span of control of supervisors is modified by its indirect influence in the opposite direction mediated by the differentiation in the structure associated with size. However, the positive direct effect of large size substantially outweighs its negative indirect effects on the span of control of supervisors. Hence, local offices exhibit an economy of scale in supervisory personnel, just as, but in more pronounced form than, agency headquarters do. One might even say that the savings in supervisory manpower realized by large size are what enables large organizations to afford the extra managerial manpower required for their complex structures. At the same time, the manpower cost of structural complexity probably limits its development. It has been suggested in the literature that size decreases, and complexity increases, the administrative ratio in organizations.[20] This is the case with respect to the

20. Theodore R. Anderson and Seymour Warkov, "Organizational Size and Functional Complexity," *American Sociological Review*, 26 (1961): 23–28. Louis R. Pondy interprets his parallel findings by suggesting that the mar-

managerial ratio in the local offices as well as the agency headquarters of employment security agencies. The main reasons for it seem to be the more efficient aggregation of subordinates under supervisors made possible by large size, on the one hand, and the extra time of supervisors taken up by communication and coordination as the result of complexity, on the other.

Conclusions

To conclude, the interrelated characteristics of local offices will be compared with those of entire agencies, or their headquarters, after first briefly summarizing the main findings on local offices. The size of an office exerts a pervasive influence on its other characteristics. It affects every one of the conditions in local offices examined: division of labor, mechanization, levels, sections, manager's span of control, clerical ratio, and first-line supervisors' span of control as well as supervisory ratio. Both the over-all and the direct effect of size are substantial and more important than any other influences on all these variables but two, mechanization and clerical ratio. The two aspects of instrumental conditions—division of labor and mechanization—are positively related in local offices, and large size fosters the advancement of these two expressions of universalistic instrumentalism.[21] The number of occupational positions, which is the indicator of the division of labor, reinforces the influences of the number of employees, which is the indicator of size, on vertical differentiation, horizontal differentiation, and manager's span of control in local offices.

The taller the hierarchical pyramid in an office, the slimmer it tends to be, notwithstanding the fact that large size promotes expansion in both vertical and horizontal directions. A larger number of hierarchical levels, though the entire range of variation is merely between three and five levels, not only reduces the number of sections and the span of control of the office manager but also narrows the width of the pyramid at the bottom as reflected in the span of control of first-line supervisors. While there is no relationship between number of sections and the manager's span of control when other factors are held constant, the same antecedent conditions influ-

---

ginal productivity of administrative personnel decreases with size and increases with complexity; "Effects of Size, Complexity, and Ownership on Administrative Intensity," *Administrative Science Quarterly*, 14 (1969): 47–60.

21. Talcott Parsons introduced the distinction between universalism and particularism in "The Professions and Social Structure," originally published in 1939 and reprinted in his *Essays in Sociology* (Glencoe: Free Press, 1949), pp. 185–199.

ence the two. Although large size promotes both vertical differentiation into multilevel hierarchies and horizontal differentiation into many sections, it generally does the one in some offices and the other in others, and both dimensions of differentiation narrow the span of control of supervisors, but they also typically do so in different local offices. The problems created by a complex structure increase requirements for supervisory personnel, and so do the problems created by complex responsibilities. The extra supervisory manpower required by the complex structures in large offices, however, is far surpassed by the savings in supervisory manpower made possible by large size itself.

The interdependence of elements in the organization of local offices reveals many parallels with that in the organization of entire agencies, though there are some differences too. It is rather surprising that size exerts the strongest and most pervasive influence on other organizational characteristics and yet has consistent effects across a wide range of differences in organizational size. Local offices vary in size from 5 to 225 employees, whereas agencies vary from 50 to more than 9,000 employees, an average of one third of whom are at the headquarters. Nevertheless, differences in size affect the structure of agencies and that of local offices in essentially identical ways. The large size of either an agency or a local office generates differentiation of occupational positions, hierarchical levels, and functional subdivisions; it fosters mechanization, in the form of automation in agencies and electric typewriters in offices; it widens the span of control of the top executive; and it reduces the supervisory ratio. Its indirect effects on the clerical ratio are also similar, but the clerical ratio is the only variable on which its influences are not virtually identical. Moreover, the expanding size of local offices as well as that of the entire agency not only increases the number of structural components along various lines into which the organizational unit becomes differentiated but also the average size of these components, as indicated by the declining slope of the regression lines of number of structural components of any sort on size.

Organizational characteristics other than size also have consonant influences in local offices and the agency as a whole. The division of labor raises the clerical ratio in both. Vertical differentiation into multilevel hierarchies reduces horizontal differentiation into functional subdivisions in both (divisions in agencies and sections in local offices), and either vertical or horizontal differentiation increase the supervisory ratio in both. These parallel relationships as well as those that are not alike for agencies and local offices can be examined by comparing the following tables: for mechanization, Tables 3–2 and 7–5; for levels, Tables 3–3 and 7–6; for major subdivisions, Tables 3–4 and 7–7; for top executive's span of control, Tables 3–5 and 7–8; and for supervisory ratio, Tables 4–1 and 7–10 (reversing signs in the latter, or using instead the values supplied in note 17).

The major difference observable in these tables is that occupational differentiation reinforces several of the influences of size in local offices but not in entire agencies, specifically, those on mechanization, levels, major subdivisions (sections), and top executive's span of control. The possibility cannot be excluded that these discrepancies are a methodological artifact, owing to differences in the number of cases and hence the standard errors, the variables controlled, multicollinearity, or some unknown problem, although our attempts to bring to the fore through various combinations of controls similar influences of the division of labor in entire agencies were unsuccessful. The discrepancies therefore may be substantively meaningful. The number of occupational positions is more closely related to the number of employees in the entire roof organizations than in their component branches, and it may for this reason exert an independent influence reinforcing that of size in the branches but not in the roof organizations, where its significance is absorbed, so to speak, by the predominant influence of size.

The two indications of mechanization, the automation of operations in the agency and the use of electric typewriters in local offices, are evidently quite different, and it is hardly astounding that their significance for the organization is not the same. Automation slightly promotes the development of multilevel hierarchies and reduces the clerical ratio in agencies, whereas modern office machines in local offices have neither of these effects. On the other hand, the use of electric typewriters is related to a wide span of control of the manager in local offices, whereas automation has no similar relationships with span of control of agency director. A final discrepancy is clearly a methodological artifact (see Tables 3–5 and 7–8): the conclusion that multiple levels reduce the span of control of the manager in local offices and not that of the director in agencies is not based on differences in the values of the standardized regression coefficients but on the fact that the b^* of $-.26$ in local offices is seven times its standard error whereas that of $-.27$ in agencies is not quite one-and-a-half times its standard error, owing to differences in the number of cases.[22]

In short, the organizational characteristics on which comparable data are available exhibit interrelations that are largely similar in employment security agencies (or their headquarters) and within their local branches.

---

22. The division of labor and the clerical ratio exert no direct influence on the supervisory ratio in local offices, though they do on the span of control of first-line supervisors, and neither do they influence the supervisory ratio in agency headquarters.

The influences exerted by size on other organizational conditions are essentially the same, and so are the influences of vertical and of horizontal structural differentiation. The effects of occupational differentiation on the clerical ratio are also parallel, but occupational differentiation reinforces the influence of size on several characteristics of local offices without having such reinforcing effects on the corresponding agency characteristics, perhaps because its stronger correlation with size in agencies than in offices blots out such reinforcing influences. This is the major discrepancy discovered, aside from the fact that automation influences the shape of the pyramid and the clerical ratio in agencies, whereas modern office equipment has no similar effects in local offices. Having now compared the interdependence between characteristics in agencies and in local offices, treating the two as independent sets of cases for this purpose, we proceed in the next chapter to examine how the characteristics of local offices are affected by those of the agency to which they belong. The questions raised are how the organizational context in which offices are rooted and the environmental context in which they are located influence their organizational attributes.

CHAPTER 8

Contexts of Organizations

The employment security agency constitutes the organizational context in which the local offices in the state are embedded. Though local offices have a degree of autonomy, the fundamental administrative decisions concerning their organization and operations and, particularly, their budget are made at the agency headquarters. We have no information on the process of decision-making, but we can study how the characteristics of the roof organization influence those of its component branches. Tracing these influences of the agency context on the organizational characteristics of local offices is the first objective of this chapter.

The agency of which they are part is not the only significant social context for local offices, however. Another is the environment of the community in which they are located, just as the state environment has been seen to affect the organization of the entire agency. The analysis of the influences of the community environment on local offices is this chapter's second objective. Finally, the conditions in the state may also affect the character of local offices. To be sure, one would expect the effects of the remote state environment on local offices to be mostly indirect, mediated by the local environment or the characteristics of the agency, and this turns out to be the case. Only those influences of the state environment are presented that are direct and not completely mediated by some other external variable under investigation.

The procedure used for the contextual analysis of the influence of

205

agency attributes on office attributes is to classify every local office by the characteristics of the agency to which it belongs, as well as by its own, and then to use the contextual variables together with the office variables in multiple regression analysis. Variations among local offices within a state cannot be influenced by contextual variables, because the values of these variables are identical for every local office in a given state. The 1,201 local offices can therefore assume only a maximum of fifty-one different values with respect to contextual variables (fifty-one rather than fifty-three because the 1,201 local offices exclude those from two jurisdictions). But the procedure does not ignore the variations among offices within a state in their own characteristics, and it consequently provides a more conservative estimate of contextual influences than would be obtained by alternative procedures. This can be illustrated by applying two alternatives to the analysis of the influence of agency size on office size. The zero-order correlation between the contextual variable of agency size and the size of the 1,201 offices is .32, whereas the zero-order correlation for the fifty-three agencies between their own size and the mean size of the local offices in them is .65. The reason for the great difference is that the former correlation is depressed by the within-state variance in size of offices, whereas the latter ignores this variance. The substantive meaning is that the method of contextual analysis directs attention to the extent to which the entire variability among local offices is influenced by their organizational context, which is different from asking what the relationships are between agency characteristics and average office characteristics.[1]

Information on the community environment is based on census sources, notably the *County and City Data Book*. There are, of course, differences in the local environment among the various offices in a state, but all those in the same community are described by the same environmental variables. For offices located in places with more than 25,000 inhabitants, the city is

1. The zero-order correlations between two agency characteristics treated as contextual variables, which can be found in the second matrix in Appendix F, differ from the true zero-order correlations between these agency characteristics shown in the first matrix in Appendix F. The reason for the differences is that in the former correlations the values for each agency are weighted by its size (strictly, by the number of its local offices under investigation). When ninety-seven contextual correlations were compared with regular ones for the larger and the smaller half of the agencies, eighty-seven of them resembled those of the larger agencies. The term "context" is used here in the conventional sense of referring to conditions external to the unit under consideration (local office), not in the specialized sense in which it is used in D. S. Pugh et al., "The Context of Organization Structures," *Administrative Science Quarterly*, 14 (1969): 91–114.

considered to be the community context, and for offices located in smaller places, the entire county is.[2] This decision was necessitated by the fact that the sources do not supply data on places with fewer than 25,000 inhabitants, though there is reason to assume that offices in small towns often also serve the surrounding countryside, which makes the decision not completely arbitrary. A dummy variable is used to indicate that county rather than city was coded as the environmental context. The use of this dummy variable in the regression analysis (whenever it makes an appreciable difference) results in the influence of city size being split between the dummy variable (reversing sign) and the variable of population size, and the two must be interpreted together. Most community variables are based on data from the 1960 U.S. Census. The influences of the state environment on local offices are analyzed by the same procedure as those of the agency context.

The multiple regression analysis treats a given office characteristic as the dependent variable and introduces as independent variables those referring to the agency context, the community context, and the context of the state environment, as well as the relevant antecedent conditions within the local office itself. Thus, there is a considerable number of independent variables in most regression problems. To keep this number within bounds, contextual variables that do not have a zero-order correlation of more than .20 with the dependent variable are not considered, except in a few cases in which theoretical considerations make it advisable to include them. But smaller partial regression coefficients are accepted as meaningful, using the same criteria as those used in Chapter 7.

Inasmuch as no reliable measures for the services provided in every local office are available, the only way to infer how office characteristics influence services is from the relationships between these characteristics and the services performed in the entire agency. Hence, though agency services as well as other agency variables are always treated as independent variables in the regression analysis (which is necessitated by the technique of contextual analysis), the relationships will sometimes be interpreted as indicative of the influence of office attributes on services. Otherwise, both agency and community context are assumed to precede the characteristics of local offices in the causal sequence, and the state environment is assumed to precede both of them. No assumptions are made concerning the relative precedence of agency context and community environment.

2. Alaska and Puerto Rico have no counties; election districts and *municipios,* respectively, are used to code environmental characteristics for offices in small communities in these two jurisdictions.

Subdivision of Work

The subdivision of work among structural components along several dimensions is a process of central significance in organizations, and many of the conditions in local offices can be considered expressions of this process. The average size of the offices in an agency relative to its own size reflects the extent to which the administration of services to clients is concentrated in a few places or subdivided among many. The degree to which the over-all responsibilities are subdivided into specialized ones is manifest in three characteristics of local offices: the fact that the office itself has specialized functions, the division of labor in it, and the number of different sections to which different responsibilities are assigned. Mechanization and the clerical ratio, though not themselves aspects of subdivision, are much affected by the division of labor, as we have seen. How does the agency context influence these conditions indicative of the organization of work in local offices, and what influences do the contexts of the community and the state environment have?

The factor that makes the most important difference for the size of local offices is their being located in a big city. Table 8–1 shows that three indicators of community urbanization—population density, not having fewer than 25,000 inhabitants, and population size—are positively related to office size, and the differences between the zero-order correlations and the regression coefficients are largely owing to overlap among the three variables. A large proportion of men and women of foreign stock in a city does not affect office size, on the other hand, inasmuch as the zero-order correlation of .29 between the two variables disappears when other conditions are controlled, mostly owing to urbanization of the community (the three measures of which account for a reduction of .24 in the coefficient). Though the more specialized local offices are larger than the others ($r = .25$), this is simply the result of the fact that most specialized offices are found in large cities, which is indicated by the lack of a positive relationship under controls owing, as decomposition reveals, to the three community urbanization measures (.25). Thus, specialization as such does not influence office size. The larger and more densely populated a city, the larger are the employment security offices in it, and the more likely are they to be specialized.

Because highly urbanized states have, of course, disproportionately large numbers of highly urbanized communities with large offices, it follows that urban states have more large local offices than comparatively rural states. Even when the urbanization of the communities and several other conditions are controlled, however, the degree of urbanization of the state is seen in Table 8–1 to have some net effect on the size of local offices. This type of influence—that of the prevalence of a characteristic in the environment on a dependent variable when the characteristic itself is held constant

TABLE 8-1. *Multiple Regression of* **Local Office Size** *on Antecedent Conditions*

Independent Variable	Standardized Regression Coefficient	Zero-Order Correlation
State Environment		
% Urban	.12*	.28
Community Environment		
Population Density	.29**	.43
Town under 25,000	−.21**	−.31
Population	.10**	.31
% Foreign Stock	−.04	.29
Agency Context		
Size	.03	.32
Extent of Personnel Regulations	.19**	.28
Automation	−.06	.31
Employee-Client Ratio in Benefit Function	−.10**	−.12
Local Office		
Specialization	−.02	.25

Multiple R = .54; n = 1,201
*Greater than twice its standard error.
**Greater than three times its standard error.

—has been called a "structural effect." [3] Why does the prevalence of urban communities in the state raise the size of a local office even after holding constant the urbanization of the community where the office is located? If there are many large cities in a state, establishing relatively large offices becomes the norm in the agency, and this norm appears to exert an independent influence on the size of local offices. In states with few big cities, correspondingly, smaller local offices are standard, and this standard

3. Peter M. Blau, "Structural Effects," *American Sociological Review*, 25 (1960): 178–193. See also Paul F. Lazarsfeld and Herbert Menzel, "On the Relation between Individual and Collective Properties," in Amitai Etzioni, ed., *Complex Organizations* (New York: Holt, Rinehart & Winston, 1961), pp. 422–440.

seems also to reduce the size of local offices in the big cities where larger offices could be established.

Formalized personnel procedures in the civil service system under which the agency operates appear to be another factor that promotes the creation of larger local offices. Table 8–1 shows that extensive personnel regulations are the aspect of the organizational context that has the greatest direct effect on office size. Formalized personnel procedures limit the discretion of office managers in making appointments and help assure that all employees meet minimum qualifications. They thereby reduce the risk of delegating responsibilities and thus encourage their delegation, as we have seen in Chapter 5. The influence of an extensive body of personnel regulations on the size of local branches may be explained in the same way. The spatial separation from the agency headquarters inevitably gives the managers of local branches a certain amount of autonomy. One way to limit the scope of their responsibilities is to restrict the size of the personnel complement over which they exercise authority. Because extensive personnel regulations reduce the risk decentralization entails for the agency management, they foster the development of larger local offices that make it possible to take advantage of the economy of scale, though doing so gives broader responsibilities to individual office managers.

Large agencies tend to establish larger local offices than do small agencies. Decomposition indicates that the main reasons for this gross effect of agency size on branch size (.32) is that large agencies, compared to small ones, operate under civil service systems with more extensive regulations (.14) and are located in more urbanized states (.08) with more densely populated communities (.08). Though Table 8–1 shows that the standardized regression coefficient of agency size is inconsequential (.03), one should not conclude that its correlation with office size is spurious, because neither extensive regulations nor community density can be considered the antecedents of agency size and because the results of decomposition with so many control variables must be interpreted with caution. This need for caution is illustrated by the different results obtained in the decomposition of two variables in Table 8–1 and in that of the same two variables in the regression of office size on them alone. In Table 8–1, singling out the influences of two independent variables, the gross effect of agency size on office size is much reduced by extent of regulations (.14), whereas the gross effect of extent of regulations on office size is little reduced by agency size (.02). However, if another regression is computed of office size on only these two variables, the effect of agency size on office size is less reduced by extent of regulations (.08) than the effect of extent of regulations on office size is reduced by agency size (.18), with the result that the direct effect of office size on agency size now appears greater ($b^* = .24$) than that of extent of regulations ($b^* = .10$).[4] In short, the relative influences of agency size and extent of personnel regulations on office size in this regression problem are the opposite of those in Table 8–1, though decomposition does not reveal the other variables in Table 8–1 to account for that.

The plausible conclusion is that agency size does influence office size, though in good part because the preponderance of urbanized communities in the states in which large agencies operate encourages the establishment of large offices. Similarly, the positive association between automation in the agency and the size of its local offices vanishes when other conditions are controlled. Though the question just raised may also be raised concerning this finding, there is no direct evidence in this case to counterindicate the conclusion that office size is increased not so much by automation itself as by the conditions with which it is associated, such as extensive personnel regulations, large agency size, and urbanization.

The large size of local offices in an employment security agency apparently contributes to operating economy, at least in terms of man-hours. Table 8–1 shows that the ratio of employees to clients in the benefit function of the agency is inversely related to the size of local offices. This is one of the cases mentioned above in which a relationship is interpreted as resulting from the influence of the office characteristic on that of the agency. The savings in supervisory manpower realized in larger offices, as we have seen in Chapter 7, possibly supplemented by other savings in personnel, help reduce the cost in man-hours of the agency's benefit operations. Given this economic advantage of larger branches, conditions that help increase the size of branches have economic advantages too. Extensive personnel regulations are such a condition, and they have in fact been found also to reduce the employee-client ratio in benefit operations (Table 4–8).

The fact that an office has specialized functions is one of three expressions of specialization, the other two being the division of labor and the number of functional sections in it. Both the specialization of the office and the division of labor within it encourage the development of many sections. Assuming that the specialized function of an office is an antecedent of all its other characteristics, specialization cannot be influenced by any office variables, and the empirical data indicate that none of the agency characteristics exert a considerable influence on it. But Table 8–2 shows that two conditions in the community, which are manifest in six specific

---

4. The standard error for both regression coefficients in this problem is .04. The results are essentially the same if office specialization is controlled.

TABLE 8-2. *Multiple Regression of* Local Office Specialization *on Antecedent Conditions*

Independent Variable	Standardized Regression Coefficient	Zero-Order Correlation
Community Environment		
Town under 25,000	−.26**	−.44
Population	.10**	.28
Population Density	.15**	.44
% Foreign Stock	.14**	.32
% Blacks	.18**	.23
Median Family Income	.09**	.23

Multiple $R = .56$; $n = 1,201$
**Greater than three times its standard error.

variables, affect the establishment of specialized offices. First, specialized employment security offices are primarily found in large cities as indicated by three variables: the community's not having fewer than 25,000 people, its population density, and the size of its population. The second set of variables influencing specialized branches refers to the heterogeneity of a city's population.

The ethnic and socioeconomic heterogeneity of the population in big cities encourages the establishment of specialized employment offices. A large proportion of blacks and of persons of foreign stock reflect ethnic heterogeneity, and the finding that high income and a large proportion of blacks exert parallel influences implies that the underlying factor is socioeconomic heterogeneity. Part of the influence of heterogeneity on specialized offices results from the fact that the populations in big cities are more heterogeneous than those in small towns, but the three variables indicative of heterogeneity exert some independent influence on specialization when city size and population density are controlled. If there are many people in a community looking for professional and other white-collar jobs as well as many looking for unskilled work, there are good reasons to create specialized employment offices. Yet, though the specialization of branches in heterogeneous communities is warranted on strictly rational grounds, it unquestionably brings about greater ethnic segregation in employment offices, with mostly blacks being served in some and mostly whites in others. Specialized offices in big heterogeneous cities are sometimes explicitly designed to provide more extensive services to underprivileged ethnic minorities, as illustrated by the youth opportunity centers, but the ethnic segregation in specialized offices also opens the door to inequitable treatment, just as the segregated schools that are the by-product of neighborhood segregation create inequities in education.

The interpretation that a heterogeneous population fosters the establishment of specialized employment offices has been inferred partly from the finding that both a high proportion of blacks and a high income level in a community are associated with specialization of local offices. This interpretation can be tested directly, because it implies that these two independent variables combined have an interaction effect on specialization. If the underlying factor leading to the creation of specialized offices is the heterogeneity of the population, as the interpretation assumes, it follows that the joint occurrence of many blacks and high incomes in a community, and not the occurrence of either without the other, is what leads to the establishment of specialized offices. The multiple regression problem in Table 8–3 tests this interpretation by adding the product term, per cent black

TABLE 8-3. *Multiple Regression of* Local Office Specialization *on Antecedent Conditions*

Independent Variable	Standardized Regression Coefficient	Zero-Order Correlation	Metric Regression Coefficient
Community Environment			
Town under 25,000	−.24**	−.44	−.42427**
Population	.09*	.28	.00004*
Population Density	.14**	.44	.00014**
% Foreign Stock	.14**	.32	.00810**
% Blacks	−.14	.23	−.00884
Median Family Income	.04	.23	.00274
% Blacks X Median Income	.33**	.33	.00044**

Multiple R = .57; n = 1,201

  *Greater than twice its standard error.

**Greater than three times its standard error.

times median income, to the independent variables previously considered in Table 8–2. The findings clearly support the interpretation. Neither the proportion of blacks nor the income level in the community alone significantly affects the likelihood that specialized offices are found there; only the combination of both represented by the product term does. Communities with heterogeneous populations, including many blacks, most of whom are poor, and many well-off middle-class people, most of whom are white, are most likely to have specialized employment offices, which keep these groups apart.

Occupational specialization within a local office, in contrast to the specialization of the office itself, is less affected by the community environment than by the agency context. The differentiation of occupational positions in the agency relative to its size is the aspect of the agency context that most influences the subdivision of labor within local offices. The matrix of formal positions in the agency constitutes the resource of available specialties on which local offices in a sense draw in establishing their division of labor. Table 8–4 shows that the agency's division of labor and

TABLE 8-4. *Multiple Regression of* **Local Office Division of Labor** *on Antecedent Conditions*

Independent Variable	Standardized Regression Coefficient	Zero-Order Correlation
Community Environment		
Population Density	−.09**	.24
Town under 25,000	−.02	−.30
Agency Context		
Size	−.43**	−.00
Division of Labor	.28**	.17
Clerical Ratio	.12**	.21
Local Office		
ES Function	.06*	.15
Size (Log)	.68**	.62

Multiple R = .70; n = 1,201

*Greater than twice its standard error.
**Greater than three times its standard error.

clerical ratio, both of which reflect the degree of subdivision of formal positions, raise the division of labor in local offices. Agency size also exerts an indirect positive influence on the division of labor in local branches, mediated by agency division of labor (.22) and branch size (.23), as decomposition shows, but this positive indirect effect is balanced by the negative direct effect of agency size on office division of labor (b^* = − .43). This finding must be interpreted together with the direct effect of agency division of labor. The larger the total number of employees in an agency relative to its division of labor, the less abundant is the proportionate supply of formal positions on which the many and large local offices that typically exist in such a large agency can draw, which depresses their division of labor, just as an abundant supply of positions raises it. To be sure, the same positions can be used in all offices, but it requires a larger complement of different positions to meet the more varied occupational needs of many large than the less diverse needs of few small offices.

The division of labor in offices is more pronounced in densely populated cities, because offices are larger there than in less urban communities (.24). But population density also has some negative direct effect on the division of labor (− .09), possibly because comparatively fewer specialized services are provided in highly urbanized centers with their large loads of unskilled clients. Table 8–4 also reveals that the strong impact of the size of an office and the slight influence of its function on its division of labor persist when contextual conditions are controlled.

The shape of the pyramid in local offices is not much affected by the agency context or the external environment, which implies that this core of the structure is to a degree protected from external influences not only in roof organizations, as we saw in Chapter 6, but also in their local components, and this protection extends even to the influences of the roof organization itself. Neither number of levels nor office manager's span of control has a zero-order correlation as high as .20 with any external variable but one. The exception is that the office structure is somewhat more differentiated—in terms of levels, sections, and manager's span of control —in cities with more than 25,000 inhabitants than in smaller towns, and population density exerts an additional influence on the differentiation into sections.[5]

The complex structure of urbanized communities is reflected in a more differentiated structure of employment security offices, notably a larger number of functional sections, which facilitate accommodation to the employment needs of a diverse clientele. (The assumption that sections are functional subdivisions is supported by the direct relationship between occupational differentiation and sections shown in Table 7–7.) The number of sections in an office is also greater if operations in an agency are automated than if they are not ($r = .22$), mostly because the offices in automated agencies are larger (.15). But automation also has a slight direct effect on number of sections ($b^* = .05$), which possibly also reflects the

---

5. In the multiple regression of number of sections on eight independent variables, the five in Table 7–7 plus three others, the standardized regression coefficients of the three new variables are: population density, .13**; population more than 25,000, − .05 *; and automation, .05 *. The three zero-order correlations, in order, are .43, − .35, .22. The standardized regression coefficients for the five variables in Table 7–7 persist when these three external variables are controlled in slightly reduced form, except that the one for electric typewriters is increased to .07*. (One asterisk refers to a value more than twice, and two asterisks to one more than three times, the standard error.)

principle that organizational differentiation is an adjustment to external complexity. This principle [6] is supported by the earlier findings that the complex environment of urbanized states promotes differentiation in agencies, as well as by the present findings that both the complexity of urban communities and the complexity of the agency's technology promote differentiation in local offices.

The substantial positive relationship between occupational differentiation and the use of electric typewriters in local offices has been interpreted as an expression of a universalistic orientation toward technical efficiency. Though informal ways of management with a personal touch may be preferable in small undifferentiated structures, an impersonal universalistic approach is required in large differentiated ones, and such an approach enhances concern with technical improvements and efficiency. Some support for this interpretation is furnished by the finding presented in Table 8–5

TABLE 8-5. *Multiple Regression of* **Local Office Electric Typewriters** *on Antecedent Conditions*

Independent Variable	Standardized Regression Coefficient	Zero-Order Correlation
State Environment		
% Government Employees	.22**	.24
Agency Context		
Supervisory Ratio at Headquarters	.13**	.22
Placements per Opening	.18**	.22
Local Office		
ES Function	.07*	.15
Size	.16**	.25
Division of Labor	.29**	.37

Multiple R = .52; n = 1,188
  *Greater than twice its standard error.
**Greater than three times it standard error.

that the placement productivity in the agency is directly related to the prevalence of electric typewriters in local offices. It does not seem very likely that these office machines actually improve productivity. A more plausible interpretation is that both effective pressure to maximize placement productivity and modern office machines are manifestations of a

6. As previously noted, this principle is the main theme in Paul R. Lawrence and Jay W. Lorsch, *Organization and Environment* (Boston: Graduate School of Business Administration, Harvard University, 1967).

universalistic orientation toward technical efficiency among managers of local offices as well as on the part of top management. This orientation may in turn further productivity, whether one assumes many placements to be indicative of actual efficiency or of excessive concern with production quantity.

Differentiation and production pressure promote a universalistic orientation in terms of technical efficiency among managers, and investment in modern machines symbolizes this orientation, according to the interpretation, which accounts for the relationships of electric typewriters with occupational differentiation and with high productivity. The same connection between differentiation and universalism is observable for entire agencies in the positive relationships of multilevel hierarchies and of many sections per division with automation (Tables 3–3 and 3–6), and particularly in the positive effect of sections per division on placement productivity (Table 4–7). The last relationship, the reasons for which were previously not clear, can now be explained within the new framework that structural differentiation fosters an emphasis on universalistic criteria of efficiency that are reflected in production quantity as well as modern technology.

Can the other two contextual variables that Table 8–5 reveals to be positively related to the prevalence of electric typewriters be encompassed by this interpretation? The two are the supervisory ratio in the agency and the ratio of state government employees to the state's population. Though these two ratios are not expressions of universalism, they both are indicative of a willingness to incur costs to make investments in government services, presumably for the sake of long-run improvements, and electric typewriters are also such investments. An inclination to make long-range investments in the state government and in the agency makes it easier for the manager of a local office to obtain modern office equipment, and the universalistic orientation that tends to prevail in a highly differentiated structure increases his interest in doing so.

Finally, Table 8–6 presents the data on the conditions that affect the clerical ratio in local offices. It has already been discussed that the proportion of clerical jobs is greater in unemployment insurance than in employment service offices and that it depends on the division of labor. The table shows that these influences of the office's function and its division of labor continue to be evident when external conditions are controlled, although the regression data suppress the interaction effect disclosed by Table 7–3, which indicated that the influence of the division of labor on the clerical ratio is essentially confined to offices with unemployment insurance responsibilities. However, controlling environmental conditions reveals some decline in the clerical ratio with increasing size (Table 8–6),

TABLE 8-6. *Multiple Regression of* **Local Office Clerical Ratio** *on Antecedent Conditions*

Independent Variable	Standardized Regression Coefficient	Zero-Order Correlation
State Environment		
Western Region	−.07*	−.23
Community Environment		
Population	.08*	.24
Population Density	−.05	.26
Town under 25,000	−.02	−.12
% Foreign Stocks	.32**	.40
Agency Context		
Size	−.35**	.08
Division of Labor	.39**	.32
% Interviewers with B.A.	.12**	.30
Delegation to Local Managers	−.06	−.30
Local Office		
ES Function	−.27**	−.27
Size	−.06*	.06
Division of Labor	.14**	.20

Multiple $R = .63$; $n = 1,201$

*Greater than twice its standard error.

**Greater than three times its standard error.

which is concealed in the absence of these statistical controls.[7] The large size of an office, by promoting the division of labor, indirectly raises the clerical ratio slightly (.07), but its direct effect is to reduce this ratio slightly again (−.06). Two interpretations of the direct effect are possible: either large size effects greater economies in clerical than in other personnel, or a large number of employees relative to the number of occupational positions reduces the clerical ratio, just as a large number of positions relative to employees raises it. The second interpretation has the advantage of subsuming several findings under one principle.

---

7. Decomposition shows that the two factors essentially responsible for the difference between the zero-order correlation (.06) and the standardized regression coefficient (−.06) are office division of labor (.07) and per cent foreign stock (.09), with the mediating influences of agency size (−.11) and division of labor (.11) cancelling each other. Hence, without controlling the environmental variable of per cent foreign stock the relationship is virtually nil.

The agency's division of labor and its size exert influences on the clerical ratio in local offices that are parallel to, but much more pronounced than, the office's own division of labor and its size.[8] The larger the number of formal positions in the repertory of the agency available to local offices, the greater the chances are that several formal positions simple enough to be filled by clerks exist that are appropriate for the particular situations in most offices. By the same token, the larger the scope of the agency's entire operations, as indicated by its size, relative to the supply of different positions in the agency, the smaller is the likelihood that most offices, operating in different situations, are able to find many appropriate positions that can be filled by clerks. In parallel fashion, a pronounced division of labor in an office routinizes many jobs sufficiently for them to be performed by clerks. However, if the scope of operations of the office reflected by its size is excessively large relative to the number of differentiated occupational positions, only a comparatively small proportion of jobs can be performed by clerks. Because the matrix of occupational positions available relative to the total scope of operations in the agency limits the development of the division of labor in local offices relative to their size (as shown in Table 8–4), the agency's division of labor and size affect the clerical ratio much more than the office's own (Table 8–6).

Another relationship between an agency-wide characteristic and the clerical ratio in local offices reveals a different form of the division of labor. The more college graduates there are among the interviewers in the agency, virtually all of whom work in local offices, the greater is the proportion of clerks in local offices. This finding suggests a form of the subdivision of work that differs from that expressed in the measure of division of labor, namely, the bifurcation of skills. Some agencies have more highly skilled as well as more unskilled employees in their local offices than others, which means that their personnel is more differentiated in terms of skills. The full analysis of this bifurcation of skills is reserved for Chapter 9.

The delegation of considerable responsibilities in an agency to the managers of local offices is negatively related to the clerical ratio in these offices, and a slight negative relationship persists when other conditions are

8. Interestingly enough, office division of labor mediates practically none of the influence of agency division of labor on office clerical ratio (.02). Agency size directly reduces the clerical ratio ($-.36$) but indirectly, via agency division of labor, raises it again (.31). Agency clerical ratio has not been included in this regression problem, although it is correlated with office clerical ratio (.59), because the two variables are tautological and including the agency clerical ratio simply reduces all other relationships.

controlled (Table 8–6).[9] The clerical ratio is lower in employment than in unemployment insurance offices, and managers of employment offices probably require more autonomy. But this is unlikely to account for the negative relationship, which persists when function is roughly controlled in the regression analysis, and which moreover is observable in all five types of offices.[10] One would have expected the greater routinization of the duties in the offices of an agency to encourage rather than discourage delegation of responsibilities to office managers, just as routine duties lead to a wider span of control of first-line supervisors. The reason for the discrepancy may be that routine duties facilitate the job of supervision but their prevalence in an office is indicative of a fragmentation of responsibilities that makes the job of management more difficult. The greater internal problems with which office managers must deal as the result of the fragmentation of duties reflected in a high clerical ratio may discourage, though this is sheer conjecture, the delegation of extra responsibilities to these managers.

The employment of many clerks in an organization depends not only on its need for them but also on the supply of them in the labor market, and an ethnically mixed population with many men and women of foreign stock is an abundant source of clerks. This inference derived from the analysis of the influence of state environment on agency clerical ratio in Table 6–6 is confirmed by the finding in Table 8–6 that a high proportion of persons of foreign stock in the local community substantially increases the proportion of clerks in the employment security office. Note that the same conditions in communities that are correlated with clerical ratio—urbanization and foreign stock—are also correlated with office size (Table 8–1). Only urbanization influences office size, however, and foreign stock has no relationship with it once urbanization is controlled, whereas primarily foreign stock influences clerical ratio and only one of three meas-

---

9. The standardized regression coefficient is .0001 short of being twice its standard error (.0314). The inverse zero-order correlation between delegation of responsibilities to office managers and clerical ratio in the entire agency is considerably less strong (−.17) than that shown in Table 8–6 (−.30), which implies that the clerical ratio in local offices rather than at the headquarters is the important factor.

10. But other conditions are not controlled in the cross-tabulations with type. The proportion of local offices with a high clerical ratio decreases with increased delegation of responsibilities to office managers from 42 per cent (of 399) to 34 per cent (of 233) in General LO's; from 27 per cent (97) to 13 per cent (27) in ES LO's; from 38 per cent (91) to 8 per cent (47) in Specialized ES LO's; from 57 per cent (130) to 28 per cent (40) in UI LO's; and from 15 per cent (78) to 2 per cent (43) in YOC's.

ures of urbanization is weakly related to it once foreign stock is controlled. Offices in small towns cannot hire as many clerks as those in large cities, because fewer people in less urban places are candidates for clerical jobs, and the major reason for the greater availability of clerks in big cities is their ethnic heterogeneity, not simply urbanization in general. One other environmental condition affects the clerical ratio: offices in Western states employ fewer clerks than those in the three other regions.

Personnel Economies

The supervisory ratio and the span of control of first-line supervisors in local offices depend mostly on the characteristics of these offices, but the agency context and the community environment exert some additional influence on them. Because all the effects on the ratio and the span-of-control measure are, with minor exceptions, parallel, the procedure adopted in Chapter 7 is again followed, and data are presented only on the mean span of control of first-line supervisors, which is the more refined measure. The findings in Table 8–7, compared to those in Table 7–10, show

TABLE 8-7. *Multiple Regression of Local Office* **Mean Span of Control of First-Line Supervisors** *on Antecedent Conditions*

Independent Variable	Standardized Regression Coefficient	Zero-Order Correlation
Community Environment		
Population Density	−.07**	.24
Agency Context		
Size	.27**	.52
Extent of Personnel Regulations	.03	.44
Automation	−.06	.44
Supervisory Ratio	−.01	−.25
Employee-Client Ratio in Benefit		
Function	−.06**	−.21
Local Office		
ES Function	−.10**	−.08
Size (Log)	1.16**	.66
Division of Labor	−.01	.32
Levels	−.44**	.25
Sections	−.36**	.25
Clerical Ratio	.06**	.19

Multiple R = .84; n = 1,201
**Greater than three times its standard error.

that controlling external conditions does not alter the relationships between other office characteristics and the span of control of supervisors very much, though there is enough modification to require revision
of one of the earlier conclusions. Let us briefly review these internal
influences.

The structural complexity produced by either vertical or horizontal differentiation in local offices narrows the supervisory span of control, because problems of coordination and communication in complex structures
make demands on the time of supervisors that leave them less time for direct supervision of subordinates. The complexity of the task also reduces
the number of subordinates per first-line supervisor; the office's responsibility for employment services is one indicator of task complexity, and its
low clerical ratio is another. The large size of an office indirectly increases
the supervisory personnel needed for a given number of operating employees, owing to the structural complexity it produces, but it directly decreases the required supervisory component, owing to the economy of
scale. Inasmuch as the direct effect of size widening the supervisory span
of control is greater than its indirect effects narrowing it, considerable savings in supervisory manpower are realized in large offices. All these relationships persist, though most are slightly reduced, when agency and community conditions are controlled, but the division of labor in the office is
seen to exert no direct influence on the span of control of supervisors
when these external conditions are taken into account.[11] To be sure, the
division of labor in the office narrows the supervisory span of control indirectly through its influence on the differentiation of levels ($-.18$) and sections ($-.17$), though these influences are concealed in the positive zero-order correlation by the strong spurious positive association between division
of labor and span of control produced by office size ($.72$). Occupational
differentiation raises the supervisory ratio because of the structural complexity it engenders, but the earlier inference that it partly does so directly
because of the heterogeneity of duties it entails is not supported by the
data.

Turning now to the organizational context, Table 8–7 shows that the

---

11. Decomposition shows that the difference between the standardized regression coefficient of the division of labor in Table 7–10 ($-.11$) and in Table
8–7 ($-.01$) is not due to the fact that any of the external conditions
controlled appreciably reduces the relationship. Instead, it results from the
fact that these controls reduce the influence of size and thus lessen the significance controlling size has for the relationship between division of labor
and supervisory span of control from $.84$ to $.72$, which accounts for most
of the difference in the standardized regression coefficient.

size of an agency has a pronounced effect on the span of control of supervisors at the very bottom of the hierarchy in local offices. The larger an agency, the wider is the span of control of first-line supervisors. More than one quarter of the variance in the mean span of control of first-line supervisors in 1,201 offices is accounted for by differences in the size of the fifty-one agencies to which they belong. Part of the influence of agency size on the ratio of operating employees to supervisors is indirect, mediated by the size of local offices (.39; counteracted by levels, $-.06$; and sections, $-.06$), and part is direct (.27). Thus, the large size of an agency effects great savings in supervisory manpower not only at the headquarters, as we saw in Table 4–1, but also in local offices, directly as well as indirectly. The reason for the indirect effect is that the larger local offices that prevail in larger agencies make it easier to establish larger work groups of employees with similar duties under each supervisor.

The direct influence of agency size, controlling office size, on the span of control of supervisors in offices may be interpreted as a structural effect. Though this concept was originally introduced to refer to the influence on individual behavior of the prevalence of individuals with a given characteristic in a social structure when the individual's own characteristic is controlled, thus revealing the external influence of the social environment on human behavior, here we have the second illustration of another type of structural effect, one that is on a higher level of social system. The prevalence of *organizational* components (here, offices) with a given independent attribute (size) in a larger organization influences a dependent attribute of these components (supervisory span) when each component's own independent attribute (office size) is controlled. Since more subordinates tend to be assigned to the average first-line supervisor in large than in small offices, and since large agencies have more large offices than small agencies, a wide span of control tends to become standard in large agencies, and this standard exerts pressures in offices of all sizes to assign more subordinates to supervisors than would otherwise be the case. In the same way, *mutatis mutandis,* a narrow supervisory span of control tends to become standard in the various offices of small agencies, reflecting a structural effect of the prevalence of small offices.

The automation of operations in an agency exhibits a strong zero-order correlation with the average span of control of supervisors in local offices (.44), which decomposition shows to be the result of a variety of influences. Part of this association is spurious, produced by the effect of agency size on both automation and supervisory span of control (.23). One indirect effect of automation is to widen the span of control of supervisors because the comparatively large local offices in large automated agencies have supervisors with a disproportionately wide span of control (.38).[12] But this positive indirect effect is diminished by the negative indirect effects owing to the complexity of these larger offices (levels, $-.06$; sections, $-.08$), and by a slight negative direct effect ($-.06$).[13] On the one hand, therefore, the span of control of supervisors is wider in automated than in other agencies, the reason being that automated agencies are larger and have larger local offices. On the other hand, however, automation changes the nature of the duties performed and creates new problems, primarily at the agency headquarters, where the computer is located, but secondarily also in branch offices, where work must be adapted to the requirements of the computer. Local offices in automated agencies tend to adapt to these new problems by adding a section and thus becoming more differentiated, as we saw above, and by reducing the ratio of subordinates to supervisors, partly as the result of this differentiation and in part independently of it.

Extensive personnel regulations encourage the establishment of larger local offices, as we have seen above. They thereby indirectly widen the span of control of supervisors and thus achieve savings in the proportion of supervisory personnel needed in local offices (Table 8–7), though they have no direct effect on the supervisory ratio.[14] Another agency characteristic entered into this regression problem is the supervisory ratio at the headquarters, which is inversely correlated with the supervisory span of control and directly with the supervisory ratio in local offices, in order to ascertain whether these correlations reveal that some agencies have a general tendency to employ higher proportions of supervisors than others. Such a tendency is not pronounced, though a slight one may exist. When other conditions are controlled, the headquarters supervisory ratio is unrelated to the office supervisory span of control, as the table shows, but it reveals a persistent small relationship with the office supervisory ratio ($b * = .06$). Most of the association between the supervisory ratio at the

---

12. Although Table 8–1 indicates that automation has no effect on office size when other conditions are controlled, decomposition of the data in Table 8–7 reveals a strong influence of automation on the supervisory span of control mediated by office size. Neither the other variables controlled nor the difference in the measure of size (raw vs. log) seems to be responsible for these inconsistent results.

13. The standardized regression coefficient falls short .0024 of being twice its standard error (.0308), but its substantive interest nevertheless makes it worthwhile to consider.

14. Decomposition shows that the zero-order correlation of .44 is mostly the result of the mediating effect of office size (.32) and the effect of agency size (.20). These figures indicate that a substantial indirect positive effect persists after agency size is controlled.

headquarters and that in local branches is the result of the effects of agency size and office size, and there is unexpectedly little evidence of blanket agency policies or standards that affect the proportion of supervisors throughout the organization.

A wide span of control of first-line supervisors in local offices produces appreciable savings in the total man-hour costs of benefit operations in the agency. The employee-client ratio in the agency's benefit function, which is shown as an independent variable in Table 8–7, is actually assumed to be the dependent variable affected by the span of control of office supervisors. The difference between the zero-order correlation of these two variables (−.21) and the standardized regression coefficient (−.06) is largely owing to office size (−.13), which indicates that most of the negative relationship is mediated by size but that part of it is direct. The supervisory ratio at the agency *headquarters* reveals no corresponding correlation with the man-hours required for benefit operations (.03),[15] although a greater share of unemployment benefit than of employment service activities is carried out at the headquarters. Apparently, administrative overhead in local offices and particularly the span of control of the many first-line supervisors there have special significance for the agency's operating economy. An important means for keeping the man-hour expenditures of the organization down is to maintain a wide span of control of supervisors in the various branches, both by establishing branches large enough to facilitate the assignment of quite a few subordinates to every supervisor (as reflected in the indirect relationship) and by finding ways to extend the supervisory span of control in offices of a given size (as reflected in the direct one).

A last condition shown in Table 8–7 to influence the span of control of supervisors is the urbanization (population density) of the community in which the office is located.[16] A diverse urbanized environment makes administrative demands on employment security offices that narrow the supervisory span of control, directly and also indirectly by increasing the structural complexity of the offices, but the large size of offices in highly urbanized cities counteracts these negative effects, with the result that the zero-order correlation between population density and span of control is positive (.24). Decomposition reveals that the positive association between

15. But the supervisory ratio in local offices, which is the reverse of the supervisory span of control, does: $r = .15$; $b^* = .05$, with a standard error of .02.

16. The zero-order correlations of supervisor's span of control with size of the city's population (.33), per cent foreign stock (.35), and median income (.27) disappear when other conditions are controlled, with office size being responsible in all three cases.

location in densely populated cities and supervisory span of control owing to the large size of the offices in these cities would be much greater (.49) were it not diminished by the negative influence a complex urban environment has on the number of subordinates per supervisor. The local offices in the most urbanized metropolitan centers are not only larger than others but also more differentiated—particularly into many sections, as noted earlier—and their more differentiated structure narrows the span of control of supervisors (mediated by levels, $-.08$, and by sections, $-.15$). In addition, the complexity of the urbanized environment has a direct effect narrowing this span of control ($-.07$). In short, the diverse needs employment security offices in highly urbanized centers must meet constrain them to develop a more differentiated structure and to free supervisors, by narrowing their span of control, to devote more time to the problems of coordination in the more complex structure and to the other problems created by the complex external environment.

The analysis of the intricate relationships in Table 8–7, which has now been completed, makes it possible to infer some of the processes that govern the attainment of personnel economies in these government bureaus. The assumption made in Chapter 7 that a wide span of control of first-line supervisors in local offices creates over-all manpower economies is supported by the empirical finding that it is inversely related to the ratio of total agency employees to clients in the benefit function. Because work on employment services is more concentrated in local offices than work on unemployment benefits, it seems likely that the supervisory span of control in these local offices achieves at least as much over-all savings in manpower in the employment service function, for which we have no measure. The large size of local offices plays a crucial role in widening the span of control of the supervisors in it and hence in the resulting personnel economies in operations. The chain of influence may be reconstructed in the following way: operating economy depends on low administrative overhead; a wide span of control of first-line supervisors in all the branches of an organization is a major element in low overhead; a wide span of control of supervisors depends on large branches. Ultimately, therefore, conditions in the organization that influence the size of branches are significant for improving operating economy, at least in terms of man-hours.

Office size exerts the dominant influence on the average span of control of first-line supervisors, accounting for 44 per cent of its variance. The positive effect of large-scale operations on the number of subordinates per supervisor substantially exceeds the negative effect of task complexity. Given this strong impact of office size, conditions in the agency or in the environment that exert considerable influence on the size of local offices thereby invariably widen the span of control of supervisors. This is the case regardless of whether these conditions also have a positive direct effect on the supervisory span of control, as agency size does, or no direct effect, as extensive personnel regulations do, or a negative direct effect, as automation and the urbanization of the local community do. Supervisory time is needed to adjust to the complexity imposed on local offices by automation in the agency or by a diverse urban environment, which is manifest in the negative influences of these two variables on the span of control of supervisors. Although automation has a negative, and extent of personnel regulations no direct effect on the supervisory span of control in local offices, both widen it indirectly owing to their association with the large size of offices, and these indirect influences are reflected in the improvements in operating economy automation and extensive personnel regulations achieve, as shown in Table 6–11.

The four major influences on the span of control of supervisors are all purely structural: the size of the office, its vertical differentiation into levels, its horizontal differentiation into sections, and the size of the agency. The demands on the time of supervisors made by the structural complexity large size generates diminish the savings in supervisory man-hours large size makes it possible to realize. The size of the agency exerts a stronger influence than any of its other characteristics on the supervisory span of control in its branches, indirectly by affecting the size of branches, as well as directly and thus complementing the influence of branch size. The question arises why this strong effect of agency size on supervisory manpower in local offices is not reflected in a substantial negative zero-order correlation with the employee-client ratio in Table 6–11 (which is only −.15), whereas the lesser effects of automation and personnel regulations are. The reason may be that not only the size of branches but also their number increases with increasing agency size. The very fact that the need for supervisory personnel declines as the size of an office expands implies that this need arises as an organization becomes more subdivided into geographically dispersed branches. It appears that the extra supervisory manpower required by large roof organizations for their large number of branches virtually absorbs the savings in supervisory manpower achieved by the large size of these branches.

Agency Context and Environment

The subject of this chapter is the examination of the influences on local offices exerted by the organizational context of the agencies to which they belong and the environmental context of the communities in which they are located. The intensive analysis of the complicated connections among a good many variables in the preceding two sections, however, makes it difficult to see the forest for the trees. It is worthwhile, therefore, to review the substantive findings at some length. Since the discussion of the tables was organized in terms of each dependent variable, we shall again change the perspective in this review of the findings and look at the data from the standpoint of each independent variable and the various influences on local offices it exerts, starting with the characteristics of the agency context and then proceeding to the conditions in the community and in the state environment.

Extensive regulations that stipulate the procedures to be followed are impersonal mechanisms of control that substitute to a degree for personal control exercised through supervision and managerial directives. This is probably the case for other bodies of rules as well as for the personnel regulations here examined. Formalized personnel regulations reduce the risk of decentralization—more indirectly than operating rules—by setting standards to guide the decisions of appointing officials and by maintaining uniform minimum qualifications of the officials appointed. These processes were inferred from the earlier finding that an extensive system of such regulations fosters delegation of responsibilities to middle managers at the headquarters and to local managers (Tables 5–1 and 5–3). The physical distance of local offices from the headquarters inevitably gives their managers some autonomy, and the greater the complement of personnel in a local office, the broader is the comparatively autonomous authority its manager exercises. Extensive personnel regulations, inasmuch as they reduce the risk top management incurs by delegating authority to local managers, may encourage the development of larger local offices in an agency (Table 8–1). By so doing, they indirectly promote a wider span of control of first-line supervisors, which largely depends on office size (Table 8–7). The savings in the supervisory personnel of local offices extensive personnel regulations help realize are in turn undoubtedly responsible for at least some of the improvements in the general manpower economy these regulations produce (Table 6–11).

Larger agencies have on the average larger local offices than smaller agencies (Table 8–1). The reason is that the increase in the number of local offices with increasing agency size does not keep pace with the increase in agency size, which implies that both the average size and the number of local offices increase as agency size does. The large size of an agency widens the span of control of the supervisors in local offices (Table 8–7), in part owing to the larger size of most local offices in larger agencies and in part independently of office size. The latter may well reflect a structural effect of the prevalence of large offices with first-line supervisors who have a wide span of control in large agencies, which make a wide span of control the norm that influences the practice in offices regardless of their size. And a narrow span becomes in similar ways the norm in small agencies. The reduction in the supervisory ratio achieved by large agency size is not fully reflected in a reduction in the employee-client ratio in benefit operations, either because the greater supervisory overhead required by the larger *number* of local offices in large agencies consumes most of the savings resulting from their larger size, or because large agencies have a disproportionately large complement of unemployment benefit personnel at their headquarters. Both may well be the case.

The division of labor in the agency, operationally defined by the number of official occupational positions or job titles, constitutes the repository of formal positions available to local offices. Although these positions are not scarce commodities and the same one can be used by all local offices, formal positions not existing in the repertory of the agency's division of labor cannot be used by any office. An insufficient number of different official positions in the agency relative to its scope of operation has the result that some local offices cannot make all the different formal appointments their particular situation would warrant and that their duty assignments are little differentiated or only informally differentiated. Hence, a large number of occupational positions in the agency relative to its scope of operations, as indicated by its size, raises the division of labor in local offices, and so does a small scope of agency operations relative to the number of occupational positions (Table 8–4). The greater latitude in making appointments in local offices created by an ample supply of formal positions in the agency relative to its scope of operations makes it possible to fill positions with clerical personnel that have to be filled by more skilled employees if there is less opportunity for occupational differentiation. This is reflected in a strong positive influence of the agency's division of labor and a strong negative influence of its size relative to its division of labor on the clerical ratio in local offices (Table 8–6).

The technological complexities the automation of operations entails, though they affect the work at the headquarters most, have repercussions for local offices. These offices tend to adjust to the new problems automation creates by adding a section (not necessarily with responsibility for tasks related to the computer) and by reducing the number of employees per supervisor to free the time of supervisors to deal with the problems of coordination in the more differentiated structure and perhaps to deal directly with problems of automated operations (Table 8–7). These negative implications of automation for the span of control of supervisors in local offices are outweighed, however, by the positive relationship between auto-mation and this span of control owing to the comparatively large size of the local offices in large automated agencies.

Several empirical findings can be explained on the basis of the assump-tion that there are differences between agencies, and indeed between state governments, in the inclination to make investments in personnel and in facilities for the sake of long-run improvements in services. The positive relationships of the supervisory ratio at the agency headquarters with the supervisory ratio, and with the availability of electric typewriters, in local offices can be interpreted to signify that differences in management's will-ingness to make such investments are manifest in local offices as well as at the headquarters (Tables 8–5 and 8–7). One might suspect the underlying factor to be the financial resources to make investments, but neither agency funds nor government expenditures in the state are positively related to su-pervisory ratio.[17] However, fundamental differences among state govern-ments may well be an underlying factor, as suggested by the finding that the ratio of state government employees to population in the state, which is indicative of the general inclination in the state to invest in government services, is also related to the prevalence of electric typewriters in the of-fices of the employment security agency. The conjecture that modern office machines reflects a universalistic orientation toward technical efficiency, advanced to explain the relationship between differentiation and modern mechanical equipment, is supported by the positive relationship between placement productivity and such equipment in an agency's local offices (Table 8–5).

Two attributes of local offices affect the manpower required in the agency to administer unemployment benefits to a given number of clients, and they may well have similar effects on the manpower requirements of employment services, though we have no measure of the latter. The large size of local branches reduces manpower requirements for benefit opera-tions (Table 8–1), and so does a wide span of control of the first-line su-pervisors in these branches (Table 8–7). These two influences are not un-related. The average span of control of supervisors is much wider in large than in small local offices, and the consequent savings large office size achieves in supervisory personnel produces over-all savings in manpower. Although the procedure used in the regression analysis for technical rea-

---

17. Government expenditure in the state is negatively correlated with supervi-sory ratio ($-.30$) and positively with supervisory span of control ($.39$) in local offices, but these relationships vanish when other conditions are con-trolled (b^* for ratio, $-.01$; for span, $-.03$), with office size largely respon-sible (ratio, $-.38$; span, $.32$).

sons made it appear that some of the influence of the supervisory span of control on manpower requirements is mediated by office size, the more plausible conceptualization is that a wide span of control of supervisors effects savings in manpower directly and large office size does so indirectly by promoting a wider span of control. In fact, the negative gross effect of the supervisory span of control on the employee-client ratio in benefit operations ($-.21$) exceeds that of office size on it ($-.12$). Nevertheless, conditions in the agency that are closely related to office size and thereby exert a substantial influence on the span of control of supervisors typically also improve the over-all personnel economy of benefit operations. Extensive personnel regulations and automation are examples (Tables 8–7 and 6–11). But there are two exceptions. Agency size has a pronounced impact on the span of control of supervisors in local offices but exerts no corresponding influence on the employee-client ratio, possibly because the manpower savings resulting from the large size of offices are neutralized by the manpower costs resulting from their large number in large agencies. And the staff ratio does not influence the supervisory span of control in local offices but does increase the employee-client ratio, undoubtedly because a large staff increases personnel overhead primarily at the headquarters.

Turning now to the influences of the community environment, what makes most differences for local offices is whether they are located in big cities with teeming populations or in small towns that are more sparsely settled. (The three expressions of urbanization—population density and two referring to city size—frequently, though not always, have parallel effects.) Specialized employment security offices are mostly established in cities where concentrated and heterogeneous populations justify the existence of several different offices (Table 8–2). The offices in a big city, though there are several of them, are also larger on the average than the single office found in most smaller cities (Table 8–1). In other words, both the number and the average size of local offices increase with increasing community size, just as both do with increasing agency size, and just as is the case for increases in both number and mean size of other structural components with increasing agency size.

The large size of the offices in the most urbanized places leads, as one would expect, to the emergence of a structure that is more differentiated into multiple levels and many sections than the structure of the smaller offices in less urban places. There are some indications, however, that urbanization directly promotes differentiation, notably into many sections, beyond that attributable to the larger office size in urbanized places, which implies that employment security offices adjust to the diverse demands of a complex urban environment by developing a complex structure. Another manifestation of the adjustments required by the greater demands made on these offices by a diversified population is that urbanization raises the ratio of supervisory personnel to operating officials, though this effect is outweighed by the savings in supervisory personnel resulting from the larger size of offices in more urbanized places (Table 8–7). Urbanization fosters structural differentiation within offices as well as differentiation among the offices in a community, and its gross effect on occupational differentiation is also positive, but its net effect on occupational differentiation is slightly negative (Table 8–4). The reason may be that, whereas the diverse demands of urbanized populations engender complexities, the availability of clerks in urban labor markets simplifies the division of labor.

Local offices in big cities employ larger proportions of clerks than those in small towns, primarily because of the greater ethnic heterogeneity of big cities, as indicated by the proportion of foreign stock in their population (Table 8–6). The second generation contains disproportionate numbers of young men and women from poor homes with ambition but few resources to move up in the world, who look on clerical jobs as desirable opportunities compared to the drudgery of unskilled labor. Such young people constitute a pool of candidates for clerical jobs in the labor market, which facilitates the recruitment of clerks in employment security offices. Though the proportion of men and women of foreign descent in a community has most effect on the supply of clerical labor reflected in the clerical ratio, the size of a city exerts some additional independent influence. The socioeconomic as well as the ethnic heterogeneity of a community, moreover, encourages the establishment of specialized employment security offices in it, as indicated by the greater prevalence of specialized offices in ethnically mixed communities and in those that contain both many blacks and many affluent families (Tables 8–2 and 8–3). Whereas the specialization of offices in heterogeneous cities makes it possible to provide more extensive services to deprived ethnic minorities, as exemplified by youth opportunity centers, it also leads to ethnic segregation in employment offices and thus entails the danger that the most underprivileged in overcrowded offices do not receive services of the same quality as others.

Most of the influences of the state environment on local offices are indirect, channeled through characteristics of the agency or conditions in the local environment. For instance, the size of the state's population, the proportion of unemployed among them, and government expenditures per capita are positively correlated with the average size of local offices, because the size of the agency, the extent of its personnel regulations, and the urbanization of local communities are affected by these three conditions in the state and in turn influence the size of local offices. The same three characteristics of the state environment are also correlated with a wide span of control of office supervisors, because the larger size of the agencies and the larger size of the local offices associated with these three factors widen the supervisory span of control. Aside from these indirect effects, which are of little interest and have not been included in the analysis, the broader environment exerts only a few direct influences on office attributes. Thus, a comparatively large state government, which may be a sign of a willingness to invest in government services, leads to greater investments in electric typewriters in local offices (Table 8–5), and clerks are for some reason less utilized in the offices of Western states than in those in the rest of the country (Table 8–6). Finally, the urbanization of the state exhibits a positive relationship with the size of local offices, which is not entirely accountable for by the many big cities in urbanized states with their disproportionately large offices, for it persists within cities of a given size (Table 8–1). The prevalence in a state of big cities with large offices, or small towns with small ones, seems to establish a normative standard in the agency that exerts an independent effect on the size of its branches. This is an illustration of a structural effect in which the individual units are not human beings in a group but substructures in a larger structure.

The influence of the agency context on local offices is more pronounced than that of the external environment, except in the case of office size. Given the large variability among the offices in a state, however, on which we relied in the analysis that treated offices as independent units in Chapter 7, agency characteristics, which ignore this intrastate variability, cannot account for a very large portion of the total variance among offices. Adding agency variables to office variables raises the variation accounted for in office size, division of labor, and mechanization about 10 per cent each.[18] Specifically, it raises that of office size from 6 to 16 per cent, with environmental conditions increasing it to 30 per cent; it raises that of division of labor from 39 to 48 per cent, with environmental conditions contributing nothing further; and it raises that of electric typewriters from 15 to 24 per cent, with environmental conditions increasing it to 28 per cent. Neither the agency context nor environmental conditions make much additional contribution to the variance accounted for by antecedent characteristics of offices in their number of levels (48 per cent), of sections (44 per cent), or their managers' span of control (18 per cent). The clerical ratio

18. The estimates of the variations accounted for here is simply R^2, because the large number of cases made it appear unnecessary to apply corrections for degrees of freedom eliminated.

in local offices is most affected by agency characteristics, which add 18 to the 14 per cent accounted for by office characteristics, with environmental conditions adding another 6 to raise the total to 38 per cent. Because 65 per cent of the variance in the supervisory span of control is accounted for by conditions in the local office, agency conditions raise it only little, to 71 per cent, with environmental conditions making no consequential independent contribution.

Such figures as these can be easily misleading, however, unless one remembers that they refer only to the direct influences exerted by agency characteristics and ignore their indirect influences mediated by office characteristics. To illustrate: whereas all agency characteristics add only 6 per cent to the variation in supervisory span of control accounted for by office characteristics, agency size alone can account for 27 per cent of the variation in this span, but most of its influence is indirect, mediated by office size. The neglect of the important indirect influences by procedures confining themselves to amount of additional variance explained is what prompted the preference for the use of regression coefficients and decomposition in this monograph. It should also be remembered that the figures refer to the portion of the *total* variation in office characteristics accounted for by the specified agency characteristics, which is necessarily less than the portion of the *mean* office variation the same agency characteristics can explain. For example, agency size accounts for only 10 per cent of the total variance in office size but for fully 42 per cent of the variance in mean office size among agencies.

Conclusions

The findings have been fully reviewed in the preceding section. In conclusion, attention is centered on the comparison of the influences exerted by the community environment on local offices with those exerted by the state environment on agencies. Reference is to some of the data in this chapter and those in Chapter 6.

The size of the population in the community where an office is located exerts a considerable influence on its size (Table 8–1), but the size of the state's population exerts a much more predominant influence on the agency's size (Table 6–1). The zero-order correlation is .31 in the first and .95 in the second case. The reason for the difference is that large cities contain several employment security offices, with the result that the demand for services created by population pressure is not so evident in the scope of any single office as in that of the state agency. Urbanization, which is indicated by per cent urban in the state and by population density in the community, is strongly correlated with agency size (.48) and with office size (.43). But the dominant influence of a state's population suppresses the relationship between urbanization and agency size under controls, whereas a city's urbanization (population density) has a direct effect on office size when other conditions are controlled, which is reinforced by a direct effect of a state's urbanization. The proportion of persons of foreign stock in the environment reveals also highly similar correlations with agency size (.32) and office size (.29), though in this instance a small direct effect is evident under controls for agencies and not for local offices. Thus, both local branches and entire agencies tend to be particularly large if their social environment is highly urbanized and ethnically heterogeneous, though what affects office size directly is urbanization and what affects agency size directly is ethnic heterogeneity.

The only environmental condition discovered to influence the mechanization of office equipment in local branches, as indicated by electric typewriters, is the relative size of the state government (Table 8–5). Interestingly enough, the same variable also reveals a positive relationship with the very different measure of mechanization in agencies, namely, automation. This relationship has not been previously reported, because it is only evident when population size is controlled, and the convention adopted in Chapter 6 was not to control state's population because of the multicollinearity produced by its high correlation with agency size. But ignoring this convention for a moment to direct attention to a suggestive parallel, we find that the standardized regression coefficient of state government employees per population and automation, controlling state's population, is .20, which is virtually identical with that shown in Table 8–5 for the same independent variable and electric typewriters (.22). The relative size of the state government, whether because it manifests a readiness to invest in government services or for some other reason, seems to further the acquisition of advanced technological equipment of such diverse sorts as computers and electric typewriters.

The external environment does not exert much influence on the internal differentiation in roof organizations or on that in its component branches, and what little influence has been observed is quite similar for both organizational units. The lack of evidence of substantial effects of community conditions on the division of labor, levels, and sections in local offices confirms the inference derived from parallel findings in agencies that the internal structure is apparently somewhat protected, and perhaps overprotected, by its boundaries from environmental stimuli. But structural differentiation is not completely insulated from environmental influences. Urbanization in the state intensifies the division of labor in the agency (Table 6–3), and urbanization (population density) in the city intensifies that of the local office indirectly through its influence on office size, though it has a slight negative direct effect (Table 8–4). Urbanization in the state also promotes the development of multilevel hierarchies and many divisions at the agency headquarters (Tables 6–4 and 6–5). The fact that a city has more than 25,000 inhabitants exerts a slight influence on multiple levels in offices, and it as well as population density exerts some influence on the number of sections. The influences are small, and they are not exactly parallel except for those of urbanization on horizontal differentiation (divisions or sections). Yet, by and large, local offices adjust to a complex urban environment with its diversified demands by developing a more differentiated structure, just as state agencies do.

Labor market conditions in the local community and the entire state exert similar influences. Local offices in big cities with a high proportion of persons of foreign stock employ more clerks than those in other places, and the main reason is that the proportion of foreign stock seems to increase the labor supply of clerks and thus exerts a pronounced influence on the clerical ratio, with the size of the community exerting only a small additional influence on it (Table 8–6). These community differences are mirrored in corresponding ones among states. The proportion of foreign stock in the state raises the clerical ratio in the agency, and in this case the relationship between urbanization and clerical ratio is no longer evident when other conditions are controlled (Table 6–6).

The effects of urbanization on the supervisory ratio at the agency headquarters and in local offices are also somewhat parallel. The urbanization in the community reduces the supervisory ratio in the employment security office indirectly through its influence on office size and slightly raises it directly (Table 8–7, reversing signs). The relationship between state's urbanization and supervisory ratio at the agency headquarters is insignificantly small and has for this reason not been reported in Chapter 6, but it reveals a corresponding pattern, with a negative zero-order correlation ($-.20$) and a positive standardized regression coefficient when size (in logarithmic transformation) is controlled (.10). Although this relationship is insignificantly small given the small number of cases of agencies, the two coefficients are of about the same magnitude as the corresponding ones for local offices.[19] The complex demands of an urban environment slightly raise the supervisory ratio, but the larger size of organizations or their branches in

19. To permit exact comparison: the community's population density and the supervisory ratio in local offices exhibit a zero-order correlation of $-.21$ and a standardized regression coefficient, controlling only office size (in logarithmic transformation), of .07.

urban environments overrides this effect by reducing the supervisory ratio.

In sum, the influences exerted by the state environment on employment security agencies and those exerted by the local environment on their branch offices reveal gratifyingly many parallels, though there are some differences too. Thus, the population concentration in a community exerts some independent influence on the size of local offices, their division of labor, and their clerical ratios, whereas the state's urbanization has no corresponding direct effect on the entire agency. The only other major differences, aside from the greater influence of population size on agency size than on office size, are that the proportion of foreign stock influences agency size slightly and that education in the state influences the supervisory ratio at the agency headquarters slightly, whereas no similar influences are observable in local offices. On the other hand, both agency size and office size are larger in highly urbanized environments with large and ethnically heterogeneous populations. A relatively large state government furthers the introduction of modern mechanical equipment in agencies as well as in local offices. The core structure at the agency headquarters and that in local offices both are little affected by external conditions and both become somewhat more differentiated in urbanized environments. The clerical ratio in branches depends on the proportion of foreign stock in the local labor markets, just as that in the entire organization depends on the corresponding proportion in the state-wide labor market, and the supervisory ratio at the headquarters and in the branches is affected in parallel ways by urbanization.

CHAPTER 9

Personnel Qualifications

This chapter presents an analysis of the relationship between skill level and organizational features in employment security agencies, with special emphasis on the conditions that have bearing on the qualifications of the interviewers in local offices, who are directly responsible for administering services to clients. The major variable is the amount of college education of interviewers. This measure does not indicate specialized professional training; the specialized skills required for the various interviewing jobs are provided by in-service training. However, a college degree is generally considered a good background for the job, though most agencies accept experience in related fields as a substitute for completion of college. In the average agency, about one half of the interviewers have college degrees.

Inasmuch as the work of interviewers is carried out in local offices, it is of interest to relate their qualifications to differences among local offices as well as those among agencies. Unfortunately, our research design did not make it possible to collect data on the education of the interviewers in all local offices. But less than one year before the date of our survey, data collection was completed for a special study of interviewers carried out by the Bureau of Employment Security (BES) in cooperation with the Division of State Merit Systems (DSMS) of the Department of Health, Education and Welfare (BES-DSMS study), who kindly put their data at our disposal.[1] After their information had been satisfactorily matched with ours, the average education of interviewers in a local office was available for less than one half of the offices under consideration. It is supplemented by the proportion of clerks as a second index of skill level in the office, which we have for all offices. The use of these two different measures makes it possible to examine the relationship between highly skilled and routine jobs in an office as well as to ascertain whether these two indicators—one referring to personnel training and the other to job complexity—have similar or different implications for the office structure.

The conditions that give rise to the bifurcation of skills to which reference was made in Chapter 8 are one of the topics treated in this chapter. Another topic is the question of what factors contribute to a government bureau's ability to attract and retain personnel with superior qualifications and consequently with good opportunities to obtain jobs elsewhere. A final problem to be analyzed is how the skill level in an office affects its authority structure. First, however, it is necessary to describe briefly the procedure for deriving the measure of education of interviewers in offices.

Bifurcation of Skills

The interviewer represents the basic professional position responsible for administering services to clients in employment security agencies, comparable to the role of the physician in a hospital, albeit without the specialized technical training of the latter. Roughly one third of the employees in local offices are interviewers. Inasmuch as every agency classifies its jobs in its own way, which positions should be included in the category of interviewers is not self-evident. Before the BES-DSMS study of interviewers could be undertaken, an extensive investigation of the duties of various jobs was carried out to determine comparable criteria for identifying the position of "interviewer." Of the eight categories decided upon, the three largest, which comprise nearly three quarters of all interviewers, are placement interviewer, who furnishes services to job applicants, and claims taker and claims examiner, who administer services and check the eligibility of claimants of unemployment insurance. The most educated group are the specialized employment counselors (one of the smaller categories). About three fifths of the interviewers are engaged in employment services

---

1. We are grateful to Albert Aronson, Director, and Lorraine Eyde, Research Psychologist, Division of State Merit Systems, Department of Health, Education and Welfare, and to Robert Droege at the Bureau of Employment Security, for making these data available to us and discussing the research with us.

and two fifths in unemployment insurance services. Virtually all interviewers work in local offices, except in a few small agencies where, owing to the lack of a sufficient number of specialized occupational positions, a small number of employees classified as interviewers are used for duties at the headquarters.

Though forty-eight jurisdictions participated in this initial phase of the research, only thirty-one states cooperated with the final BES-DSMS study from which our data on interviewers' education are derived. (The study as well as its preliminary phase is described in Appendix B.) Of the total number of 4,939 respondents, who constitute 73 per cent of all those defined as interviewers, we were able to match 3,889 with 728 local offices, but 170 of these local offices are among the simple ones excluded from the analysis. Hence, data on the education of interviewers are available for 558 of the 1,201 offices under investigation. The measure is the mean number of years of education of all interviewers in an office, and the mean number of interviewers on which it is based is six. In the smallest offices, the measure may refer to the education of only one interviewer (10 per cent) or only two (12 per cent).

The 558 offices with data on interviewers' education are clearly not a representative sample of all 1,201 employment security offices that meet minimum criteria of size and complexity, because all states did not participate in the BES–DSMS study, all interviewers in the participating states are not included, and all those included could not be matched with their local office. To check how much bias is introduced by this attrition in several stages, the means of the major characteristics of the 558 and of all 1,201 offices are compared. There is surprisingly little difference. The subgroup mean departs from the total mean by less than one tenth of a standard deviation with respect to size (number of employees), division of labor (number of positions), electric typewriters, number of levels, number of sections, and span of control of office manager. The main difference is that the subgroup of offices contains fewer specialized ones than the total (the mean score of degree of specialization is .42, whereas it is .70 for the total), largely because it includes only one youth opportunity center. The three other differences are within two tenths of a standard deviation: the mean of the subgroup is larger for the per cent clerks (22.8 vs. 20.3), smaller for the per cent supervisors (19.8 vs. 21.0), and larger for the span of control of first-line supervisors (5.6 vs. 5.0).

The average amount of education of interviewers is two years of college, with claims takers averaging only one year and specialized counselors more than three years of college education. To put it another way, the agency mean for proportion of interviewers with college degrees is 54 per cent. More than one half of the interviewers are men. One third of the placement interviewers and about one quarter in most other categories have been with the agency fewer than three years. On the other hand, between one fifth and one third of the interviewers in various categories have more than sixteen years of seniority. The average age is forty-four years. The interviewers in General LO's, ES LO's and UI LO's hardly differ in their average education, but those in Specialized ES LO's have typically one more year of college education than the rest.

Local offices with an intermediate degree of division of labor have interviewers with better educational qualifications than either those with little or those with much occupational differentiation. This curvilinear relationship implies that an office cannot take advantage of personnel with superior qualifications without a modicum of occupational specialization, but that its need for highly qualified personnel is reduced if great fragmentation of positions routinizes the duties of many. (Among small local offices with fewer than twenty employees, the education of interviewers averages two or more years of college in 46 per cent of the thirty-seven cases with five to seven occupational positions, but in none of the ten with fewer and in only 37 per cent of the nineteen with more positions. In larger offices with twenty or more employees, similarly, occupational differentiation first raises the likelihood of a high average education of interviewers from 50 per cent [eight cases] to 62 per cent [sixty] and then drops it again to 52 per cent [163].) Both insufficient and excessive division of labor are associated with lower qualifications of the personnel.

Local offices vary not only in the division of labor but also in the bifurcation of skills, by which is meant that offices who employ more highly skilled personnel also employ more unskilled personnel than others. This tendency was mentioned in Chapter 8, but contingency tables reveal that it is confined to those offices that employ clerks extensively and utilize them as production personnel, specifically, unemployment insurance offices. Among UI LO's, the thirty-nine above the median with respect to educational level of their interviewers are much more likely to employ many clerks (74 per cent) than the thirty-eight with less educated interviewers (42 per cent). In the other types of local offices, there is no similar positive relationship between qualifications of interviewers and clerical ratio.[2]

---

2. The proportions with a high clerical ratio among offices with more and less well-educated interviewers, respectively, are 34 per cent (of 202) and 37 per cent (181) for General LO's; 35 per cent (17) and 40 per cent (20) for ES LO's; 40 per cent (42) and 42 per cent (12) for Specialized ES LO's. The same differences are evident in covariance analysis: with size and division of labor controlled, the partial correlation between interviewers' education and clerical ratio is .18 in UI LO's but .02 or less in the other types.

Although clerks are extensively used in production functions at the head-quarters too, there are no interviewers there, and although there are interviewers in other types of offices, clerks there are used in smaller numbers, mostly for administrative support. Because the bifurcation of skills probably affects variations in personnel among the subunits of an agency but differences within units only in UI LO's, there is a modest correlation for the entire agency between qualifications of interviewers and clerical ratio.[3]

The bifurcation of skills implies that organizations staffed by professionals with high qualifications are more likely than others to utilize a large proportion of clerks. The employment of many skilled experts in some positions depends on the large-scale employment of unskilled clerks in others, which in turn requires that clerks be used in basic operations and not merely in administrative support for these operations. The savings in salary costs achieved by the extensive utilization of clerical personnel, made possible by assigning the routine tasks in the organization to clerks instead of assigning them as part-time work to skilled personnel, frees budgetary resources that enable the organization to attract better qualified personnel to perform the more difficult duties. The nexus is akin to one we have encountered before: the savings in managerial manpower made possible by large size enable agencies and their local offices to afford the extra managerial manpower needed to cope with the problems of coordination and communication in large and differentiated structures. The conjecture that the employment of interviewers with superior qualifications for the more complex jobs exerts constraints to achieve savings in the performance of the more routine duties receives some support from the interaction effect of interviewers' education and the existence of modern office equipment on the clerical ratio.

Whether modern office machines designed to improve the efficiency of clerical work actually reduce the clerical manpower in a local office depends on the qualifications of its interviewers. Electric typewriters can raise the efficiency of typists, and their presence is probably indicative of that of other modern office equipment, which too can raise clerical efficiency. But modern office machines are also a convenience and a status symbol, which office managers may seek to acquire even when the volume

---

3. The proportion of interviewers with college degrees in the agency, treated as a contextual variable, has been shown by Table 8–6 to be positively related to the clerical ratio in local offices ($r = .30$; $b^* = .12$). For entire agencies, the correlation between the two variables is less ($.20$), and it is further reduced when automation, division of labor, and size are controlled ($b^* = .11$), which is why it was not used in the regression problem in Table 4–3.

of clerical work does not require it. In employment offices, moreover, electric typewriters might be used solely or primarily to test the typing aptitudes of applicants without exploiting their potential for improving the efficiency of the office's own work. Table 9–1 shows that the availability

TABLE 9-1. **Per Cent of Local Offices with a High Clerical Ratio,** *as Affected by Education of Interviewers and Electric Typewriters*

| | Mean Education of Interviewers | |
	Less than Two Years	**Two Years or More**
Electric Typewriters		
None	42	54
	(164)	(149)
One or More	32	25
	(112)	(132)

of electric typewriters reduces the prevalence of a high proportion of clerks substantially in those offices that employ better qualified interviewers but not appreciably in those that have less qualified interviewers.[4] Just as the use of a computer in an agency lessens the need for clerical personnel (Table 4–3), so does the use of modern office machines in local branches, though in this case only if the interviewing staff is highly educated.[5]

To employ a complement of interviewers with superior education, adequate salaries must be offered, which creates pressures to effect savings in other personnel by using modern office equipment to best advantage,

4. In a covariance design with size and the division of labor controlled, the partial correlation between prevalence of electric typewriters and clerical ratio is −.15 for offices with highly educated and −.04 for those with less well-educated interviewers. The same result is obtained by still another procedure: if the product term, interviewers' education times electric typewriters, is introduced into the multiple regression of clerical ratio on these two variables and division of labor, size, and ES function, the product term has a negative regression coefficient that exceeds twice its standard error. Finally, cross-tabulations within the four types of local offices (there are no educational data on the fifth, YOC's) reveal the same pattern as in Table 9–1 in three types—all but UI LO's.

5. A decline in the clerical ratio resulting from improved technology is assumed to reflect a reduction in the total size of the personnel, whereas differences in the clerical ratio associated with other conditions, such as office function, division of labor, or education of interviewers, are assumed to reflect primarily shifts in the composition of the personnel complement.

whereas offices that get along with less educated interviewers do not experience this pressure. The inverse relationship between the availability of electric typewriters and the clerical ratio in offices with highly educated, but not in those with less well-educated, interviewers reflects this difference. The same pressure leads to the more extensive use of clerks in local offices if their function permits it, as manifest in the positive relationship between education of interviewers and clerical ratio in UI LO's. The general principle is that the bifurcation of skills helps organizations to employ highly trained personnel for the performance of their most difficult responsibilities by utilizing personnel more efficiently in the performance of routine duties. Such efficiency can be attained by relieving professionals of routine work and assigning it to clerks and by utilizing modern technology to lower the manpower requirements of routine work.

Retention of Qualified Personnel

Turnover is a perennial problem in government bureaus, and not in them alone. The loss of the most qualified personnel through turnover is a particularly serious problem. The annual rate of separation for all employees, averaged over a three-year period for all agencies, is 27 per cent. The range among the different agencies is from 10 to 69 per cent. Of the interviewers appointed in the entire country during the fiscal year preceding our survey, 13 per cent were separated in that year. Because the latter figure refers to separations *within* the year of appointment, it should be doubled, or nearly so, to translate it into an annual separation rate, which indicates that turnover among interviewers is about the same as that among other employees. Most of these separations are resignations; only 10 per cent are involuntary, resulting from the termination of the appointment by the agency during the probation period. Interviewers with superior qualifications are more likely to leave the agency within a short time after their appointment than others. The rate of separations within the year of appointment is 15 per cent for interviewers with a college degree and 9 per cent for those without one.[6]

The tendency of the employees with the best qualifications to resign from their jobs with government agencies in disproportionate numbers is a problem of great concern. There has been much discussion of whether state government salaries are to blame, which often are not competitive

---

6. *Analysis of Appointments, Separations, Promotions: Public Assistance Workers and Employment Security Interviewers* (Washington, D.C.: Department of Health, Education and Welfare, Division of State Merit Systems, 1966), Table 7, p. 23.

with federal wages or those in private industry, or whether other conditions in government bureaus are the cause, perhaps bureaucratic restrictions that stifle initiative, or civil service requirements that prevent rapid advancement, or conversely nonmerit appointments that discourage those relying on their superior qualifications. But it should be pointed out that the mere fact that employees with the highest education are most likely to leave these agencies does not necessarily prove that employment or working conditions in them are particularly bad. The better a man's training and qualifications, the greater his opportunities in the labor market are, barring discrimination against him. Hence, employees with superior skills and abilities are most likely to continue to find better jobs than their present one, almost regardless of what their present job is, unless, of course, they obtained it through connections or by accident and it is much better than what their qualifications warrant. The best educated and best qualified persons may well be generally most likely to move from job to job and from place to place.[7] Discrimination on ethnic or other irrelevant grounds interferes with the superior opportunities of the most able, and government bureaus operating under civil service benefit from this by having more than their share of highly skilled employees of minority groups who are discriminated against by private employers.

Saying that the most promising employees are most likely to quit other jobs as well as those in employment security agencies, however, is not saying that their doing so is no reason for concern in these agencies. The disproportionately high resignation rates of the most qualified employees generates a process of negative selection, which skims the cream off the top and leaves in the organization those employees who are unable to find jobs elsewhere.[8] This process of negative selection affects all employers whose employees are protected against arbitrary dismissal, as are civil servants, workers with strong unions, faculty members, and informally also the managers and other white-collar employees in many large companies. An essential requirement for maintaining a complement of highly skilled em-

7. For example, John F. Marsh presents positive correlations between education and changes in jobs among engineers in engineering and scientific fields; "The Engineers and the Price System," Ph.D. dissertation, University of Chicago, 1967.

8. Disproportionately high resignation rates characterize not only the most educated interviewers but also those with the highest scores on their entrance examinations and those with the highest scores on an extensive series of job knowledge tests administered in the course of the BES-DSMS study. Ironically, the interviewers who know most about their job in employment security are more likely to quit this job than those who know little about it.

ployees is to stem this negative selection resulting from the superior alternative opportunities of those whose skills are in greatest demand. To do so, conditions must be created in the organization that are attractive to the highly qualified employees who can find jobs elsewhere and that discourage them from actually leaving for other jobs. Let us examine what conditions in employment security agencies and their local offices help them to attract and to retain large numbers of highly educated interviewers.

The proportion of interviewers with college degrees in the entire agency is affected by entrance requirements, salaries, and adherence to civil service standards in making appointments. Stricter educational requirements for the position of interviewer are positively correlated with the actual educational attainments of its incumbents, as one would expect, but the correlation is unexpectedly low (.31), with requirements accounting for only 10 per cent of the variation in actual qualifications. Setting high requirements can only raise the floor of minimum training but not bring men and women with superior training into the agency. For college graduates to be attracted to jobs in employment security, salaries must be high enough to compete with those elsewhere, which is manifest in a zero-order correlation of .29 between interviewers' salary and the per cent B.A.'s among them. Firm adherence to civil service standards in making appointments also raises the educational level of the interviewers in the agency ($r = .26$). This finding belies the frequently heard accusation that the rigidity of the civil service system impedes optimum personnel selection. What lowers the educational qualifications of the personnel is, on the contrary, the recurrent departure from civil service requirements permitted or even necessitated by a weak civil service system with inadequate provisions to fill all positions with permanent appointments. The prevalence of temporary and provisional appointments, which can later often be converted into permanent ones, does not raise the qualifications of the personnel, despite the freedom from normal civil service restrictions, but lowers them. These three positive relationships persist in the multiple regression analysis with all three conditions as independent variables and per cent interviewers with college degrees as the dependent one (b*, for requirements, .25; for salary, .26; for civil service appointments, .20).[9]

These three differences in employment conditions among agencies probably affect primarily the chances that college graduates start to work as employment security interviewers, though they perhaps also influence the

---

9. All three regression coefficients are between one-and-a-half times and twice their standard error. The multiple correlation is .45.

chances that they remain in their jobs rather than leave them quickly for others. Low salaries may prompt college graduates to quit their jobs as interviewers as soon as they can find better ones, and so may the prevalence of colleagues with much lower educational attainments than their own resulting from low requirements and frequent deviations from merit standards of civil service in making appointments. But the retention of highly qualified interviewers is undoubtedly affected at least as much by differences in their particular working conditions as by these differences in employment conditions. Given the higher separation rates of the most educated interviewers, factors that influence their retention assume special significance. To infer what conditions influence the retention of the best educated interviewers, data are presented in Table 9–2 on the characteris-

TABLE 9-2. *Multiple Regression of* **Local Office Education of Interviewers** *on Antecedent Conditions*[a]

Independent Variable	Standardized Regression Coefficient	Zero-Order Correlation
Community Environment		
Population Density	.19**	.24
Median Education	.01	.07
Agency Context		
Salary of Interviewers	.02	.20
Placements per Opening	−.13*	−.21
Employee-Client Ratio in Benefit Function	−.22**	−.25
Local Office		
Specialization	.05	.19
Size	−.12	.23
Sections	.20**	.26

Multiple R = .41; n = 558

*Greater than twice its standard error.

**Greater than three times its standard error.

[a]The matrix of zero-order correlations between the independent variables in this table is presented at the end of Appendix B.

tics of local offices and of their agency contexts that are related to the educational level of interviewers.[10]

Table 9–2 shows that the characteristic of local offices most closely related to the educational level of its interviewers is its differentiation into a

10. The matrix of zero-order correlations for the independent variables in Table 9–2 is presented at the end of Appendix B.

fair number of functional sections instead of just a few. Interviewers in specialized local offices also are better educated than those in general offices ($r = .19$), but this difference essentially results from the greater number of specialized offices in metropolitan centers of population concentration (.10) and the greater subdivision of specialized offices into sections (.07); when these two conditions are controlled the education of interviewers in specialized offices is no longer superior to that in general ones. Similarly, the positive zero-order correlation between office size and educational level (.23) is entirely accounted for by the larger size of offices in densely populated cities (.09) and the greater number of sections in large offices (.13). Size as such, independent of other conditions, does not have a positive effect on the educational level of interviewers but, if anything, a slightly negative one ($b^* = -.12$). In other words, educational qualifications in specialized and in large offices are higher than in others only because the former are located in urban centers and because they are subdivided into more sections.

Why does differentiation into functional sections raise the educational level of interviewers? The larger the number of functional sections in an office, with a narrower range of responsibilities in each section, the greater probably is the likelihood that the assignments of interviewers too are narrower and more specialized. Specialized duties may well require better qualified personnel than general ones. But the findings also imply that offices in which the functional differentiation of sections results in specialized assignments are more successful than others in retaining their most qualified interviewers, which invites the conjecture that highly educated employees prefer specialized tasks to diverse duties. One might also speculate whether the congenial colleagues in the more homogeneous work groups in offices with numerous sections make the job more attractive and for this reason help retain educated interviewers.

Let us now turn to the influence on interviewer qualifications of the community environment. Table 9–2 shows that offices in urbanized centers have better educated interviewers than those in less densely populated towns, but that the educational level of the city's population is unrelated to that of the employment security interviewers. It has been previously noted that many highly educated people are most likely to be found in places where there are outstanding employment opportunities for persons with higher education. An obvious example is a college town. If the demand for the services of men and women with superior education keeps abreast of the supply of them, many educated people in a community do not make it any easier for the employment security office to attract and retain highly educated interviewers. The supply of, and demand for, employees with college education appear to be less well balanced in metropolitan centers than elsewhere. The educational attainments in big cities with concentrated populations are superior to those in more sparsely populated smaller places, and though employment opportunities for persons with higher education are also superior in big cities, there may be an excessive supply of educated labor in the most urbanized communities that enables employment security offices there to hire and keep better educated interviewers than can offices elsewhere. Even if the total supply of educated labor does not especially exceed the demand for it in metropolitan centers, moreover, these places are likely to contain proportionately large numbers of educated blacks and members of other minorities who are discriminated against by private employers, and this too improves the opportunity of government offices to maintain a complement of highly educated employees.

The condition with the most pronounced relationship to the educational qualifications of interviewers in local offices is a low employee-client ratio in the agency's benefit function, as Table 9–2 shows. It is tempting to interpret this finding as indicating that the superior qualifications of the core personnel in local offices improve the efficiency of benefit operations, and possibly of other operations as well. Another finding makes this interpretation questionable, however: the educational qualifications of interviewers are inversely related to the placement productivity in the agency.[11] Paradoxically, therefore, the qualifications of interviewers improve the efficiency of unemployment benefit operations but impede the effectiveness of employment services, on the assumption that these two measures are equally unambiguous indications of the effectiveness of services in the two functions. The paradox can be resolved by analyzing this assumption.

Inasmuch as unemployment benefit operations are primarily an administrative task and variations in the quality of services are relatively minor, efficiency is a major objective, and the employee-client ratio is a fair measure of an important aspect of it. The situation is quite different with respect to employment services, which is primarily a professional rather than administrative task, and in which productive efficiency is by no means an unequivocal objective. Whether to maximize the sheer number of placements or to provide more intensive professional employment services instead is a much disputed issue, and the most professionally oriented interviewers tend to line up on the side of quality in opposition to quantity. An emphasis on placement quantity in the agency may also reflect a

---

11. For the 53 agencies, per cent of interviewers with college degrees exhibits lower correlations with the employee-client ratio in the benefit function $(-.08)$ and with placements per opening $(-.06)$ than those for local offices shown in Table 9–2. The reason probably is that large agencies contribute disproportionately to the relationships in the table.

predominant concern with the needs of employers, who tend to demand quick referrals of large numbers of unskilled applicants from the public employment agency, whereas an emphasis on the quality of placements may manifest a stronger interest in the needs of job applicants. Whether a public employment agency indeed best fulfills its obligation to the most underprivileged segment of the population by providing intensive services to limited numbers rather than by concentrating on finding some work for large numbers is a moot question, which need not be answered here. Suffice it to say that the more educated and professionally oriented employment interviewers typically express a preference for placement service of superior quality and depreciate endeavors to maximize the sheer number of placements. Given this orientation, the prevalence of highly educated employment interviewers may depress placement quantity, for these interviewers are most concerned with quality, whereas the prevalence of highly educated unemployment interviewers, for whom there is no similar conflict between quantity and quality, improves operating efficiency. It is possible, however, that the causal nexus is the reverse.

The retention of the interviewers with the best educational qualifications, who have the greatest opportunities for getting jobs elsewhere, requires that working conditions are satisfactory for them. If they feel that administrative inefficiency wastes their skills, they will not experience much work satisfaction, and neither will they if they are under administrative pressure to perform tasks in ways that violate their principles of how the work should be performed. The expeditious and efficient conduct of unemployment insurance operations, which is a relatively undisputed *desideratum,* creates working conditions that are appreciated by educated persons trained to disapprove of waste and inefficiency. But pressure to maximize placement quantity is not considered a sign of efficiency by educated interviewers, who typically think of themselves as professionals responsible for furnishing more intensive placement service of superior quality to applicants. Hence, such pressure is probably resented and lowers work satisfaction. The efficiency of management, on the one hand, and its respect for the professional interests of interviewers and its refusal to sacrifice them for the sake of efficiency, on the other, create working conditions that may help retain the most educated personnel in employment security offices. But this combination of a strong concern with efficiency in unemployment insurance operations and a willingness to disregard it in employment services is not typical.[12]

---

12. There is a slight negative correlation between employee-client ratio in benefit function and placements per opening for the fifty-three agencies ($-.16$), which suggests that the two factors are more or less independent of each other.

The positive correlation between interviewers' salaries and their educational qualifications (.20) is reduced to close to nil when other conditions are controlled, as Table 9–2 shows, and decomposition reveals that the employee-client ratio (.08) and placements per opening (.07) are largely responsible. The interpretation of this result depends on the causal assumption accepted for the relationships of interviewers' education with the two service measures. If one assumes that highly educated interviewers improve the efficiency of benefit operations but reduce the quantity of placements in favor of high quality, the two service measures are dependent, not intervening, variables, and their role as mediating influences should be disregarded. Following this assumption, the conclusion is that higher salaries directly attract better educated interviewers. But the data on salaries have another implication if one accepts the last interpretation that expeditious unemployment insurance operations and lack of pressure to make many placements in employment operations create advantageous working conditions that help retain the most qualified interviewers. In this case the two measures are intervening variables. Hence, the data imply that high salaries reflect a general concern of management with making employment and working conditions attractive for interviewers, and the generally more satisfying working conditions in agencies that pay higher salaries are what keep highly qualified interviewers from quitting their jobs at the same high rates as they do in other agencies.

Skill Level and Authority Structure

In a study of government bureaus of another type, one of the authors of this book concludes that superior skills of the personnel increase the number of levels and narrow the span of control of first-line supervisors in the organization.[13] Research based on the same data by Meyer shows that it is within the divisions of these bureaus that the skills of the personnel and the span of control of first-line supervisors are inversely related.[14] The data from employment security offices require some revision of this conclusion, though they support it in part. The measure of skill level in the earlier research is average education of the personnel. In the present analysis, two expressions of differences in skill levels among employment security offices are used. The first, which is highly similar to the earlier measure, is the mean education of interviewers, who are the employees with primary responsibility for serving clients. The second is the clerical ratio

13. Peter M. Blau, "The Hierarchy of Authority in Organizations," *American Journal of Sociology*, 73 (1968): 461–463.
14. Marshall W. Meyer, "Expertness and the Span of Control," *American Sociological Review*, 33 (1968): 948–949.

in an office. These two indications of differences in skills jointly affect hierarchical differentiation into levels, and either interacts with differentiation in influencing the span of control of first-line supervisors.

The education of interviewers in an employment security office exhibits only a weak positive correlation with the number of levels in the hierarchy (.14), and the clerical ratio is not at all associated with the number of levels (−.02). But Table 9–3 indicates that the two manifestations of the

TABLE 9-3. **Per Cent of Local Offices with Many Levels**[a], *as Affected by Education of Interviewers and the Clerical Ratio*

| Clerical Ratio | Mean Education of Interviewers | |
	Less than Two Years	**Two Years or More**
0-.22	35	31
	(171)	(167)
.23-.73	12	26
	(105)	(115)

[a]Residual from its regression line on size.

skills in a local office together affect hierarchical differentiation.[15] Specifically, if a large proportion of clerks combines with a low level of education of interviewers to depress the available skills in an office, a multilevel hierarchy is less likely to develop than if the office has either fewer clerks or better educated interviewers or both. Variations among types of offices do not account for this interaction effect.[16] Superior qualifications of an office's personnel, with either few untrained clerks or a highly educated interviewing staff, make the performance of tasks more reliable and thus the top manager less reluctant to become removed by intervening levels from the operating level, just as the automation of operations does at the agency headquarters.

15. The disproportionate number of offices with negative values for the residuals of number of levels from its regression line on size indicates that size has not been effectively controlled. But size does not distort these findings, as their replication when different procedures are used will show.
16. Although the clerical ratio is highest in UI LO's and only there related to the education of interviewers, there are no differences between UI LO's and all types in mean years of college of interviewers (1.9 vs. 1.9), or mean number of levels (3.32 vs. 3.26), and there is little difference in mean size (28.4 vs. 26.7). Neither is there an appreciable relationship between interviewers' education and levels in any of the types.

The data in Table 9–3 also imply that the bifurcation of skills discussed earlier in this chapter is contingent on a multilevel hierarchy and does not occur in simple structures. The percentages must be computed a different way to make this apparent. Among offices with many levels relative to their size, those with better educated interviewers are more likely to have a high clerical ratio (37 per cent) than those with less well-educated interviewers (18 per cent), but among offices with few levels, there is no corresponding difference (46 and 42 per cent). Hierarchical differentiation in the office structure appears to promote the bifurcation of skills.

The two indicators of the skills involved in the duties of a local office do not have the same direct effects on the mean span of control of first-line supervisors, but they combine with differentiation in parallel ways to have the same interaction effects on this span of control. Though a small proportion of clerks narrows the supervisory span of control, as we have seen (Table 8–7), superior educational qualifications of interviewers do not. As a matter of fact, there is a weak positive zero-order correlation between interviewers' average education and supervisors' average span of control in a local office (.10). However, the two expressions of superior skills in an office—*few* clerks and *high* education of interviewers—exert similar conditional influences on the number of subordinates per first-line supervisor. That is, either variable conditions the influences of two separate aspects of differentiation on the supervisory span of control as the other does, producing parallel interaction effects, except that the clerical ratio has somewhat more impact than the education of interviewers. Hence, the analysis presents the data on clerical ratio in full, with those on interviewers' education being relegated to footnotes. The interaction effects are complex and require detailed discussion.

Hierarchical differentiation into multiple levels, which makes extra demands on the time of supervisors, narrows their span of control more in offices with many clerks than in those with a low clerical ratio, as Table 9–4 indicates.[17] Looking at the data the other way, an increase in the proportion of clerks widens the span of control of supervisors in offices with few hierarchical levels but hardly at all in those with multilevel hierarchies.[18] The savings in supervision time that more routine duties make possi-

---

17. Similarly, an increase in levels reduces the likelihood of a wide span of control of supervisors only from 53 to 41 per cent in offices with highly educated interviewers but from 58 to 37 per cent in those with poorly educated interviewers (which corresponds to a high clerical ratio). The case base of the four percentages, in order, is 201, 81, 203, and 73.

18. There are some variations in detail among types, though most of the pattern is observable in four of the five types, all but YOC's.

TABLE 9-4.   **Per Cent of Local Offices with a High Mean Span of Control of First-Line Supervisors**[a], *as Affected by Levels and the Clerical Ratio*

Clerical Ratio	Hierarchical Levels[b]				Difference
	Few		Many		
0-.22	44		31		−13
		(574)		(254)	
.23-.73	60		37		−23
		(294)		(79)	
Difference	+16		+6		

[a]Residual from its regression on the logarithm of size.
[b]Residual from its regression line on size.

TABLE 9-5.   **Per Cent of Local Offices with a High Mean Span of Control of First-Line Supervisors**[a], *as Affected by Division of Labor and the Clerical Ratio*

Clerical Ratio	Division of Labor[a]				Difference
	Low		High		
0-.22	47		31		−16
		(459)		(369)	
.23-.73	54		56		+2
		(163)		(210)	
Difference	+7		+25		

[a]Residual from its regression line on the logarithm of size.

ble are largely absorbed by the extra supervisory time required for coordination and communication in offices with differentiated hierarchies. For a wide mean span of control of first-line supervisors to prevail in local offices, it is necessary not only that many jobs are simple but that the hierarchical structure is simple too lest problems of coordination in a differentiated structure take up much of the time of supervisors.

The case of occupational differentiation is quite different, as Table 9–5 shows, though there are some underlying similarities. A pronounced division of labor narrows the span of control of first-line supervisors in offices with a small proportion of clerical jobs but not in those in which much work is routine enough to be performed by clerks.[19] Reading Table 9–5 in the other direction, an expansion of clerical jobs raises the chances of a wide supervisory span of control little if the division of labor is rudimentary but substantially if it is advanced. When there is much routine work performed by clerks, the mean span of control of supervisors is wide in the majority of offices regardless of the division of labor. When there is little routine work, however, the heterogeneity among jobs created by the division of labor lessens the likelihood that the supervisory span of control is wide. Either many routine jobs or little diversity among jobs suffices to make it fairly likely that supervisors have a wide span of control, and it is the combination of few routine jobs and much differentiation among jobs in an office that makes it unlikely that its first-line supervisors have a wide span of control. The data suggest that it is possible for a man to supervise a considerable number of subordinates with different duties, provided that they are quite routine, and also a considerable number of subordinates with difficult duties, provided that they are alike. But he cannot supervise so many if their jobs are both complex and diverse.

Much hierarchical as well as little occupational differentiation attenuates the influence of the proportion of routine clerical jobs on the span of control of supervisors. The reason for the attenuating influence of much hierarchical differentiation is that the supervisory span is *rarely* wide in offices with multiple levels whatever their clerical ratio, whereas the reason for attenuating influence of little occupational differentiation is that the supervisory span is *often* wide in offices with a low division of labor regardless of their clerical ratio. A basic similarity between Tables 9–4 and 9–5 is that the local offices with the narrowest average span of supervisory control are those with little clerical work and much differentiation, whether hierarchical or occupational differentiation is considered. It so happens that the proportion of offices meeting these two conditions that have a wide mean span of control is in both instances exactly 31 per cent. What enlarges this proportion is not the same in the two tables, however. An increase in the amount of clerical work raises the chances of a wide span of control in offices with marked hierarchical differentiation only little (from 31 to 37 per cent) but in offices with marked occupational differ-

---

19. Education of interviewers again reveals the same pattern as clerical ratio in attenuated form. The division of labor reduces the proportion of local offices with a wide span of supervisory control from 56 to 41 per cent if interviewers have superior education but only from 56 to 49 per cent if they do not. The case base of the four percentages, in order, is 156, 126, 114, and 162.

entiation much (from 31 to 56 per cent). The dominant influence of hierarchical differentiation, which makes great demands for coordination and communication on the time of supervisors, largely overrides that of much routine work on the number of subordinates per supervisor. A considerable amount of routine clerical work must combine with little hierarchical differentiation to make it likely that a wide span of supervisory control prevails. Both conditions are necessary for the majority of local offices to have many subordinates per first-line supervisor.

Table 9–5, on occupational differentiation, presents a different picture. Only if extensive occupational differentiation produces few routine clerical positions is the supervisory span of control in the office typically narrow. The majority of offices with substantial proportions of simple jobs clerks can perform have many subordinates per first-line supervisor, whatever their division of labor is, and the proportion of offices with many subordinates per supervisor is not much less if the division of labor is simple though clerical jobs are few. In short, either the homogeneity resulting from little *occupational* differentiation or a considerable amount of clerical work suffices to make it likely that the supervisory span of control in an office is wide, whereas both little *hierarchical* differentiation and considerable clerical work are necessary for this to be likely.

Contingency tables make such specific differences between interaction effects on a dependent variable clearly apparent, whereas these differences are not so readily discernible when product terms in multiple regression analysis are used, at least not to those of us who are not expert statisticians. On the other hand, regression analysis employing product terms supplies knowledge about interaction effects that cannot be obtained from contingency tables. First, it tests the assumption that the interaction effects manifest in cross-tabulations are not merely accidental results of the way variables have been dichotomized. Second, regression analysis makes it possible to control several other conditions influencing the dependent variable and thus to ascertain whether the observed interaction effects are the product of correlated biases, for example, the fact that type of office function is associated with division of labor, clerical ratio, and supervisory span of control. A third question that arises and can be answered by regression procedures is whether the two interaction effects discussed, which have one variable in common, are really two independent joint influences or whether both simply reflect the same underlying forces. Specifically, because the division of labor is known to influence the supervisory span of control primarily indirectly through its influence on differentiation into levels and sections in the office, one may suspect that its combined effect with the clerical ratio on the span of control is no longer evident when the interaction effect of levels and clerical ratio on the span of control is taken into account.[20]

In addition to testing the inferences about interaction effects derived from contingency tables, regression analysis using product terms furnishes important information about the threshold at which the conditioning effect of one independent variable turns the positive influence of another into a negative influence, or vice versa. It also tells us whether there is such a threshold creating a turning point within the range of existing variation. Let us look again at the data in the contingency tables to explicate this principle. Table 9–4 implies that an increase in the clerical ratio raises the likelihood of a wide supervisory span of control more in offices with few levels (a difference of 16 per cent) than in those with many (6 per cent). Assuming the regression analysis to confirm this basic pattern, we can ask whether the effect of the clerical ratio on the supervisory span of control becomes nil, or even negative, in the offices with a large number of levels. If it eventually does become negative, we can further ask what the average number of levels is at which its influence turns from positive to negative. Corresponding questions can be asked about the way the influence of the clerical ratio on the supervisory span of control is modified by the division of labor, and concerning the ways the influence of hierarchical, and that of occupational, differentiation are conditioned by the clerical ratio. To present one more example: Table 9–5 suggests that occupational differentiation reduces the likelihood of a wide span of control of supervisors only if there are few clerks (− 16 per cent) and not if there are many (+ 2 per cent). What is the threshold of routine clerical jobs the expanding division of labor must produce before its negative effect on the supervisory span of control, owing to structural complexity, turns into a positive effect, owing to task routinization?

Table 9–6 presents the results of the multiple regression of mean span of supervisory control on the conditions in local offices previously shown to influence it (Table 7–10) and on the two product terms, levels times clerical ratio, and division of labor times clerical ratio. Either product term has a regression coefficient that is more than three times its standard error when office function and other major influences on the number of subordinates per supervisor are controlled, which confirms the conclusions based on the two contingency tables.[21] Specifically, Table 9–4 implies that the joint effect of both independent variables strengthens the negative ef-

20. The number of sections does not interact with education of interviewers or with clerical ratio in affecting the span of control of supervisors.

21. Covariance analysis also yields parallel results. Offices were divided into three equal categories on the basis of their clerical ratio. With size (log)

TABLE 9-6.   *Multiple Regression of* Mean Span of Control of First-Line Supervisors *on Local Office Antecedent Conditions*

Independent Variable	Standardized Regression Coefficient	Zero-Order Correlation	Metric Regression Coefficient
ES Function	−.11**	−.08	−.5095**
LO Size (Log)	1.34**	.66	12.6807**
Division of Labor	−.22**	.32	−.2526**
Levels	−.37**	.25	−2.2228**
Sections	−.42**	.25	−1.0363**
Clerical Ratio	.28*	.19	6.2126*
Division of Labor X Clerical Ratio	.25**	.31	.6135**
Levels X Clerical Ratio	−.44**	.23	−2.9121**

Multiple R = .81; n = 1,201

 *Greater than twice its standard error.

**Greater than three times its standard error.

fect of levels (−13 vs. −23 per cent) and weakens the positive effect of the clerical ratio (+16 vs. +6 per cent), and the negative sign of the product term, levels times clerical ratio, indicates that this is the case. Similarly, Table 9–5 implies that the joint effect of both independent variables attenuates the negative effect of the division of labor (−16 vs. +2 per cent) and accentuates the positive effect of the clerical ratio (+7 vs. +25 per cent), and the positive sign of the product term, division of labor times clerical ratio, demonstrates that this too is the case.

The joint effect of two variables may reinforce or counteract the effect of either on a dependent variable. If the coefficients of a variable and its product term have the same sign, it indicates reinforcement; if they have opposite signs, it indicates counteraction. Only counteraction can produce a threshold level at which the influence of a factor turns into its opposite. The procedure for determining a threshold has been described in Chapter 7, though the concept of threshold was not used there. In brief, given the opposite sign, the ratio of the metric regression coefficient of a variable to that of its product term with another indicates the threshold in terms of

---

and sections controlled, the partial correlations between number of levels and supervisory span of control decrease as the clerical ratio *declines* from −.51 to −.46 to −.40, whereas the partial correlations of division of labor and supervisors' mean span of control decrease as the clerical ratio *increases* from −.18 to −.17 to an inconsequential −.01 in the offices with the highest clerical ratio. These two patterns correspond quite closely to those in Tables 9–4 and 9–5.

the second variable at which the influence of the first changes direction. The data in Table 9–6 reveal two reinforcing effects and two counteracting effects, one of which reaches a threshold.

The negative influence of a multilevel hierarchy on the supervisory span of control is reinforced if an office has a large proportion of clerks, which suggests that problems of coordination in a differentiated structure are particularly acute and time-consuming for supervisors if many employees have low skills. Although the routine jobs of clerks require less supervision than more difficult jobs, clerks seem to rely more on supervisors for coordination than other employees whose superior skills and wider perspectives may enable them to contribute to coordination by fitting their own work into the framework of the responsibilities of the office. Whereas the negative joint effect of levels and clerical ratio reinforces the negative effect of a multilevel hierarchy itself, it counteracts the positive effect of the clerical ratio itself on the supervisory span of control. As a matter of fact, the result of dividing the metric regression coefficient of proportion of clerks by that of its product term with levels is only 2.1, which literally would mean that the clerical ratio widens the supervisory span of control only in offices with two levels and narrows it in those with three or more. But this result is misleading, because it fails to take into account the fact that the clerical ratio is also represented elsewhere in the regression problem, in combination with the division of labor. The influences of the proportion of clerks on the supervisory span of control represented by two different combinations of variables must be interpreted together.

The positive effect of the proportion of clerks on the number of subordinates per supervisor in an office is reinforced by a pronounced division of labor, as the positive coefficients for both the main effect of the clerical ratio and its interaction effect with division of labor indicate. The cross-classification in Table 9–5 helps explain this finding. If the division of labor is rudimentary and many jobs in an office are alike, supervisors tend to have a wide span of control even when few of the jobs are routine clerical ones. But if a pronounced division of labor creates great diversity among jobs, supervisors cannot be in charge of many subordinates unless their work is quite routine, which strengthens the influence of the clerical ratio on the average supervisory span of control. Now we can interpret the finding mentioned at the end of the last paragraph within the context of the new finding.

A large amount of routine clerical work in an office widens the mean span of control of supervisors, particularly if a large diversity of jobs would otherwise require a narrow span of control. Abstracting from this effect of the routine nature of clerical work on supervision, however, the lesser skills of clerks to integrate their own work with that of others in the office intensifies problems of coordination for supervisors and consequently narrows their span of control in differentiated structures with three or more hierarchical levels, which includes all offices here under investigation, though by no means all employment security offices in the country. In short, a large proportion of clerical employees reduces the supervisory man-hours needed for supervision but raises those needed for coordination.

The division of labor also has conflicting implications for supervision, because it makes the structure more complex in the process of simplifying many jobs. The demands made on supervisors by the problems of coordination that occupational differentiation produces are counteracted by the lesser demands on their time resulting from the enlargement of routine duties occupational differentiation brings about. This is evident in Table 9–6 in the negative main effect of the division of labor and its positive interaction effect with the clerical ratio on the supervisory span of control.[22] The greater the proportion of jobs the division of labor routinizes, the more does its consequent widening effect on the span of control of supervisors counteract its basic narrowing effect, and ultimately the positive effect predominates over the negative one. The threshold at which the narrowing effect of the division of labor turns into a widening effect on the supervisory span of control is obtained by dividing its metric regression coefficient by that of its product term with the clerical ratio; the result is .41. When the division of labor has routinized jobs sufficiently for 41 per cent of them to be filled by clerks, a threshold tends to be reached, and though increasing occupational differentiation up to this point narrows the supervisory span of control, on the average, after this point it widens it. Not many employment security offices have that large a proportion of clerks, but some do.[23] Even before this threshold is reached, of course, the routinization of work the division of labor effects reduces the supervisory manpower that would be otherwise required in the complex structures it generates.

---

22. Though external conditions have not been controlled in Table 9–6, the regression coefficients for division of labor and its product term are too large to make it likely that such controls would make them less than twice their standard error.
23. A clerical ratio of 41 per cent is about one and one-half standard deviations above the mean, which implies that between 6 and 7 per cent of the local offices have that many clerks, about eighty of those analyzed and 150 in the country.

Conclusions

Differentiation takes numerous forms in organizations, and one of them is the bifurcation of skills. The more extensively clerks are used to perform the routine duties in an office, provided there is much routine work, the higher generally are the qualifications of the personnel employed to perform the comparatively complex professional responsibilities. The reason for this tendency toward bipolarization of skills probably is that the savings in the salary budget realized by filling a larger proportion of positions with clerks are needed to offer the higher salaries that attract professionals with superior qualifications. The same principle, that the employment of expensive skilled manpower in complex jobs depends on the efficient utilization of manpower in routine jobs, is reflected in the finding that employment security offices that have highly educated interviewers take advantage of modern office equipment to save clerical manpower, but the offices with less qualified interviewers do not. The bifuration of skills occurs primarily in offices with multilevel hierarchies and not in those with a simple undifferentiated structure, which indicates that these two forms of differentiation occur together, just as occupational differentiation is associated with both vertical and horizontal differentiation in the structure.

The complexity of the tasks and the complexity of the structure in an office interact in intricate ways in their effects on supervision. Product terms in regression analysis as well as contingency tables have been used to discern these interconnections. A large proportion of simple clerical jobs in an office widens the average span of control of its first-line supervisors. Occupational differentiation reinforces this positive effect of the clerical ratio on span of control, but hierarchical differentiation suppresses it. These findings are more easily understood by treating the clerical ratio as the condition that modifies the influences of the two kinds of differentiation, rather than vice versa.

The negative effect of hierarchical differentiation on the number of subordinates per supervisor is reinforced by a large proportion of clerks. Thus, problems of coordination in a differentiated structure consume more time of supervisors if their subordinates are clerks than if they are not (although routine clerical work as such makes less demand on the time of supervisors), probably because employees with superior qualifications are trained to put their own work into a broader context, and their consequent contributions to coordination reduce the problems of coordination that confront supervisors. The negative effect of occupational differentiation on the number of subordinates per supervisor, in contrast, is counteracted by a large proportion of clerks. The subdivision of labor simultaneously makes the structure more, and many duties less, complex. Occupational differentiation, just like hierarchical differentiation, engenders problems of coordination that raise requirements for supervisory manpower, but the simplification of jobs occupational differentiation produces diminishes requirements for supervisory manpower. If the division of labor generates many specialties without at the same time generating many routine jobs, it increases the need for supervisory manpower substantially. The more effective the division of labor is in separating routine from complex tasks and consequently simplifying the duties of many jobs—which is possible only if the amount of routine work in the office is considerable—the more do the savings in supervisory manpower it thereby effects suppress the increments in supervisory manpower differentiation requires. The threshold is reached in employment security offices when more than two fifths of the personnel are clerks, from which point on the over-all effect of the division of labor on the supervisory span of control tends to be positive rather than negative.

The freedom of employees to move from job to job in pursuit of better opportunities has the inevitable result that organizations tend to lose their most qualified employees in disproportionate numbers; men whose qualifications are in general demand are most likely to keep on finding better jobs than their present one. Discrimination on ethnic grounds interferes with the opportunity of members of minority groups to obtain the best jobs for which their training qualifies them, and government bureaus that do not practice discrimination obtain a windfall profit in the labor market by being able to hire more than their share of highly qualified members of ethnic minorities. This may be one of the reasons why interviewers in employment security offices in big cities are better educated than those in less urbanized places, where there are few highly educated members of ethnic minorities.

The high rates of turnover of the best trained personnel make those conditions in an organization that are capable of attracting and retaining them particularly important. What conditions these are has been inferred from their association with the educational level of the interviewers in an office, though it should be noted that these inferences about preferences and motives are highly speculative. The homogeneous colleague groups and the specialized responsibilities in offices with many functional sections seem to constitute more congenial working conditions for interviewers with college degrees than assignments in offices with few sections in which a greater variety of responsibilities is performed. Though congenial colleagues in a homogeneous work group may make the atmosphere in the office more pleasant, highly educated persons typically are oriented to deriving their major job satisfaction from the work itself, and they tend to become alienated from their jobs if they feel that administrative inefficiency wastes their efforts or that administrative pressures force them to sacrifice professional standards for the sake of a large volume of work of poorer quality. Efficient unemployment insurance operations and the absence of pressures to maximize the sheer number of placements in employment services appear to create working conditions that help retain the most educated interviewers.

CHAPTER 10

Structures and Functions

The headquarters of employment security agencies comprise divisions with different functions. We turn now from the internal analysis of local offices to that of headquarters divisions, another type of structural component of these agencies. This analysis provides an opportunity for studying how differences in function affect the formal structure. Another objective of the inquiry is to ascertain whether the regularities and interrelations observed in entire agencies and within local offices are also evident within divisions. Inasmuch as functional divisions are themselves an expression of the division of labor, it is of particular interest to determine whether the division of labor within them plays the same role as that in the entire organization.

The various headquarters divisions in the fifty-three employment security agencies can be divided into six types: (1) employment services (ES); (2) unemployment insurance (UI); (3) administrative services (AS); (4) personnel and technical (P&T); (5) data processing (DP); and (6) legal and quasijudicial services (LS). (The responsibilities of the six types have been described in Chapter 2.) Of the 566 units in all the agency headquarters whose heads report to top management, 387 meet our criterion for division and are included in the analysis.[1] Since every agency is differently

---

1. A division must have at least five employees.

organized, a headquarters may contain more than one division of a given type, or none. On the average, each of the fifty-three agencies has one ES division, one AS division, one DP unit, and one LS division. But the mean number is one and a quarter for UI divisions, because some agencies subdivide unemployment insurance into benefit and tax functions, and one and a half for P&T divisions, because agencies combine in various ways the heterogeneous staff services subsumed under this category, which includes personnel, training, reports and analysis, information, and organization, methods, and planning. In the analysis of types of divisions, therefore, some agencies are represented more than once, and in the data of all types combined, all agencies are represented several times.

The basic characteristics of the internal structure of divisions examined are the same as those investigated for entire agencies and for local offices: size, division of labor, number of levels, number of sections, clerical ratio, and supervisory ratio. Because divisions are larger than local offices, it is possible to analyze the conditions that affect the span of control on three different levels instead of two, namely, that of middle managers as well as those of the division heads and first-line supervisors. Middle managers are found in the 169 divisions with four or more levels. Supplementary data were obtained in a self-administered questionnaire distributed to division heads that asked them about staff meetings and other conferences, the decisions they make, and the influence they exert.[2] Some background characteristics, such as their seniority and their education, were provided from the agencies' personnel files. (The operational definitions of the variables and the statistics for the six types of divisions are presented in Appendix H.)

As a first step, the differences between the six types of divisions are described on the basis of a comparison of means. These differences are then used to construct a typology of function and a typology of structure. The next topic is the analysis of various aspects of differentiation to discover the similarities and dissimilarities among the six functions, on the one hand, and between the internal structure of divisions and the encompassing structure of agencies, on the other. Finally, division management is examined, with special emphasis on the ways the complexity of the structure and the complexity of the function influence the supervisory span of control on various levels. The procedure primarily used is comparison of zero-order correlations, controlling size as well as type, inasmuch as multiple regression analysis becomes cumbersome if each problem must be done for

---

2. Returns were received from 284, or 73 per cent, of the heads of the 387 major divisions included in the analysis.

seven groups, each of the six types as well as all combined. Some multiple regression problems are presented, however, notably to discern conflicting influences concealed in simple correlations and to check whether relationships between divisional characteristics persist when corresponding agency characteristics are controlled. It should be noted that comparisons of different types (between-type) pertain largely to differences within an agency, whereas the analysis of variations in each type (within-type) refers mostly to differences among agencies.

Types of Divisions

The six functions under consideration are representative of the divisions found at the headquarters of American employment security agencies, but most agency headquarters do not contain exactly these six divisions. All agencies have divisions in charge of the two basic line functions, unemployment insurance and employment services, and usually there is one of each. Two of the four staff functions, administrative and legal services, are also represented by a single division in the majority of cases. The responsibilities classified under personnel and technical, however, are typically divided among several small headquarters units, one or two of which tend to be large enough to meet our criterion for inclusion in the analysis, and data-processing is frequently not a separate division but a subunit in the UI or AS division. (For an illustrative organizational chart of an agency headquarters, see Figure D–2 in Appendix D; for the description of variables and basic statistics by type, see Appendix H.)

The 387 major functional divisions in all employment security agencies have an average of fifty-two employees, although the average of personnel in all headquarters subdivisions, including the smallest ones here excluded, is less than forty. Table 10–1 shows that the UI division, one of the two line functions, is typically by far the largest, and the P&T and LS divisions are generally the smallest ones. The ES division, the second line function, is comparatively small. But it must be remembered that the two line divisions at the headquarters, in contrast to the four staff divisions, contain only a small proportion of the total personnel in the line functions, most of whom are stationed in local offices. In the average agency, more than 90 per cent of the employment service personnel and two thirds of the unemployment insurance personnel work in local offices, not at the headquarters. The present discussion is confined to the personnel and structure of the major headquarters divisions themselves.

In the average division, the fifty-two employees occupy ten different formal positions. The mean number of levels in all divisions is 3.5, and that

TABLE 10-1. *Mean Characteristics of Six Types of Divisions*

	1 ES	2 UI	3 AS	4 P&T	5 DP	6 LS	7 All
Size	32.4	128.2	47.4	24.2	49.4	22.3	51.8
Occupational Positions (Division of Labor)	10.1	14.1	12.1	6.9	8.0	5.3	9.6
Levels	3.3	4.5	3.6	3.1	3.5	2.8	3.5
Sections	2.8	3.4	2.7	2.2	2.5	.9	2.5
Clerical Ratio	29.0	54.0	64.0	44.7	83.7	51.5	53.0
Supervisory Ratio	32.7	19.8	24.0	21.9	16.0	19.0	22.6
Span of Control							
Division Head	7.5	6.2	5.9	5.8	5.9	6.0	6.2
Middle Manager[a]	5.2	6.3	4.7	5.1	5.6	6.4	5.6
First-Line Supervisor	4.5	6.3	4.5	4.4	8.3	6.0	5.5
Regular Staff Meetings[b]	.77	.41	.35	.31	.29	.36	.45
Controlling Size							
Occupational Positions[c] (Division of Labor)	.92	.39	2.58	−.74	−2.62	−1.37	−0.00
Levels[c]	−0.10	.09	.15	−.00	−.19	−.00	.00
Sections[c]	.44	−.28	.27	.30	−.29	−.68	.00
Supervisory Ratio[d]	9.60	−.81	1.32	−1.48	−6.67	−4.35	−.00
Number of Cases	68	71	67	77	51	53	387

[a]The number of cases for the seven columns are 27, 54, 35, 18, 25, 10, 169.
[b]The number of cases for the seven columns are 61, 61, 57, 61, 7, 25, 272.
[c]Residual from its regression line on the logarithm of size.
[d]Residual from its regression line on size.

of sections is 2.5.[3] Table 10–1 shows that the largest type of division—UI
—has the largest number of occupational positions, of levels, and of
sections, and the two smallest types—P&T and LS—have the smallest
numbers of all three structural components, as one would expect. Hence,
differentiation along these three dimensions is indicated, in the lower part
of Table 10–1, by the residuals of the three variables' regression lines on
the logarithm of size. The DP unit is the least differentiated when size is
controlled in this manner,[4] and the AS division is the most differentiated of the six types (on two of the three measures). Relative to its size, the

---

3. All two-level divisions are defined as having no sections.
4. Data-processing is treated as a division to single it out for attention, as
   noted, although it is part of another division in most agencies and an
   independent division in only twelve. If the DP unit is not a division, its
   personnel was deleted from the division to which it belonged and the two
   were treated separately in the computation of the various measures.

ES division appears to be more differentiated than the UI division into occupational positions and sections, though not into hierarchical levels.

Executive responsibilities and professional staff functions constitute only a small portion of the work at the headquarters, the bulk of which is routine. Table 10–1 indicates that the majority of the employees in the average headquarters division are clerks, in contrast to only one fifth of those in the average local office. There are great variations among types of divisions, however, with more than four fifths of the personnel in the DP unit and less than one third of that in the ES division consisting of clerks. Though more of the work in headquarters divisions is routine, the mean proportion of supervisors in them is about the same as that in local offices (23 per cent and 21 per cent, respectively). A likely reason is that skills are more bifurcated at the headquarters, with a greater proportion of both complex (administrative and professional) and simple (clerical) jobs than in local offices. Variations in the supervisory ratio among types of divisions correspond, in reverse, to those in the clerical ratio, with the smallest supervisory ratio being found in DP units and the largest in ES divisions, which reflects the growing need for supervisors with increasing complexity of duties. The mean span of control of first-line supervisors is widest in DP units, as one would expect on the basis of the high proportion of routine clerical duties there, but it is no narrower in ES divisions than in two other types with higher proportions of clerical positions, and the span of control of the division head is wider in ES divisions than in any other type. These differences must be further clarified when size and other conditions as well as function are taken into account, and so must the variations in the span of control of middle managers.

Let us sketch brief profiles of the outstanding attributes of the two line divisions on the basis of the means in Table 10–1. The first thing to be noted is that the characteristics of the ES division and those of the UI division differ sharply. The ES division, which contains the largest proportion of supervisors and the smallest proportion of clerks, consists mostly of managers and professionals in charge of administering and planning the employment services of the agency carried out by a personnel complement in local offices twelve times the size of the headquarters group. (Some ES divisions comprise mostly supervisory personnel.) This headquarters contingent of managers and experts is organized into a larger number of sections relative to its size than any other division, and its head has a wider span of control than any other division head. A final distinctive feature of ES divisions is that regular staff meetings are more likely to be scheduled for this group of highly skilled personnel than in other types of divisions.

The UI division at the headquarters, on the other hand, encompasses not only the management and planning staff of the agency's unemployment insurance operations but also all operating personnel in the tax function and some of that in the benefit function. As a result, the average UI division is much larger than other types, notwithstanding the fact that a number of agencies have more than one UI division. Corresponding to its large size, there are more occupational positions, levels, and sections in the UI division, though relative to its size only one of these three dimensions of differentiation is pronounced—that into hierarchical levels. Of all division heads, those in charge of unemployment insurance have the longest seniority as division heads and as civil servants, averaging ten years in their present position and twenty-six with the agency.

What are the distinctive traits of the four staff divisions? Administrative services include a great variety of responsibilities, which is reflected in a larger number of occupational positions in the average AS division relative to its size than in the other five types. Vertical as well as occupational differentiation tends to be most pronounced in the AS division. Many jobs in it are routine and performed by clerks, though not so many as in the DP unit. Despite the simpler duties, the structural complexity of the typical AS division generated by differentiation narrows the span of control of supervisors. When size is controlled, the span of control of both middle managers and first-line supervisors is narrower in the AS division than in any other type. Though personnel and technical services are also varied, the division of labor in the average P&T division is not pronounced, probably because many agencies do not assign all of these services to the same division. Most characteristics of the P&T division are close to the average for all types.

The DP unit, which is not an independent division in most agencies, has a simple structure in accordance with the predominance of simple duties in it, and the simple structure and the simple duties reduce the need for supervision. It has the largest proportion of clerks of all types, the least occupational and the least hierarchical differentiation, the lowest proportion of supervisors, and its first-line supervisors have the widest span of control. Extensive legal services are not needed, and the LS divisions are smaller than other types, with correspondingly few occupational positions, levels, and sections. Indeed, they are quite often not subdivided into sections at all, and the number of their sections is disproportionately low even when their small size is taken into account. The head of an LS division, who is usually a lawyer, is better educated than the heads of other divisions, and he expresses least interest in exercising administrative influence within his division.

A typology of functions can be constructed by cross-classifying the re-

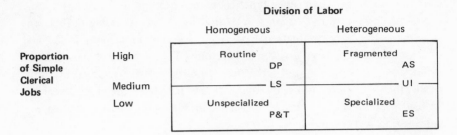

FIGURE 10–1 Typology of Function

sponsibilities of divisions in terms of two dimensions—whether the work is simple or complex, and whether the jobs are homogeneous or specialized. These two dimensions yield four types: (1) routine functions, which are simple and homogeneous; (2) fragmented functions, which are simple but heterogeneous; (3) unspecialized functions, which require higher skills and are homogeneous; and (4) specialized functions, which require higher skills of diverse kinds. The number of occupational positions relative to that expected on the basis of the division's size furnishes a measure of occupational heterogeneity. The proportion of clerical jobs provides a measure of the extent to which the work is simple (but as the distribution of the clerical ratio among the six kinds of divisions in Table 10–1 indicates that a dichotomy would create a distorted picture, a trichotomy is used instead). Figure 10–1 shows that four of the six kinds of divisions represent the four functional types quite well. Data-processing is the prototype of a routine function; administrative services are a polar case of a fragmented function; personnel and technical services illustrate an unspecialized function; and employment services typify a specialized function. UI and LS divisions tend to have an intermediate clerical ratio. The most pronounced occupational heterogeneity in the UI division stamps it as a comparatively pure case of a heterogeneous function. Inasmuch as more than half of the jobs in the LS division can be performed by clerks and its basic responsibilities require advanced professional training, legal services may be considered a bifurcated function.

Cross-classification of the vertical and the horizontal dimension of differentiation in divisions yields a typology of structure. The four types are: (1) undifferentiated structures, with few levels and few sections; (2) tall pyramids, with few sections and a multilevel hierarchy; (3) squat pyramids, which are short and wide; and (4) differentiated structures, which have both many levels and many sections. The operational criteria are whether the number of levels and of sections, respectively, exceed that expected on the basis of the division's size (see Table 10–1). Figure 10–2 shows that the six empirical cases distribute themselves among these four types, which is not what the earlier findings would have led one to expect. Data-processing is an extreme case of an undifferentiated structure, and legal services represent this type in somewhat less extreme form. Administrative services are the prototype of a structure differentiated in both dimensions. Employment services, and to a less extent personnel and technical services, exhibit a squat pyramid. Unemployment insurance, finally, manifests a tall pyramid.

If the six types of divisions are compared, there is no relationship between vertical and horizontal differentiation, inasmuch as there are empirical cases in all four cells of the cross-classification of the two dimensions of differentiation. This conflicts with the earlier findings that number of levels and number of sections are inversely related among entire agencies as well as local offices when size is controlled, as it has been here. The question arises whether no inverse relationship between vertical and horizontal differentiation exists among divisions or whether one is observable within each of the six types. A parallel question can be raised concerning the relationship between the division of labor and the clerical ratio. In both agencies and local offices, the division of labor and the clerical ratio are positively associated. But the comparison of types of divisions in Figure 10–1 indicates no such relationship, inasmuch as the empirical cases fall into all cells, not only those in the minor diagonal. Is the association between division of labor and clerical ratio different among headquarters divisions than among entire agencies and local offices? If so, why? To answer these questions, we must analyze the relationships in all divi-

Hierarchical Differentiation

		Low	High
Horizontal Differentiation	Low	Undifferentiated DP, LS	Tall UI
	High	Squat ES, P&T	Differentiated AS

FIGURE 10–2 Typology of Structure

sions instead of merely comparing the six types. Before doing so, however, let us look at the connection between the typologies.

A routinized function, in which most jobs are homogeneous and simple, seems to find expression in an undifferentiated structure, with comparatively few levels and few sections. Figures 10–1 and 10–2 show that data-processing represents this combination in pure form, and legal services do to a lesser degree. A fragmented function, in which there is a great variety of mostly simple jobs, in contrast, appears to give rise to a highly differentiated structure in both dimensions, as illustrated by administrative services. A complex function that contains few simple clerical jobs seems to make the division head reluctant to let hierarchical levels separate him from direct contact with the professionals performing the work, whatever the division of labor, and the pyramid tends to be squat. Employment services illustrate this connection, and so do personnel and technical services. A heterogeneous function primarily distinguished by a pronounced division of labor, like unemployment insurance, appears to promote a structure with a tall pyramid.

In sum, if a function is simple enough for most of the work to be performed by clerks, the degree of heterogeneity among jobs tends to govern the extent to which the structure becomes differentiated into both hierarchical levels and functional sections. But if the function is complex and the majority of duties require training and skills, multilevel hierarchies are unlikely to develop, regardless of the degree of specialization among jobs produced by the division of labor. These conclusions based on comparisons of typologies, however, are necessarily tentative and raise questions that only more refined analysis of differences within as well as between types can answer. Granted that the fragmented function is more differentiated in either direction than the routinized functions are, do vertical and horizontal differentiation within these types also exhibit a positive association, contrary to the findings for agencies and for local offices? Does the division of labor affect differentiation into multilevel hierarchies and many sections only in some types of divisions, in all the types, or in none of them? Why is the routinizing effect of the division of labor, which in agencies and in branches raises the clerical ratio, not observable, or even reversed, among divisions, as implied by the findings that the function with the highest proportion of clerks (data-processing) has the least pronounced division of labor whereas the function with the lowest proportion of clerks (employment services) is one of the two with most division of labor?

Functional Differentiation

Large size generates structural differentiation within divisions of all types, just as it generates differentiation in the formal structure of entire agencies and in that of local offices. The larger a division, the more it is differentiated into occupational positions, hierarchical levels, and functional sections. All three relationships are substantial within all six types of division without a single exception, as the correlations in the top rows in Table 10–2 show, although the precise strength of the association var-

TABLE 10-2. *Zero-Order Correlations in Six Types of Divisions*

	1 ES	2 UI	3 AS	4 P&T	5 DP	6 LS	7 All
Size and							
Division of Labor	.49	.64	.74	.70	.72	.74	.65
Levels	.75	.70	.76	.75	.67	.73	.71
Sections	.44	.31	.60	.55	.29	.47	.40
Log Size and							
Division of Labor	.69	.76	.85	.67	.70	.87	.77
Levels	.80	.84	.88	.81	.78	.82	.86
Sections	.69	.59	.84	.79	.60	.75	.72
Division of Labor[a] and							
Levels[a]	−.10	.10	.05	.21	.14	.22	.13
Sections[a]	.20	.02	.12	−.40	−.02	.44	.09
Levels[a] and[b]							
Sections[a]	−.32	−.26	−.15	−.41	−.40	−.29	−.28
Number of Cases	68	71	67	77	51	53	387

[a]Residual from its regression line on the logarithm of size.
[b]All cases with two levels have been eliminated. The number of cases for the seven columns are 55, 67, 54, 58, 44, 30, 308.

ies, of course. The scatter diagrams of the regressions on size of number of occupational positions, number of levels, and number of sections reveal logarithmic curves. Logarithmic transformation of size improves the correlations for all divisions combined considerably, and the data in Table 10–2 indicate that these improvements are manifest within four of the six types for the division of labor, and within all six for both levels and sections.

As the size of divisions increases, therefore, both the number and the average size of the structural components within a division increase, and this is the case within all types of divisions and with respect to three distinct kinds of structural components—positions, levels, and sections. Hence, size promotes differentiation within divisions of all kinds at decelerating rates. The pattern is exactly the same as that found in local offices and in entire agencies. The variables characterizing local offices are entirely independent of those characterizing headquarters divisions, though agency characteristics are only in part independent of those of divisions. The size of a functional division depends on the size of the agency of which it is part; but the number of sections within a division is not necessarily greater—in fact, one would expect it to be smaller—if the agency headquarters has many than if it has few divisions; and the maximum number of levels at the agency headquarters, which is usually that in the UI division, has an intrinsic connection with the number of levels within only one of the six types.

The conclusion to which the findings point is that the patterns of differentiation in formal organizations are partly the result of, and partly replicated by, corresponding patterns of differentiation within its various segments, whether headquarters divisions or local branches are considered. The large size of an employment security agency expands the number as well as the average size of its various structural components, such as headquarters divisions and local offices, and the large size of these components in turn expands the number as well as the size of their structural subunits. The process of differentiation at decelerating rates with the increasing size of an organization repeats itself within the organizational components it has generated. It is a process of successive organizational fission, which assumes the same form within the substructures as in the encompassing structures.

What are the interrelations among these three aspects of differentiation in functional divisions? We have seen earlier that the division of labor exerts an independent positive influence, when size is controlled, on both number of levels and number of sections in local offices but on neither vertical nor horizontal differentiation in the entire agencies. The pattern within divisions is similar to that for the agency headquarters: the division of labor exerts little if any independent influence on vertical or horizontal differentiation in divisions. Its positive correlations, with size (in logarithmic transformation) controlled, are only .13 with number of levels and .09 with number of sections, and Table 10–2 shows that the correlations within the six types are not consistent. The number of occupational positions reinforces the influence of the number of employees on structural differentiation only in the smallest organizational segments of employment security agencies—their local offices.

Vertical and horizontal differentiation in divisions are inversely related when size is controlled, which replicates the findings obtained for entire agency headquarters and for local offices. Table 10–2 indicates that this inverse correlation is observable within all six types of divisions as well as for the combined total.[5] Why then did the earlier comparison of the six types of function fail to reveal this inverse relationship between number of levels and number of sections, controlled for size? [6] Apparently, levels and sections are inversely related when divisions in different agencies are compared, as is done in the within-type analysis, but not when the various functional divisions within an agency are compared, as is done when contrasting differences between types.

Although a function may be comparatively much differentiated in both directions, as exemplified by administrative services, or in neither, as illustrated by data-processing, within each function hierarchical differentiation into multiple levels tends to reduce the number of sections into which a division is horizontally differentiated. A multilevel hierarchy relieves the division head of the heavy administrative load created by many section chiefs who directly report to him. This significance of multiple levels is further indicated by the finding (see Table 10–4 below, p. 283) that many levels narrow the span of control of division heads, for all divisions combined and for each type separately. Here again we see that the process of differentiation in organizations repeats itself within the differentiated units. Multiple levels develop in agencies to relieve top management of excessive administrative burdens, and they do so by reducing the number of divisions. The existence of few divisions generally increases the number of sections within them (Table 3–6), creating internal pressures in divisions to multiply hierarchical levels to reduce the division heads' administrative burdens.

Not all interrelations between elements in divisions parallel those in total agencies and local offices, however. The influence of the division of labor on the clerical ratio in functional divisions is not the same as that observed in the two other organizational systems, nor is it the same in all

5. Two-level divisions have been eliminated, because they have by definition fewer sections (namely none) than divisions with three or more levels.

6. The data in Table 10–1, on which Figure 10–2 is based, include two-level divisions, but those in Table 10–2 do not. If the same data as those in Table 10–1 are used (including two-level divisions), the correlation between levels and sections, controlling size (log) for all divisions combined is lower ($-.13$), and the correlations for the six types fluctuate more. But it would not alter the point made in the text, in that four of the six inverse within-type correlations are again more pronounced than the one for all types combined.

divisions, and the effect of size on the clerical ratio also reveals some note-worthy variations. These distinctive effects are most clearly seen in multiple regression analysis, which makes it possible to control simultaneously agency size and agency clerical ratio in order to ascertain whether these two aspects of the agency context modify the influence of the division's occupational differentiation and size (in logarithmic transformation) on its clerical ratio. Table 10–3 presents the results of the seven regression problems, for each of the six types and for all divisions combined. The relationships between division characteristics are hardly affected by controlling agency size and clerical ratio. The proportion of clerks in the agency is related to that in most types of divisions, though not strongly. Agency size has no appreciable effect on the clerical ratio in divisions. Let us examine the influence of the division's size before analyzing that of its occupational differentiation on the clerical ratio.

Larger divisions contain higher proportions of clerks than smaller ones, and when the division of labor is controlled, the net effect of size on the clerical ratio is seen to be substantial, but it is confined to four types of division and not observable in the other two. Employment services and personnel and technical ones are the only two functions that have, on the average, less than a majority of clerical employees, as Table 10–1 shows, and these are the only two types of divisions in which increasing size does not raise the proportion of clerks, as Table 10–3 shows. We have seen earlier that large size effects savings in administrative overhead. If the professional personnel constitutes a minority among a majority of clerks, increasing size reduces the proportion of these professional specialists needed (manifest in a positive relation of size and clerical ratio), just as it reduces the proportion of managers needed. But if the majority of the personnel are professional—that is, neither clerical nor managerial—they constitute the basic work force rather than the specialized support of the clerical work force. Although large size under these conditions may well result in savings in professional manpower too, they are no greater than the savings in clerical manpower resulting from it. Indeed, they may be smaller. Hence, in divisions with a majority of professionals, size has no positive effect on the clerical ratio. And in local offices, where the proportion of nonclerical personnel is generally still larger (the mean being only 20 per cent clerks), size was seen to have a slight negative effect on the clerical ratio when other conditions are controlled (Table 8–6), quite possibly because in most offices clerks are primarily utilized for administrative support, and large size reduces administrative overhead. In short, whether a minority of professionals supports the basic work of a majority of clerks or a minority of clerks supports the work of a majority of profes-

TABLE 10-3. *Multiple Regression of **Clerical Ratio** in Six Types of Divisions on Antecedent Conditions*[a]

Independent Variable	ES	UI	AS	P&T	DP	LS	All
	Standardized Regression Coefficients						
Agency Context							
Size	.17	.23*	−.04	.19	−.11	−.10	−.02
Clerical Ratio	.10	.30*	.25*	.17	−.09	.08	.10*
Division							
Size (Log)	−.03	.42*	.48*	−.09	.53*	.18	.42**
Division of Labor	.07	−.22	−.30	.11	−.65**	.22	−.24**
	Zero-Order Correlations						
Agency Context							
Size	.18	.32	.10	.18	−.16	.18	.08
Clerical Ratio	.13	.36	.26	.18	.02	.22	.12
Division							
Size (Log)	.09	.38	.24	.04	−.03	.33	.23
Division of Labor	.06	.16	.12	.07	−.35	.34	.08
Multiple R	.21	.55	.37	.26	.48	.37	.29
Number of Cases	68	71	67	77	51	53	387

*Greater than twice its standard error.

**Greater than three times its standard error.

[a]The matrix of zero-order correlations between the independent variables in this table is presented at the end of Appendix H.

sionals, large size apparently reduces the proportionate size of the supportive force.

The inverse relationship between division of labor and clerical ratio observable for all divisions, which contrasts with the direct effect of the division of labor on the clerical ratio in entire agencies and in local offices, is only manifest in three of the six functional types. There is, if anything, a slight positive relationship between occupational differentiation and proportion of clerks in ES divisions, P&T divisions, and LS divisions. The three functions in which occupational differentiation reduces the clerical ratio are unemployment insurance, administrative services, and data-processing, all of which, on the average, contain a majority of clerks and are above the median in the size of their total personnel. The analysis in Chapter 5 of the distribution of positions in data-processing indicated that what typically produces a reduction in the proportion of clerks in this unit is the addition of computer programmers, operators, and other specialists consequent to the introduction of automation. Though we have no similar data on specific positions in UI and AS divisions, it is quite possible that the addition of specialized responsibilities of one sort or another is also a main factor there that reduces the ratio of clerks.

If a new responsibility is assigned to a division and experts in several specialities are needed to perform it, as illustrated by the responsibility for computers in data-processing, one would expect the number of occupational specialties to increase and the ratio of clerical to nonclerical personnel to decrease. In other words, a larger number of responsibilities or subfunctions in a functional division is assumed, by this interpretation, to produce an inverse relationship between occupational differentiation and clerical ratio. The reason that such an inverse relationship is found only in UI and AS divisions (aside from DP units, for the reason already given) may be that these two functions contain a greater variety of distinct responsibilities than do ES, P&T, and LS divisions. An independent measure available only for the three staff divisions confirms the inference that administrative services encompass more subfunctions than either personnel and technical or legal services.[7]

Why is occupational differentiation negatively related to the proportion of clerical jobs for divisions but positively for entire agencies and for local offices? To answer this question, it must be noted that the negative relationship exhibited by the data for all divisions results in part from corresponding negative relationships in three of the six types, as just discussed, and in part from between-type differences. The negative between-type association, which is primarily indicative of differences within each agency, is illustrated by the polar cases of data-processing, with the highest clerical ratio and the lowest division of labor, and employment services, with the lowest clerical ratio and the second-highest division of labor. It is also reflected in the fact that the standardized regression coefficient for all divisions, which expresses both the between-type and the within-type relationships between occupational differentiation and clerical ratio, is more pronounced $(-.24)$ than the mean for the standardized regression coefficients of the six types $(-.13)$, which indicates the average within-type relationship.

Functional differentiation among the divisions in an organization is a form of division of labor, which is distinct from the one manifest in the

---

7. The personnel time reports of the agencies list thirteen different subfunctions performed by the three staff divisions. A weighted score was computed based on the number of these assigned to a division, with weights ranging from zero to four, depending on the extent of the responsibility the division has for the subfunction. The means are 20.0 for AS, 8.0 for P&T, and 1.8 for LS divisions.

measure of number of occupational positions. The process of functional differentiation may be envisaged, reconstructing a developmental sequence from cross-sectional data, to affect initially individual positions and subsequently also whole segments of the organization. The differentiation of duties into more complex and more routine ones increases the proportion of positions that can be filled by clerks, which is indicated by the positive effect of the division of labor on the clerical ratio in the total organization. Further functional differentiation entails the assignment of different kinds of duties with varying skill requirements not merely to different individuals but to different divisions or sections. In the terminology of Gulick, "process," or the nature of the work performed, assumes growing importance relative to "purpose," or the end-product to be achieved, as the principle on the basis of which tasks are assigned to various parts of the organization.[8] The concentration of data-processing activities or of office services in one unit, whatever the purpose to which the work performed there is put, exemplifies this principle of organizing subunits in terms of process.

This further functional differentiation among substructures involves the allocation of most routine duties to some divisions and most complex ones to others, just as the initial differentiation among persons involves the assignment of most routine tasks to some individual positions and most complex ones to others. The divisions in which most of the work is routine can employ many clerks and need little formal differentiation of positions for these simple jobs. The divisions in which much of the work is complex cannot utilize many clerks and tend to require personnel with different specialized qualifications to perform the various complex duties. This is reflected in an inverse relationship of the division of labor and the clerical ratio among the various types of divisions as well as within some types, not only for the reason suggested above, but also because a group of divisions here classified under the same type may include some with more complex and others with more routine responsibilities. For instance, there are more specialties and fewer clerks in those data-processing units utilizing computers than in the ones that are not automated.

Divisions are not self-contained organizations but functionally specialized segments of organizations, which accounts for the paradox that the negative relationship between occupational differentiation and clerical ratio in divisions and their positive relationships in agencies both reflect

---

8. Luther Gulick et al., *Papers on the Science of Administration* (New York: Institute of Public Administration, 1937), pp. 15–25.

the process of functional differentiation. By segregating the routine tasks that can be performed by clerks from the complex ones that require specialized training, task differentiation among positions increases the proportion of clerks in the total organization, which is evident in the comparison of *different* organizations. But by further segregating most routine clerical duties in some functional divisions and most complex duties performed by a variety of specialists in others, task differentiation among functional segments produces a negative relationship between occupational specialization and the proportion of clerks in these segments, which is primarily manifest in differences among functions in the *same* organization. The negative relationship between occupational differentiation and routinization among divisions, however, does not in any way negate the positive effect of occupational differentiation on routinization among positions, which continues to be observable for the total organization.

Local offices are not functionally interdependent segments, as divisions are, and General LO's are not even specialized but all-purpose geographical branches. One would consequently expect a positive association between division of labor and clerical ratio in local offices, and such a positive relationship has been reported in Table 7–3, though only in General and UI LO's, and not in the three specialized types of employment offices. The interpretation advanced in Chapter 7 was that clerks are not used extensively enough in employment offices for the division of labor to raise their proportion. But the finding may also reflect the principle that the positive relationship between division of labor and clerical ratio is only evident in relatively self-contained organizational units and not in functionally differentiated segments of organizations.

Division Management

Division heads are oldtimers with many years of experience in the agency. On the average, they have been with the agency for nearly a quarter of a century. Seniority, whether because of the experience it brings or the loyalty it demonstrates, counts heavily in the scope of influence of division heads, whereas education counts little. The seniority of the division head is positively correlated with the division's size (.26 for all divisions, ranging from .19 to .42 for the six types). The within-type differences are indicative of variations among agencies and thus show that it takes longer to become a division head in a big agency with large divisions than in a small agency with small ones. Comparisons between types imply that it also takes longer in a given agency to become the top manager of a larger than of a smaller division. On the average, the heads of the two line divisions, who are in charge of local office as well as headquarters personnel, had been with the agency longest when initially appointed (seventeen years in the ES, sixteen in the UI division), and the head of the largest staff function had nearly as much seniority when appointed (fifteen years), but the heads of the three smaller staff functions were appointed several years earlier in their careers. Holding constant size, moreover, seniority tends to widen the division head's span of control and increase his influence over administrative decisions in his division, but superior education does neither.[9]

Recent successors to the position of division head are more likely than oldtimers to schedule regular meetings with their senior staff, mostly section chiefs. The correlation between tenure in the position and the dummy variable of whether staff meetings are regularly scheduled (rather than only when necessary) is −.16 for all divisions. Most likely, regular meetings help recent successors to the top managerial position in the division to get acquainted with their subordinates, to establish informal working relations with them, and to institute new policies or changes in procedures. The dummy variable of whether periodic staff meetings are scheduled or not is negatively correlated with the clerical ratio in the division (−.21) and positively with the supervisory ratio, controlling size (.15). However, these correlations are essentially the product of between-type differences and not replicated within types of divisions. In 77 per cent of ES divisions, which have the lowest proportion of clerks and the highest proportion of supervisors, staff meetings are regularly scheduled, in contrast to 41 per cent or less for all other types (see Table 10–1). The *frequency* with which staff meetings are held does not reveal similar differences.

Why is the bureaucratic procedure of following a regular schedule of meetings most prevalent in the division with most professional and managerial personnel, whose superior skills and complex duties would lead one to expect that their exercise of discretion be least restricted by administrative rules? Complex responsibilities may well require more regular communication and consultation among experts than simple ones. But this should be reflected primarily in disproportionately frequent staff meetings in ES divisions, whereas the empirical data indicate that meetings there are more likely to be regularly scheduled but no more frequent than in other types of divisions with less skilled personnel. Hence, something

---

9. For all divisions combined, seniority (residual from its regression line on size) has a correlation of .14 with the division head's span of control and one of .15 with his influence over promotion decisions. The division head's years of education have a correlation of −.01 with his span of control and of −.08 with his influence over promotion decisions.

about maintaining a regular schedule of meetings instead of calling one whenever necessary apparently accounts for the difference. The ES division is often the only one that includes supervisors in the field, which is one reason why its meetings are scheduled in advance. Another possible reason pertains to the nature of the duties.

Routine duties require less concentration for long periods than complex ones, which means that interrupting the work of employees by calling a meeting on short notice is more disruptive and harmful if their job is complex than if it is routine. Though such interruptions might be welcomed by persons whose duties are monotonous, they are likely to be resented by those involved in a difficult task. Complex professional and managerial responsibilities are more in need of protection against disruption by formal administrative procedures than simple responsibilities, and a regular schedule of meetings provides such protection. The paradoxical conclusion implied by these conjectures is that administrative regulations— presumably of other kinds than meeting schedules as well—are more prevalent if skilled employees perform professional work than if unskilled ones perform routine tasks. Some data in support of this speculation will be supplied in Chapter 12.

Turning now to the conditions in divisions that influence the structure of supervision, we start by examining the effects of the division's size. The four measures of supervision are: the span of control of the division head; the span of control of middle managers (that is, section chiefs who are not first-line supervisors); the span of control of first-line supervisors over employees at the lowest level; and the ratio of supervisors in the division (which is a rough summary measure of the other three). Since we have already seen that large size reduces the managerial ratio at the agency headquarters (Table 4–1) as well as in branch offices (Table 7–10), it does not come as a surprise that the size of headquarters divisions is also negatively correlated with the proportion of supervisors in them. Table 10–4 shows that size and supervisory ratio are negatively correlated in all six types of divisions because large size widens the span of control of division heads, that of middle managers, and that of first-line supervisors, though in the case of the division head's span of control the effect is primarily evident when size is logarithmically transformed. Only two of twenty-four correlations of the logarithm of size with four measures of supervision in six types of divisions do not conform to the dominant pattern.

The complexity of a division's internal structure generated by large size raises requirements for managerial manpower and reduces the number of subordinates under a supervisor, which also replicates the findings for entire agency headquarters and for local offices. Table 10–4 shows that

TABLE 10-4. *Zero-Order Correlations (Supervision) in Six Types of Divisions*

	ES	UI	AS	P&T	DP	LS	All
Size and							
Span of Control of							
Division Head	.12	.10	.22	.18	−.10	.23	.07
Middle Managers[a]	.29	.02	.20	.70	.13	.92	.22
First-Line Supervisors[b]	.60	.47	.50	.28	.29	.53	.40
Supervisory Ratio	−.28	−.35	−.16	−.12	−.14	−.31	−.20
Log Size and							
Span of Control of							
Division Head	.28	.24	.30	.36	−.08	.49	.22
Middle Managers[a]	.43	.05	.17	.66	.22	.78	.32
First-Line Supervisors[b]	.54	.39	.48	.42	.46	.69	.45
Supervisory Ratio	−.38	−.39	−.12	−.14	−.18	−.36	−.23
Levels[c] and							
Span of Control of							
Division Head	−.61	−.11	−.29	−.56	−.30	−.51	−.39
Middle Managers[a,c]	−.41	−.08	.05	−.58	−.26	−.06	−.18
First-Line Supervisors[b,d]	.00	−.31	−.45	−.55	−.19	−.53	−.32
Supervisory Ratio[d]	−.10	.43	.33	.69	.53	.68	.27
Sections[c] and							
Span of Control of							
Division Head	−.04	.25	.15	−.01	.26	−.18	.10
Middle Managers[a,c]	−.28	.13	−.42	−.36	−.15	−.76	−.18
First-Line Supervisors[b,d]	−.51	−.04	−.22	−.25	−.31	−.48	−.30
Supervisory Ratio[d]	−.11	−.05	.28	.36	.18	.44	.19
Number of Cases	68	71	67	77	51	53	387

[a]The number of cases in the seven columns are 27, 54, 35, 18, 25, 10, 169.

[b]The number of cases in the seven columns are 55, 67, 54, 58, 44, 30, 308.

[c]Residual from its regression line on the logarithm of size.

[d]Residual from its regression line on size.

both vertical (levels) and horizontal (sections) differentiation reduce the average span of control of supervisors on all three levels and thereby increase the ratio of supervisors for all divisions combined and, with a few exceptions, within each of the six types.[10] Fluctuations in detail must be expected, but the departures from the main pattern indicated by within-type correlations that are more than .10 lower than that for all divisions should be examined. A multilevel hierarchy narrows the span of control

10. Size is controlled for every variable with which it is correlated .20 or more, and the logarithm of size is used in effecting the control if its correlation with the variable is more than .10 greater than that of raw size.

of division heads, except that it does so very little in UI divisions. It narrows the span of control of middle managers in varying degree within four of the six types, though it does not have this effect in AS and LS divisions. And it narrows the span of control of first-line supervisors, considerably for all divisions and within four of the six types, though less in DP units and not at all in ES divisions. The supervisory ratio, which is most affected by the span of control of the first-line supervisors (who are more numerous than division heads and middle managers combined), increases substantially with the increasing number of levels in the division within five of the six types as well as for all six combined, the exception being ES divisions.

The number of sections in a division has a spurious positive nexus with the span of control of division heads, because the number of section chiefs is included in the number of subordinates defining this span. Such a positive correlation is only evident in the three larger and not in the three smaller types, ES, P&T, and LS divisions, undoubtedly because heads of small divisions are more likely than those of large ones to be in charge of several nonsupervisory employees, which makes the total number of subordinates more independent of the number of section chiefs. Table 10–4 indicates, however, that many sections, just as many levels, narrow the span of control of middle managers and of first-line supervisors and raise the supervisory ratio for all divisions combined and within most of the six types. In this case, the main exceptions are that many sections do not affect the span of control of either middle managers or first-line supervisors in UI divisions, and they consequently do not influence the supervisory ratio in unemployment insurance. Besides, sections and supervisory ratio are not positively correlated in ES divisions, but this last exception should be disregarded as an artifact of coding, because most of the *lowest-level* personnel in a few small ES divisions, being field supervisors over local offices, is included in the supervisory component. If the thirteen two-level ES divisions are excluded, the correlation between sections and supervisory ratio, controlling size, is positive (.25).

The basic pattern is clearly the same as that previously observed in two other organizational systems: differentiation within divisions in either direction makes demands on managers that reduce the number of subordinates they can supervise. This finds expression on all levels of supervision and in all of the different functions within an agency. Most of the deviations from this dominant pattern reveal regularities that can themselves be explained in terms of the same fundamental principle. Multiple levels do not narrow the span of control of middle managers in AS and LS divisions, whereas they do otherwise. However, they narrow the span of control of first-line supervisors more in AS ($-.45$) and in LS divisions ($-.53$) than they generally do ($-.32$). In ES divisions, a multilevel hierarchy does not narrow the span of control of first-line supervisors, but it narrows instead the span of control of middle managers more there ($-.41$) than usually ($-.18$), as well as that of the division head ($-.61$ vs. $-.39$). The weaker negative effect that the number of hierarchical levels in DP units has on the span of control of first-line supervisors is also compensated for on other levels, as indicated by the finding that the positive effect of hierarchical levels on the supervisory ratio is greater in DP units ($.53$) than in all divisions combined ($.27$).

If a multilevel hierarchy fails for one reason or another to reduce the span of control of supervisors on one level it tends to compensate for it by producing extraordinary reductions in the span of control of supervisors on a different level. Numerous hierarchical levels raise the proportion of managers by definition, and they simultaneously intensify problems of coordinating and communication in the hierarchy. When other conditions prevent arrangements that enable supervisors on one level to meet the demands on their time made by these problems created by differentiation, supervisors on another level seem to have to make up for it. This principle of compensation can explain all but one of the exceptional cases in which multiple levels fail to reduce the span of control on any supervisory level in any of the types. The remaining exception is that levels in UI divisions exert little negative influence on the span of control of the division head. The two deviant cases in which many sections fail to narrow the supervisory span of control (leaving aside their influence on the division head's span of control discussed above) also involve the UI division. Many sections narrow neither the middle managers' nor the first-line supervisors' span of control in UI divisions. The supervisory ratio in UI divisions is consequently not positively associated with horizontal differentiation, as it is in other types.

Why does differentiation, notably horizontal differentiation into sections, not make the same demands on supervisory manpower in UI divisions as in other types? A possible reason, which is clearly *ad hoc,* is that these divisions usually consist of two quite distinct functions, unemployment insurance taxes and unemployment benefits. Though these two functions are sometimes in two different divisions, they are in the same one in the large majority of agencies (thirty-eight of fifty-three). If a division consists of two parts with little interdependence, the measure of horizontal differentiation exaggerates the need for coordination, inasmuch as it is the *interdependence* among differentiated units that makes coordination necessary. A low degree of interdependence in a division is therefore likely to attenuate the demand for managerial manpower created by differentiation.

Further clarification of the basic findings requires once more resort to multiple regression analysis. The first question to be answered by using this procedure is whether the direct effect of size on managerial manpower and its indirect effect mediated by structural complexity assume the same pattern within divisions of each type as they do for the total agency head-quarters and for local offices. If so, it would imply that differences among functions within an agency have little significance for the impact on super-vision of size, differentiation into levels, and differentiation into sections. A second issue is posed by the fact that large and complex divisions of all types are, of course, usually found in larger rather than smaller agencies. To determine the independent influence the size and complexity of *divisions* exert on supervision, both the size of the agency and the supervisory ratio at the agency headquarters are controlled in the regression analysis.[11] Finally, we want to know how supervision is influenced by the heterogene-ity of jobs produced by the division of labor and by the routinization of jobs manifest in the clerical ratio, and whether these influences are inde-pendent of, or confounded with, those of size and structural complexity. Hence, these two variables are included in the regression problems. Table 10–5 presents the results of the seven regression analyses, for the six types and all of them combined, using first-line supervisors' span of control as the dependent variable.[12]

The data clearly show that the influences of a division's size and internal complexity on the span of control of first-line supervisors are independent of the size of the agency to which the division belongs and of the propor-tion of supervisors in the total agency headquarters. The large size of divi-sions of all types has a strong direct effect widening the supervisory span of control. The internal differentiation of the division into levels and that into sections both have substantial direct effects narrowing the supervisory span of control. Decomposition of the data for all divisions reveals that the negative indirect effects of size mediated by the vertical ($-.41$) and hori-

---

11. The two measures of differentiation of the agency headquarters are not controlled, because they are largely independent of differentiation within divisions. The number of divisions is different from the number of sections within these divisions, and the maximum number of levels at the agency headquarters is different from the maximum number of levels in all but one of the divisions (usually the UI division). In fact, if levels and divi-sions at agency headquarters are added to the variables in Table 10–5, results are little altered.

12. The logarithmic transformation of size is used, although the criterion for doing so is not quite met (see Table 10–4), consistent with the procedure employed for the agency (Table 4–1) and for local offices (Table 7–10).

TABLE 10-5. *Multiple Regression of* **Mean Span of Control of First-Line Supervisors** *in Six Types of Divisions on Antecedent Conditions*[a]

Independent Variable	ES	UI	AS	P&T	DP	LS	All
	Standardized Regression Coefficients						
Agency Context							
Size	.45**	.04	.36*	−.05	−.19	−.25	.06
Supervisory Ratio	−.09	−.29*	.03	−.10	−.12	−.23	−.15*
Division							
Size (Log)	.56*	.67*	1.18**	1.23**	1.00**	1.43**	1.05**
Division of Labor	−.01	.06	−.12	.22	−.12	.02	−.11
Sections	−.44**	−.29*	−.43*	−.59**	−.45*	−.56**	−.42**
Levels	−.19	−.43*	−.66**	−.83**	−.28	−.58*	−.48**
Clerical Ratio	.02	.02	.05	.03	−.02	.21	.15**
	Zero-Order Correlations						
Agency Context							
Size	.72	.31	.55	.12	.34	.34	.34
Supervisory Ratio	−.41	−.49	−.31	−.30	−.33	−.54	−.36
Division							
Size (Log)	.54	.39	.48	.42	.46	.69	.45
Division of Labor	.21	.31	.32	−.42	.20	.47	.20
Sections	−.17	.01	.18	.05	−.07	.30	−.02
Levels	.40	.15	.19	−.03	.25	.39	.22
Clerical Ratio	.17	.24	.32	.01	.14	.38	.34
Multiple R	.81	.60	.73	.79	.61	.85	.69
Number of Cases	55	67	54	58	44	30	308

*Greater than twice its standard error.
**Greater than three times its standard error.

[a]The matrix of zero-order correlations between the independent variables in this table is presented at the end of Appendix H. The number of cases is smaller than in Table 10-3 because two-level divisions, in which all employees report directly to the division head, have no first-line supervisors.

zontal (−.30) differentiation it generates are what reduces its strong direct positive effect (1.05) to a still substantial positive over-all effect (.45) on the number of subordinates per first-line supervisor, and that controlling agency size (.02) and agency supervisory ratio (.03) has little bearing on this effect.

The influence of agency size on the span of control of first-line supervisors is largely mediated by the size of divisions, and so is the influence of the supervisory ratio at the agency headquarters. The zero-order correlations between agency size and supervisory span of control in divisions are .31 or larger in five of the six types of division and .34 for all combined. The main reason that first-line supervisors have a wider span of control in large agencies is that divisions are larger in these than in small agencies, as indicated by the regression coefficients of agency size and by decomposition. Only in two types (ES and AS divisions) does agency size exert an independent direct effect widening the supervisory span of control. Turning to the other contextual variable, the higher the ratio of supervisors in the entire headquarters, the higher is the ratio of supervisors and the narrower is their span of control in particular divisions, as the negative correlations in Table 10–5 show. Most of this relationship is owing to the influence of division size, but the regression coefficients indicate that a slight relationship persists under controls.[13] This relationship together with a parallel one observed in local offices in Chapter 8 implies the existence of an explicit policy or an implicit tendency throughout an agency to employ either relatively many supervisors with narrow, or relatively few with wide, spans of control, though this tendency is not very pronounced.

The findings on divisions confirm and refine the conclusions previously derived from the analysis of agencies and that of local offices. The large size of roof organizations lowers, and the structural differentiation it generates raises, requirements for supervisory manpower primarily because the components into which large organizations become differentiated are themselves comparatively large and internally differentiated. The internal complexity of large functional divisions and large local offices enhances the need for supervisors and narrows their span of control, but not so much as the large scale of operations reduces the need for supervisors by widening their span of control. The size and complexity of the subunits within divisions may in turn be responsible for these effects. Consequently, remote as the work groups on the bottom of the hierarchy of an organization's headquarters and branches are, the size of these work groups under a supervisor and hence the proportionate need for first-line supervisors are much influenced by the total organization's scale of operations and complexity. Although most of the effect of agency size on the subordinates per first-line supervisor is indirect and mediated by the size of subunits, some of it is direct, in local offices (Table 8–7) and in two types of divisions (Table 10–5). This suggests that the prevalence of large units with many, or small ones with few, subordinates per supervisor in organizations, depending on their own size, has a structural effect creating standards that exert an independent influence on the number of subordinates assigned to each supervisor. The need for extra supervisory manpower to contribute to coordination and communication in differentiated hierarchies is so ada-

---

13. In the multiple regression problem with *division's supervisory ratio* as the dependent variable and the same independent variables, the standardized regression coefficients for *agency's* supervisory ratio are ES, .14; UI, .52**; AS, .41**; P&T, .20*; DP, .22; LS, .15; and all combined, .21**.

mant that its not being met by reducing the span of control of supervisors on one level tends to be compensated for by disproportionately great reductions in the supervisory span of control on another level.[14]

The complexity of the duties influences requirements for supervisory personnel less than the complexity of the structure does. Table 10–5 shows that the proportion of routine clerical jobs is positively correlated with a wide span of control of first-line supervisors for all divisions (.34). But most of this association is spurious, decomposition reveals, owing to the influence of the division's size (.24), and the remaining direct relationship expressed by the standardized regression coefficient (.15) is essentially the result of between-type variations, inasmuch as the mean of the six regression coefficients indicative of the net within-type relationships is an inconsequential .05.[15] This does not mean that supervisors in charge of highly routine clerical work do not have a wider span of control than other supervisors. As a matter of fact, it was mentioned in Chapter 5 that the supervisors of the very simple job of keypunching have twice as many subordinates on the average (12.3) than supervisors generally. What the data do imply is that the important differences in task complexity among functions and the associated differences in the clerical ratio among functional divisions reflect all the variations in the span of control of first-line supervisors that can be accounted for by the clerical ratio. They also imply that the additional differences in the clerical ratio within a given function do not accurately express differences in task complexity but result from other factors and hence do not affect the supervisory span of control. In other words, variations in task complexity among the different functions within an agency are important for supervision but variations between agencies are not, which corresponds to the fact that different divisions have fundamentally different responsibilities but all agencies have essentially the same.

---

14. It should be noted that if agency headquarters were perfectly symmetrical pyramids, with equal numbers of levels throughout and with the same span of control for all managers and supervisors on every level, the span of control would be a mathematical function of size and the number of levels. The means in Table 10–1 show, however, that there are considerable variations among divisions in both number of levels and average span of control, not to speak of the additional variations within divisions. These variations make the empirical findings that size and levels influence the span of control not mathematically inevitable and thus of substantive interest, and they also make it possible for other factors to influence the span of control, as Table 10–5 shows.
15. The within-type correlations in the table are close to nil in five of six cases.

The division of labor may increase the need for supervisory manpower through the differentiation in the structure or through the heterogeneity of duties it produces. We shall assume that its effect on supervision mediated by the two other measures of differentiation signifies the former and that its remaining net effect signifies the influence of heterogeneity. The positive zero-order correlation between division of labor and supervisory span of control in Table 10–5 is spurious (.20 for all types), and decomposition indicates that once size is controlled (.81) the division of labor can be seen to narrow the span of control of supervisors owing to its association with multiple levels ($-.34$) and many sections ($-.25$). Since the standardized regression coefficient ($-.11$) is less than twice its standard error, the results suggest it is the structural complexity that the division of labor generates rather than the heterogeneity that it entails that narrows the span of control of supervisors. However, differences in the division of labor *among* the six types parallel their differences in the ratio of supervisors. The rank orders of the six type of divisions on mean number of occupational positions and mean proportion of supervisors, both controlled for size, are virtually identical (see Table 10–1, lower section). There is only one reversal in ranks, which produces a rank-order correlation of .94. The variations in the degree of occupational heterogeneity or specialization among different functions within an agency affect the need for supervision, but the remaining variations in a given function among different agencies have little import for supervision.

The fundamental differences in the complexity of the work and the occupational specialization of employees among major functions in employment security agencies overshadow in significance the minor differences in these respects among the divisions performing the same function. The differentiation of the divisions in an agency on the basis of the nature of the work process expresses an advanced form of the division of labor and leads to the concentration of routine clerical work in some divisions and of work requiring various specialized qualifications in others. Functions with a preponderance of clerks performing routine work need few supervisors, and functions with a variety of occupational specialists need many, and the variations in the precise proportion of clerks and in the precise number of different specialties among divisions performing similar functions have little effect on the need for supervisors. The size and structural complexity of divisions, in sharp contrast, have strong effects on the requirements for supervisors and their span of control that are independent of function and evident in divisions of all types, whatever their function. Whether the implications of the division of labor for structural complexity and for task heterogeneity are analytically separated, or whether the influences of vertical and horizontal differentiation are compared with those of a prevalence of routine clerical work, the conclusions are the same: the significance of structural complexity exceeds that of task complexity for supervisory manpower, at least in employment security agencies, in which variations among functions are confined to segments within the organization, and the functions of the organizations themselves are basically identical.

Conclusions

The six functions that have been analyzed are representative of the divisions found at the headquarters of employment security agencies in the United States, although there are great variations among agencies and few have exactly one each of these six divisions and no more at their headquarters. A basic difference between the headquarters divisions in charge of the two line functions is that hardly any of the employment services, but a considerable part of routine unemployment insurance operations, are carried out at the headquarters itself rather than in local offices, and this is reflected in differences in the personnel composition, for example, in the proportion of clerks. Using the clerical ratio as an indicator of the routine nature of the work in a division, the four staff functions are also clearly distinguishable: the work in data-processing is most routine, followed by administrative services, with legal services ranking third, and the personnel and technical function involving the least amount of clerical work. Another important factor that distinguishes functions is the degree of occupational differentiation among their positions. Occupational differentiation and clerical ratio, which are positively related for total agencies, are negatively related for types of divisions, and this contrast reveals the process of functional differentiation within agencies.

The functional differentiation of divisions in organizations expresses the division of labor in another form from that of the occupational differentiation of individual positions. The subdivision of labor segregates routine tasks that can be performed by clerks from complex ones that require specialized skills and allocates them to different positions, which is manifest in a positive association between occupational differentiation and clerical ratio. A higher-order subdivision of labor is achieved, however, by allocating most routine tasks to some divisions in the organizations and most complex ones requiring specialized skills to others, with the result that some types of divisions contain many clerks and few specialists and others few clerks and a variety of specialists, which is reflected in a negative association between clerical ratio and occupational differentiation among divisions of various types. Agencies with the most advanced occupational differentiation employ more clerks than other agencies, but the functions within an agency that use the most clerks exhibit less occupational differentiation than others.

Complex work makes greater demands on the time of supervisors than simple work, and it takes more time to supervise a variety of specialists than a homogeneous group of subordinates. These considerations imply that the clerical ratio widens, and occupational differentiation narrows, the span of control of supervisors. Such direct effects are indeed observed for all types of divisions, but they are owing to between-type differences, and no corresponding effects are in evidence within the six types. The implication of this pattern is that the major differences in task complexity and specialization among functionally differentiated divisions within each agency influence the need for supervision as expected and that the remaining differences in these respects within types—that is, among the divisions performing the same function in different agencies—have no further significance for supervision.

Variations among functions do not always exert the dominant influence, however. The influence of size on structural differentiation is independent of function, and so are many interrelations within the formal structure. The large size of a division promotes both vertical differentiation into multilevel hierarchies and horizontal differentiation into many sections in all six functions, and the number of levels is inversely related to the number of sections when size is controlled in all six. The comparison of average types is misleading in these respects. It implies that levels and sections are unrelated and that division of labor is related to them both, whereas regression analysis shows that levels and sections are inversely related and that the division of labor exerts no consistent direct effect on either (with size controlled in all cases). Thus, the internal differentiation in divisions exhibits the same traits as the differentiation of the headquarters as a whole and that in local branches: vertical and horizontal differentiation both depend on size but are inversely related to each other in all three instances.

The effects of size and of the structural complexity it generates on supervision are also independent of function. Whatever the type of division, vertical differentiation and horizontal differentiation increase requirements for supervisory manpower and reduce the span of control of supervisors on all levels in order to meet these requirements. Inasmuch as large divisions are more differentiated than small ones, large size indirectly raises requirements for supervisory personnel, but the economies in supervision that a large scale of operations makes possible outweigh these indirect negative effects, so that large size achieves over-all savings in managerial personnel. These findings on divisions replicate and help explicate parallel ones obtained in the analysis of total agencies (Table 4–1) and of local offices (Table 7–10). Large organizations need proportionately fewer supervisors than small ones, despite the fact that they are more differentiated, because their subunits are larger, and larger subunits permit a greater number of subordinates per supervisor on all levels. The supervisory ratio is not the only one that declines with increasing size; we have seen earlier that the ratio of administrative staff does too (Table 4–2). The new data suggest that the ratio of supportive personnel of any kind decreases with increasing size. Whether the majority of the personnel is clerical and a minority of professionals may be considered to support the basically clerical work, as in four of six types of divisions; or whether the majority consists of professionals and a minority of clerks provides administrative support, as in most local offices; in either case, the proportion of the minority declines with growing size. Large size seems to reduce overhead support by a minority regardless of the nature and skill level of the supportive service.

Both vertical and horizontal differentiation extend the time of managers required for coordination and consequently reduce the number of subordinates per supervisor in all six functions on all three managerial levels examined. To be sure, there are some exceptions to this predominant pattern, but these are themselves instructive. In four of the five deviant cases in which hierarchical differentiation does not reduce the supervisory span of control on one level, it produces a compensatingly stronger reduction in it on one or more other levels. The remaining exception as well as the only two exceptions pertaining to sections involves the UI division, possibly because the low degree of interdependence between its unemployment tax and benefit functions lessens the need for coordination below that which differentiation would lead one to expect. A final point is this: inasmuch as the same interrelations have been observed in divisions with a considerable variety of functions, the conjecture may not be completely unwarranted that these interrelations reveal general principles not confined to employment security agencies but also applicable to organizations with different functions.

PART FOUR

Toward a Theory of Organizations

A scientific system consists of a set of hypotheses
which form a deductive system; that is, which is arranged
in such a way that from some of the hypotheses as
premises all the other hypotheses logically follow. . . .
It is not necessary for these higher-level hypotheses to
be established independently of the law which they
explain; all that is required for them to provide an
explanation is that they should be regarded as established
and that the law should logically follow from them . . . it
is absurd to suppose that the scientific explanation of a
lower-level law by deducing it from a higher-level
law does not give some intellectual satisfaction even
if no explanation is known of the higher-level law itself.

BRAITHWAITE, *Scientific Explanation*

CHAPTER 11

Generalizations

Much empirical material has been analyzed in this book, and numerous interpretations of findings have been offered. We explained the research results as best we could and hope of course that the conjectures suggested are valid and will be confirmed in subsequent research. But it would be too much to hope that all interpretations advanced will prove to be correct, inasmuch as some were highly inferential and some were based on meager evidence. However, several regularities have been observed consistently in a great variety of contexts—so much so that the reader may have grown tired of the repeated accounts of them. These consistent patterns imply the existence of general underlying principles that can provide a systematic theoretical explanation of the formal structure of organizations.

The conception of systematic theory adopted is explicated by Braithwaite.[1] An empirical proposition concerning the relationship between two or more variables is explained by subsuming it under a more general proposition from which it can be logically derived. A deductive theory is a set

---

1. Richard B. Braithwaite, *Scientific Explanation* (Cambridge, Eng.: University Press, 1953). See also Karl R. Popper, *The Logic of Scientific Inquiry* (New York: Basic Books, 1959); and Carl G. Hempel and Paul Oppenheim, "The Logic of Explanation," *Philosophy of Science,* 15 (1948): 135–175.

of such logically interrelated propositions, all of which pertain to connections between at least two variables, and the least general of which, but only these, must be empirically demonstrable. "A scientific theory is a deductive system in which observable consequences logically follow from the conjunction of observed facts with the set of fundamental hypotheses in the system." [2] The theoretical hypotheses that explain the empirical findings cannot be directly tested, nor can they be definitively confirmed. They can only be established as probably valid by the successful predictions they make, that is, by the fact that the propositions that logically follow from them are substantiated by empirical evidence. Generalizations are in turn explained by subsuming them under still more general ones, so that the theoretical system may have propositions on several levels of abstraction. These principles apply not only to universal hypotheses—if A, then B— but also to the statistical ones characteristic of the social sciences—the more A, the more likely is B.

The explanatory thrust of a formal theory of this kind resides completely in the generality of the theoretical propositions and in the fact that the empirical findings can be deduced from them in strict logic. Theorizing in the social sciences usually assumes, not this form of a deductive model, but what Kaplan calls the "pattern model," according to which "something is explained when it is so related to a set of other elements that together they constitute a unified system." [3] The psychological experience of gaining understanding by the sudden insight the theory brings of how parts fit neatly into a whole is largely missing in deductive theorizing. Instead, the objective is to discover a few theoretical generalizations from which many different empirical propositions can be derived. Strange as it may seem, the higher-level hypotheses that explain the lower-level propositions are accepted as valid purely on the basis that they do explain them, in the specific sense that they logically imply them, and without independent empirical evidence, whereas acceptance of the lower-level propositions that need to be explained is contingent on empirical evidence. [4] Indeed, the reason for developing the deductive system is to empower empirical findings that confirm lower-level hypotheses indirectly to establish an abstract body of explanatory theory. And providing empirical evidence for any lower-level proposition strengthens confidence in all propositions. In Braithwaite's words:

---

2. Braithwaite, *Scientific Explanation,* p. 22.
3. Abraham Kaplan, *The Conduct of Inquiry* (San Francisco: Chandler, 1964), p. 333.
4. Braithwaite, *Scientific Explanation,* p. 303.

One of the main purposes in organizing scientific hypotheses into a deductive system is in order that the direct evidence for each lower-level hypothesis may become indirect evidence for all the other lowest-level hypotheses; although no amount of empirical evidence suffices to prove any of the hypotheses in the system, yet any piece of evidence for any part of the system helps toward establishing the whole of the system.[5]

This chapter attempts to start building a deductive theory of the formal structure of organizations. At first, a theoretical generalization is inferred from a large number of empirical findings. This generalization subsumes many empirically demonstrated propositions, that is, it logically implies them and hence explains them. Next, several middle-level propositions are deduced from the generalizations, and empirical findings supporting these generalizations are cited. These empirical findings for the deduced propositions indirectly help establish the basic one from which they were deduced. In elaborating the theory, another highest-level generalization is advanced, and the middle-range propositions and empirical findings that can be logically derived are discussed. There are several cross-connections between propositions in the two sets and some alternative ways of deriving a given proposition from others, which strengthen the interdependence in the theoretical system. To be sure, this formal theory does not encompass all empirical observations presented in the book. It is confined to those empirical relationships that are so strong and that are observable in such a variety of conditions that there is sound reason to suspect that general principles about organizations are manifest in these findings. In particular, moreover, it is confined to structural regularities found to be independent of function.

But can one construct a theory about organizations in general, even about limited aspects of them, without research on all types of different organizations? The answer is: one not only can, one must. If theorists were to wait until all the evidence were in, no theory would ever be developed, because all the evidence is never in. It is impossible to study all types of organizations. We have investigated the organizational structure in more than 1,500 component organizations, although they all belong to fifty-three roof organizations, and all of these are of a single type. It is, of course, possible to conduct research on more than one type of organization, but it is impossible to study a representative sample of all types, for there is no universe of types from which such a sample could be drawn. The theory advanced on the basis of data from one type of organization must be tested in other types, and a limited empirical test of this kind will be presented in

---

5. Ibid., pp. 17–18.

Chapter 12. One reason for restricting the formal theory to inferences from the most trustworthy data is that doing so gives us some confidence that the underlying principles are applicable to work organizations in general. Future research will tell whether this confidence is warranted.

Building a formal theory of organizations is a slow process, and here we only make a start. A number of substantial findings of theoretical interest —for example concerning technology and decentralization—are not encompassed by the formal theory, because we were not able to develop a deductive system of propositions under which they could be subsumed. This is a second, practical reason for the limited scope of the formal theory. The presentation of the deductive theory in the next two sections is therefore complemented by some less rigorous theorizing in the following section. There the discussion deals with the conflicting forces in organizations and the processes of adjustment to these forces, as inferred from the empirical findings. In conclusion, some issues posed by deductive theorizing in sociology are raised.

Deductive Theory

The formal structure of organizations is conceptualized here more narrowly than is usually the case. The term "social structure" is often used broadly, and sometimes loosely, to refer to the common value orientations of people, the traditional institutions in a society, cultural norms and role expectations, and nearly everything that pertains to life in groups. But it has a more specific meaning. A structure is, according to the dictionary, "something composed of parts." [6] The gist of a social structure is that people differ in status and social affiliation, that they occupy different positions and ranks, and that they belong to different groups and subunits of various sorts. The fact that the members of a collectivity are differentiated on the basis of several independent dimensions is the foundation of the collectivity's social structure. This differentiation into components along various lines in the formal structure of organizations is the object of this analysis. The theory centers attention on the social forces that govern the interrelations among differentiated elements in a formal structure and ignores the psychological forces that motivate the behavior of individual managers and other employees. The assumption is that fundamental structural conditions exert constraints on the members of organizations that make their administrative decisions virtually independent of their psychological dispositions. Formal structures consequently exhibit regularities

---

6. *Webster's New World Dictionary* (Cleveland: World, 1960).

that can be studied in their own right without investigating the motives of the individuals in organizations.

Formal organizations cope with the difficult problems large-scale operations create by subdividing responsibilities in numerous ways and thereby facilitating the work of any operating employee, any manager, and any subunit in the organization. The division of labor typifies the improvement in performance attainable through subdivision. The more completely simple tasks are separated from various kinds of complex ones, the easier it is for unskilled employees to perform the routine duties and for skilled employees to acquire the specialized training and experience to perform the different complex ones. Further subdivision of responsibilities occurs among functional divisions, enabling each one to concentrate on certain kinds of work. Local branches may be established in different places to facilitate serving clients in various areas, and these branches may become functionally specialized. The management of such a differentiated structure requires that managerial responsibilities too become subdivided among managers and supervisors on different hierarchical levels.

Weber recognized the vital importance the subdivision of responsibilities has for administrative organizations and placed it first in his famous enumeration of the characteristics of modern bureaucracy: "I. There is the principle of fixed and official jurisdictional areas . . . 1. The regular activities required for the purposes of the bureaucratically governed structure are distributed in a fixed way as official duties." [7] Consistent with this focus on a structure of differentiated responsibilities is his emphasis on the division of labor, specialized competence, and particularly the hierarchy of authority.[8] An apparent implication of this stress on structural differences is that the analysis of differentiation in the formal structure constitutes the core of the systematic study of formal organizations, but Weber himself does not pursue this line of inquiry. It is the central concern of the theory that we now start to present.

Increasing size generates structural differentiation in organizations along various dimensions at decelerating rates (1). This fundamental generalization is inferred from a large number of empirical findings. It logically implies these findings, and thereby explains them, and from it can be deduced several middle-range propositions, which subsume additional empirical findings. One can consider this first theoretical principle about organizations to comprise three parts, in which case the various middle-level and

7. Max Weber, *Essays in Sociology* (New York: Oxford University Press, 1946), p. 196.
8. Ibid., pp. 196–197; and Max Weber, *The Theory of Social and Economic Organization* (New York: Oxford University Press, 1947), pp. 330–331.

lower-level propositions are derived from the conjunction of these three highest-level ones. In this alternative formulation, the three highest-level propositions composing the first general principle about the formal structure of organizations are: (1A) large size promotes structural differentiation; (1B) large size promotes differentiation along several different lines; and (1C) the rate of differentiation declines with expanding size. The assumption is that these generalizations apply to the segments within organizations as well as to total organizations, which can be made explicit in a fourth proposition: (1D) the segments into which an organization is differentiated become internally differentiated in parallel manner.

The terms used must be explicitly defined. Reference is to formally established work organizations, which have specified objectives and are composed of paid employees. The number of these employees define the size of the organization and likewise the maximum degree of differentiation possible in the structure, inasmuch as there cannot be more social subunits than incumbents. A dimension of differentiation is any criterion in terms of which the members of the organization are formally divided into various positions, such as occupational specialties; ranks, such as managerial levels; and horizontal segments, such as branches, divisions, or sections. [The internal differentiation noted in proposition (1D) occurs within the differentiated segments of organizations and not within the differentiated positions or hierarchical ranks.] A structural component is any distinct official status—for example, employment interviewer or first-line supervisor —or any subunit within the organization—for example, local branch or functional division. The term "differentiation" refers exclusively to the number of structural components that are formally distinguished in terms of a single criterion or dimension, for instance, the number of occupational positions or of hierarchical levels or of local offices or of headquarters divisions. No over-all index of differentiation in all dimensions is used.[9] The structural components of a given kind in an organization or within its segments can vary not only in number but also in size, which is defined, just as the size of the total organization, in terms of number of employees.

A considerable number of empirical findings on employment security agencies can be explained by the general principle that differentiation in organizations increases at decreasing rates with increasing size, and none of the relevant evidence conflicts with this generalization. When total state

---

9. In the preliminary analysis of headquarters divisions, a measure of structural differentiation encompassing both levels and sections was used, but it did not yield any information not revealed by the two separate measures of number of levels and number of sections, and hence it has not been presented.

agencies are compared, increases in size are accompanied by initially rapid and subsequently more gradual increases in the number of local branches into which the agency is spatially differentiated; the number of occupational positions expressing the division of labor; the number of levels in the hierarchy; the number of functional divisions at the headquarters; and the number of sections per division. This pattern of growing differentiation at declining rates with expanding size is manifest in a logarithmic slope of the regression lines of the number of structural components on size in the scatter diagrams, whatever the criterion of structural component.[10]

The internal differentiation within the segments that have become differentiated in the total agency assumes the same form. Local offices become differentiated at declining rates as their size increases. Specifically, office size is correlated with number of occupational positions (.51), number of hierarchical levels (.68), and number of functional sections (.61), and all three regression lines exhibit logarithmic curves.[11] Similar logarithmic curves characterize the differentiation within the functional divisions at the agency headquarters. The larger a division is, the larger is the number of its occupational positions, hierarchical levels, and functional sections, and differences between very small and medium-sized divisions have again more impact on variations in these three aspects of differentiation than differences between medium-sized and very large divisions. Moreover, this pattern of differentiation at decelerating rates with increasing size is observable in six separate types of divisions with basically different functions,[12] which suggests that it is independent of function and thus provides some support for the assumption that the same pattern will be found in other organizations that have different functions from those of employment security agencies.

The first proposition that can be derived from the fundamental generalization is the following: *as the size of organizations increases, its marginal influence on differentiation decreases* (1.1). As a matter of fact, this is hardly a derived proposition, because it is merely a restatement of one part (1C) of the original general principle. But by translating the initial proposition into different concepts, the new proposition directs attention to a distinctive implication and an important parallel with the economic principle of diminishing returns or, in technical terms, of the eventually dimin-

---

10. See Figures 3–1, 3–3, 3–5, and 3–7.
11. For an example, see Figure 7–1.
12. The pattern of differentiation at decelerating rates is reflected in the differences between the correlations of raw size and those of the logarithm of size with various measures of differentiation shown in the first six rows of Table 10–2.

ishing marginal physical productivity. In Boulding's words: "As we increase the quantity of any one input which is combined with a fixed quantity of the other inputs, the marginal physical productivity of the variable input must eventually decline." [13]

In a factory, production output can be raised by adding workers, but the marginal increment in output resulting from adding more and more workers without changing plant size and equipment eventually declines. In parallel fashion, a larger complement of employees in an organization makes its structure more differentiated, but as the number of employees and the differentiation of the structure increase, the marginal influence of a given increase in personnel on further differentiation declines. It seems that the differentiation produced by the expanding size of organizations stems the power of additional expansions in size to make the structure still more differentiated.

But why does the marginal influence of size on differentiation in organizations decline? If the analogy with the economic principle of diminishing returns is appropriate, it should provide some clues for answering this question. The reason for the eventually declining marginal productivity of increments in only one type of economic input is that such increments create an imbalance of inputs and the growing need for other inputs depresses productivity. For example, additional workers cannot be efficiently utilized in production without parallel increases in equipment and space. The influence of increasing organizational size on differentiation can be conceptualized as producing in similar fashion a growing need that diminishes the influence of further increases in size.

The existence of differentiation in a formal organization implies a need for coordination. There are at least two inputs, using the terminology of economics, on which the development of structural differentiation in organization depends. The first is a sufficient number of employees (the measure of size) to fill the different positions and man the various subunits, and the second is an adequate administrative machinery to meet problems of coordination. The advancing differentiation to which an increasing number of employees gives rise intensifies the need for coordination in the organization, and this need restrains the further development of differentiation, which is reflected in the declining marginal influence of increasing size on differentiation. The implication of these considerations extrapolated from economic theory is that differentiation in organizations creates pressures to find ways to meet the need for coordination. We shall later re-

13. Kenneth E. Boulding, *Economic Analysis,* 3d ed. (New York: Harper, 1955), p. 589.

turn to the analysis of this problem, after discussing five other propositions that can be derived from the first basic generalization.

The second derived proposition is that *the larger an organization is, the larger is the average size of its structural components of all kinds* (1.2). This proposition logically follows from the principle of the decelerating rate of differentiation with increasing organizational size (1C), which is graphically expressed by the decline in the slopes (the logarithmic curves) of the regression lines of the number of structural components of various kinds on size. In a diagram with total size or number of employees on the horizontal axis and number of structural components on the vertical axis, the average size of the structural components of an agency represented by a point is indicated by the ratio of the horizontal to the vertical coordinate of this point. As the positive slope of the regression line declines, this ratio is larger for most large than for most small agencies.[14] If the increases in the number of structural components do not keep pace with the increase in organizational size producing them, which is what their declining rate signifies, it necessarily follows that the average size of these components becomes larger as the size of the total organization does. Even in those cases in which the decline in the slope of the regression line is not pronounced, the average size of the structural components is strongly associated with the size of the organization. Two examples are the mean size of local branches, which has a zero-order correlation with agency size of .65, and the number of incumbents of the average occupational position, which is correlated .94 with agency size.

Thus, the large size of an organization raises the average size as well as the number of its structural components. Large agencies tend to have more and larger local offices than small agencies, more and larger headquarters divisions, and the same holds true for each of their structural components. The large size of the local offices within an agency and of its headquarters divisions, whatever their function, in turn tends to increase both the number and the average size of sections, and both the number of managerial ranks and of occupational positions and the mean number of employees occupying each rank and each position. Indeed, this principle is not confined to the organizational context: the larger a city is, the larger tends to be both the size and the number of the employment security offices in it.

This double effect of organizational size has the paradoxical result that

---

14. This can be readily seen by looking at the regression lines in any of the scatter diagrams in Figures 3–1, 3–3, 3–5, 3–7, or 7–1. For a point moving along this line from left to right, the horizontal coordinate increases more rapidly than the vertical one, which means that the ratio of the first to the second increases.

large offices and headquarters divisions constitute at the same time a more homogeneous and a more heterogeneous occupational environment for most employees than small ones. For larger offices or divisions contain comparatively many employees in nearly every occupational specialty, providing a congenial ingroup of colleagues for most employees, which is often not available in small organizational units, and they simultaneously contain a relatively great variety of different specialties, enhancing opportunities for stimulating contacts with people whose training and experience are unlike one's own. However, the greater opportunity for social interaction with a colleague ingroup in large offices may prove so attractive that social contacts with persons from different specialties are rarer there than in small ones, despite the fact that opportunities for outgroup contacts are better in large offices too.

The proposition that the average size of structural components is associated with the size of the organization (1.2) has been derived from the proposition that differentiation, or the number of structural components, increases at a decreasing rate with increasing organizational size (1C). But would it not make more sense to consider the former proposition (1.2) the higher-order one and derive the latter (1C) from it? After all, it is intuitively understandable that the broader scope of operations of larger employment security agencies requires them to have more employment interviewers, more file clerks, and more employees in nearly every position than small agencies have, and the same applies to other structural components. But, the fact that the mean size of structural components increases with increasing organizational size (1.2) does not necessarily imply that the increase in the number of components with increasing organizational size occurs at a decreasing rate (1C), whereas the fact that the latter is the case necessarily implies that the former must be. This is why the proposition that the rate of structural differentiation decreases with increasing size is considered the fundamental one that explains why larger agencies have larger structural components of all kinds than smaller ones.

A third derived proposition is that *the proportionate size of the average structural component, as distinguished from its absolute size, decreases with increases in organizational size* (1.3). This follows directly from (1A): if the number of structural components, the criterion of differentiation, increases as organizational size does, the proportion of all employees who are in the average component must decrease. Hence, most groups or categories of employees in big organizations are larger in absolute numbers but constitute a smaller proportion of the total personnel than in small organizations. The consequence that logically follows from the premise is merely that the *mean* proportionate size of all employee complements in terms of a given dimension decreases with increasing organizational size, not that the proportion of any particular personnel complement does.

But we may reformulate this proposition (1.3) into a probability statement about groupings of employees: chance expectations are that the proportionate size of any personnel complement decreases with increasing organizational size, *ceteris paribus*. The empirical data show that this proposition applies to various kinds of administrative overhead or supportive service for the majority work force. The proportionate size of the administrative staff is inversely related to organizational size, and so is the proportion of supervisory personnel, not only for entire agencies but also for their local branches and for their headquarters divisions regardless of function.[15] (The adjectives "supervisory" and "managerial" are used interchangeably for personnel complements that include supervisors and managers on all levels, as in this case.) When a certain personnel complement is singled out for attention—the staff or the supervisory component—and exhibits the expected decrease in proportionate size with increasing organizational size, the remainder of the total personnel—the line or the nonsupervisory employees—must naturally reveal a complementary increase in proportionate size. This is mathematically inevitable, and it indicates that the reformulated proposition (1.3) cannot possibly apply to both parts of a dichotomy. Generally, the proportionate size of any supportive service provided by a distinctive minority to the majority work force is likely to decline with increasing organizational size.

Another proposition can be derived either from the last one (1.3) or from the one preceding (1.2): *the supervisory span of control is wider the larger the organization is* (1.4). If chances are that the proportionate size of any organizational component declines with increasing size (1.3), and if this applies to the proportion of supervisors, it follows that the number of subordinates per supervisor, or the span of control, must expand with increasing size (1.4). Besides, if the absolute average size of any structural component or grouping of employees probably increases with increasing size (1.2), and if this applies to the various work groups each under a supervisor, it follows that the size of the group under a supervisor, or his span of control, tends to expand with increasing size (1.4). Here implications are extended beyond the limits of strictly logical deduction from the premises. What two parts of the initial generalization (1A and 1C) logically imply is that the statistical probability is that the size of any personnel component increases in absolute numbers and decreases as a propor-

15. The zero-order correlations are: agency size (log) and staff ratio, $-.60$; agency size (log) and supervisory ratio, $-.45$; office size (log) and supervisory ratio, $-.64$; division size (log) and supervisory ratio, ranging for the six functional types from $-.12$ to $-.39$.

tion of the total as organizational size increases. (The inferences for mean absolute and proportionate size for all components have been translated into probabilities for any.) Whether these derived propositions apply to a particular personnel component, such as the supervisory personnel on a given level, must be empirically ascertained. If the evidence is negative, it would not falsify the theory, though it would weaken it. If the evidence is positive, it strengthens the theory and extends it beyond the limits of its purely logical implications by taking into account the empirical data confirming this particular application of the merely probabilistic deduction from the theory.[16]

The empirical data on employment security agencies confirm the proposition that the span of control of supervisors expands with increasing organizational size. This is the case for all levels of managers and supervisors examined in these agencies and their subunits. The larger an agency, the wider is the span of control of its director and the average span of control of its division heads. The larger a headquarters division, whatever its function, the wider is the span of control of its division head, the average span of control of its middle managers, and the average span of control of its first-line supervisors. The larger a local office, the wider is the span of control of the office manager and that of the average first-line supervisor.[17] Moreover, the size of the total organization has an independent effect widening the supervisory span of control when the size of local offices is controlled.[18] Big organizations and their larger headquarters divisions and

---

16. Two kinds of statistical or probability statements must be distinguished, theoretical and empirical ones. On the one hand, it is only probable that any given large agency has a lower proportion of supervisors than any given small agency does, because the correlation is less than 1.00. This empirical probability is not what is referred to in the text. On the other hand, and this is what is discussed above, it is only probable that the ratio of supervisory personnel is inversely related to agency size, because the theory only predicts that the proportionate size of most components of the agency is inversely related to its own size and merely that it is probable that such an inverse relationship will be observed with respect to any particular component, such as that of supervisory personnel.
17. The zero-order correlations of size (log) of the respective organizational units and mean span of control of various managers are: agency director, .39; head of division, .22 for all types combined; middle managers in divisions, ranging, with one exception (.05) from .17 to .79; first-line supervisors in divisions, ranging from .39 to .69 in the six types; managers of local offices, .40; and first-line supervisors in local offices, .66.
18. The standardized regression coefficient between agency size and mean span of control of first-line supervisors in local offices, with office size and a number of other conditions controlled, is .27; see Table 8–7.

local branches tend to have more employees in any given position with similar duties than small organizations with their smaller subunits, as we have seen, which makes it possible to use supervisors more efficiently in large units by assigning more subordinates with similar duties to each supervisor. The additional influence of the size of the total organization, independent of that of the size of the office, on the number of subordinates per supervisor may reveal a structural effect.[19] The prevalence of a wide span of supervisory control in large organizations, owing to the large size of most of their branch offices, creates a normative standard that exerts an influence in its own right increasing the number of subordinates assigned to supervisors regardless of the size of the office, and the same is the case, *mutatis mutandis,* for the prevalence of a narrow supervisory span of control in small organizations with their smaller branches. (To be sure, the supervisory span of control is also affected by other conditions, such as the nature of the duties.)

Organizations exhibit an economy of scale in management overhead (1.5). This proposition is implicit in the two foregoing ones. For if the proportion of supervisory personnel on all levels declines with size (1.3) and their span of control expands with size (1.4), this means that large-scale operations reduce the proportionate size of the administrative overhead, specifically, of the complement of managers and supervisors. In fact, the relative size of administrative overhead of other kinds, such as staff and supportive personnel, also declines with increasing size, as has been noted. The question arises whether the economy of scale in administrative overhead produces over-all personnel economies with increasing scale of operations. The data on employment security agencies are equivocal on this point. The only index of personnel economy available, the ratio of all employees engaged in unemployment benefit operations to the number of clients served by them, is inversely correlated with size, but the correlation is too small ($-.14$) to place any confidence in it with a case base of only fifty-three agencies. Logarithmic transformation of size raises the correlation to $-.24$, which suggests that large size might reduce the man-hour costs of benefit operations slightly. Whereas this finding is inconclusive, the numerous findings that indicate that the relative size of management and other administrative overhead declines with increasing organizational size are not. Large-scale operations make it possible to realize economies in managerial and supervisory manpower. This can be explained in terms of the generalization that the number of structural compo-

---

19. Peter M. Blau, "Structural Effects," *American Sociological Review,* 25 (1960): 178–193.

nents increases at a declining rate with increasing size (1), which implies that the *size* of work groups under a supervisor, just as that of most personnel components, increases with increasing size, whereas the *proportion* of supervisors, just as that of most personnel components, decreases with increasing size, and these relationships account for the economy of scale in management.

A final derived proposition in this set is that *the economy of scale in administrative overhead itself declines with increasing organizational size* (1.6). This proposition follows indirectly from two parts of the basic generalization (1A and 1C) in conjunction with one derived proposition (1.3). If the number of structural components increases with increasing organizational size (1A), the statistical expectation is that the proportionate size of any particular personnel component decreases with size. In fact, as we have seen, the proportion of supervisory personnel and that of staff personnel do decrease as size increases (1.3). But since the increase in the number of components with expanding size occurs at a declining rate (1C), the decrease in the proportionate size of the average component implicit in this increase in number must also occur at a declining rate with expanding organizational size. Reformulation in terms of statistical probability yields the proposition that chance expectations are that the proportionate size of any particular personnel complement decreases at a decelerating rate as organizations become larger.

Whether this statistical proposition about most personnel components holds true for the supervisory and the staff component is an empirical question, and the answer is that it does. The proportion of staff personnel decreases at a declining rate as organizational size increases, and so does the proportion of supervisory personnel both in local offices and at the agency headquarters, as the scatter diagrams show.[20] The marginal power of organizational size to effect economies in administrative overhead diminishes with growing size, just as its marginal power to generate structural differentiation does. Both of these patterns are implied, and in this technical sense can be explained, by the generalization that the number of structural components in an organization increases at a declining rate with expanding size.

---

20. See Figures 4–1, 4–3, and 7–2. The same pattern is observable in the scatter diagrams for divisions; a rough indication of these curves, which underestimates them, is provided by the finding that the negative correlation of the supervisory ratio with log size is at least slightly more pronounced than its negative correlation with raw size in five of the six types of divisions (Table 10–4).

Elaboration

The structure of formal organizations seems to undergo repeated social fission with growth. In a large organization responsibilities tend to be subdivided to facilitate their performance, and it thereby becomes differentiated into a number of structural components of diverse sorts. The larger an organization, however, the larger is typically not only the number but also the average size of the components into which it is differentiated. These larger segments of larger organizations, in turn, tend to become internally differentiated along various lines. Thus, the process of social fission recurs within the differentiated units it has originally produced. Differentiation lessens the difficulties the performance of duties entails by reducing the scope of the responsibilities assigned to any individual or unit, but it simultaneously enhances the complexity of the structure. Social fission makes duties less complex at the expense of greater structural complexity.

The extensive subdivision of responsibilities that the large size of an organization promotes has the result that many individual employees have the same duties and entire units have similar ones, which effects savings in supervisory manpower. At the same time, however, the greater structural complexity implicit in the pronounced subdivision of large organizations intensifies problems of communication and coordination, which make new demands on the time of managers and supervisors on all levels. The administrative problems engendered by the complexity of differentiated structures are likely to have feedback effects that create resistance to the further development of differentiation. This resistance produced by feedback may be the reason why the influence of organizational size on differentiation declines with increasing size. The expanding size of an organization is a social force that effects differentiation. (We infer the dynamics engendered by expanding size from cross-sectional data on variations in size.) The more differentiated an organization already is, the more resistance such a force may have to overcome to produce still more differentiation, and the more of an expansion in size it therefore takes to produce a given increment in differentiation.

In short, the very subdivision of responsibilities, through which large organizations facilitate the performance of duties and reduce the need for supervision, creates structural complexities in the highly differentiated organizations and new problems of communication and coordination for supervisory personnel. The formal theory that has been presented accounts for the effect of size on savings in supervisory manpower (1.4, 1.5) as well as for its effect on differentiation that makes the structure more complex (1A). But it does not encompass the demands made on the time of supervisors by problems of coordination in a complex structure. To be sure, the analysis of the proposition that the marginal influence of size on differentiation declines (1.1) has already led to the inference that differentiation engenders administrative problems. Nevertheless, this principle cannot be deduced from the first basic generalizations and hence requires the postulation of another.

Structural differentiation in organizations raises requirements for managerial manpower (2), because the intensified problems of communication and coordination in complex structures demand managerial attention. This second fundamental generalization of the deductive theory subsumes in its first part many empirical findings, whereas the second part introduces theoretical terms not independently measured in the research but inferred from the first part to explain the nexus between its terms. The assumptions are that differentiation makes an organization more complex; that a complex structure engenders problems of communication and coordination; that managers, the staff, and even first-line supervisors spend time dealing with these problems; and that consequently more supervisory and administrative manpower is needed in highly differentiated than in less differentiated structures. Although these assumptions of the intervening connections are not empirically tested, the implications of the conclusion are. If, in accordance with the inferred assumptions, much of the time of supervisors on all levels in the most differentiated structures is occupied with problems of communication and coordination, it follows that these supervisors have less time left for guiding and reviewing the work of subordinates.

Hence, the more differentiated the formal structure, the more administrative personnel of all kinds should be found in an organization of a given size, and the narrower should be the span of control of first-line supervisors as well as higher managers. This is precisely the pattern the empirical findings reveal. Vertical differentiation into levels and horizontal differentiation into divisions or sections are both positively related to the proportion of supervisors among the total personnel, controlling size, in the whole organization, in local branches, and in the six functional types of headquarters divisions. They are also positively related to the proportionate size of the administrative staff in agencies of a given size. Moreover, both vertical and horizontal differentiation, with size held constant, are negatively related to the span of control of managers and supervisors on different levels in local offices and in headquarters divisions, regardless of function.[21]

---

21. For agencies, see Tables 4–1 and 4–2; for local offices, Table 7–10; for divisions, Tables 10–4 and 10–5.

The finding that the second generalization, and its derivations discussed below, are supported when the span of control of supervisors on a given level is substituted for the ratio of all supervisors is of special importance. The more levels organizations of a given size have, the higher is necessarily their supervisory ratio, that is, the proportion of their personnel above the operating level. Consequently, the question arises whether the observed relationship between number of levels and supervisory ratio merely reflects this mathematical nexus, which would make it trivial, and a similar question can be raised concerning the relationship between number of divisions and supervisory ratio. The positive relationship of either number of levels or number of divisions (or sections) with the supervisory span of control, which is not affected by this mathematical nexus, gives a negative answer to this question and clearly shows that there is an empirical connection that is not tautological. These empirical data support the principle that hierarchical as well as horizontal differentiation, presumably by creating problems of coordination, make demands on the time of managers and thereby enlarge the management component.

One implied proposition is that *the large size of an organization indirectly raises requirements for managerial manpower through the structural differentiation it generates* (2.1). If increasing organizational size generates differentiation (1A), and if differentiation raises requirements for supervisory manpower (2), it follows that the indirect effect of size must be to raise these requirements. Decomposition of the zero-order correlations of size with various indicators of supervisory or administrative manpower in multiple regression analysis makes it possible to isolate the indirect effects of size mediated by differentiation from its direct effects. In every problem analyzed, the empirical findings confirm the prediction that the indirect effects of size mediated by both vertical differentiation into levels and horizontal differentiation into divisions or sections raise the ratio of supervisory or administrative to total personnel. This is the case whether the dependent variable under consideration is the staff ratio or the supervisory ratio at the agency headquarters, or the ratio of all supervisors or the span of control of first-line supervisors in any of the six types of functional divisions or in local branches. In all these instances, the indirect effects of size mediated by the differentiation it generates and its direct effects are in opposite directions. The savings in administrative overhead large-scale operations make possible are counteracted by the expansion in administrative overhead the structural complexity of large organizations necessitates.

Another derived proposition is that *the direct effects of large organizational size of producing savings in managerial manpower exceed its indirect effects of raising managerial overhead owing to the structural complexity it generates* (2.2). This is a logical consequence of propositions

(1.5) and (2.1). If the over-all effect of large size realizes economies in management overhead, and if size, by fostering differentiation, indirectly increases management overhead, it follows that its effect of reducing overhead must outweigh this indirect effect. All the decompositions of the zero-order correlations of size with various measures of management referred to in the preceding paragraph reflect this, as they inevitably must. For example, the direct effect of agency size on the supervisory ratio at the agency headquarters, which is represented by the standardized regression coefficient when three measures of differentiation are controlled, is -1.13, whereas its over-all effect is $-.45$, the difference resulting from the strong counteracting effect mediated by differentiation.[22] For the staff ratio at the headquarters, with the same conditions controlled, the direct effect of size is -1.04, and its over-all effect is $-.60$, revealing again a substantial indirect counteracting effect owing to structural differentiation. The direct and indirect effects of the size of a division on its ratio of supervisors and of the size of a local office on its supervisory ratio reveal parallel differences.[23] *Ceteris paribus,* a large scale of operations would effect tremendous savings in administrative overhead, but these savings are much reduced by the structural complexity of large organizations. Consistently, however, the economies of scale exceed the costs of complexity, so that large organizations, despite their greater structural complexity, require proportionately less management manpower than small ones.

There are additional crosswise connections between propositions that strengthen the interdependence in the theoretical system. The last two propositions, for instance, can be derived in an alternative manner. The economy of scale in managerial manpower (1.5) is evident within branch offices and headquarters divisions, in accordance with the proposition (1D)

22. The three aspects of differentiation controlled that account for the difference are number of levels, number of divisions, and number of sections per division (see Tables 4–1 and 4–2).
23. In the multiple regression analysis for all divisions combined, with the same conditions controlled as those in Table 10–5, the standardized regression coefficient indicating the direct effect of division size (log) on supervisory *ratio* is $-.77$, and the zero-order correlation indicative of the over-all effect is only $-.23$, with differentiation into levels (.34) and sections (.21) being responsible for most of the difference. The separate regression analyses for the six types reveal parallel findings. In the analysis of local offices (with levels, sections, specialization, manager's span of control, and division of labor controlled), the standardized regression coefficient of office size (log) on the supervisory *ratio* is -1.43, but this enormous direct effect is reduced to an over-all effect, represented by the zero-order correlation, of $-.64$, largely owing to differentiation into levels (.41) and sections (.40).

that the initial generalization (1), and thus the consequences deduced from it, apply to the segments of the organization. The fact that large size promotes differentiation of the organization into increasing numbers of offices and divisions (1A) implies that these segments are smaller than they would be in the absence of such differentiation (though they are larger than corresponding segments in small organizations). If differentiation reduces the size of offices and divisions, and if smaller segments require more managerial manpower than larger ones, it follows that the extensive differentiation in large organizations diminishes the economies in managerial manpower large size would otherwise achieve. This principle, that large organizational size indirectly reduces the economies in management overhead it directly produces, is embodied, in different language, in propositions (2.1) and (2.2). Whereas the structural differentiation of large organizations raises the cost in managerial manpower of large-scale operations, however, it simultaneously enhances the economy of scale, that is, the *rate* at which an increase in scale achieves economies.

The last proposition to be derived is that *the differentiation of large organizations into segments arrests the decline in the economy of scale in managerial manpower with increasing size,* that is, the decline in the decrease in the proportion of managerial personnel with increasing size (2.3). The derivation of this proposition is rather complicated and must be approached in several steps. It is not as well knit into the system as the other propositions are, and it should be regarded as a conjecture. Let us first note another cross-connection. The growing requirements for managerial manpower resulting from the structural differentiation engendered by expanding size (2.1) increasingly impinge upon the savings in managerial manpower that a large scale of operations realizes (1.5), which helps explain why the economy of scale in management overhead tends to decline as size and complexity increase (1.6). But there is a major exception to this tendency of the economy of scale in management to decline, and the new proposition is designed to account for it.

The concept of economy of scale in managerial manpower refers to the fact that the proportion of various kinds of administrative personnel decreases with increasing size of the organization or its segment. The operational indication is a negative correlation between any of these proportions and size, which is represented on a graph by a negative slope of the regression line of the proportion on size. These negative correlations and slopes are evident in all empirical cases: size of local branch and proportion of all managerial personnel, or its size and ratio of first-line supervisors to operating employees (which is the reverse of the span of control of first-line supervisors); size of functional division and ratio of all managerial

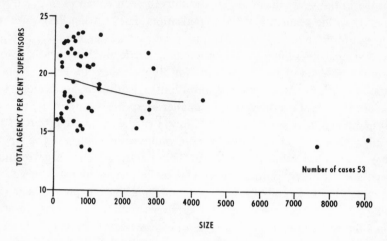

FIGURE 11–1   Scatter Diagram of Total Per Cent Supervisors and Size

personnel, or its size and ratio of supervisors to subordinates on three levels (without exception for all divisions combined; with a few if the six types are separately examined); size of total agency and proportion of staff personnel, its size and proportion of managerial personnel at the headquarters, or its size and proportion of managerial personnel in the total organization.

A decline in this economy of scale means that the rate of decrease in the ratio of managerial personnel itself decreases with increasing size. This is reflected on a graph by the curve of the regression line of the ratio on size, which shows that the ratio of overhead personnel drops first sharply and then more gradually with increasing size. The ratio of managerial personnel in local offices illustrates a decrease at such a decreasing rate (Figure 7–2), and so does the ratio of the staff personnel (Figure 4–3) and of the supervisors at the agency headquarters (Figure 4–1), and the same pattern is observable in most other relationships mentioned in the above paragraph. The major exception [24] is that the proportion of managerial personnel in the total agency does not reveal such a declining rate but a fairly linear decrease as agency size increases, which is shown in Figure 11–1.[25]

---

24. There may be some additional exceptions in the six types of divisions for some of the specific measures of span of control, because these scatter diagrams have not been drawn.

25. The previous analysis has dealt with the supervisory ratio at the headquarters and those in local offices separately, because the structures of the headquarters and that of local offices are different and there is no systematic way to combine the measures of structural differentiation.

Although this appears to be a deviant case, the principle it expresses can be deduced from the propositions in the theory.

In local offices, the smallest organizational unit examined, the proportion of all supervisory personnel drops rapidly as size increases from ten or less to about fifty employees, but it drops much more slowly with further increases to one and two hundred employees (see Figure 7–2). From a projection of this trend, one would expect that further increases in size to several thousand employees are hardly accompanied by any decline in the proportion of supervisory personnel. As the size of the entire organization increases from about one hundred to several thousand employees, however, the total proportion of supervisory personnel decreases on the average at a fairly constant rather than declining rate, as Figure 11–1 reveals, though there is much scatter. While the average decline is not pronounced, it is by no means inconsequential; the zero-order correlation is − .34, which compares with a correlation of − .46 between size of office and its proportion of supervisors. (However, the latter correlation is raised to − .64 if size is logarithmically transformed. In contrast, the former correlation is reduced to − .23 by such a transformation, which is another indication that the regression line does not exhibit a logarithmic curve.) Why does the decrease in the proportion of managerial personnel with increasing size, which is already very gradual as size (of offices) expands beyond fifty employees, not virtually cease as size (of agencies) expands from several hundred to several thousand? Why is there again a considerable decrease in this larger size range? The answer suggested by the theory is that the differentiation of large organizations into many branch offices (and divisions), though raising the over-all proportion of managers needed, simultaneously restores the economy of scale in management overhead, that is, it recreates the decline in the proportion of managerial personnel with increasing size that is observed among very small organizational units.

The savings in managerial manpower realized by the large size of an organizational segment (1.5) are more and more counteracted by the growing need for managerial manpower in the increasingly differentiated structures generated by expanding size (2.1). This is why the rate of savings in managerial manpower with size tends to decline with increasing size of organizational units (1.6). In other words, the *rate* of savings in management overhead with expanding size is higher among comparatively small than among comparatively large organizational segments, although, or perhaps because, the management overhead is bigger in small than in large organizational segments. Differentiation in a large organization (1A) means that it consists of relatively many smaller rather than relatively few larger organizational segments, such as local offices. Inasmuch as the *rate* of savings in management overhead is higher in smaller than in larger organizational segments, the reduction in the size of segments created by differentiation raises overhead but simultaneously raises the rate of savings in it and thus checks the decline in the economy of scale with respect to management overhead.

Inferred Processes

A formal theory of the formal structure of formal organizations has been presented. Its subjects are formally established organizations with paid employees, not emergent groupings or voluntary associations of people. It is confined to the analysis of the formal structure of organizations, ignoring the informal relations and the behavior of individuals within them. And the endeavor has been to develop a formal theory, though not one couched in mathematical terms, by inferring from many empirical findings a minimum number of generalizations that through their implications can logically account for these findings concerning structural differentiation. The two basic generalizations, which together with nine propositions deducible from them sufficed for this purpose, are: (1) the increasing size of organizations generates structural differentiation along various dimensions at decelerating rates; and (2) structural differentiation enlarges the administrative component in organizations.

The concluding review of the theory rearranges the order of presentation of propositions to call attention to alternative connections between them and to some of the unmeasured terms assumed to underlie these connections. Organizing the work of men means subdividing it into component elements. In a formal organization, explicit procedures exist for systematically subdividing the work necessary to achieve its objectives. Different tasks are assigned to different positions; specialized functions are allocated to various divisions and sections; branches may be created in dispersed locations; administrative responsibilities are subdivided among staff personnel and managers on various hierarchical levels. The larger an organization and the scope of its responsibilities, the more pronounced is its differentiation along these lines (1A, 1B), and the same is the case for its subunits (1D). But large-scale operations, despite the greater subdivision of work, also involve a larger volume of most duties than operations on a smaller scale. Hence, large organizations tend to have larger as well as more structural components of various sorts than small organizations (1.2).

The pronounced differentiation of responsibilities in large organizations enhances simultaneously intraunit homogeneity and interunit heterogeneity. Inasmuch as the amount of work required in most specialties is greater in large organizations, there are comparatively many employees performing homogeneous tasks in large organizations. The large homogeneous personnel components in large organizations simplify supervision and administration, which is reflected in a wider span of control of supervisors (1.4) and a lower administrative ratio (1.3) than in small organizations. Consequently, organizations exhibit an economy of scale in administrative manpower (1.5). At the same time, however, the heterogeneity among organizational components produced by differentiation creates problems of coordination and pressures to expand the administrative personnel to meet these problems (2). In this formulation, the unmeasured concepts of intraunit homogeneity and interunit heterogeneity have been introduced to explain why large size has two opposite effects on administrative overhead, reducing it owing to the enlarged scale of similar tasks, and raising it owing to the differentiation among parts.

By generating differentiation, then, large size indirectly raises administrative overhead (2.1), and if its influence on differentiation were unrestrained, large organizations might well have disproportionately large administrative machineries, in accordance with the bureaucratic stereotype. The facts of the case are different, however. The administrative ratio decreases with expanding organizational size, notwithstanding the increased administrative ratio resulting from the differentiation in large organizations (2.2). Two feedback effects of the management costs of differentiation may be inferred, which counteract the influences of size on administration and on differentiation, respectively. The first of these apparently reduces the savings in administrative manpower resulting from a large scale of operations, as implied by the decline in the rate of decrease in managerial overhead with increasing organizational size (1.6). (Whereas differentiation into local branches may keep the rate of overhead savings with increasing size constant [2.3], it also raises the amount of overhead.) The second feedback process probably attributable to the administrative problems engendered by differentiation creates resistance to further differentiation, which is reflected in the diminishing marginal influence of expanding size on differentiation (1.1) and the declining rate at which size promotes differentiation (1C).

In short, feedback processes seem to keep the amount of differentiation produced by increasing organizational size below the level at which the additional management costs of coordination would equal the administrative savings realized by the larger scale of operations. Hence, organizations exhibit an economy of scale in administration, despite the extra administrative overhead required by the pronounced differentiation in large organizations, but this economy of scale declines with increasing size, on account of this extra overhead due to differentiation. The feedback effects inferred, though not directly observable, can explain why the influence of size on differentiation as well as its influence on management economy declines with increasing size. Figure 11–2 presents these connections graphically.

Two points emerge from this review of the theory: the size of organizations exerts profound influences on their structure, and its influences are sometimes in opposite directions. In employment security agencies, as a matter of fact, the influence of size extends to most of the organizational characteristics examined, including salaries, automation and mechanization of operations, standardization of procedures, decentralization of decisions, and services administered—as well as structural differentiation along all lines considered. In a number of instances, size has direct and indirect effects in opposite directions on the same organizational attribute, or two indirect influences in opposite directions. These cases reveal conflicting forces in the organization, and their analysis makes it possible to infer the dynamics set in motion by contradictory conditions and the resulting processes of organizational adjustment. We turn now to a further examination of such conflicting forces and the processes that can be inferred from them. Though theoretical interpretations are advanced in this analysis, the theorizing is less rigorous than in the foregoing discussion, and it is not formalized into a deductive system.

Sometimes, the indirect effects of size that counteract its direct effects may be interpreted as readjustments to problems the direct effects have produced, but this inference of adjustment is by no means always warranted. In the example incorporated into the deductive theory, the differentiation of large organizations into components of various kinds to facilitate the performance of responsibilities engenders problems of commu-

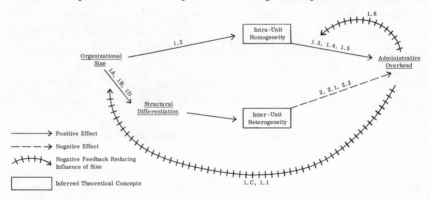

FIGURE 11–2   Chart of Connections

nication and coordination that raise management overhead. It would be true but trivial to say that the employment of more supervisors and a larger administrative staff have the function to meet the problems a complex structure creates. The basic process here is not one of adjustment; on the contrary, a process necessary for large organizations to operate— extensive subdivision of responsibilities in several ways—has a by-product —structural complexity—that creates rather than solves problems.

A case of adjustment is illustrated by the relationship between vertical and horizontal differentiation in the formal structure. In organizations or organizational units of a given size, the larger the number of hierarchical levels, the smaller does the number of functional divisions or sections directly under top management tend to be.[26] The inference is that many major divisions (or sections) overburden top management with purely administrative chores and leave insufficient time for such executive responsibilities as long-range planning and external communication. The addition of a hierarchical level is undoubtedly often deliberately designed to relieve top executives of these supervisory burdens by appointing a few heads of "superdivisions" to whom the former heads of divisions now report and who alone report to the top executives. Thus, an increase in levels reduces the number of major subunits immediately under top management. The large size of an organization (or organizational segment) directly increases the number of these major subunits, thereby intensifying administrative problems for top management, but it indirectly reduces their number by promoting hierarchical differentiation, thereby relieving the problems it has created.

Decentralization of administrative responsibilities by top executives to middle managers appears to depend on two factors: the pressure to decentralize created by a large volume of responsibilities and the reduction in the risk incurred by decentralization resulting from mechanisms of control that assure reliable operations. The large size of an organization not only increases the pressure to decentralize some of the voluminous administrative responsibilities but also magnifies the risk of decentralization, inasmuch as managerial decisions in big organizations affecting large numbers have more import than decisions in small ones. These cross pressures are evident in the empirical findings on employment security agencies. One of their manifestations is that large size discourages official delegation of formal authority but at the same time leads to inadvertent decentralization, as it were—the expansion of influence that accrues to middle managers. An-

---

26. This is the case for entire agencies (see Table 3–4), all six types of divisions (Table 10–2), and local offices (Table 7–7).

other expression of these conflicting pressures is that large size directly discourages official delegation of authority but simultaneously gives rise to conditions, such as automation, that reduce the risk of delegation and encourage it, with the result that size indirectly promotes official delegation.[27] The pressure of large size actually gives rise to explicit delegation of authority primarily if it is complemented by mechanisms that reduce the risk of delegation, like automation or civil service regulations that improve the reliability of employees.

Feedback processes affecting delegation of responsibilities can be inferred. The data suggest that effective services to clients in large agencies, though not in small ones, depend on considerable delegation of responsibilities to the managers of local offices and that this delegation to local levels in large agencies, though not in small ones, depends on automation, which is an impersonal mechanism that lessens the risk of delegation. The empirical evidence also shows that more large agencies than small ones have instituted automation.[28] Operations in local offices seem to have feedback effects that promote the development of the conditions needed to improve them, as indicated by the greater likelihood for automation to be instituted and for it to foster delegation to local offices in the very organizations, large ones, in which service operations suffer without such delegation.

To be sure, the explicit purpose of installing computers is not to foster delegation of decisions to local managers. The point made is rather that one of the pressures promoting the adoption of automation in large agencies is that in them operations can be improved by delegation to local levels, which automation facilitates. The main explicit reason why automation is more likely to be introduced in large than in small agencies is undoubtedly their larger volume of routine administrative work, which can be done by computers. Automation achieves savings in personnel by substituting machines for men, as suggested by the findings that it achieves reductions in both the proportion of clerks among employees and the ratio of employees to clients in the unemployment benefit function. Although computers in these agencies are used mostly for unemployment insurance operations and hardly at all for employment services, automation enlarges the volume of employment services in the organization.[29] By replacing personnel with

---

27. See Tables 5–2 and 5–4 and the analysis of the influence of size on decentralization on pp. 128–136.
28. See Tables 5–5 and 5–7; the correlation between size and the dummy variable of whether or not operations are automated is .30.
29. See Tables 4–3 (reduction in clerical ratio), 4–8 (reduction in employee-client ratio), and 4–5 (enlargement of employment services).

machines in the performance of routine tasks, automation frees resources and consequently enables an organization to expand the volume of its complex services that cannot be done by computers.

Automation plays an important part in the adaptation of large agencies to their large volume of work and their complex structure. The extent of unemployment insurance services the agency administers is beyond its own control, whereas the extent of employment services and particularly that of counseling services provided to job applicants are within its own control. The large volume of unemployment insurance activities in large agencies tends to preempt administrative attention and lessen the emphasis on the relatively more professional employment services. Automation takes much of the routine work in unemployment insurance off the shoulders of the personnel and relieves management from having to administer a large complement of clerical employees, and it therefore leads to more concentration on employment services. Occupational differentiation in large agencies raises the man-hour costs of unemployment benefit operations, but large agencies nowadays typically react to this economic problem by instituting automation, which reduces man-hour costs, with the result that these costs are, if anything, lower in large than in small agencies. But more important than automation for keeping the man-hour expenditures of large agencies down despite their complexity is the small size of their administrative overhead.

The conditions that affect the proportionate size of the administrative staff in employment security agencies are the same as those that affect the proportion of their managerial personnel: large size lowers both, differentiation raises both, and the economies large scale achieves exceed the diseconomies the differentiation of large organizations produces. But the ratio of staff personnel has distinctive implications for the services administered, not shared by the ratio of managerial personnel. The larger the relative size of the administrative staff, the less emphasis there is in an agency on employment services in general and special vocational counseling of job applicants in particular. This suggests that a large staff component is better suited for the more administrative work in unemployment insurance than for the comparatively more professional work in employment services. However, a large administrative staff raises the cost in hours of unemployment benefit operations.[30] To be sure, one might expect a relatively large overhead component to raise man-hour expenditures. Yet only the proportionate size of the staff component does so, not that of the manage-

---

30. See Tables 4–2 (determinants of staff ratio), 4–5, 4–6, and 4–8 (consequences of staff ratio for services).

rial component. It appears that a large management component produces personnel economies that pay for its own personnel, at least in terms of man-hours, whereas a large staff component does not. As far as could be ascertained by the four measures used, a disproportionately large staff has only disadvantages for services, which arouses the suspicion that it is maintained not so much to meet the needs of the public the agency serves as to satisfy political ambitions and help build bureaucratic empires.

Adjustment is not inevitable, and the concept must not be used loosely for anything that might be thought of as benefiting an organization in one way or another, lest it give the impression that adjustment is inevitable.[31] By adjustment is meant here that problems that arise under a certain condition have feedback effects that overcome these problems: the empirical indication that there is feedback adjustment is that the condition's indirect effects counteract its direct ones. A number of such feedback processes leading to adjustment have been inferred from the empirical findings. Large organizations become differentiated into many divisions or sections immediately under top management, and the excessive administrative load this places on top management has feedback effects that stimulate hierarchical differentiation and thereby reduce the number of divisions or sections. The administrative cost of differentiation results in feedback that stems further differentiation.

Decentralization provides more complicated instances of feedback processes. The pressure from a large volume of responsibilities to decentralize decision-making tends to be resisted by top management for fear of the risk doing so entails. But large size simultaneously promotes the development of conditions, such as automation, that reduce the risk of delegation of responsibilities and thereby encourage it. Specifically, effective services in large agencies seem to depend on delegation of responsibilities to local managers, and delegation to local managers in large agencies seems to depend on automation. Feedback effects may be inferred from the fact that large agencies are usually automated, which implies that large size creates the condition without which effective services in large agencies would not prevail. Finally, the differentiation in large agencies raises man-hour expenditures, but the relatively smaller staff and prevailing automation in large agencies reduce their expenditures in man-hours for benefit operations, despite their greater differentiation, below that of small agencies.

There are good grounds why adjustments often occur as problems arise in such work organizations as government bureaus or private firms, whose members are employees paid a salary in order to perform tasks. Adjust-

---

31. Such loose usage of the term "function" has brought it into disrepute.

ments are often deliberately instituted to meet problems. For work organizations are the prototype of social systems in which an instrumental orientation toward the rational performance of tasks in terms of universalistic criteria of efficiency predominates, and they are the prototype of social systems governed in part by explicit design. There is no mysterious teleological force that creates a functional equilibrium, but universalistically oriented managers and operating employees tend to react to problems that come up by trying to find ways to adjust conditions to them. Although informal relations among colleagues and paternalistic leadership practices introduce particularistic elements into work situations,[32] this is most likely to be the case in small undifferentiated offices. The structural differentiation of large organizations seems to constrain management to be more impersonal and intensifies the strain toward instrumental universalism.[33]

The analysis here has been confined to the relationships between organizational characteristics, notably size, differentiation in the structure, and the management manpower needed to effect coordination, though a number of other variables have also been considered, for example, automation, merit standards, decentralization, and the services rendered. It is worth repeating that these formal structures exhibit regularities that are independent of the individuals in them and that can be studied without inquiring why individual managers make certain decisions. Saying so does not involve an anthropomorphic assumption that organizations act as human beings do. What happens in organizations occurs, of course, only because human beings make decisions and take action. And differences between individuals—their orientations and leadership qualities and other attributes—unquestionably affect the course of events in organizations. Taking these psychological factors into consideration would help explain some differences among organizations left here unexplained, but it seems most doubtful that these factors can account for nearly as much of the variance in organizational characteristics as the antecedent organizational conditions examined do.

We challenge anyone who questions this statement to account for as

---

32. For the original discussion of the distinction between universalism and particularism, see Talcott Parsons, *Essays in Sociology* (Glencoe: Free Press, 1949), pp. 185–199.

33. This conjecture is suggested by the findings that various measures of differentiation are positively associated with such expressions of a universalistic orientation toward technical efficiency as high productivity (Table 4–7) and the introduction of technological innovations, specifically, computers (Tables 3–3 and 3–6) and electric typewriters (Table 8–5). But not all expressions of differentiation exhibit such associations.

much variation in the managerial ratio in organizations with differences in leadership qualities and other personality traits as can be explained with differences in size and differentiation. One reason personality factors are less important than structural conditions in affecting the characteristics of organizations is that it is justified to assume that the members of work organizations make rational decisions about their instrumental activities in terms of universalistic criteria. But a still more important reason is that the structure exerts constraints that limit the alternatives of individuals. If an organization is large, it cannot operate unless responsibilities are subdivided in various ways; if such differentiation into structural components occurs, increased structural complexity is implicit in it; and utter confusion would reign if management would fail to react to increased structural complexity by appointing more supervisors to effect coordination.

The existence of these structural regularities by no means implies, however, that all organizations have achieved a functional equilibrium of perfect adjustment. There are clearly considerable differences among employment security agencies, and among other types of organizations, and not all are equally well organized to provide services to the public, or to achieve other objectives. For example, a disproportionately large staff component seems to be detrimental to effective service operations. Besides, not all of the regularities in the formal structure reveal adjustment; regularities may, on the contrary, be indicative of conditions that create problems. Thus, the structural complexity generated by large size is not a type of adjustment but a condition that creates problems of communication and coordination requiring adjustment. Last but not least, even interrelations among elements in the structure that constitute a satisfactory adjustment for the organization itself are not necessarily beneficial for the society in which the organization functions. As a matter of fact, the high degree of efficiency achieved by huge and complex organizations in today's world has created a new form of power that poses serious problems for a democratic society. We shall return to this problem at the end of Chapter 12.

Conclusions

An endeavor to start building a deductive theory of the formal structure of work organizations has been presented in this chapter, based on the preceding quantitative analysis of empirical data on the fifty-three employment security agencies in the United States, their 387 headquarters divisions, and their 1,201 local branches (excluding the smallest and simplest). A substantial number of empirical uniformities has been subsumed under two fundamental generalizations, both of which pertain to differentiation in the structure of formal organizations. Nine middle-range propositions have been derived from the two most general ones, and empirical findings have been cited that confirm the implied propositions. In conclusion, some questions raised by this theory of the structure of organizations are briefly discussed.

One basic question is whether the generalizations are valid and apply to organizations other than the ones from which they were derived. The empirical data that serve as the material for building a theory naturally cannot also be used to test it. Independent testing requires research findings from other organizations, and one such test based on empirical data from 416 government bureaus of a different type is reported in the next chapter. The claim that the theory is applicable to organizations in general can only be corroborated in the future if research on various types of private firms as well as other kinds of government bureaus fails to turn up evidence to contradict it. No doubt, quantitative information on other types of organizations will indicate the need for some sort of revision. Another question concerns not the empirical validity but the logical consistency of the theoretical system of propositions. The logical inferences and deductions connecting the propositions in the theory are rather complicated, as has been surely noticed, and it is for others than we to tell whether we have been successful in building a tight logical system.

The deductive theorist is recurrently confronted by the dilemma of having to choose between deriving propositions that are tautological and deriving them in ways that do not strictly conform to the logical criteria of deduction, narrowly construed. For if a proposition can be deduced in strictest logic from another, it is already contained in the other and hence the two are a tautology. For example, the proposition that the marginal influence of size on differentiation declines with size (1.1), which was derived from the generalization that increasing size generates differentiation at decreasing rates (1C), can be considered redundant because it restates in different terms what the initial proposition already indicates.[34] On the other hand, if a derived proposition goes beyond using new terms and refers to a new relationship between terms not contained in the initial generalization, the derivation probably is not a strictly logical deduction in the narrow sense. (However, a new relationship can be deduced in strictest logic from the conjunction of two propositions: if size promotes differentiation [1A], and if differentiation raises requirements for managerial

34. Hempel and Oppenheim state that this kind of deduction does not make the "explanation trivially circular"; "The Logic of Explanation," p. 162, n. 31.

manpower [2], it follows that size indirectly raises these requirements [2.1].) Thus, a new relationship not contained in the generalization that size promotes differentiation (1A) is indicated by the proposition derived from it that the proportionate size of any structural component is, according to statistical expectations, likely to decline with increasing organizational size (1.3). But this new element is introduced precisely by going one step beyond the purely logical deduction that the mean proportionate size of structural components must decline if their number increases with size, which is again a tautology. By translating the proposition about mean proportion of components into a probability statement about the proportionate size of any component and applying it to administrative components we add something new, but we also depart from pure logic. It would appear that such strictly limited departures from pure logic greatly enhance the scope of an empirical theory with few fundamental propositions.

A controversy in the philosophy of science is whether the sheer fact that a generalization can be formulated from which other propositions logically follow is sufficient for the former to constitute a scientific explanation of the latter or whether something else is necessary. Braithwaite takes the first position and states: "It is scarcely too much to say that this [logical nexus] is the whole truth about the explanation of scientific laws." [35] Kaplan, citing this statement, disagrees by noting that this "*is,* I am afraid, too much to say." [36] He goes on to quote Campbell to the effect that what else is needed for a theory to explain is "that it shall add to our ideas, and that the ideas it adds shall be acceptable." [37] Although Kaplan does not explicitly say so, the implication is that the deductive model does not fully explain unless complemented by what he elsewhere calls the "pattern model" of theory, which indicates how various elements meaningfully fit together into a whole.[38] An illustration would be that the generalization that organizational differentiation raises requirements for managerial manpower is further clarified by adding that more managerial personnel is needed to effect coordination in a complex structure, which makes the formal proposition meaningful and understandable in terms of our human experience.

To pose the issue squarely for sociology: does the explanation of empir-

---

35. Braithwaite, *Scientific Explanation,* p. 343. He makes this statement immediately following the second of the three sentences cited to introduce Part Four.
36. Kaplan, *The Conduct of Inquiry,* p. 342 (italics in original).
37. The quotation is from Norman Campbell, *What Is Science?* (New York: Dover, 1952), p. 83.
38. Kaplan, *The Conduct of Inquiry,* pp. 325–336.

ical regularities in social structures on the basis of a system of propositions from which they can be deduced have to be supplemented by *Verstehen,* by a meaningful understanding in terms of human experience of the relationships in the generalizations? A sound argument can be advanced for an affirmative answer. After all, the characteristics of social structures are the result of patterns of human conduct. The fundamental principles that explain the connections between characteristics of social structure would, therefore, be expected to strike human beings as meaningful and comprehensible if they reflect on their own experiences in social life. General principles that do not would be suspect. This is particularly so as long as we do not yet have well established and widely accepted generalizations in the social sciences. But once a science has established such generally accepted laws, like the law of gravity in physics, they shape human perception and become part of human experience. This day lies still in the future for sociology. When it comes, however, the insightful understanding a new generalization about social structure provides will probably have its source, not in its connection with everyday experience, but in its connection with other generalizations already firmly established. Although social theories in the meantime command more confidence if they are understandable in terms of common experience, this does not imply that they should be psychological theories. The challenge for sociologists is to develop systematic theories of social structures that treat the regularities in them in their own right. The foregoing chapter endeavors to meet this challenge.

CHAPTER 12

Implications

Two quite different implications of the analysis of organizations that have been presented are discussed in this concluding chapter. First, the implications of the theory formulated in Chapter 11 are tested by ascertaining whether the generalizations inferred from the empirical regularities in employment security agencies accurately predict the empirical interrelations in the structure of another type of organization. In this initial test of the theory, it is applied in a quantitative study of organizations that are also government bureaus, but the nature of these bureaus is very different from that of employment security agencies. If the generalizations derived from research on one type of government organization are validated in research on a second type, it has been demonstrated that the theory is at least not confined to the empirical data used in building it. Future research in private firms of various sorts as well as still other public organizations must determine how widely the theory is applicable. In addition, some inferences not incorporated into the formal theory are also tested with the new data.

The broader implications of the study of formal organizations are discussed in a more speculative vein in the last two sections of the chapter. The basic issue is that of the connection between organizations and societies. One facet of this issue is whether the principles that govern differentiation in formal organizations have any similarity with the principles that

330

govern differentiation and stratification in societies at large. A very different question is that of the role impersonal modern organizations play in the power structure of today's societies. The thesis is advanced that contemporary organizations constitute a new form of power exercised through insidious controls and that new democratic institutions are needed to harness this power for the commonweal. Here we are in the realm of pure speculation, of course. But, as Homans has said, the last part of a book

> should resemble a primitive orgy after harvest. The work may have come to an end, but the worker cannot let go all at once. . . . Accordingly, he is allowed a time of licence, when he may say all sorts of things he would think twice before saying in more sober moments, when he is no longer bound by logic and evidence but free to speculate about what he has done.[1]

Testing the Theory

The deductive theory presented has been constructed inductively. Inferences were drawn from the empirical uniformities observed in employment security agencies to develop a body of propositions that logically imply these uniformities. Except for possible faults in logic, therefore, the empirical findings on employment security agencies must correspond to the implications of the theoretical generalizations. Independent testing requires that the generalizations be applied to new sets of data on a variety of other organizations. As a first test, the hypotheses implied by the theory are examined in another type of government organization, namely, the major finance departments of 416 state and local governments in the United States. The responsibilities of these departments vary, because many jurisdictions maintain more than one finance department and data were obtained only from its major one; those of most departments include maintaining the financial records of the government, auditing disbursements, investment management, and fixed-asset accounting.

Though these organizations are also government bureaus, they differ fundamentally from employment security agencies. Their responsibilities are quite different, do not involve contacts with clients but with other government departments, and are more varied than those of employment security agencies. The large majority of these finance departments are not agencies of state governments, as employment security agencies are, but of municipal (246) or county (128) governments, with only a minority (42) being state finance departments. Thus, there is variation in jurisdiction as

---

1. George C. Homans, *Social Behavior* (New York: Harcourt, Brace & World, 1961), p. 378.

well as in responsibilities among finance departments, but not among employment security agencies. Moreover, the finance departments do not operate directly under specific federal statutes, and their funds are not allocated to them by a bureau of the federal government. They are also much smaller than employment security agencies, with an average size of seventy, compared to one of nearly 1,200, and they have no local branches. In these respects, they are more similar to the local offices or headquarters divisions of employment security agencies than to the agencies themselves. The range in size is very wide, from 5 to 1,714, and the distribution is highly skewed to the right (6.3).

The data for the 256 larger and more complex finance departments were collected in personal interviews with informants administered by the interviewing staff of the National Opinion Research Center, and those for the 160 smaller and simpler departments were collected by mail questionnaires.[2] Included are most of the major finance departments in American cities with a population of more than 50,000, counties with a population of more than 100,000, and states.[3] The information obtained through mail questionnaires is neither so complete nor so reliable as that obtained in personal interviews. Nevertheless, both sets of data are combined in the analysis, because extensive comparison indicated that the questionnaire data on the major structural characteristics of concern here are sufficiently reliable. (A description of the variables used from this study and a matrix of their zero-order correlations are presented in Appendix I. It can be seen there that the operational measures of some of the variables, though still comparable, are not exactly the same as those in employment security agencies.)

---

2. For a discussion of research procedures and results (based on the data obtained in interviews only), see Marshall W. Meyer, "Authority Structures and the Practice of Authority in Formal Organization," Ph.D. dissertation, University of Chicago, 1968. We are grateful for Meyer's assistance and that of Jacques Gellard in this research.

3. Preliminary questionnaires were sent to all these 656 jurisdictions to ascertain what finance departments they have and to identify their major one. No returns were received from 69, and the returns of 60 others indicated that there is no finance department with five or more employees. Of the remaining 527, data were obtained from 416, or 79 per cent. Only eight of the 264 finance departments selected for personal interviews did not cooperate, whereas 39 per cent of the mail questionnaires were either not returned or had to be discarded for lack of adequate information. Because the over-all return rate of 79 per cent is the result of a nearly perfect return rate for the larger and a return rate of 61 per cent for the smaller finance departments, the data are biased in favor of larger departments. (See also Appendix I.)

The first basic generalization stipulates that the increasing size of organizations generates structural differentiation along various lines at decelerating rates. One set of implied hypotheses is that the size of finance departments is positively associated with the division of labor, the number of hierarchical levels, and the number of functional divisions. (These departments have no local offices, and their small size made it impractical to analyze sections within divisions.) Indeed, the data indicate such correlations. The zero-order correlation of size and the division of labor is the strongest of the three (.81), which is also the case for employment security agencies (.78). Another prediction of the first generalization is that the regression lines of these three indicators of differentiation on size exhibit a declining positive slope. All three scatter diagrams reveal the predicted logarithmic curves. The curvature for division of labor, which is shown in Figure 12–1, is least pronounced, with that for hierarchical levels being intermediate and that for functional divisions being most pronounced, which corresponds exactly to the differences in degree of curvature for these three aspects of differentiation in employment security agencies. Logarithmic transformation of size produces a curve in the opposite direction for the division of labor and does not improve the correlation (.80). But this transformation produces fairly straight regression lines for the two other measures of differentiation and improves the correlations of size with number of levels from .55 to .66 and with number of divisions from .50 to .73.

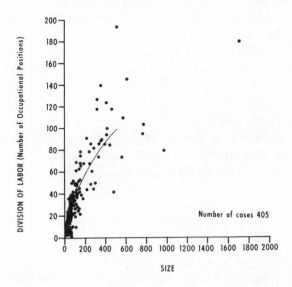

FIGURE 12–1   Scatter Diagram of Division of Labor and Department Size

These findings replicate those observed in employment security agencies. Even the magnitude of two of the three associations with size is very similar, though that of divisions is more pronounced in finance departments. Size in logarithmic transformation accounts for between 44 and 64 per cent of the variances in these three aspects of differentiation in finance departments, and between 30 and 67 per cent of those in employment security agencies. These data on finance departments support not only the generalization that differentiation along several dimensions increases at declining rates with expanding size but also the propositions implied by it. Specifically, they show that the marginal influence of size on differentiation diminishes with expanding size (1.1). They also indicate that the average size as well as the number of structural components increases with size (1.2), because this inevitably follows from the declining rate at which the number of components increases as size does. Larger finance departments, compared to smaller ones, have typically both more formal occupational positions and more incumbents in each, both more hierarchical ranks and more officials per rank, and both more and larger divisions. Furthermore, the research results reveal that the proportionate size of the average personnel complement in an occupational position, on a hierarchical level, and in a division decreases with the increasing size of finance departments (1.3), for an increase in the number of structural components inevitably spells a decrease in their mean proportion of the total.

Does the implied statistical expectation that the proportionate size of any given personnel complement decreases with increasing departmental size apply specifically to the complement of managerial personnel? Unfortunately, poor questionnaire construction makes it impossible to devise accurate measures of managerial manpower. Of the three measures—per cent managerial personnel, and span of control of middle managers and of first-line supervisors—the one for the span of control of first-line supervisors probably is most accurate.[4] (No information on staff personnel was collected.) The theory asserts that the supervisory span of control is wider in large than in small organizations (1.4). This is so in finance departments. The zero-order correlation between departmental size and number of operating employees at the bottom level of the hierarchy per first-line supervisor is .49.

---

4. The responses make it impossible to distinguish nonsupervisory personnel located above the bottom level, such as consultants to the department director, from managerial personnel. Since the information on the nonsupervisory employees on the bottom level is accurate, and since there are more first-line supervisors than middle managers, this error probably biases the measure of span of control of first-line supervisors least.

Inasmuch as first-line supervisors constitute the bulk of the managerial personnel, particularly in relatively small organizations, the finding that the number of subordinates per first-line supervisor increases with size in finance departments provides some support for the proposition that management overhead exhibits an economy of scale (1.5). The scatter diagram shows that the span of control of first-line supervisors expands at first rapidly and then more and more gradually with increasing size. The curvature is not very pronounced, about as much as that of the division of labor is, and logarithmic transformation of size produces a curve in the opposite direction and hardly improves the correlation (.51). If the number of subordinates per first-line supervisors increases at a declining rate as departmental size increases, the ratio of these supervisors to operating employees at the lowest level must decrease also at a declining rate with increasing size. Thus, the economy of scale in management overhead diminishes as finance departments become larger, at least as far as first-line supervisors are concerned, in accordance with proposition (1.6).

The second basic generalization of the theory is that structural differentiation in organizations raises requirements for managerial manpower. Problems of communication and coordination in the complex structures created by differentiation make demands on the time of first-line supervisors as well as on that of higher administrative officials. The consequent hypotheses specify that both multilevel hierarchies and the existence of many functional divisions in finance departments narrow the average span of control of first-line supervisors. Table 12–1 shows that vertical differen-

TABLE 12-1. *Multiple Regression of* **Mean Span of Control of First-Line Supervisors** *in Finance Departments on Departmental Conditions*

Independent Variable	Standardized Regression Coefficient	Zero-Order Correlation
Size (Log)	1.08**	.51
Levels (Mean)	−.25**	.32
Divisions	−.55**	.17

Multiple R = .62; $n = 415$
**Greater than three times its standard error.

tiation into levels and horizontal differentiation into divisions have independent effects narrowing the mean span of control of first-line supervisors in finance departments, confirming the hypotheses.[5]

5. The effect of number of divisions is stronger than that of number of levels, which is unlike the findings in employment security agencies and in their

Three middle-range propositions have been derived from the second basic generalization in conjunction with some of the earlier ones. First, large organizationai size, by generating structural differentiation, indirectly raises the need for managerial manpower (2.1). Second, the economies in management realized by large scale exceed the higher management cost incurred owing to the structural complexity of large organizations (2.2). Third, the differentiation of large organizations into separate segments, such as local branches, counteracts the otherwise observable decline in the economy of scale in management overhead with increasing size (2.3). The last one of these three generalizations cannot be tested in finance departments, because they have no local branches, but the other two can be.

The implied hypotheses are: first, the indirect effects of large size mediated by multiple levels and many divisions narrow the mean span of control of first-line supervisors in finance departments; and second, the direct effect of large size widening the supervisory span of control exceeds these indirect effects narrowing it. Evidence confirming the second of these two hypotheses is provided by the comparison of the standardized regression coefficient and the zero-order correlation of size with span of control in Table 12–1, which shows that the direct effect of size expanding the average span of control of first-line supervisors is considerably greater than its total effect. The difference is owing to the two dimensions of structural differentiation, the only other variables in the regression problem, which confirms the first hypothesis. Specifically, the large size of finance departments indirectly narrows the span of control of first-line supervisors partly because of the vertical ($-.17$) and particularly because of the horizontal differentiation ($-.40$) it promotes. The structural complexity generated by the large size of these government bureaus creates problems that supervisors must attend to, and it therefore reduces the economies in supervisory personnel effected by a large scale of operations, but it does not completely eliminate these economies.

The data on finance departments clearly confirm the hypotheses implied by the theory and closely replicate the empirical regularities observed in employment security agencies and their subunits, which served as the foun-

---

subunits (see Tables 4–1, reversing signs, 7–10, and 10–5). The data for agency headquarters in Table 4–1 are not strictly comparable, because the effect of horizontal differentiation in the table is split between two variables, number of divisions and sections per division, but this factor does not account for the discrepancy. A possible reason for it may be a difference in the measure of vertical differentiation: in employment security agencies, it is the maximum number of levels of any division; in finance departments, the average number of all divisions, which has less variance than the maximum.

dation for constructing the theory. In both kinds of government organizations, different though they are, large size fosters differentiation in several dimensions at declining rates. The structural complexity engendered by differentiation creates problems of communication and coordination that take up the time of supervisors, thus raising requirements for administrative manpower. But the economies in administrative overhead a large scale of operations makes possible exceed the additional overhead cost the complexity of large structures requires. The rate at which increasing size effects economies in supervisory manpower declines with size, just as the rate at which it promotes structural differentiation does. All these propositions are equally applicable to finance departments and to employment security agencies. The theory's ability accurately to predict the research findings on finance departments does not demonstrate its general validity, of course. What it does demonstrate is that the generalizations inferred from the empirical uniformities in one type of government organization correctly predict the uniformities in an entirely different kind of government organization, which implies that these propositions refer to principles not confined to any particular type, an implication already suggested by the comparable data on six different functional divisions in employment security agencies. That is all the theory can claim so far. How generally applicable it is only future research on a variety of organizations can tell.

Testing Further Inferences

Numerous empirical findings on employment security agencies and the interpretations inferred from them have not been incorporated into the formal theory of the structure of organizations. It is of interest to utilize the data on finance departments to test a few of these additional inferences. As a start, let us quickly glance at a bit of supportive evidence, hardly deserving to be called a test, for a conjecture that conflicts with common sense. The finding that a regular schedule of staff meetings is most likely to be kept in the employment security division whose personnel has the highest qualification prompted the surmise in Chapter 10 that administrative procedures are generally not less but more prevalent the higher the skills of employees, because complex work is more in need of protection against disruption than routine work. The use of procedure manuals in finance departments is a more direct measure of explicit operating procedures than a regular schedule of meetings; no such measure is available for employment security agencies. The implied hypothesis that the educational qualifications of employees (per cent with college degrees) are positively related to extent of use of procedure manuals is confirmed by the data, and though the correlation is not strong (.10), it persists when a variety of other conditions are controlled. Resort to explicitly formulated procedures apparently increases with superior qualifications, contrary to common sense but in accordance with the hypothesis.

To return to the analysis of formal structure, one underlying principle is that complexity of one sort breeds complexity of another in organizations. The complex problems confronting an organization with a large scope of responsibilities are met by subdividing these responsibilities, which makes the work of individuals and of subunits less complex but the structure of the organization more complex. The division of labor represents this simplification of duties through subdivision at the expense of greater structural complexity, and so does the assignment of separate functions in the work process to different divisions in the organization. A large number of divisions expands the administrative burden of top management and infringes on other executive responsibilities, such as long-range planning and external communication. To relieve top executives of excessive administrative detail, an intervening level of managers in charge of superdivisions is often introduced, to whom the previous division heads report, and who alone report directly to top management. Thus, the complexity in the structure resulting from many divisions is counteracted by adding to the hierarchical levels, creating another complexity in the structure.

According to this inference, vertical differentiation into levels and horizontal differentiation into divisions, although both depend on organizational size, are inversely related to each other when size is controlled. Such an inverse relationship between the two dimensions of structural differentiation was observed in employment security agencies (Table 3–4) as well as within their local offices (Table 7–7) and divisions (Table 10–2), and Table 12–2 shows that it is also observable in finance departments. As a

TABLE 12-2. *Multiple Regression of* **Divisions** *in Finance Departments on Departmental Conditions*

Independent Variable	Standardized Regression Coefficient	Zero-Order Correlation
Size (Log)	1.05**	.73
Division of Labor	−.10	.52
Levels (Mean)	−.37**	.26

Multiple R = .78; n = 416
**Greater than three times its standard error.

matter of fact, this relationship had been discovered in an earlier analysis of the data on finance departments before it was found to be also evident in employment security agencies and their subunits.[6] In any case, hierarchical differentiation into multilevel hierarchies appears to reduce the number of major divisions and thereby to lessen the administrative load of top management in different kinds of organizations and organizational subunits. Tall organizational pyramids tend to be slim at the top, as indicated by few divisions, and at the bottom too, as indicated by few subordinates per first-line supervisor.

The structure of large organizations is, on the whole, more differentiated both vertically and horizontally than that of small ones, but the more large size produces vertical differentiation into levels in an organization the less likely it is to be accompanied by horizontal differentiation into many divisions or sections.[7] The next question is what conditions in an organization stimulate the development of differentiation in its structure primarily in a vertical rather than horizontal direction. It has been suggested that impersonal mechanisms of control make operations more reliable, lessen top management's reluctance to become far removed from the operating level, and consequently encourage the emergence of a multilevel hierarchy. The empirical finding that provided direct support for this inference was that automation, which is such an impersonal control mechanism, slightly fosters hierarchical differentiation in employment security agencies (Table 3–3). But inasmuch as the standardized regression coefficient indicating this effect of automation on multiple levels barely met the criterion of acceptance, given the small number of employment security agencies, it is especially important to ascertain whether the inference is supported by the research on finance departments, with a case base nearly eight times that of the number of agencies. A somewhat different measure of automation is used in the study of finance departments, which may be called the "scope of automation." It is the proportion of selected responsibilities for which computers are utilized (for the operational measure, see Appendix I).

Table 12–3 indicates that automation promotes the development of

6. But most of the propositions in the deductive theory (except for the positive association of size with measures of differentiation) had been inferred from the findings of the study of employment security agencies, and it was not known in advance whether the data on finance departments would support them.
7. This interpretation is supported by the negative effect of the product term, size times levels, on the number of sections in local offices, which counteracts the positive effects of size and of number of levels (Table 7–9).

TABLE 12-3. *Multiple Regression of **Mean Hierarchical Levels** in Finance Departments on Departmental Conditions*

Independent Variable	Standardized Regression Coefficient	Zero-Order Correlation
Size (Log)	.42**	.66
Division of Labor	.22**	.60
Scope of Automation	.14**	.42

Multiple R = .68; n = 415
**Greater than three times its standard error.

multilevel hierarchies in finance departments,[8] as it does in employment security agencies. Large departments typically use computers more widely ($r = .49$) and have taller hierarchies (.66) than small ones, producing a spurious correlation between the two, but automation exerts some independent positive effect on the number of hierarchical levels in departments of a given size, as the standardized regression coefficient indicates. Although the magnitude of this effect of the use of computers on number of levels in finance departments is no greater than that in employment security agencies (compare Tables 12–3 and 3–3), we can place more confidence in the regression coefficient representing it, because the number of finance departments is so much larger. These findings support the inference that the greater reliability of automated operations furthers hierarchical differentiation in the structure of organizations.

A pronounced division of labor also fosters hierarchical differentiation in finance departments, as can be seen in Table 12–3. The division of labor has no such effect in employment security agencies (Table 3–3), though it does in their local offices (Table 7–6). In these local offices, the division of labor also encourages horizontal differentiation into sections (Table 7–7), which is neither the case for the headquarters of employment security agencies nor in finance departments. If anything, the division of labor reduces horizontal differentiation into divisions in finance departments (Table 12–2), though the fact that the standardized regression coef-

---

8. This finding, based on an earlier analysis of 254 of these finance departments, was mentioned in Chapter 3. Inasmuch as the measure of scope of automation in finance departments is less strongly correlated with size and with division of labor than the automation measure in employment security agencies, it does not create such serious problems of multicollinearity and could be used in Table 12–3, whereas problems of multicollinearity necessitated substituting the dichotomous for the thirteen-category variable of automation in Table 3–3.

ficient does not reach the criterion of acceptance makes it preferable to disregard this relationship. The number of occupational positions among which employees are distributed (division of labor) reinforces the influence of the number of employees (size) on both dimensions of structural differentiation in local offices, on neither dimension in employment security agencies as a whole, and on vertical but not on horizontal differentiation in finance departments. More precisely, the over-all influence the size of finance departments exerts on hierarchical levels (.66) is partly direct (.42) and partly mediated by the division of labor (.17) (and to a slight extent mediated by automation [.07]), inasmuch as the division of labor exerts an independent influence on the levels in the hierarchy.

Thus, occupational differentiation exerts an independent influence on both dimensions of structural differentiation in local offices, on one of the dimensions in finance departments, and on neither dimension in entire employment security agencies. A possible reason for the difference is sheer size, inasmuch as local offices are smaller and entire agencies (or even their headquarters alone) are larger on the average than finance departments. The large size of an organization leads to the subdivision of responsibilities and thereby creates differentiation of several kinds. The most immediate and strongest expression of this process is the differentiation of duties among various formal positions, and more indirect expressions are the differentiation into functional subunits and into managerial levels. The assumption is that hierarchical differentiation into managerial levels occurs in reaction to problems engendered by functional differentiation into many divisions or sections and that this functional differentiation into subunits in turn was a reaction to the problems of organizing a differentiated work force, which itself was a means for meeting the problem of a large volume of different tasks. In a small organization, this process has not yet advanced far, and the number of different positions to which employees are allocated exerts a distinct influence on differentiation into functional sections and managerial levels, complementing that of number of employees. In a larger organization, the process has advanced further; functional divisions and sections have become differentiated to absorb, as it were, the differentiated work force, and hierarchical levels have become differentiated in reaction to the administrative problems created by functional differentiation. The interpretation assumes that vertical as well as horizontal differentiation in large organizations have typically advanced enough to take care of the problems produced by occupational differentiation, and the latter consequently no longer has an independent influence on the former.

In short, the difference in the influence of the division of labor on structural differentiation among local offices, finance departments, and entire employment security agencies is essentially attributed to differences in their size, and some conjectures have been offered as to why this may be so. Three cases do not make a generalization, however, even if each of the "cases" consists of a large number of organizations. But the interpretation that size is the factor responsible for the difference can be tested in finance departments, which nearly span the size ranges of local offices and agency headquarters. The two implied hypotheses are that the independent positive influences of the division of labor on number of divisions and on number of levels decrease with increasing size. (This cannot be shown on simple scatter diagrams, because three variables instead of two are involved in each hypothesis.) Translated into operational terms, the interaction of the division of labor and size represented by their product term is expected to counteract the positive influences of division of labor on functional divisions and on hierarchical levels. The results of the two regression analyses are presented in Table 12–4 for divisions and in Table 12–5 for levels.[9]

The findings confirm both hypotheses. Table 12–4 shows that the division of labor itself exerts a positive influence on horizontal differentiation into divisions in finance departments, reinforcing that of size. (This is not evident in Table 12–2, because the product term is not taken into account there.) But this positive influence is more and more counteracted by the negative interaction effect the expanding division of labor has jointly with expanding size. The ratio of the metric regression coefficient of the division of labor to that of its product term with size reveals the threshold at which its positive direct effect is turned, by its counteracting joint effect with size, into a negative effect. The result of dividing the two coefficients is 219, which means that the threshold is reached, on the average, in finance departments with 219 employees, which is about one standard deviation (137) above the mean size of these departments (70). The ratio of the regression coefficient of size to that of the product term is 168:1, which shows that the positive effect of increasing size on horizontal differentiation is never neutralized by the negative joint effect, because it would

---

9. Size is used in raw form in Tables 12–4 and 12–5. If its logarithmic transformation is used instead, the regression coefficients of division of labor and of the product term do not reach acceptable levels. This implies that the logarithm of size can account for the effect that size in combination with the division of labor exerts on structural differentiation. But this transformation conceals how size interacts with the division of labor it generates to affect structural differentiation, that is to say, how its direct effect is reinforced in small but counteracted in large organizations by the division of labor, which may well help produce the logarithmic curve.

TABLE 12-4. *Multiple Regression of* **Divisions** *in Finance Departments on Departmental Conditions*

Independent Variable	Standardized Regression Coefficient	Zero-Order Correlation	Metric Regression Coefficient
Size	1.15**	.50	.02568**
Division of Labor	.29**	.52	.03345**
Size X Division of Labor	−.97**	.29	−.00015**

Multiple R = .66; n = 416
**Greater than three times its standard error.

TABLE 12-5. *Multiple Regression of* **Mean Hierarchical Levels** *in Finance Departments on Departmental Conditions*

Independent Variable	Standardized Regression Coefficient	Zero-Order Correlation	Metric Regression Coefficient
Size	.50**	.55	.03346**
Division of Labor	.45**	.60	.15589**
Size X Division of Labor	−.34**	.43	−.00016**

Multiple R = .63; n = 415
**Greater than three times its standard error.

be so neutralized only in organizations with more than 168 divisions, which is an empirically impossible number.

The division of labor, the expansion of which closely follows that of size, initially reinforces the effect of size on horizontal differentiation, but a pronounced division of labor combines with the large organizational size that produces it increasingly to counteract this positive reinforcing effect, with the result that in large organizations the division of labor does not foster and may even impede horizontal differentiation. Table 12–5 indicates that the same applies to vertical differentiation. The strong positive effect of the division of labor on hierarchical differentiation, which reinforces that of size, is counteracted by the interaction effect of the division of labor and size together. But in this case, the threshold at which the positive reinforcing effect of the division of labor on hierarchical levels is completely neutralized by its joint counteracting effect is reached much later, only in organizations with more than 956 employees. Very few finance departments are that large. (The point at which the positive effect of size on hierarchical differentiation is counteracted by the joint effect is again far beyond the realm of possibility—205 levels.)

The findings imply that the independent effect of the division of labor on both dimensions of structural differentiation, just as the effects of size on them, declines with expanding size and the consequent expansion of the division of labor.[10] In relatively small organizations, be they employment security offices or small finance departments, the number of different positions into which employees are divided complements the impact of the number of employees on horizontal as well as vertical differentiation in the structure. The resulting horizontal differentiation into functional subunits is a form of division of labor that reduces the problems of occupational differentiation and blunts its further influence on the structure. When organizations reach this range of size and functional complexity, occupational differentiation no longer has an independent influence on horizontal but still has one on vertical differentiation, as indicated in finance departments by the weaker influence of occupational differentiation on number of divisions than number of levels and by the higher threshold at which its positive influence on levels, compared to its influence on divisions, is completely suppressed. The administrative problems created by functional differentiation into many divisions, and indirectly by occupational differentiation, further hierarchical differentiation, which reduces these problems and blunts the forces producing them. This is reflected in the findings that horizontal differentiation is negatively related to vertical differentiation, particularly in large organizations (compare the coefficients for levels in Tables 3–4 and 7–7), and that occupational differentiation no longer has an independent positive effect on hierarchical differentiation in large organizations, be they employment security agencies or the largest finance departments.[11] One reason why the influence of size on structural differentiation declines with increasing size may be that the expanding division of labor that accompanies expanding size initially reinforces and mediates but ultimately counteracts this influence of size.

---

10. The decline in the effects of size with increasing size on each aspect of differentiation is indicated on a two-dimensional scatter plot by a logarithmic curve. To reveal the decline in the effect of the division of labor with increasing size on a measure of structural differentiation requires a three-variable procedure, as that employed in regression analysis including a product term. A three-dimensional scatter diagram would reveal this too.

11. The basic assumptions of this interpretation conform to a number of findings in employment security agencies and their local offices and are tested in finance departments (Tables 12–4 and 12–5), but there are additional implications in the argument that still require testing through more refined analysis.

New Forms of Power

Turning now in a more speculative mood to the broader implications of this inquiry into the structure of organizations, we may begin by asking whether the theoretical propositions advanced about differentiation in formal organizations are in any way similar to the principles that govern differentiation and stratification in societies. A basic distinction between formal organizations and societies must be recognized at the outset: the former are "enacted" social systems, in Sumner's terms, whereas the latter are "crescive" systems.[12] In other words, formal organizations are deliberately established to achieve specified objectives, and while their objectives may change in the course of their history, the accomplishment of explicit objectives remains their *raison d'être*. Societies have no particular objectives in the same sense, and their differentiated structure is the emergent product of diverse and often conflicting forces, not of formally enacted provisions. The distinction is an analytical one and must not be reified or exaggerated, inasmuch as social forces beyond the control of individual administrators affect the structure of organizations and planned actions of governments and powerful groups affect that of societies.

Societies are characterized by a division of labor, and so are formal organizations. Durkheim summarizes his theory of the causes of the division of labor in societies in the following words: "The division of labor varies in direct ratio with the volume and density of societies," [13] having defined volume as the number of members in a society and density as their concentration that leads to much social interaction among them. The predominant influence of the number of members in an organization on its division of labor corresponds to the first of these two principles. No indication of social density in organizations is available in the research. But on the plausible assumptions that employees in organizations are more concentrated and interact more than people randomly selected from the society at large and that the division of labor in organizations is especially pronounced, the conditions in organizations would also support Durkheim's second principle. Be that as it may, Durkheim's first principle about the causes of the division of labor in society doubtlessly applies to formal organizations.

The differentiation of power and privilege in the stratification systems of societies is also somewhat analogous to the differentiation of managerial authority in the hierarchies of organizations. A basic principle of Lenski's

---

12. William G. Sumner, *Folkways* (Boston: Ginn, 1907), p. 54.
13. Emile Durkheim, *The Division of Labor in Society* (Glencoe: Free Press, 1947), p. 262 (original in italics).

theory of stratification is that "the degree of inequality in distributive systems will vary directly with the size of a society's surplus." [14] This principle that surplus is required for inequality to develop is homologous to the inference from the theory here presented that the savings in supervisory manpower a large scale of operations effects in an organization free the resources needed for the development of a differentiated hierarchy and the appointment of managers on various levels required by such a hierarchy. The underlying forces are not the same, however. Perhaps more important than this analogy are some other parallels between Lenski's analysis and ours and a fundamental issue they raise.

After examining advanced industrial as well as several kinds of simpler societies, Lenski revises his original principle and suggests that the relationship between technology and surplus, on the one hand, and inequality, on the other, is curvilinear.[15] Technological advances that produce surplus beyond the necessities for survival and subsistence in the society give rise to inequality, and further technological progress intensifies inequality. In the most advanced industrial societies with the greatest surplus, however, there is less inequality than at an intermediate stage of technological development. One reason Lenski gives for this reversal of the trend toward inequality is that the complexity of modern industrial society makes it impossible for the ruling group "to maintain effective control over those beneath them." [16] For the sake of efficiency and productivity, some authority must be delegated, which leads to "the diffusion of power and privilege." [17]

The situation in organizations is similar, as we have seen: large size and complexity create pressures to decentralize authority; an advanced technology, such as automation, is a main factor promoting the delegation of authority; and productivity in large organizations appears to suffer without such delegation. At the end of the analysis of these factors in Chapter 5 the issue was raised whether greater delegation of responsibilities necessarily means a loss of power on the part of top management. Lenski's analysis poses the same issue with respect to power in society. Indeed, it is implicit in a second reason he gives for the lesser inequality in modern industrial society: "In an expanding economy, an elite can make economic concessions in *relative* terms without necessarily suffering any loss in *absolute* terms." [18] But if the wealth of the wealthy increases as the income of

14. Gerhard Lenski, *Power and Privilege* (New York: McGraw-Hill, 1966), p. 85 (original in italics).
15. Ibid., pp. 308–318.
16. Ibid., p. 313.
17. Ibid., p. 314.
18. Ibid. (italics in original).

the poorer and middle strata does, what is the implication of this for their relative economic power?

Most of the facts are not in dispute. Middle managers in large organizations do exercise more authority and more influence than those in small ones, and the discretion of employees on lower levels also may well be greater in large organizations. Similarly, there can be no doubt that the citizens of modern democracies are more affluent, have more political rights, and are less dominated by the arbitrary will of a ruler than the subjects of a feudal lord or of a tribal chieftain. But does this mean that the top executives of the largest organizations exercise less control either within the organization or outside it than the executives in small organizations or feudal princes or tribal chieftains or even political tyrants? Is not the power of control over our lives and destinies that the heads of the military establishment and of giant corporations exercise far greater than the power a Caligula or a Genghis Khan has wielded? This is the paradox: we today are freer from coercion through the power of command of superiors than most people have been, yet men in positions of power today probably exercise more control than any tyrant ever has.

New forms of power have been emerging that are exercised within modern organizations and through them in contemporary society. These new forms of organizational control can be clarified by contrasting them with old-fashioned bureaucratic power. Weber's great contribution to the understanding of modern organizations is that he discerned incipient trends, which have only become manifest since his time, and that he recognized that organizations take advantage of a variety of mechanisms of control, ranging from obviously bureaucratic ones, such as command authority and discipline, to quite unbureaucratic ones, such as the controlling power rooted in expert knowledge.[19] His limitation is that he failed to make explicit analytical distinctions between these different control mechanisms and subsumed them all under his ideal type.[20] This failure prevented him from exploiting his profound insights fully and from realizing that tradi-

19. Max Weber, *Essays in Sociology* (New York: Oxford University Press, 1946), pp. 196–244, and *The Theory of Social and Economic Organization* (New York: Oxford University Press, 1947), pp. 324–341.
20. Talcott Parsons has emphasized the advantages of analytical over type concepts and specifically criticized Weber for failing to distinguish between the authority based on administrative position and that based on professional competence; for the first, see his *The Structure of Social Action* (New York: McGraw-Hill, 1937), pp. 27–42, 606–610; for the second, see his "Introduction" to Weber, *The Theory of Social and Economic Organization*, pp. 58–60, note, and Alvin W. Gouldner, *Patterns of Industrial Bureaucracy* (Glencoe: Free Press, 1954), pp. 22–24.

tional bureaucratic controls were in the process of becoming transformed into different ones. To be sure, several mechanisms of control occur together in organizations, but the analytical distinctions between them are necessary to examine how they combine and which ones become predominant in certain places and at certain times.

The prototype of bureaucratic control is the authority exercised through a chain of command, in which superiors give orders subordinates are obligated to obey. This is the mechanism of organizational control Weber emphasizes most, and its polar example is the Prussian army of his time, which lends some justification to Friedrich's criticism that Weber's analysis of bureaucracy "vibrates with something of the Prussian enthusiasm for the military organization." [21] An essential element in the exercise of control through a chain of command is rigorous discipline enforced through coercive sanctions. Weber explicitly states "that military discipline is the ideal model for the modern capitalist factory," [22] and he implies that Puritanism is an important source of the discipline in modern armies.[23] Discipline is the means that transforms the simplest kind of human control— that of a man who gets others to do what he wills, which is limited to a single person's span of attention—into a control mechanism for large organizations. The transmission of orders through a long chain of communication links in an organizational hierarchy is likely to be a slow process and to distort these orders unless strict discipline reigns. But though there are similarities between the command authority of the general and that of the factory manager, and between the disciplined performance required of soldiers and of workers, the rigid obedience the general demands of his troops, the virtually unrestricted power of sanction he has over them, and the deference he expects of them are quite unlike the conditions characteristic of the management of modern factories.

A second mechanism of control in organizations discussed by Weber is the establishment of explicit regulations and procedures that govern decisions and operations. Discipline refers to compliance with rules and regulations as well as to compliance with orders from superiors. Moreover, standing orders of those in positions of authority become rules or, as they are called in the army, "standard operating procedures," which must be regularly followed. Hence, there is a close connection between conformity with rules and control through a chain of command in organizations, which is illustrated by the strong emphasis on strict compliance with de-

---

21. Carl J. Friedrich, *Authority* (Nomos I) (Cambridge: Harvard University Press, 1958), p. 31.
22. Weber, *Essays in Sociology*, p. 261.
23. Ibid., pp. 256–257.

tailed rules as well as on the chain of command in military organizations. Nevertheless, rules restrict the arbitrary exercise of power by the dominant group, because rules are relatively general in two senses of the term, both of which Weber notes: they refer to the principles underlying decisions rather than a particular decision, and they tend to apply to everybody in the system, rulers as well as ruled. Freedom of action is less restrained if superiors establish rules stipulating criteria for decision-making than if they issue commands as to how specific decisions must be carried out. Besides, once a management or dominant group has established a rule that is to its advantage, its individual members cannot easily escape from being bound by the rule even if they would like to in particular instances, because it is to the advantage of the group as a whole to uphold the rule.[24] Hence, a rule, though it be established purely in terms of the self-interest of an elite, limits the arbitrary exercise of power by the members of the elite.

A control mechanism of special importance in modern work organizations is the incentive system. Weber discusses the significance of salaries and of career advancements for making employees dependent on the organization and thus constraining them to submit to the authority exercised in it. But his focus on public bureaucracies has the result that he pays no attention to the ways these rewards are directly tied to performance as incentives in many private firms and in recent times increasingly also in government bureaus. Pure cases of this control of performance through incentives are piece rates in factories and sales commissions in merchandising firms. A modified form, applicable to any type of work, is the systematic periodic review of the performance of employees, often on the basis of statistical records of performance, and the use of this information in adjusting salaries and in making promotions. The control exercised through the chances for an impending promotion clearly is more indirect and entails less imposition of another's will on one's action than that exercised through a chain of command with coercive sanctions to enforce disciplined compliance.

The technology enters the control system of an organization in two different respects. First, the machine technology constrains the performance of workers and is a tool in the hands of management for controlling operations. A clear example is the regulation of productivity by the speed of the assembly line in a factory. A more complex illustration is provided by the design of the automated set-up in a white-collar office, which constrains the work of the employees preparing the input and those processing the

24. See Lenski, *Power and Privilege,* p. 55.

output of the computer. Automation in factories plays a similar role. Second, the technical knowledge of the experts employed by an organization is the source of their ability to perform complex tasks and keep in control of the situation. By hiring the appropriate professionals with the expert knowledge required for the performance of various responsibilities, management indirectly controls operations and reduces the need for alternative mechanisms of control, such as close supervision through a chain of command or detailed rules for less skilled employees to follow. In addition, employing experts makes it possible to discharge responsibilities that otherwise simply could not be undertaken. Weber placed much stress on the significance of expert knowledge in organizations: "The role of technical qualifications in bureaucratic organizations is continually increasing." [25] And again: "Bureaucratic administration means fundamentally the exercise of control on the basis of knowledge." [26]

From the perspective of management, the importance of expertise in modern organizations means that the recruitment of employees with the required technical skills becomes a crucial responsibility and a major mechanism of control. An organization can be governed by recruiting anybody and everybody and then using a chain of command to rule them with an iron hand or installing a technology that harnesses them to machines. But an organization can also be managed by recruiting selectively only those employees that have the technical qualifications and professional interest to perform on their own the various tasks for which the organization is responsible and then give them discretion to do what needs to be done within the broad framework of basic policies and administrative guidelines. This is how research institutes and universities are run. Though the specialists in these organizations are never told how to do things and rarely what to do, senior administrators maintain long-range control over operations by recruiting certain specialists rather than others. As a matter of fact, administrative control becomes still more indirect if the organization is large and comprises specialists in many different fields, because under these conditions top administrators cannot make recruitment decisions themselves but must delegate responsibility for them too.

The allocation of personnel and other resources is the ultimate mechanism of organizational control, not only in the sense that it is fundamental and nearly always complements other mechanisms, but also in the sense that reliance primarily on it is the polar opposite of Weberian bureaucratic control through a chain of command backed with coercive sanctions. Take

25. Weber, *The Theory of Social and Economic Organization*, p. 335.
26. Ibid., p. 339.

major universities as an extreme example. The faculty's responsibilities for teaching and research are not supervised by administrators; tenure provisions make it impossible to discharge senior faculty members whose performance fails to meet expected standards; and most personnel decisions are in effect made by departmental faculties, because senior administrators cannot easily, and rarely do, exercise their veto power over these decisions. Nevertheless, senior administrators control the direction in which universities are moving and the work that is being done in them in the long run, because they allocate the funds that determine which fields can expand and which ones must contract. Whereas major universities are atypical organizations, of course, and most other organizations are not administered as they are, they provide an extreme instance of indirect forms of administrative control in organizations.

Combinations of several of the mechanisms of control outlined are found in most organizations, but the emerging trend seems to be a decreasing reliance on control through a chain of command and an increasing tendency to rely on indirect kinds of control. While incentive systems and machine technologies are probably the most prevalent mechanisms of organizational control today, controls through recruitment of qualified personnel and allocation of resources assume major significance in organizations with the most specialized personnel, which may well be indicative of their growing future importance. These indirect forms of control are more compatible with democratic values than is the bureaucratic authority exercised through a chain of command in which subordinates are compelled to obey the orders of superiors. However disagreeable the need to keep up with a piece-rate system or a machine is, it does not violate the democratic conception of man, as submission to the commands of a drill sergeant does. In the extreme case, these constraints disappear too, and employees are free to do the work they are professionally trained to do and interested in doing in their own way, and managerial controls are primarily exercised indirectly through selective recruitment and through the decisions that determine the expansion and contraction of various personnel complements. That type of power suffices to govern the organization, though there is virtually no domination of any individuals in it. The extreme case of organizations composed of specialized professionals working with dedication and free of external constraints, though rare, is a polar example of a more general principle: inasmuch as indirect forms of control are more compatible than army-type submission to commands with our values of human freedom and integrity, they reduce resistance, which makes them more effective means of control.

The new forms of power that are developing in modern society are closely connected with the great efficiency of indirect mechanisms of organizational control. Slave drivers have gone out of fashion not because they were so cruel but because they were so inefficient. Men can be controlled much more effectively by tying their economic needs and interests to their performance on behalf of employers. Calling this wage slavery is a half-truth, which correctly indicates that workers dependent on their wages can be exploited as slaves can be, and which conveniently ignores the basic differences between economic exploitation and slavery. The efforts of men can be controlled still far more efficiently than through wages alone by mobilizing their professional commitments to the work they can do best and like to do most and by putting these highly motivated energies and skills at the disposal of organizations. There is a tremendous gain in freedom for individuals, just as there is in the step from slavery to working for wages, and there are simultaneously great advantages that accrue to organizations and give them new potentials for expanded power, just as did the change from slaves to employees. The professionalization of organizations, by which is meant that decisions are made by technical experts both interested and qualified in specialized fields of competence, enhances the internal efficiency and the external power of organizations. In speculating about the implications of this, we have in mind the power exercised by giant organizations, such as the U.S. Army or U.S. Steel.

Power on a large scale, and thus excepting that in small tribes and small groups, is indubitably always exercised with the aid of organizations. The new forms of power, however, are not so much exercised by individuals through organizations as by organizations through individuals. This is not anthropomorphism; on the contrary, attributing the power of organizations to strong leaders is. Administrative decisions are naturally made by individuals, and the decisions of senior administrators of large organizations entail the exercise of much power. But we suspect that even top corporation or military officers are tools of their organization, not the other way around, in the specific sense that their administrative decisions are made to further the interests of the organization rather than their immediate self-interests, which they can ignore because their own long-range interests are linked to those of the organization. Besides, not all important administrative decisions in an organization are made by one individual at the top, and it is often impossible to say which individuals wield the power exercised by an organization without being completely arbitrary. The power is rooted in the structure of the organization. No individual has it, and individuals merely make the decisions through which this power is exercised as incumbents of positions in the formal structure.

The new forms of power rooted in the structure of organizations pose a serious threat in a democratic society. For democratic institutions have been designed to curb the power of individuals or political institutions, such as the federal government, and not that of organizations, such as corporations or military services. How serious the threat is is indicated by a well-known warning of the late President Eisenhower, who hardly can be accused of harboring an ingrained prejudice against the military or against private enterprise:

> In the councils of government we must guard against the acquisition of unwarranted influence, whether sought or unsought, by the military-industrial complex. The potential for the disastrous rise of misplaced power exists and will persist. We must never let the weight of this combination endanger our liberties or democratic processes.[27]

It is the contention here that we shall not be able to meet this danger until we recognize its basic nature and realize that what is required is a readjustment of our democratic institutions to make them capable of controlling the power of organizations.

Insidious Control

The power exercised in new forms within and by big organizations rests on insidious control—control that is "more dangerous than seems evident" [28] for democracy and that is not readily identifiable as power. It is deceptive, because it does not entail the experience of being oppressed by the arbitrary will of a despot and sometimes not even the need to comply with directives of superiors, but merely the internalized obligation to perform tasks in accordance with standards of workmanship. It is elusive, because there is usually nobody who can be held accountable for the actions of powerful organizations that may harm thousands or millions. It is unresponsive to democratic constraints, because it is often not recognized as power and has developed historically more recently than our basic democratic institutions, which are not constituted to protect people's freedom against it. The insidious character of the new forms of power is the source of their strength and of their danger.

The surmise that the controlling influence of giant organizations in modern society is insidious is not meant to imply that a sinister power elite conspires to subdue the populace. Nor is the suggestion that the persons responsible for influential decisions can frequently not be located intended

---

27. Dwight D. Eisenhower, Farewell Address to the Nation, January 17, 1961.
28. *Webster's New World Dictionary* (Cleveland: World, 1960).

to imply that bureaucratic buck-passing and the shielding of the real powers behind the throne by underlings keep decision-makers from public
view. Quite the contrary, the position taken here is that to blame in such
manner the diabolical plots of selfish men for the basic problems of power
in contemporary society is completely mistaken. There are undoubtedly
corrupt and power-hungry men in high places who conspire to dominate
others at any price. But evil men are not what produces the fundamental
problem of power in today's society in our view. What does is the structure of organizations and the systems of interrelated organizations in modern society, including the fact that these organizations command the loyal-
ties of many decent men who often quite selflessly discharge their responsibilities in the interest of their organization.

Organizations are complex structures of decision-making. The research
in this book has already made this evident, and it must be remembered
that the giant organizations comprising the military-industrial complex we
are discussing now are more than 100 times as large as employment security agencies. The considerations advanced here apply also to the power
that exists in organizations with the most benign objectives, for example,
the Roman Catholic Church, which is more than 100 times as large as the
corporate giants. The power wielded by a huge and complex organization
does not simply rest on the decisions of its top executive, regardless of
how dominant a person he is, but it is the joint result of the judgments of
many officials, past and present. Furthermore, there is a tight web of intricate connections among big corporations and between them and the dominant military or political organizations, with the stocks of most companies
owned by others, interlocking directorates, consultation arrangements, and
senior military officers and government officials being often recruited from
private corporations or moving later to lucrative posts in corporations.
The outlawed trust of companies is a horse and buggy by comparison with
this powerful combination.

There are two reasons why the search for the men to be held accountable for the actions of powerful corporations is a chimera: first, as just
noted, the complex structures of decision-making make it frequently impossible to locate the individuals in diverse places whose judgments were
the ultimate source of a given action; second, when they can be located,
they are usually specialized experts whose judgments rest on technical
grounds of efficiency, which makes it almost meaningless to hold them responsible for any deleterious consequences that may result from their judgments. The pressure to make the most rational decision in terms of the interest of the organization requires that the recommendations experts make
on the basis of their technical competence govern as much as possible such

decisions of organizations as whether to shut down a plant and lay off its workers; in which city to build a new plant; whether to back the British pound against inflation or not; or in which company's stock to invest funds.

Decisions like these have far-reaching implications for the lives of people, and sometimes they have deleterious consequences for society. But if experts have reached their recommendations on the basis of technical judgments, they cannot be censured for having arrived at these conclusions, because there is no animus in them, technical criteria govern them, and other experts would have reached the same conclusions. Whereas not all administrative decisions are based on purely technical grounds and exclude all political considerations, it is in the interest of organizations to make most decisions largely on these grounds.[29] Inasmuch as experts judge issues in terms of universal criteria of rationality and efficiency, they cannot be blamed for the conclusions they reach, even though these conclusions may lead to actions of powerful organizations that are contrary to the interest of most people. We must stop looking for villains to blame for the ills of modern society. But as a democratic nation, we must at the same time protect the interest of the commonweal against the actions of powerful organizations and their combinations by finding ways to regulate these formal structures themselves without worrying which particular individuals in them to hold responsible.

Selective recruitment and allocation of personnel resources as mechanisms of internal control in organizations also pose a problem for a democratic society. The employees in an organization benefit from the greater freedom they have if management resorts little to control through a chain of command or detailed rules and relies primarily on this kind of control through gate-keeping, that is, determining how large a personnel complement to recruit for each of the various responsibilities and the qualifications required, and then letting those hired largely work at their own discretion. Surely, these are the organizations in which most of us like to work. But the advantages the insiders gain entail some cost, and those who are kept out pay the cost, simply by being kept out of these preferable places of employment. If a management mistreats its own workers in some ways, they may organize themselves and jointly force management to make

---

29. Although Weber has been justly criticized for failing to make the analytical distinction between the authority based on administrative office and that based on professional competence, as noted (note 20), and one of us (Blau) has previously joined in this criticism, he foresaw correctly that the merger of the two kinds of authority is what makes the modern administrative organization such an efficient tool for power.

concessions, as the union movement illustrates. But if the persons who suffer from the treatment of management remain outside the organization, they have no such recourse. It would appear to be the responsibility of a democratic society to protect these outsiders. Indeed, laws prohibiting discrimination in employment against ethnic minorities do precisely that in one area.

These speculations are not entirely unrelated to the inquiry into organizations that has been presented. A main theme emphasized throughout the book has been that the formal structure of organizations exhibits regularities of its own. Although organizations are made up of people, of course, and what happens in them is the result of decisions of human beings, regularities are observable in their structure that seem to be independent of the personalities and psychological dispositions of individual members. Much empirical material has been presented to support this thesis. It is supported by the very fact that a large portion of the variance in structural characteristics could be accounted for by organizational antecedents without taking into account differences between individuals at all. Hence, a common theme of the sociological analysis of the book and the political speculations in the last few pages is, in short, that organizations are not people.

Democratic institutions are established to maintain the sovereignty and protect the liberty of people against encroachment by other people and particularly by the institutionalized structures other people have built. In the eighteenth century, the main threat to popular sovereignty and individual freedom were tyrannical governments (except for slavery, which was essentially ignored), and the democratic institutions Jefferson and the other fathers of the American Revolution developed were primarily designed to deal with this threat. These men could not have anticipated the threat to human freedom in the twentieth century created by the military-industrial complex, by giant corporations with millions of dollars at their disposal and a military establishment that devours many billions every year. Instead of adapting democratic institutions to this growing threat, we have perverted them and used the very provisions intended to protect people against domination by powerful impersonal structures to protect these structures against people, through legal fictions like the one that corporations are persons.

Marx and his followers have criticized all along the exploitation of people by capitalistic enterprises, imperialist armies, and government bureaucracies. Though true enough, what needs to be added is that economic exploitation is not the only issue, and neither is it the main one in technologically advanced countries near the end of the twentieth century.

The oppression of Manchester workers by sweatshop owners and that of Russian soldiers by the tsarist army were blatant. Nowadays the control exercised by organizations is generally more insidious, but regardless of how subtle and easy to take these indirect controls are and how little economic exploitation they involve, the domination of society by combines of huge organizations is a threat to democracy.

Unless we take seriously the simple fact that organizations are not people, we as citizens shall not be able to meet this threat to democracy, and we as sociologists shall not be able to meet the main challenge our discipline poses. To put it another way: in our sociological analysis as well as our political thinking, it is time that we "push men finally out," [30] to place proper emphasis on the study of social structure in sociology, and to recognize the power of organizations as the main threat to liberty in modern society. The enemy is not an exploitative capitalist or an imperialist general or a narrow-minded bureaucrat. It is no man. It is the efficient structure of modern organizations, which enables the giant ones and their combinations to dominate our lives, our fortunes, and our honor. To restore the liberty of men, we must free them from the domination of powerful organizations, just as eighteenth-century men needed to be freed from domination by tyrannical governments. To do so requires that we stop pretending that organizations are people and protecting them as if they were people. It also requires that we stop looking for villains on whom to place blame and begin to realize that a democratic society is entitled to prevent organizations from engaging in actions that are harmful to the commonweal whether the men who decide on such action are evil or well-intentioned. Their intentions are irrelevant; what is important is to reassert the sovereignty of the people over organizations by instituting democratic restraints on these organizations.

To offer specific suggestions on how this can best be done would go far beyond the scope of this book and the qualifications of its authors. The objectives of the book have been to present a systematic analysis of research on formal organizations and develop a theory that can explain a good number of the empirical findings. This theory did not deal with the problems organizations pose in a democracy. But if our assumptions are correct that the problems for a democracy created by the new forms of organizational power are insidious and that they are rooted in the structure

---

30. We are here paraphrasing the title of a paper by Homans, just as our concept of "new forms of power" paraphrases the title of a book by Mills; see George C. Homans, "Bringing Men Back In," *American Sociological Review,* 29 (1964): 809–818, and C. Wright Mills, *New Men of Power* (New York: Harcourt, Brace, 1948).

of organizations, learning to understand this structure is a first step in solving these problems. We hope that our analysis contributes to such an understanding. Whereas the research data on employment security agencies do not pertain to the giant organizations that endanger democracy, we would have been remiss had we not at least called attention to these dangers inherent in the structure of organizations, though doing so entailed speculations that went far beyond the research evidence or the formal theory derived from it.

Appendices

APPENDIX A

Jurisdictions with Two Agencies

In most states, a single agency is responsible for both unemployment insurance and public employment services. But responsibility for these two functions is split between two agencies in four jurisdictions—those of Arizona, North Dakota, Wisconsin, and the District of Columbia. In these four cases, separate information was collected in interviews with informants in both the employment services and the unemployment insurance agency. The question arose how these four special cases should be treated in the analysis. The decision made was to combine the data for the two agencies in these four jurisdictions and treat each as a single organization. This appendix describes the four situations, outlines the reasons for the decisions to treat these pairs of agencies as single organizations, and indicates the procedures used for combining data into single variables.

In *Arizona,* the administrators of the State Employment Service and the Unemployment Compensation Division both report to a three-man Employment Security Commission. The director of the State Employment Service said in his interview that he discusses policy matters with the Employment Security Commission and gets their "perfunctory" approval on "personnel actions." The deputy director of the Unemployment Compensation Division stated that the Employment Security Commission gives final approval in personnel matters, is the final appeals authority, and is responsible for the general policy and scope of employment security in the state. The deputy felt that the commission supervised the Unemployment Compensation Division "somewhat closely" and that it does "dictate policy"; the Employment Service director said that the commission supervises "not at all closely." (The fact that the commission is housed in the same office

361

building with the Unemployment Insurance Division may well account for the difference.) According to our interview schedule, the commission also initiated and directed the "most important change in the agency that occurred in the last five years." The top executive control and coordination of employment security in Arizona, therefore, is vested in a three-man commission that is more or less closely involved in managing the activities of both employment service and unemployment compensation.

Most of the administrative, staff, and technical functions are divided between the two programs. However, there still remain some functions that cut across agency boundaries. The legal section serves both programs but the chief reports directly to the commission. The Unemployment Compensation Division is responsible for computer services for both programs, including processing payrolls and computations for employment service research and current reports. The data-processing unit also handles the labor market and turnover statistics program in conjunction with employment service personnel. On the other hand, the field supervisor for the unemployment compensation program reported that the employment service staff is responsible for "laying out the basic physical plan for all local offices," including the unemployment offices. Although the various functions have been separated in Arizona to a large degree, there is, nonetheless, considerable overlap, probably owing to the facts that the two programs have historically developed together and that they are jointly administered by one commission.

In March 1965, *North Dakota* still listed a State Employment Service and an Unemployment Compensation Division located at separate addresses in the same building, whose administrators reported to the Workmen's Compensation Bureau. However, a major reorganization was inaugurated the following summer. By January 1966, the month in which our interviews were begun, a new Bureau of Employment Security had been established, a director had been appointed, and organization charts had been revised. Under the new organizational plan the former director of unemployment insurance became the director of the North Dakota Employment Security Bureau; as such he reported directly to the governor rather than the Workmen's Compensation Bureau. The director of employment services now reported to the head of the Employment Security Bureau. Although the dust had not settled at the time of the interviews, this state definitely had one integrated agency responsible for the two programs.

The organizational picture presented by the situation in *Wisconsin* is similar to that in Arizona: a three-man Industrial Commission provides integration of the top level of two separate agencies. Wisconsin has a proud tradition of having been a pioneer in unemployment insurance legislation, and it also enjoys an excellent reputation for employment services. Partly for these reasons, Wisconsin's administrators would undoubtedly resist any allegations that theirs is an integrated organization and emphasize that there are two separate and distinct agencies. Notwithstanding this public image, however, the managing and operating activities of the employment service and unemployment insurance programs in Wisconsin reveal considerable organizational integration. Three functions—personnel, data-processing, and information services—are combined in one division and performed as joint staff services for all the programs of the Industrial Commission, including employment service and unemployment insurance. As an indication of the influence and importance of these coordinating structures, it should be noted that one of the commissioners along with the director of the joint staff services division and the personnel officer were the three respondents who together answered all the questions in the interviews intended for the directors of the employment service and unemployment insurance programs. It would be a contradiction of such organizational facts to consider the two programs to be administered by two totally separate agencies. Wisconsin, too, may be considered a single, if loosely integrated, organization.

The "Directory of State Employment Security Agency Officials" for 1965 states: "In the *District of Columbia* the Employment Service is administered by the federal government. There is no District of Columbia official responsible for matters involving both programs" (p. 3, italics ours —eds.). The director of the Employment Service reports to an official in the U.S. Employment Service and the director of unemployment compensation reports to the District of Columbia Unemployment Compensation Board. Our organization charts, interview schedules, and functional descriptions do not indicate that there is much official contact between the two directors. Physically, however, there is considerable integration of the two programs in that the entire unemployment insurance operation (including the one claims office that serves the whole district) as well as all phases of employment service (including six of the seven local employment offices) are housed in the same building. We are left with the irony that the only agency that carries out virtually all of its operations, including local office functions, under one roof comes closest to being two separate and distinct organizations. Given the necessary procedural cooperation between the two functions and the informal communication that results from physical proximity, it is not entirely unjustified to treat the two agencies in the District of Columbia also as a single organization, though the grounds for doing so are weakest in this case.

There is no entirely satisfactory solution that makes these four jurisdictions with two agencies fully comparable to the other forty-nine jurisdictions with only one agency. The decision to combine the pair of agencies into one organization in these four cases is based on the conviction that doing so distorts empirical conditions less than either eliminating the four cases from the analysis or letting each be represented by two agencies. Though this decision is somewhat arbitrary, notably with respect to the District of Columbia, analysis reveals that the structure of these combined organizations is not much different from that of many of the other forty-nine agencies. For example, the two programs, unemployment insurance and employment services, are also carried out in separate local offices in many of the jurisdictions that have only one agency. Specifically, local operations for the two functions are completely integrated in seventeen agencies, completely separated in nine jurisdictions, and mixed in the rest. Arizona, the District of Columbia, and Wisconsin are among the nine states that have separate local offices for ES and UI and that also have field supervisors specialized by program. At the operational level, then, there are six other agencies that separate the programs to the same degree as these three. (North Dakota's agency now has all integrated local offices and unspecialized field supervisors.)

A comparison of other structural characteristics reveals that when the agency as a whole is considered, the differences between the split agencies and the others are further minimized. For example, Arizona has 23 more local offices than would be expected given the size of the agency, and Wisconsin has 16 more than expected given its size. But Ohio has 28, Illinois 35, and Texas 41 more offices than expected given their size. On the other hand, the District of Columbia has 19 fewer offices than would be expected on the basis of its size, and Massachusetts has 20 fewer than expected given its size. The number of job titles represented in the entire Arizona agency (94) and the number in the Wisconsin agency (105) are both very close to the median for all the agencies under analysis (96). (Data for the District of Columbia are not available for this variable.) There are six hierarchical levels in the Arizona headquarters and five in both Wisconsin and the District of Columbia; the average agency headquarters has six levels. However, the unique attributes of these agencies have not been lost by considering them single organizations. For instance, Wisconsin and Texas have the greatest number of divisions in the central headquarters (13) of all the agencies although the combined Wisconsin agency has many fewer employees than the one in Texas, and though more than half of the employment security agencies have more personnel than that in Arizona, only three of them have more headquarters divisions (one of these being Wisconsin's).

Finally, it is necessary briefly to describe the procedures used for constructing the variables in these cases in which two agencies were combined. Eight measures posed no problems because the data were combined in the sources; these are the variables listed in Appendix C as numbers 2, 4, 5, 6, 7, 8, 15, and 46. The scores for eleven other variables were computed by simply adding the figures; for example, the number of personnel working in the employment service was added to the number in unemployment insurance to produce a score for the size of the entire agency. Size is the denominator for several ratios, the numerators of which were also produced by adding the data. This procedure supplied variables number 1 and 42, 9, 11, 13, 14, 16, 17, 18, 21, and 44 in Appendix C. The service measures (variables 23, 24, 25, and 26) are derived from production records that are the same for all fifty-three agencies.

Some of the measures required special decisions in handling. Civil service appointments were reported separately for Arizona (but for no other jurisdictions), and in this case we computed the weighted average (variable 3). Computers are always used agency-wide, and the scores for variables 6 and 43 were derived in the normal way. The number of hierarchical levels (variable 10) was based on the division with the longest chain of command regardless of whether it is part of the ES or UI agency. The director's span of control (variable 12) was computed for Arizona, the District of Columbia, and Wisconsin by summing the number of officials reporting to both agency directors and dividing by two. For variable 19, delegation of personnel decisions, the responses of both personnel officers were considered. When two or more positions were given in response to the question, and if there were no additional comments to clarify the role of the various participants in the decision, the position with the highest status was coded. For variable 20, delegation of budget decisions, the responses of both directors were considered in order to get a picture of the budget-making process for the integrated agency. The score was then coded according to the same procedure used for the other agencies. Variable 22, delegation to LO manager, is the number of decisions out of five for which the LO manager has major responsibility. In order for the LO managers to be credited with having major responsibility for any of the decisions in the three agencies in question, they had to have it in both the ES and the UI offices. In summing up the number of regular contacts with other state agencies (variable 48), those which were duplicates were excluded. The number of times per year the director discusses agency matters with the governor or commissioner (variable 49) was added together for the two directors and then divided by two.

APPENDIX B

Federal Interviewer Study

The "Study on Selection Methods for Claims and Employment Interviewers in State Employment Security Agencies" was undertaken jointly by the Bureau of Employment Security and the Division of State Merit Systems (BES-DSMS study). The original research and the reports are the combined efforts of several government employees. Helen G. Price (DSMS) supervised the construction of the DSMS test batteries. Robert Droege (BES), Beatrice J. Dvorak (BES), Lorraine D. Eyde (DSMS), Hal M. Gwinn (DSMS), Josephine M. Meers (BES), and Thomas E. Paine (BES) had primary responsibility for the research design and preparation of the written reports. The data were collected from September 1962 to June 1964, and the final report was going to press in 1970. Although we finally use only one variable, education of interviewers, derived from the federal interviewer study, we submitted several others to extensive analysis in the earlier stages of our research, some of which are mentioned in Chapter 9.

The unit of analysis for the BES-DSMS study was the individual interviewer. In using these data for our analysis of local offices, the unit has to be changed from the individual to the local office itself. Thus, the variable of concern is the average number of years of education of all the interviewers in a local office. But this information is not available for all offices. Only thirty-one states cooperated with all phases of the federal study, and it was possible to match the identification codes for only 728 offices. Accordingly, of the 4,939 interviewers on whom we received punched data from the BES-DSMS research group, we could include only 3,889 in our data deck. The 728 offices were further reduced in number to 558, because they had to meet the criteria of minimum size and structural com-

366

plexity for inclusion in our analysis. In these 558 local offices, approximately 73 per cent of the total number of interviewers who were on the staff during the period from September 1962 to July 1963 (and up until the first part of 1964 in some states) provided information concerning education and other personal characteristics. Our index of educational qualifications, therefore, is based on approximately 73 per cent of the total number of interviewers who worked in the 558 offices in our sample during that one-year period. (The other 27 per cent represents the average attrition rate of interviewers during the study; see Table B–1, column 5.) The actual n's on which the aggregate measure is based in each of the local offices have a median of 5 and range from 1 to 50. In other words, in half of the 558 offices, the average number of years of education is computed from five or more observations. However, in 10.2 per cent of the offices, the average is based on only one case; in 11.6 per cent the average is based on two, in 13.4 per cent on three, and in 11.3 per cent on four cases.

The general purpose of the BES-DSMS study is to determine the validity of various tests proposed for use in the selection process of employment security interviewers. Nonsupervisory local office staff who perform claims and employment interviewing activities were included in the study; excluded were employees who (1) spent more than 40 per cent of their time on clerical assignments, (2) were employed on an intermittent basis, (3) were office managers or other working supervisors, and (4) had been working at their present job for less than six months.

A preliminary phase of the study, in which nearly all states participated, was designed to ascertain the different tasks of interviewers in various agencies. Each member of the local office interviewing staff was asked to estimate the per cent of his total work time spent on a large number of work assignments during the year. In order to assist the staff in making the estimates, checklists were provided with accompanying instructions giving examples of hours spent on an assignment each day or each week in terms of equivalent percentages of annual work time. Before completing the time estimates on the official checklist, the interviewer was asked to keep an informal tally of all his work assignments for at least one week.

A total of 14,837 local office employees from 1,668 offices in forty-seven states and the District of Columbia adequately completed checklists. Eight job duties patterns were identified, and 9,386 "interviewers" were put into one of the eight categories according to the following criteria: (1) placement interviewer ($n = 3,383$): at least 50 per cent of the work time is spent on taking job orders and providing direct placement services; (2) employment service generalist ($n = 824$): at least 10 per cent of the work

TABLE B-1. *Number of Interviewers in BES-DSMS Study and Attrition Rates by State*

Number of "Interviewers" Who:	Completed Checklists	Met Criteria as "Interviewer"	Completed Testing	Provided Complete Data for Analysis	% Attrition
Alabama	277	154	142	140	.09
Alaska	34	22	—	—	—
Arizona	133	94	76	47	.50
Arkansas	208	135	111	96	.29
California	1,144	767	668	608	.21
Colorado	198	151	119	109	.28
Connecticut	269	168	140	114	.32
Delaware	38	23	21	19	.17
District of Columbia	96	54	—	—	—
Florida	460	301	193	175	.42
Georgia	290	168	136	123	.27
Guam	—	—	—	—	—
Hawaii	39	28	—	—	—
Idaho	105	75	63	56	.25
Illinois	619	430	—	—	—
Indiana	313	193	173	159	.18
Iowa	207	121	85	72	.40
Kansas	164	93	65	64	.31
Kentucky	252	159	—	—	—
Louisiana	222	139	122	116	.17
Maine	107	67	—	—	—
Maryland	299	158	51	48	.70
Massachusetts	636	422	—	—	—
Michigan	365	259	204	198	.24
Minnesota	199	142	116	95	.33
Mississippi	197	113	94	89	.21
Missouri	424	299	—	—	—
Montana	88	60	—	—	—
Nebraska	103	68	59	52	.24
Nevada	50	36	—	—	—
New Hampshire	67	41	—	—	—
New Jersey	708	380	319	265	.30
New Mexico	—	—	—	—	—
New York	1,735	971	778	699	.28
North Carolina	380	233	192	182	.22
North Dakota	70	46	44	38	.17
Ohio	945	508	—	—	—
Oklahoma	260	179	—	—	—
Oregon	168	125	103	92	.26
Pennsylvania	1,501	1,027	899	797	.22

Continued on following page

TABLE B-1 (continued)

Number of "Interviewers" Who:	Completed Checklists	Met Criteria as "Interviewer"	Completed Testing	Provided Complete Data for Analysis	% Attrition
Puerto Rico	—	—	—	—	—
Rhode Island	147	123	—	—	—
South Carolina	199	130	117	108	.20
South Dakota	55	27	19	19	.30
Tennessee	—	—	—	—	—
Texas	—	—	—	—	—
Utah	119	79	76	76	.04
Vermont	44	36	28	18	.50
Virginia	217	122	—	—	—
Virgin Islands	—	—	—	—	—
Washington	215	146	124	111	.24
West Virginia	158	77	—	—	—
Wisconsin	283	216	190	154	.29
Wyoming	30	21	—	—	—
Totals	14,837	9,386 (6,738)[a]	5,527	4,939	
Average					.27

[a]The number of interviewers in the thirty-one states that participated in the data-gathering phase of the study.

time is spent on each of three out of five employment service activities; (3) employer relations specialist ($n = 458$): at least 50 per cent of the work time is spent on employer relations activities; (4) employment security generalist ($n = 380$): at least 10 per cent of the work time is spent on each of three functions including at least one claims and one employment service function; (5) claims examiner ($n = 1,939$): at least 50 per cent of the work time is spent on such claims activities as obtaining and evaluating information to determine eligibility or disqualification issues; (6) claims taker ($n = 1,523$): at least 50 per cent of the work time is spent on such claims activities as interviewing workers who are making initial or continued claims for unemployment insurance; (7) counselor ($n = 752$): at least 50 per cent of the work time is spent on counseling activities; and (8) farm placement specialist ($n = 127$): at least some time is spent on each of twelve activities designated as critical to the performance of the farm placement function.

The number of employees in each of the forty-eight participating states who met the criteria for inclusion in a job duties pattern is shown in Table B–1, column 2. They represent 63 per cent of all interviewing personnel who completed checklists in the early phases of the study. In order to be

TABLE B-2. *Variables and Basic Statistics*

	n	Mean	Standard Deviation	Skew
Major LO Characteristics				
B-1 (52)[a] Specialization	558	0.42	0.68	1.33
B-2 (53) LO Size	558	28.24	22.92	2.30
B-3 ([b]) Education of Interviewers	558	13.90	1.36	−0.23
B-4 (57) Sections	558	2.37	1.14	1.34
Agency Context				
B-5 (4) Salary of Interviewers	558	5,156.08	545.19	0.32
B-6 (25) Placements per Opening	558	0.71	0.07	0.34
B-7 (26) Employee-Client Ratio				
in Benefit Function	558	12.60	2.53	0.06
Community Environment				
B-8 (79) Population Density	556	526.45	798.19	3.81
B-9 ([b]) Median Education	556	10.68	1.22	−0.42

[a]The numbers in parentheses are the variable numbers assigned in Appendix C; see the variable identified for definitions, sources, and comments.

[b]These variables are used only in Chapter 9; variable B-3 is described above and variable B-9 has the same definition as variable 34 and the same source as variables 77-82 in Appendix C.

included in a job duties pattern, the interviewing staff member had to meet the first criterion of a minimum amount of work time spent on the activities included in the pattern, as well as a second criterion that stated that this minimum amount of time had to include some time spent on certain work assignments that were designated as critical to the performance of that particular function. A total of 5,451 employees did not meet these criteria and could not be placed in any of the job duties patterns; by definition, then, these staff members could not be classified as "interviewers" for the purposes of the study.

Eventually, only thirty-one states were able to take part in the next stage of the project, which involved a full day of testing for each participating employee. Higher summer workloads, vacations, and budgetary limitations prevented the other states from completing the study. A personal data sheet supplied information that included a detailed description of educational experience from which our index of average number of school years was computed. The bulk of the data, however, came from a series of job-oriented tests devised by the Division of State Merit Systems that were tailored to fit the characteristic duties of each of the job duties patterns described above. In the final analysis the test scores and the personal characteristics were related to two performance measures. Each interviewer's job performance had been rated once by a peer and again by a supervisor. The number of interviewers in each of the participating states who actually

TABLE B-3.   *Zero-Order Correlation[a] Matrix for Subsample of Local Offices*

		B-1 Spec	B-2 LO Size	B-3 Ed Ints	B-4 Sctns	B-5 Salary Intvwr	B-6 Plcmts /Opng	B-7 Emp-Cl Ratio	B-8 Pop Dnsty
B-1	Specialization	1.000							
B-2	LO Size	.345	1.000						
B-3	Education Interviewers	.192	.226	1.000					
B-4	Sections	.357	.649	.265	1.000				
B-5	Salary of Interviewers	.166	.444	.202	.184	1.000			
B-6	Placements per Opening	−.057	−.312	−.212	−.037	−.548	1.000		
B-7	Employee-Client Ratio	.012	−.286	−.247	−.157	−.348	.355	1.000	
B-8	Population Density	.545	.464	.238	.445	.227	−.121	.135	1.00
B-9	Median Education	−.033	.224	.073	.105	.293	−.145	−.318	−.116

[a]The coefficients used here are the Pearsonian r computed according to the Mesa-85 statistical system (UCSL 510, 9/1/66) obtained from the program library of the University of Chicago's Computation Center. The n's are given in Table B-2. When there are missing cases, the Mesa-85 system computes the correlations "by summing the deviation cross products defined for both variables, but using means and standard deviations based on all values defined for each variable independently" (p. 3).

completed checklists and were tested is shown in Table B–1, column 3. The numbers that formed the basis for the actual analysis are given in column 4 of Table B–1. Some final comments on these figures will consider the questions of the attrition rate and the representativeness of the sample.

The thirty-one states that participated contain 73 per cent (6,738 out of 9,386) of all the interviewers who met the criteria for inclusion in one of the job duties patterns. There was a loss of 18 per cent of the total sample within the thirty-one states during the eleven months that elapsed between the time that the checklists were completed and the data were gathered. This attrition included separations, major job changes and promotions, employees who could not be tested or rated, and an administrative decision in one state that eliminated 107 interviewers. (It should be noted that the median separation rate for all employees with permanent status in these thirty-one states for fiscal year 1963 was 15.7 per cent.) Another 558 had to be eliminated from the data-processing because of incomplete or incorrect data bringing the attrition rate for the entire period to 27 per cent (1,799 out of 6,738). The loss ranges from 4 to 50 per cent (except for the state mentioned above, which was able to test only a subsample of its eligible interviewers, producing a rate of attrition of 70 per cent).

The BES-DSMS researchers state that

> while the attrition was slightly higher in the smallest offices and in the Employment Security Generalist job duties pattern, it was concluded that the sample of 4,939 analyzed in Phase III was generally representative of the interviewing staff working in local offices of the State employment security system. The total sample and most job duties patterns reflect the heavy contribution by the three largest states: Pennsylvania, New York, and California. However, this too is representative of the total interviewer staffing in the system.[1]

Six of the 13 smallest states, 9 out of 15 medium-sized states, 11 out of the 13 large states, and 5 out of the 8 very large states that participated in the data-gathering phase were also included in the analysis of the study. "Half of the States had statewide civil service systems and half were merit system States. Different types of administration were represented, as well as a wide range of State salary structures." [2]

Repeated attrition for various reasons makes it impossible to consider the 558 local offices for which information on the average education of interviewers is available a representative sample of the entire group of 1,201 local offices. However, comparison of the characteristics of these 558 local offices with those of all 1,201 local offices reveals virtually no substantial difference, as noted in Chapter 9, which warrants the conclusion that attrition does not seem to have produced serious distorting biases.

---

1. Final report of the BES-DSMS study, in preparation, 1969, p. 13. The data contained in Table B–1 are taken from Table 1 and Appendix III of this final report. The information about the federal interviewer study contained in this appendix is taken in part from the research design and questionnaires, Bureau of Employment Security, GAL 1223 and attachment, August 13, 1968, and the various reports issued by the BES-DSMS study group.
2. Ibid.

APPENDIX C

Variables and Sources

This appendix contains a detailed description of all the variables used in the analysis of the fifty-three employment security agencies and the 1,201 local offices that met the criteria for inclusion in the study. The first section gives the operational definition and basic statistics for each of the 85 variables. The second lists the original sources of the data and adds further technical comments about coding, scaling, and reliability for the interested reader. If the index is commonly used in the literature (for example per cent blacks or per cent foreign stock), only the title accompanies the descriptive statistics in the first section and the definition given in the source is added to the reference cited in the second section. Those variables generated directly from the organizational charts are described in full in Appendix D with the aid of sample charts and models constructed for coding purposes.

Definitions and Basic Statistics

Agency Analysis

TABLE C-1. *Major Characteristics of Agencies*

	n	Mean	Standard Deviation	Skew
Parameters				
1. Size: number of full-time personnel in the agency[a] as of a given date in the first quarter of 1966.	53	1,194.7	1,675.69	3.34
2. Extent of personnel regulations: number of words in the rules book covering employment, in thousands.	51	18.4	11.01	2.45
3. Civil service appointments: number of competitive accessions divided by total accessions X 100 for fiscal years 1964, 1965, and 1966; the three percentages then averaged.	52	59.7	19.16	−0.27
4. Salary of interviewers: annual salary for new interviewers (in dollars) averaged over three review periods of six months each, ending January 1, 1965, July 1, 1965, and January 1, 1966.	52	4,762.1	608.98	0.58
Instrumental Conditions				
5. Division of labor: number of official job titles used in the agency, not counting different grades within one job title.	52	105.7	45.41	1.62
6. Automation: score based on number of computers and input/output units; coded into thirteen categories.	53	2.5	2.45	2.49
7. Educational requirements: those for the entry level interviewer position set by the state's civil service department; coded with an ordinal scale in four categories (1-4).	53	2.1	1.08	0.50
8. Educational qualifications: number of interviewers with B.A.'s appointed during 1965 divided by the total number appointed that year, X 100.	52	53.9	28.52	0.20
9. Education of division heads: sum of the number of years of college and graduate education for division heads divided by number of division heads for whom the information was reported.	51	3.5	0.89	−0.63
Shape of the Pyramid				
10. Levels: number of supervisory strata in the headquarters division with the most supervisory strata; assistant supervisors and deputies are not counted as distinct levels.	53	6.0	1.11	0.10
11. Divisions: number of major subunits in the headquarters whose head reports to the director or his deputy; a division must have at least five people.	53	6.6	2.53	0.77

Continued on following page

TABLE C-1 (continued)

	n	Mean	Standard Deviation	Skew
Shape of the Pyramid (continued)				
12. Director's span of control: sum of all division heads, special assistants, and supervisors of a divisional office (a subunit with two to four members).	53	10.2	2.91	0.67
13. Sections per division: number of sections in the headquarters divided by number of divisions; a section is a subunit in a division whose head reports to the division head.	53	2.5	0.92	0.81
14. Division heads' span of control: sum of all supervisory and nonsupervisory personnel who report directly to division heads, divided by the number of divisions.	53	6.2	1.30	0.44
Administration				
15. Standardized ratings: annual personnel rating forms coded with an ordinal scale in four categories (1-4) from least to most objective.	49	2.5	1.06	−0.14
16. Clerical ratio: sum of all clerical personnel divided by total personnel in the agency, X 100.	53	32.1	6.46	0.78
17. Supervisory ratio in agency headquarters: sum of all supervisory personnel divided by total personnel at the headquarters, X 100.	51	21.2	4.55	0.71
18. Staff ratio: number of administrative, staff, and technical equivalent positions divided by total number of equivalent positions in the agency, X 100.	52	10.7	2.80	1.20
Decentralization				
19. Delegation-personnel: locus of responsibility for hiring personnel to fill a supervisory position; coded with an ordinal scale in four categories (1-4) with a high score indicating decentralized authority.	53	2.7	0.91	−0.04
20. Delegation-budget: budget-making process coded with an ordinal scale in four categories (0-3) with a high score indicating decentralized authority.	46	1.3	1.01	−0.04
21. Decentralization-influence: number of division heads who claim influence in all major structural changes in their own division or in other subunits divided by number of division heads answering question, X 100.	49	39.6	22.21	0.56

Continued on following page

TABLE C-1 (continued)

	n	Mean	Standard Deviation	Skew
Decentralization (continued)				
22. Delegation to LO manager: out of a total of five types, the number of decisions for which LO manager has major responsibility.	53	1.3	1.10	0.64
Services				
23. Applications per employee: average number of new applications for March, June, September, and December 1966, divided by size (as defined for variable 1).	53	15.3	4.60	0.53
24. GATB's per application: average number of General Aptitude Test Batteries administered in March, June, September, and December 1966, divided by average number of new applications for the same months.	53	0.08	0.04	1.20
25. Placements per opening: average number of nonagricultural placements for March, June, September, and December 1966, divided by average number of nonagricultural openings received for the same months.	53	0.71	0.13	−2.49
26. Employee-client ratio in benefit function: number of benefit positions per 1,000 average insured unemployed, fiscal year 1965.	52	13.1	2.75	0.49

[a]"Agency" is herein defined as the entire organization including central headquarters, outstationed units, and all local offices in the jurisdiction.

TABLE C-2. *State Environment of Agencies*

	n	Mean	Standard Deviation	Skew
27. Midwestern region: dummy variable with states in Northcentral coded 1 and others 0.	51	0.26	0.44	1.16
28. Southern region: dummy variable with states in South coded 1 and others 0.	51	0.31	0.47	0.83
29. Western region: dummy variable with states in West coded 1 and others 0.	51	0.26	0.44	1.16
30. Population: 1965 estimate, in thousands.	51	3,800.4	4,118.80	2.11
31. % urban: 1960.	51	62.5	15.86	0.04
32. Median family income: 1959, in hundreds of dollars.	51	53.7	10.05	−0.38

Continued on following page

TABLE C-2 (continued)

	n	Mean	Standard Deviation	Skew
33. % manufacturing employees: number of full-time and part-time employees in manufacturing, 1963, divided by population estimate, 1963, in hundreds.	51	7.4	3.9	0.19
34. Median education: median years completed, 1960.	51	10.6	1.11	−0.25
35. % foreign stock: 1960.	51	16.6	11.39	0.51
36. % government employees: number of state government employees divided by 1965 state population estimate, both in thousands.	50	0.01	0.00	1.74
37. Expenditures per capita: state and local general expenditures per capita, 1964-1965, in dollars.	50	400.5	112.98	2.31
38. Governor's appointive power: extent of formal influence that the governor has over the appointment of the chief administrator for each of sixteen major functions and offices in the state. An interval scale (0-100) based on a six-point ordinal subscale used to score the governor's powers of appointment over each of the sixteen functions.	49	44.2	13.76	0.05
39. % insured unemployed: average weekly insured unemployment for 1966 in raw numbers divided by the population estimate for 1965 in hundreds.	51	0.49	0.26	1.52
40. Benefit duration: average potential duration of benefit payments for insured claimants, in weeks, for 1966.	52	23.6	3.13	−0.70
41. Funds/taxes: ratio of federal funds allocated to states for employment security administration to federal unemployment tax collections, fiscal year 1963, in hundreds.	52	108.4	52.16	2.03
42. Size (log): logarithm to base 10 of size (variable 1).	53	2.8	0.44	0.30
43. Automation (dummy): dummy variable with those agencies having a computer coded 1, others 0.	53	0.55	0.50	−0.20
44. Supervisory ratio in total agency: number of all supervisory personnel divided by total personnel in the agency.	53	19.0	3.03	−0.07
45. Size of government: number of state government employees, 1965, in thousands.	50	40.6	35.78	2.15

Continued on following page

TABLE C-2 (continued)

	n	Mean	Standard Deviation	Skew
46. Merit system coverage: dummy variable with those states in which the merit system or civil service department covers nearly all state employees coded 1, and other states with only partial coverage coded 0, 1963.	53	0.57	0.50	−0.27
47. Population expansion: population change, 1950 to 1960.	51	19.6	20.39	1.70

TABLE C-3. *Additional Variables in Agency Analysis*[a]

	n	Mean	Standard Deviation	Skew
48. Contacts with other state agencies: sum of state offices in regular contact with the employment security agency.	53	5.9	2.20	0.92
49. Communication with governor or commissioner: number of times per year the director discusses agency matters with his superior (the governor or the commissioner).	53	104.2	144.86	2.24
50a. Applications per initial claim: average number of new applications for March, June, September, and December 1966, divided by the average number of initial claims for the same months.	53	1.7	0.88	1.21
50b. % nonagricultural employees: number of nonagricultural employees divided by the total civilian labor force, 1960.	51	0.91	0.07	−1.42
50c. % total unemployed: number of unemployed as defined by the U.S. Census Bureau divided by the total civilian labor force, 1960.	51	5.14	1.58	2.61

[a]These characteristics are mentioned in the text, but they are not used in multiple regression problems.

Local Office Analysis

TABLE C-4. *Major Characteristics of Local Offices*

	n	Mean	Standard Deviation	Skew
Parameters				
51. ES function: ordinal scale of employment service function. The categories are only UC, zero; mixed, one; only ES, two.	1,201	1.2	0.65	−0.20

Continued on following page

TABLE C-4 (continued)

	n	Mean	Standard Deviation	Skew
Parameters (continued)				
52. Specialization: ordinal scale based on office function, ranging from 0 (least specialized) to 2 (most specialized).	1,201	0.70	0.81	0.60
53. Size: total number of personnel in the office as of a given date in the first quarter of 1966.	1,201	26.7	23.48	2.77
Instrumental Conditions				
54. Division of labor: number of official job titles represented in the office, not counting different grades within one job title.	1,201	7.1	2.57	0.70
55. Mechanization: number of electric typewriters in the office.	1,188	0.74	1.27	2.89
Shape of the Pyramid				
56. Levels: number of supervisory strata in the section with the most supervisory strata. Assistant supervisors and deputies are not counted as distinct levels.	1,201	3.3	0.49	1.31
57. Sections: number of units in the office whose head reports to the office manager or assistant manager.	1,201	2.4	1.18	1.42
58. LO manager's span of control: number of section heads and sectional officers who report to the LO manager or his assistant.	1,201	6.0	3.15	1.77
Administration				
59. Clerical ratio: sum of all clerical personnel divided by total personnel in the office, $\times$ 100.	1,201	20.3	13.2	1.29
60. Supervisory ratio: sum of all supervisory personnel divided by total personnel in the office, $\times$ 100.	1,201	21.0	7.9	0.99
61. First-line supervisors' span of control: total number of people on the lowest organizational level in the office divided by the number of supervisors to whom they report.	1,201	5.0	2.94	1.04

TABLE C-5. *Local Office Supplementary Variables*

	n	Mean	Standard Deviation	Skew
62. LO size (log): logarithm to the base 10 of LO size (variable 53).	1,201	1.3	0.31	0.38
63. LO size $\times$ levels: product term of LO size (variable 53) times levels (variable 56).	1,201	95.9	103.48	3.31

Continued on following page

TABLE C-5 (continued)

	n	Mean	Standard Deviation	Skew
64. Levels X sections: product term of levels (variable 56) X sections (variable 57).	1,201	8.0	4.57	1.46
65. Division of labor X clerical ratio: product term of division of labor (variable 54) X clerical ratio (variable 59).	1,201	1.5	1.17	1.53
66. Levels X clerical ratio: product term of levels (variable 56) X clerical ratio (variable 59).	1,201	0.67	0.44	1.47

TABLE C-6. *Agency Context of Local Offices*[a]

	n	Mean	Standard Deviation	Skew
67. Size: see variable 1.	1,201	3,125.2	2,858.85	1.06
68. Extent of personnel regulations: see variable 2.	1,194	24.7	17.82	1.86
69. Division of labor: see variable 5.	1,194	148.3	57.83	0.59
70. Automation: see variable 6.	1,201	4.8	4.02	0.80
71. Educational qualifications: see variable 8.	1,194	52.5	28.15	0.28
72. Clerical ratio: see variable 16.	1,201	32.6	7.70	0.64
73. Supervisory ratio in agency headquarters: see variable 17.	1,201	18.7	4.16	0.14
74. Delegation to LO manager: see variable 22.	1,201	1.3	1.25	0.95
75. Placements per opening: see variable 25.	1,201	0.72	0.08	0.01
76. Employee-client ratio in benefit function: see variable 26.	1,201	12.7	2.41	0.08

[a]The variables used in the contextual analysis of local offices are the same as those used in the analysis of the major characteristics of agencies. See Chapter 8 for a description of the procedures used in this type of analysis. The definitions of these variables are the same as those for the corresponding variables identified, but the statistics are not identical.

TABLE C-7. *Community Environment of Local Offices*

	n	Mean	Standard Deviation	Skew
77. Town under 25,000: dummy variable with towns under 25,000 coded 1 and cities of 25,000 and over coded 2.[a]	1,199	1.3	0.47	0.76
78. Population: of city or county; 1964 estimate, in thousands.	1,187	680.9	1,643.78	3.55

Continued on following page

TABLE C-7 (continued)

	n	Mean	Standard Deviation	Skew
79. Population density: of city or county; 1960, in tens of people/square mile.	1,188	559.1	771.99	4.13
80. Median family income: of city or county; 1960, in hundreds of dollars.	1,199	56.8	11.52	−0.66
81. % blacks: of city or county; 1960.	1,183	11.5	12.43	1.38
82. % foreign stock: of city or county; 1960.	1,188	20.9	14.32	0.34
83. % blacks X median family income: product term of per cent blacks (variable 81) X median family income (variable 80).	1,183	617.8	614.88	1.12

[a]If a local office is located in a town with less than 25,000 population, the community environment is considered the county in which the town is situated; when the population is 25,000 and over the city itself is used. This applies to variables 78-82.

TABLE C-8.   *State Environment of Local Offices*

	n	Mean	Standard Deviation	Skew
84. Western region: see variable 29.	1,190	0.20	0.40	1.54
85. % urban: see variable 31.	1,190	71.2	14.18	−0.80
86. % government employees: see variable 36.	1,183	0.01	0.00	2.34

Sources and Comments

Agency Analysis

MAJOR CHARACTERISTICS

1. Size: the payroll print-out or some official current listing of personnel such as an employee register, manning tables, or staffing patterns. Although every attempt was made to secure a listing for a definite date in the first quarter of calendar year 1966, a few are from the last quarter of 1965 and the second quarter of 1966. CORP 7 files.

Size can fluctuate from week to week. This measure "freezes" the number of personnel at the date of the official listing. Full-time intermittents were included if they were on the payroll at the time; part-time personnel were not included in the counts. In those few cases in which an active supervisory position was temporarily vacant, the position was added to the total.

2. Extent of personnel regulations: *Personnel Rules and Regulations* manual containing the written rules governing appointment, probation,

promotion, separation, and other personnel procedures, for all employees under the merit system of the state. CORP 7 files.

The score was obtained by counting the average number of words per page for a sample of pages and multiplying by the total number of pages.

3. Civil service appointments: Department of Health, Education and Welfare, Division of State Merit Systems, *Summary of Merit System Reviews,* 1964, 1965, 1966; Table 6, p. 12.

The three-year average reduces the fluctuations in the data from year to year. The correlations between individual years are .63, .62, and .67; those between an individual year and the average of the other two are .71, .74, and .71. Percentages are based on data from fiscal years 1964, 1965, and 1966.

4. Salary of interviewers: Department of Health, Education and Welfare, Division of State Merit Systems, *State Salary Ranges,* January 1, 1965, July 1, 1965, January 1, 1966, "Employment Interviewer," p. 6.

Any one year would be a satisfactory measure for this variable. The average reduces the slight fluctuations that are in the data. The correlations between the individual years are .94, .91, and .93; those between an individual year and the average of the other two are .95, .96, and .93. Interviewer's salary was chosen as the basis for this measure because this job is the entry level professional position, because it represents the basic production functions of the agency, and because it encompasses comparable duties in all agencies.

5. Division of labor: Department of Health, Education and Welfare, Division of State Merit Systems form 85–R012, "Review of Personnel Operations—Grant-Aided Agency," fiscal year 1965, item 1: "Number of classes at end of period."

This variable measures the number of task areas in an employment security agency that are specific enough to warrant an official job classification in the state civil service department's roster of job classes. Before a new classification is authorized by the civil service office for the employment security agency, it must be determined that none of the existing job classes could in fact cover the task area in question.

6. Automation: copies of rental invoices listing all electronic computers and/or conventional equipment in use in the agency. In lieu of the invoice, copies of official equipment inventory lists. CORP 7 files.

Any index of computer-automation has built-in inadequacies. For example, a highly competent team of systems analysts and programmers can operate an EDP system that will work more efficiently with less equipment than a less-skilled group can with more extensive hardware.

7. Educational requirements: official job specifications for the Inter-

viewer 1 or equivalent position issued by the individual state civil service department or merit system council. CORP 7 files.

The text was coded according to its face-value meaning: whatever requirement was listed first was considered most desired. The categories are: (1) requires merely "experience" or "high school with less than four years of experience"; (2) requires "high school and four years of additional experience, or education, or some combination of additional experience and education"; (3) requires "a B.A. degree but allowing some experience substitute"; (4) requires "a B.A. degree and not allowing any experience substitute." The interviewer position was selected for reasons listed under variable 4.

8. Educational qualifications: Department of Health, Education and Welfare, Division of State Merit Systems, *Analysis of Appointments, Separations, Promotions: Public Assistance Caseworkers and Employment Security Interviewers,* 1966, Table 15, p. 26. The table is based on information for 1965.

The interviewer position was selected for reasons listed under variable 4.

9. Education of division heads: CORP 7 interview: obtained from director or, more often, from the personnel files.

We tried to get the number of school years for all supervisors who report directly to the agency director or his deputy; this group comprises all heads of divisions and divisional offices (a division has five or more personnel and a divisional office has fewer than five). If we did not obtain data for at least half of the division heads in any agency, the case was not coded (N.A.). In the fifty-one states that had sufficient data there are 533 heads of divisions and divisional offices; we have data on 78 per cent of them. The base from which the state average was computed ranges from three to fifteen with a mean of 8.1.

10. Levels: organization charts or manning tables, explained and verified by the director, division heads, or other officials who had the accurate information, dated as closely as possible to the first quarter of calendar year 1966. CORP 7 files.

In order to include the top level of the director to whom the division heads report, another level is added to the number in the "longest" division. See Appendix D for a complete description of coding procedures, especially Figure D–4 and section 2.3.

11. Divisions: source: same as variable 10. See Appendix D for a complete description of coding procedures, especially section 2.2.

12. Director's span of control: source: same as variable 10. See Appendix D for a complete description of coding procedures, especially section 2.5.

13. Sections per division: source: same as variable 10. See Appendix D for a complete description of coding procedures, especially section 2.2.

14. Division heads' span of control: source: same as variable 10. See Appendix D for a complete description of coding procedures, especially section 2.5.

15. Standardized ratings: employment security agencies' performance rating or evaluation forms used by supervisors to rate their subordinates periodically. CORP 7 files.

The rating forms were coded according to the following four categories: (1) form requests the supervisor to give a general evaluation of the worker in a few sentences; (2) main part of the form provides for general comments and also suggests several factors to be rated "satisfactory" or not; (3) form lists several factors to be checked and asks for comments on each; and (4) form lists several factors to be scored quantitatively and does not ask for comments. An annual evaluation of employees is required by the Division of State Merit Systems for all grant-in-aid agencies, and in many states employees are evaluated once or twice during their probationary period as well. Some employment security agencies use the form provided by their state merit council, but many have modified them or drawn up original rating forms to meet their own needs.

16. Clerical ratio: sources: same as variables 1 and 10.

Most clerical job titles are easily identifiable, for example, typists, stenos, telephone operators, secretaries, and the like. We kept a record of the disputed job titles, listing whether they were eventually coded as clerical or professional. See Appendix D for a complete description of coding procedures, especially section 2.6.

17. Supervisory ratio: sources: same as variables 1 and 10. See Appendix D for a complete description of coding procedures, especially section 2.4.

18. Staff ratio: BES 84–21,[1] items 131–138, 141, 143, 151, 180, for the quarter ending March 31, 1966.

This form covers all functions carried out in an employment security agency and reports the number of equivalent positions (computed from man-hours) used to perform them during the review period. The data on the BES 84–21 report are compiled from tallies kept by all personnel in the agency. Note that the numerator of our staff ratio variable is different from the category "Administrative, Staff, and Technical Functions" used

---

1. Bureau of Employment Security, form 84-21, "Personnel Time Report." Replaced form ES-160 in 1966.

on the BES 84–21 form. We have removed the executive and field supervisory line positions as well as the positions devoted to the labor statistics program in order to have a purer measure of only staff positions. The building maintenance positions have been removed from both the numerator and denominator of our staff ratio.

19. Delegation–personnel: CORP 7 interview: "When there is a vacancy in the headquarters, who actually decides which person will be hired from a civil service eligibility list for a supervisory position?" Respondent: personnel director. CORP 7 files.

A high score means this hiring decision is decentralized to the section head or immediate supervisor (third level from the top of the supervisory hierarchy or lower). The possible rank scores are: (1) commission(er), (2) director or deputy director, (3) division head or personnel officer, and (4) section head or immediate supervisor.

20. Delegation–budget: CORP 7 interview: "Which division heads submit a budget proposal for their division?" Respondent: agency director. CORP 7 files.

The question was answered with a brief description of the budget-making process; it was coded to include the more general underlying question: "Who submits a budget proposal or participates directly in the budget process?" The possible rank scores are: (0) division heads do not participate: either the director alone, *or* the budget officer alone, prepares the budget, *or* it is drawn up through some informal procedure; (1) selected budget committee prepares the budget, *or* each division head participates when his program is involved; (2) all division heads participate; and (3) some local office personnel and headquarters section heads as well as all division heads participate.

21. Decentralization–influence: CORP 7 self-administered questionnaire: "What changes in the internal organization of your division can you make? (For example, can you add a unit or combine two into one?)" Respondents: all division heads. CORP 7 files.

The respondents for this questionnaire were all the supervisors who report to the agency director or his deputy; this group comprises all heads of divisions and divisional offices (a division has five or more personnel and a divisional office has less than five). If less than half of the division heads in any agency have answered this question, the case was dropped from the analysis (N.A.). In the forty-nine agencies that have sufficient data there are 516 heads of divisions and divisional offices; we have data on 77 per cent of them. The base from which the percentage was computed ranges from three to sixteen with a mean of 8.1.

22. Delegation to LO manager: CORP 7 interview: "Does the employ-

ment service director, field supervisors, or do local office managers have the major responsibility for the following:

A. Selection and hiring of *temporary* and *part-time* personnel after the positions have been approved.

B. Negotiating for building lease, *after* approval from the state office.

C. Laying out basic physical plan for local office, within federal and state restrictions.

D. Opening and closing existing itinerant points.

E. Approving overtime for personnel other than local office manager?" Respondent: director of employment service division. CORP 7 files.

23. Applications per employee: The average number of new applications for the four months ending each of the quarters in 1966 was computed from ES-209,[2] item 1, column 2 total (data for March); *ESS*,[3] August 1966, Table 1, column 8, p. 3 (data for June); *ESS*,[3] November 1966, Table 1, column 8, p. 3 (data for September); *ESS*,[3] February 1967, Table 1, column 8, p. 3 (data for December). The denominator is number of employees in the agency (variable 1).

The definition of "application" is given in the *Employment Security Manual* glossary: "The act by which a job seeker informs an employment service interviewer of his availability and qualifications for referral to job openings." If this information is not recorded but the applicant is immediately referred, it is not counted as an application. See Appendix E for a complete discussion of the factor analysis and reliability checks used in generating this measure.

24. GATB's per application: The average number of GATB's for the four months ending each of the quarters in 1966 was computed from: ES-209,[2] item 4, column 2 total (data for March); *ESS*,[3] August 1966, Table 3, column 8, p. 3 (data for June); *ESS*,[3] November 1966, Table 3, column 8, p. 3 (data for September); *ESS*,[3] February 1967, Table 3, column 8, p. 3 (data for December). The source and definition for average number of applications is given under variable 23.

The definition of "General Aptitude Test Battery" is given in the *Employment Security Manual* glossary: "A multi-factor or multiple-aptitude test battery used by counselors to determine the individual's potentiality for acquiring the skills involved in many broad occupational groups. The original edition, B-1001, is a combination of 15 aptitude tests measuring 10 different aptitudes." See Appendix E for a complete discussion of the factor analysis and reliability checks used in generating this measure.

2. Bureau of Employment Security, form ES-209, "Local Office Activities," state summaries.

3. U.S. Dept. of Labor, Bureau of Employment Security, Manpower Administration, *Employment Service Statistics* (*ESS*); published monthly.

25. Placements per opening: The average number of placements and openings for the four months ending each of the quarters in 1966 was computed from: ES-209,[2] item 19, column 2 total and item 14, column 2 total (data for March); *ESS,*[3] August 1966, Table 1, column 13 and Table 2, column 2 (data for June); *ESS,*[3] November 1966, Table 1, column 13 and Table 2, column 2 (data for September); *ESS,*[3] February 1967, Table 1, column 13 and Table 2, column 2 (data for December).

The definition of "placement" is given in the *Employment Security Manual* glossary:

> An acceptance by an employer of a person for a job as a direct result of employment office activities, provided the employment office has completed all of the following four steps: (a) Receipt of an order, prior to referral; (b) selection of the person to be referred without designation by the employer of any particular individual or group of individuals; (c) referral; and (d) verification from a reliable source, preferably the employer, that a person referred has been hired by the employer and has entered on the job.

The definition of "opening": "a single job for which the local office has on file a request to select an applicant or applicants." See Appendix E for a complete discussion of the factor analysis and reliability checks used in generating this measure.

26. Employee-client ratio in benefit function: memorandum issued by the Unemployment Insurance Service of the Bureau of Employment Security to all regional directors, UIS: dated November 3, 1965; subject: "Management Improvement and Cost Reduction in UIS"; Ref. GAL, No. 924.

In comparing the figures from this memorandum with those reported in the ES-160 [1] for the period ending June 30, 1965 (which we have on file), we were able to ascertain that the number of benefit positions is an average based on the four quarters of fiscal year 1965. By checking the figures given in the memo against those reported in Table 100 of *Historical Statistics of Employment Security Activities 1938–1966,* we were able to determine that the number of insured unemployed is the mean weekly average insured unemployed for fiscal year 1965. See Appendix E for a complete discussion of the factor analysis and reliability checks used in selecting this measure.

STATE ENVIRONMENT

27. Midwestern region: *CCDB,*[4] Table 1, p. 2.

The following states were coded 1: Ohio, Indiana, Illinois, Michigan,

---

4. U.S. Bureau of the Census, *County and City Data Book 1967* (Washington, D.C.: Government Printing Office, 1967). (*CCDB*)

Wisconsin, Minnesota, Iowa, Missouri, North Dakota, South Dakota, Nebraska, Kansas; all others were coded 0.

28. Southern region: *CCDB,*[4] Table 1, p. 2.

The following states were coded 1: Delaware, Maryland, District of Columbia, Virginia, West Virginia, North Carolina, South Carolina, Georgia, Florida, Kentucky, Tennessee, Alabama, Mississippi, Arkansas, Louisiana, Oklahoma, Texas; all others were coded 0.

29. Western region: *CCDB,*[4] Table 1, p. 2.

The following states were coded 1: Montana, Idaho, Wyoming, Colorado, New Mexico, Arizona, Utah, Nevada, Washington, Oregon, California, Alaska, Hawaii; all others were coded 0.

30. Population: *RMCA,*[5] 1967, 98th ed.; Table is entitled "Population Projections for State and Metropolitan Areas, 1965–1985," p. 30.

The population estimate for 1965 is based on census information, growth patterns, and annexations, and it is recorded in thousands.

31. Per cent urban: *CCDB,*[4] item 9, p. xx and Table 1, item 9, p. 2.

The urban population comprises all persons who were living in (a) incorporated places of 2,500 inhabitants or more; (b) the densely settled urban fringe, whether incorporated or not; (c) towns and townships that are not incorporated and that have either 25,000 inhabitants or more, or a population of 2,500 to 25,000 and a density of 1,500 or more per square mile; (d) counties that have no incorporated municipalities and that have a density of 1,500 persons or more per square mile; and (e) unincorporated places of 2,500 or more. Data for 1960.

32. Median family income: *CCDB,*[4] items 28–30, p. xxii and Table 1, item 28, p. 3.

Family income represents, as a single amount, the combined incomes of the head of the family and of all other members fourteen years old and over who are living with the family for the calendar year 1959.

33. Per cent manufacturing employees: numerator: *CCDB,*[4] items 64–65, p. xxvi and Table 1, item 64, p. 6. Denominator: Bureau of the Census, *Statistical Abstract of the United States,* 85th ed. (Washington, D.C.: Government Printing Office, 1964), Table 8, column 10, p. 11.

Figures for employees in manufacturing comprise all full-time and part-time "production" employees on the payrolls of operating manufacturing establishments who worked or received pay for any part of the pay period which included the twelfth and ended nearest the fifteenth of March, May, August, and November, 1963, plus all full-time and part-time

---

5. *Rand McNally Commercial Atlas and Marketing Guide* (Chicago, Ill.: Rand McNally, 1964 and 1967). (*RMCA*)

"nonproduction" employees on the payrolls at mid-March, 1963. Thus the numerator for our measure is an average (in hundreds) of the four monthly figures for production workers and the March figure for all other employees. The denominator is the population estimate for 1963 in thousands.

34. Median education: *CCDB,*[4] items 19–21, p. xxi and Table 1, item 19, p. 3.

The score for each state is based on the highest grade or number of school years completed, 1960.

35. Per cent foreign stock: *CCDB,*[4] item 11, p. xx and Table 1, item 11, p. 2.

The number of foreign born plus natives of foreign or mixed parentage is divided by the total population, 1960.

36. Per cent government employees: numerator: Bureau of the Census, *Statistical Abstract of the United States,* 87th ed. (Washington, D.C.: Government Printing Office, 1966), Table 601, column 4, p. 438. Denominator: same as denominator for variable 33.

37. Expenditures per capita: Harvey C. Mansfield, "Functions of State and Local Governments," in James W. Fesler, ed., *The 50 States and Their Local Governments* (New York: Knopf, 1967), Table 4–1, column 4, pp. 110–112.

38. Governor's appointive power: Joseph A. Schlesinger, "The Politics of the Executive," in Herbert Jacob and Kenneth N. Vines, eds., *Politics in the American States* (Boston: Little, Brown, 1965), pp. 222–225.

The value for each state is based on the governor's powers of appointment in the following major functions and offices: administration and finance, agriculture, attorney general, auditor, budget officer, conservation, controller, education, health, highways, insurance, labor, secretary of state, tax commissioner, treasurer, and welfare. For each function existing in the state, the governor's power of appointment is scored 1–5, and the ratio of the sum of these scores to the possible maximum yields the index. (The formula shown in the source, p. 223, seems to be inverted.)

39. Per cent insured unemployed: numerator: *UIS,*[6] February 1967, Table 8, column 5, p. 8. Denominator: same as variable 30.

40. Benefit duration: *UIS,*[6] February 1967, Table 8, column 12, p. 8.

41. Funds/taxes: William Haber and Merrill G. Murray, *Unemployment Insurance in the American Economy* (Homewood, Ill.: Irwin, 1966), Table 20–22, pp. 412–413.

Haber and Murray estimated the denominator of this ratio on the basis

---

6. U.S. Dept. of Labor, Bureau of Employment Security, Manpower Administration, *Unemployment Insurance Statistics (UIS)*; published monthly.

of data from the 1962 BES ES-202 reports, *Employment, Wages, and Contributions,* the BES ES-202 Taxable Wage Supplement for calendar year 1962, and *Employment and Wages,* first quarter of 1962.

42. Size (log): source and comments same as variable 1.

43. Automation (dummy): source and comments same as variable 6.

44. Supervisory ratio in total agency: source and comments same as variable 17.

45. Size of government: source and comments same as the numerator of variable 36.

46. Merit system coverage: Department of Health, Education, and Welfare, Division of State Merit Systems, *Directory of State Merit Systems* (Washington, D.C.: Government Printing Office, July 1963).

If the merit system covered over 90 per cent of state government employees, it was coded 1; all others were coded 0.

47. Population expansion: *CCDB*,[4] item 5, p. xx and Table 1, item 5, p. 2.

Census figures from 1950 are used as a base to compute the percentage change from 1950 to 1960.

48. Contacts with other state agencies: CORP 7 interview: "Does the Employment Security Agency maintain regular formal contact with the following offices: Bureau of the Budget, Purchasing Department, State's Attorney's Office, State Auditor, Treasurer?" and "Does the agency maintain regular formal contacts with any other state offices or departments? Which ones?" Respondent: director. CORP 7 files.

In adding the agencies reported in response to these questions, three offices were not included because they would necessarily be in regular formal contact with all employment security agencies, namely, the personnel, education, and welfare departments.

49. Communication with governor or commissioner: CORP 7 interview: "About how many times a month does the director discuss the agency with the (title of the person to whom the director reports, taken from question 1)?"

For our measure the reported number of times per month was multiplied by twelve.

50a Applications per initial claim: sources and definition for average number of applications: same as variable 23. The average number of initial claims for the four months ending each of the quarters in 1966 was computed from: ES-209,[2] item 29, column 2 total (data for March); *UIS*,[6] August 1966, Table 1, column 1 (data for June); *UIS*,[6] November 1966, Table 1, column 1 (data for September); *UIS*,[6] February 1967, Table 1, column 1 (data for December).

The definition of "initial claim" is given in the *Employment Security Manual* glossary:

Either a new or an additional claim. A new claim is a request for determination of insured status for purposes of establishing a new benefit year. An additional claim is a notice filed at the beginning of a second or subsequent series of claims within a benefit year, when a break in job attachment has occurred since the last claim was filed, concerning which State procedures require that separation information be obtained.

See Appendix E for a complete discussion of the factor analysis in which this variable was used.

50b Per cent nonagricultural employees: *CCDB,*[7] items 34 and 38, pp. xxi–xxii, and Table 1, items 34 and 38, p. 4.

Our measure is 1.00 minus the per cent employees in agriculture. Per cent employees in agriculture was computed by dividing the number of employees engaged in farming and agricultural services by the total civilian labor force. Data for 1960.

50c Per cent total unemployed: *CCDB,*[7] item 35, pp. xxi–xxii and Table 1, item 35, p. 4.

Persons are classified as unemployed if they were fourteen years old and over and not "at work" but looking for work. Those waiting to be called back to a job from which they had been laid off were also counted as unemployed. The base is the total civilian work force. Data for 1960. (This measure represents *total* unemployment as opposed to *insured* unemployment used in variable 39.)

Local Office Analysis

MAJOR LOCAL OFFICE CHARACTERISTICS

51. ES function: Local office organization charts or manning tables explained and verified by the employment service director or other official who had the accurate information, dated as closely as possible to the first quarter of calendar year 1966; corroborated by ES-209's.[2] CORP 7 files.

The five types of LO's discussed in Chapter 7 were given the following score on this three-point scale: UI LO's, 0; General LO's (and the few LO's combining specialized ES and UI functions), 1; ES LO's, specialized ES LO's, and YOC's, 2.

---

7. U.S. Bureau of the Census, *County and City Data Book 1962* (Washington, D.C.: Government Printing Office, 1962). (*CCDB*)

52. Specialization: sources same as variable 51.

A high score on this three-point scale means that the local office has a high degree of task specialization. General LO's, which perform both ES and UI services, were given a score of zero; the intermediate score of one characterizes ES LO's, UI LO's, and the few LO's combining specialized ES with UI activities; and a score of two was assigned to Specialized ES LO's, YOC's (which are restricted to young workers), and the few specialized UI LO's.

53. LO size: source and comments same as variables 1 and 51.

54. Division of labor: sources same as variables 1 and 51; comments same as variable 5. See Appendix D for a complete description of coding procedures, especially section 2.1.

55. Mechanization: CORP 7 interview: "Indicate the code numbers of local offices in which electric typewriters are available." Respondent: head of the fiscal section, who took the information from the official equipment inventory listing. CORP 7 files.

Sixty-one per cent of all offices have no electric typewriters.

56. Levels: source same as variable 51. See Appendix D for a complete description of coding procedures, especially section 2.3.

57. Sections: source same as variable 51. See Appendix D for a complete description of coding procedures, especially section 2.2.

58. LO manager's span of control: source same as variable 51. See Appendix D for a complete description of coding procedures, especially section 2.5.

59. Clerical ratio: sources same as variables 1 and 51; comments same as variable 16. See Appendix D for a complete description of coding procedures, especially section 2.6.

60. Supervisory ratio: sources same as variables 1 and 51. See Appendix D for a complete description of coding procedures, especially section 2.4.

61. First-line supervisors' span of control: source same as variable 51. See Appendix D for a complete description of coding procedures, especially section 2.5.

62. LO size (log): source and comments same as variable 53.

63. LO size × levels: sources and comments same as variables 53 and 56.

Product terms are computed by multiplying one variable by the other.

64. Levels × sections: sources and comments same as variables 56 and 57.

65. Division of labor × clerical ratio: sources and comments same as variables 54 and 59.

66. Levels × clerical ratio: sources and comments same as variables 56 and 59.

The variables used in the contextual analysis of local offices are the same as those used in the analysis of the major characteristics of the agencies. See Chapter 8 for a description of the procedures used in this type of analysis. The sources and comments for variables 67–76 are the same as those for the corresponding variables identified.

67. Size: identical to variable 1.
68. Extent of personnel regulations: identical to variable 2.
69. Division of labor: identical to variable 5.
70. Automation: identical to variable 6.
71. Educational qualifications: identical to variable 8.
72. Clerical ratio: identical to variable 16.
73. Supervisory ratio in agency headquarters: identical to variable 17.
74. Delegation to LO manager: identical to variable 22.
75. Placements per opening: identical to variable 25.
76. Employee-client ratio in benefit function: identical to variable 26.

COMMUNITY ENVIRONMENT

77. Town under 25,000: *RMCA*,[5] 1964, 95th ed.; for cities over 25,-000, estimates are from section entitled "State Maps and Statistics," Tables entitled "Index of Cities, Towns, Counties, Transportation Lines, Airports, Banks and Post Offices"; for counties, estimates are from section entitled "State Maps and Statistics," tables entitled "[State] Counties and SMSA's: Population and Agriculture."

78. Population: source same as variable 77. Also "Commuting Fields of Central Cities" and "Commuting Fields of Central Counties," maps prepared by Brian J. L. Berry, University of Chicago, April 1967, for the Social Science Research Council Committee on Areas for Social and Economic Statistics, in cooperation with the Bureau of the Census, U.S. Department of Commerce; project staff: Larry Bourne, Mary Earickson, Paul Schwind; cartographer: Gerald Pyle.

The cities with 25,000 or more population were easily coded by looking at the estimate for 1964. If, however, the local office is located in a town with fewer than 25,000 inhabitants, the appropriate county for which the town is a central city had to be coded as the community environment. Such towns are sometimes located near the border or even on the boundary line of a county. In these cases the maps indicating the commuting fields of central cities and central counties were consulted in order to ascertain the county most likely to be the community environment of the local office in question. Election districts for Alaska and *municipios* for Puerto Rico are used to code environmental characteristics for offices in places with fewer than 25,000 inhabitants in these two jurisdictions. (These comments apply also to variables 79–83.)

79. Population density: *CCDB*,[4] for cities over 25,000: items 201–205, p. xxxv and Table 4, item 204, pp. 464–573; for counties: items 3–4, p. xix and Table 2, item 4, pp. 12–431.

The score for each city or county gives the average number of inhabitants per square mile of land area and is coded in tens. Data for 1960.

80. Median family income: *CCDB*,[4] for cities over 25,000: items 28–30, p. xxii and Table 4, item 231, pp. 464–573; for counties: items 28–30, p. xxii and Table 2, item 28, pp. 12–431.

Data for 1960. See variable 32 for comments.

81. Per cent blacks: *CCDB*,[4] for cities over 25,000: item 10, p. xx and Table 4, item 208, pp. 464–573; for counties: item 10, p. xx and Table 2, item 10, pp. 12–431.

This classification includes persons of black and of mixed black and white descent and of mixed Indian and black descent, unless the individual is regarded as an Indian in the community. Data for 1960.

82. Per cent foreign stock: *CCDB*,[4] for cities over 25,000: item 11, p. xx and Table 4, item 210, pp. 464–573; for counties: item 11, p. xx and Table 2, item 11, pp. 12–431.

Data for 1960. See variable 35 for comments.

83. Per cent blacks × median family income: sources and comments same as variables 81 and 80.

STATE ENVIRONMENT

84. Western region: identical to variable 29.

85. Per cent urban: identical to variable 31.

86. Per cent government employees: identical to variable 36.

APPENDIX D

Organization Charts and Structural Variables

1. Federal-State Employment Security System

The thousands of offices that make up the federal-state employment security system are physically located at four different general sites. First, as the umbrella organization for the national system, the federal bureau is housed in Washington, D.C., and is organizationally a part of the U.S. Department of Labor. Second, field operations of the federal government are carried out in eleven regional offices geographically distributed throughout the United States. Third, fifty-four autonomous agencies have a central headquarters usually located in the capital city of the state or territory. Finally, there is a network of local employment security offices in each jurisdiction that is set up to minimize the traveling time of the agency's clients. Thus, every state system as well as the federal system consists of a central office acting as roof organization for a number of field offices. At the time of the survey, a federal bureau was the central headquarters for eleven regional field offices (see Figure D–1), although a recent reorganization in the Department of Labor abolished this bureau, its functions being assigned to the new Manpower Administration. But each federal regional office continues to work with the five or six state agencies in its particular area. In the average state, an agency headquarters is the roof organization for approximately forty local offices (see Figure D–2).

The entire focus of this research is on the state agency (ignoring the federal and regional offices), but we have used three distinct units of anal-

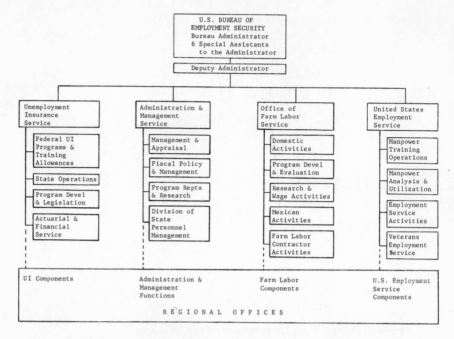

FIGURE D–1 Organization Chart for U.S. Bureau of Employment Security, October 1965

ysis: (1) the agency in its entirety, (2) the divisions or departments that comprise the agency headquarters, and (3) the local offices scattered throughout the jurisdiction, which carry out most of the production functions.

1.1. State Agency

Figure D–2 illustrates the organizational structure of a typical state agency. The executive director of the agency reports to the governor or the state commissioner of labor. In many cases the line of authority upwards goes through an industrial commission or a commission specifically set up to oversee the activities of the employment security agency.

The sample organization chart shows that the directors of the two production functions, employment services and unemployment insurance, along with the directors of the various services divisions, all report directly to the agency director. The local office managers report to the field supervisors, who in turn usually report to the employment service division director or, as in the case of the agency shown here, to the head of the field operations section. In some agencies, the field supervisors are specialized; employment service field supervisors report, then, to the employment service director, and the unemployment insurance field supervisors report to the unemployment insurance division director. The chain of command, in theory at least, extends from the governor of the state down through the central headquarters of the agency and finally to the interviewer or clerk on the lowest hierarchical level of the local office.

1.2. Divisions at Agency Headquarters

The headquarters of the agency shown in Figure D–2 has ten divisions, the heads of which report directly to the agency director. On the average a state headquarters has six or seven divisions (by coding definition a division must have five or more personnel); one agency has as few as two and another as many as thirteen divisions. The 387 divisions that met certain criteria form separate units of analysis for the research. Figure D–3 pre-

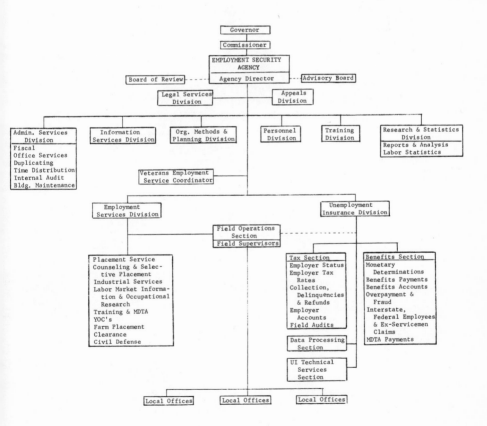

FIGURE D–2 Sample Organization Chart for State Employment Security Agency

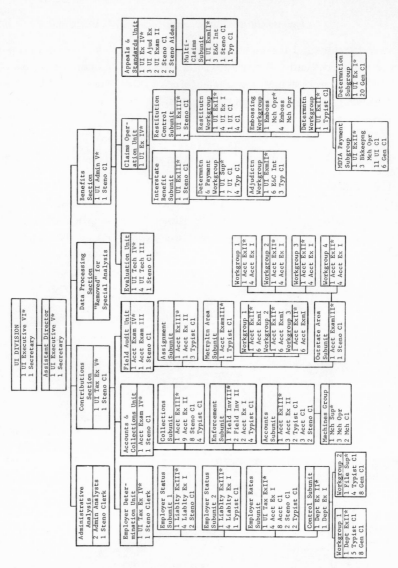

FIGURE D–3   Sample Organization Chart for Unemployment Insurance Division

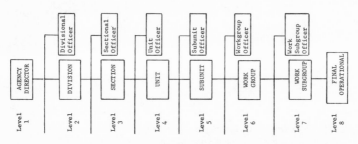

FIGURE D–4   Model Organization Chart Used for Coding
Number of Hierarchical Levels in Agency Headquarters

sents a sample chart for the unemployment insurance division, which is usually the division with the most differentiated structure in the agency. The divisions were actually the coding units for many of the variables used in analyzing agency characteristics. Thus, Figure D–3 is helpful in illustrating the definitions of the variables used in the major part of the study as well as in the analysis of divisions.

1.3. Local Offices

In a third level of analysis, the focus of attention is on the local offices that handle most of the agency's employment services and benefit functions. The following sample organization charts illustrate the most important types of local offices. Of the 1,201 offices included in our research, 53 per cent are General LO's, that is, they are responsible for both employment services and unemployment insurance programs. Figure D–5 illustrates such a local office with twenty-three personnel and three hierarchical levels. Another type is an ES LO, in which only (but all) employment service activities are performed and no unemployment insurance claims are taken. Ten per cent of our local office sample are ES LO's. In contrast, UI LO's, illustrated in Figure D–7, handle only (but all) unemployment insurance claims and no employment services; 13 per cent of the local offices sampled are this type.

In large metropolitan areas a further degree of specialization is possible. Most of the major cities throughout the United States have local employment offices that provide services for only one specific sector of the labor market. When specialization is sufficiently advanced, there is a local office for professional clientele, another for service employees, a third for industrial workers, and a fourth for clerical and sales personnel. Generally, a metropolitan area office coordinates and facilitates the activities of the various specialized local offices. Figure D–8 illustrates such a specialized ES LO, which offers employment services for clerical and sales occupations; 11 per cent of the sample are specialized ES LO's.

2. Quantitative Structural Variables from Organization Charts

About 3,000 organization charts were collected during the data-gathering phase of the study and eventually coded. These charts provided the data for the key structural variables that form the core of our analysis. Structural attributes of organizations have been operationalized in any number of ways in the literature. It becomes increasingly necessary to clearly state the operational definitions of "structural" variables and to il-

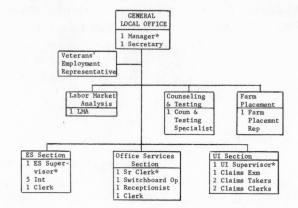

FIGURE D–5   Sample Organization Chart for General Local Office

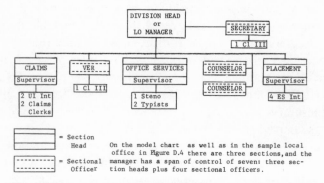

FIGURE D–6   Model Organization Chart Used for Coding the Number of Sections, and the Division Head's and Manager's Span of Control (Sections plus Sectional Officers)

lustrate them in sufficient detail so that comparative studies are possible. The following operational measures were derived from data coded directly from our organization charts. (The information contained on the organization charts was supplemented, and actually verified, by an official listing of all the employees of an agency; this official list was usually a payroll print-out that contained the name of each employee and his location in the organization, as well as his official job title.)[1]

---

1. It cannot be overemphasized that organization charts are a valuable source of research data *if*, and *only if*, they have been explained and verified by an informant who is familiar with the current operations of the organization in question. There is such a wide variety of styles for constructing charts that a researcher left to his own devices could easily impose preconceived notions onto them. See Chapter 1, pp. 15–16, for a description of the procedures used to verify the accuracy of these charts.

2.1. Division of Labor

For the analysis of the total agency this variable was not coded from organization charts. Instead, the information was provided by the state civil
service commission (via HEW form 85-R012; see the second section of
Appendix C, variable 5), which keeps a roster of all the job titles used in
each of the agencies that it services. In the divisional and local office analyses, however, the number of job titles represented in each subunit was
coded directly from the organization charts and the official listing of personnel described above. For example, in the UI division illustrated in Figure D–3 there are twenty-seven job titles without counting each grade separately, and in the local office illustrated in Figure D–5, there are fifteen
job titles without counting grades separately.

2.2. Number of Major Subunits

"Major subunits" is a generic term which applies to the first order of
horizontal structural differentiation in an organization. In other words, the
head of a major subunit always reports to the top management of an organization. In the agency analysis this variable is the number of divisions
at the headquarters. A "division" is defined as an organizational substruc-

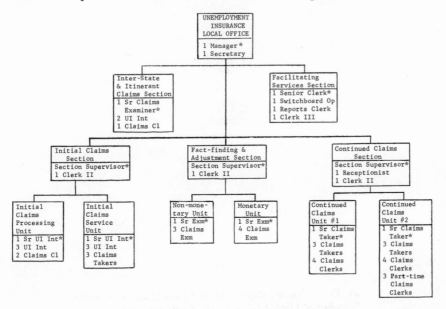

FIGURE D–7   Sample Organization Chart for Unemployment Insurance Office

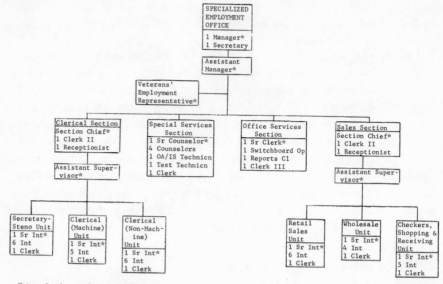

Note: In the sample Local Office, there are six hierarchical levels including the extra levels created by the use of assistant supervisors; excluding the assistant supervisors, there are only four levels. On the model chart there are five and three levels, with and without the assistant supervisory levels.

FIGURE D–8 Sample Organization Chart for Specialized Employment Service Office

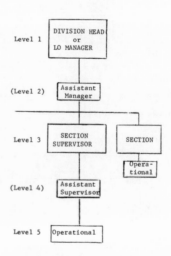

FIGURE D–9 Model Organization Chart Used for Coding Number of Hierarchical Levels Excluding Assistant Supervisors

ture that has five or more persons and that has a head who reports directly to the agency director or to his deputy. By this definition there are ten divisions in the state office headquarters of the sample agency illustrated in Figure D–2.

For the divisional and local office analyses, the major subunits are called sections. A "section" is defined as the major subunit in a headquarters division or local office whose chief reports to the division head or to the local office manager (or to their deputies), provided that it consists of a supervisor and at least one professional or two clerical subordinates. In other words, a section is any group of two or more individuals, one of whom is a supervisor reporting to either the division head or the local office manager, except that an official with a single clerical assistant is not considered a section.

Other staff members besides the heads of sections report to the top managers in the divisions and local offices. These personnel, such as secretaries and staff specialists, are referred to as sectional officers, for coding purposes. A "sectional officer" is defined as a nonsupervisory employee who reports directly to the division head or the local office manager. But when an employee has just one clerical assistant, he is also considered nonsupervisory and thus as a sectional officer. See Figure D–6 for an illustration of the distinction between sections and sectional officers. The sample division in Figure D–3 has four [2] sections, and the sample local office in Figure D–5 has three sections.

2.3. Number of Hierarchical Levels

The concept of supervisory or hierarchical levels refers to the strata in an organizational pyramid and derives from principles stated by Weber: "The principles of office hierarchy and of levels of graded authority mean a firmly ordered system of super- and sub-ordination in which there is a supervision of the lower offices by the higher ones." [3] Fayol calls it the

---

2. In the divisional analysis, the data-processing sections were removed from their parent divisions for detailed analysis. However, in computing the number of major subdivisions and division head's span of control, the data-processing sections were included. The procedures used in the analysis of the data-processing divisions are described elsewhere; see Richard A. Schoenherr, "Task Requirements and Organizational Structure," Ph.D. dissertation, University of Chicago, 1970.

3. Max Weber, *Essays in Sociology* (New York: Oxford University Press, 1946), p. 197.

scalar chain principle.[4] The number of levels of authority refers to links in the chain of command, not to skill gradations or salary grades.

In all three units of analysis the number of hierarchical levels is measured by the longest chain of command found in the organization. Thus, if the division in Figure D–3 has the longest chain of command in the agency, there would be eight hierarchical levels in that particular agency. There are six levels in the longest section of the longest division, and the seventh level is the division head, whereas the eighth, the top level in the agency, is created by the executive director (see Figure D–4). This variable is essentially the same in the divisional and local office analysis, except that the division or LO head defines the highest level.

If deputy managers or assistant supervisors are used as part of an organization's structure, the number of hierarchical levels could be measured in two ways, either counting deputies and assistants or not counting them. The latter procedure is used. Figures D–8 and D–9 illustrate that in the sample local office presented there would be six hierarchical levels including the extra levels created by the use of assistant supervisors, but because they are excluded, only four levels are counted.

2.4. Supervisory Ratio

"Supervisors" are defined as heads of organizational subunits who have line authority over those employees who report to them. Any superior to whom two or more employees report is always considered a supervisor; however, a superior with a professional job title to whom one clerical assistant reports is not considered a supervisor, whereas a clerical superior with one clerical subordinate is considered a supervisor. Functional or technical supervisors (these titles are used in a number of agencies and refer to specialists in charge of coordinating a special activity but having no line authority over those employees engaged in the activity) are not included in these counts. One criterion that was easy to apply in order to distinguish functional from line supervisors was to ascertain whether or not the supervisor in question was responsible for doing the annual performance rating of those working under him. Only bona fide line supervisors are responsible for the performance rating.

When the agency is the unit of analysis, the variable, supervisory ratio, is used in two different ways: the ratio of supervisors to all personnel at the headquarters and the ratio of supervisors to the total personnel in the

---

4. Henri Fayol, *General and Industrial Management* (London: Pitman, 1949), pp. 34–35.

entire agency (headquarters and local offices). The numerator for the first measure includes all the supervisors mentioned below for the divisional analysis plus the agency director and his deputy if there is one; for the second measure, the numerator includes, in addition, the supervisors in all local offices. The supervisory ratio in the average agency's headquarters is 21 per cent; in the total agency it is 19 per cent.

In the analysis of divisions the measure includes for its numerator all the supervisors in the division, namely, the division director, his deputy if there is one, and the heads (and their assistants) of all the subdivisions down to and including the working supervisors of the subgroups (see Figure D–4 for all the possible subdivisions within a division). Thus in the sample division in Figure D–3 there are forty supervisors (bona fide supervisors are indicated by an asterisk) and 283 total personnel, or 14 per cent [5] supervisors. For local offices, the total number of supervisors includes the local office manager and the assistant manager plus the heads (and their assistants) of all subdivisions in the local office. Thus in the sample local office illustrated in Figure D–5, there are four supervisors out of a total personnel of 23, or 17 per cent supervisors.

2.5. *Span of Control*

The "span of control" is defined as the number of subordinates who report to an individual supervisor. There are two measures of span of control used in the agency analysis: the director's span and the average span of control of division heads. The agency director's span of control includes all division heads plus all supervisors of divisional offices (defined as a small subdivision of less than five) and all single individuals who report directly to the agency director. On the sample agency chart in Figure D–2 the director's span of control is eleven, with ten division heads and one divisional office (the veterans' employment service coordinator) reporting to him. If the chart were drawn in more detail the span would probably be at least twelve, the director's secretary would increase it by one. The average span of division heads is computed by averaging the spans of control of all division heads (defined below) in the agency headquarters.

In the divisional analysis there are three measures for the span of control variable: the division head's span of control, the average span of control of middle managers, and the first-line supervisors' average span of control. The division head's span of control comprises all section heads and all sectional officers, that is, all individuals who report to the division

---

5. The actual scores for all ratios have been converted to percentages.

director or his assistant. (Whenever there is an assistant, the top supervisor and the assistant supervisor are considered one position for the purpose of the span-of-control variable.) In the sample UI division in Figure D–3 the division head and his deputy have a span of control of eight: four sections plus four sectional officers (two secretaries and two administrative analysts who together share one steno clerk).

Middle managers by definition are section heads in only those divisions that have four or more hierarchical levels. As herein operationally defined, middle managers report to the head of the division and they in turn have supervisors reporting to them. The average span of control of middle managers, therefore, is derived by summing the number of unit chiefs and unit officers (see Figure D–4 for an illustration of units and unit officers; unit officers are defined in the same way, *mutatis mutandis,* as sectional officers, see Figure D–6) and dividing the sum by the number of sections represented in the division. In the sample division of Figure D–3 there are six unit chiefs and two unit officers (two steno clerks) in the two sections; the average span of control of the middle managers, therefore, is 4.0.

A first-line supervisor monitors the activities of the operational personnel on the lowest level of an organization. Although there may be first-line supervisors on other hierarchical levels, they are not included in this measure. Thus a first-line supervisor is somewhat differently defined operationally depending on the number of hierarchical levels in a division or local office. The section heads are first-line supervisors in three-level organizations, the unit heads in four-level organizations, and the subunit heads in five-level organizations; the work group leaders are the first-line supervisors in six-level organizations and the subgroup leaders are the first-line supervisors when there are seven hierarchical levels (see Figure D–4). The average span of control of the two subgroup supervisors in the sample division in Figure D–3 is twenty.

The local office manager's span of control is operationalized in the same way as the division director's, that is, it includes all the section chiefs plus the sectional officers. The local office manager in the sample office illustrated in Figure D–5, therefore, has a span of control of eight: three section heads plus five sectional officers. Likewise the first-line supervisors' span of control in the local offices has the same operational definition as in the analysis of divisions. To illustrate: in Figure D–5, a local office with three levels, the first-line supervisors' average span of control is 4.7, the three section heads being responsible for fourteen subordinates; the first-line supervisors' span of control is 6.3 in the four-level office in Figure D–8, because the six unit heads have thirty-eight persons under them.

2.6. Clerical Ratio

Most clerical job titles were easily identifiable, for example, typists, stenographers, telephone operators, secretaries. Our codebook contains an appendix listing the decisions made when the coders considered a job title ambiguous. Implicit in this measure is the fact that we have dichotomized all job titles into professional and clerical categories. The clerical ratio is not a measure of the proportion of total personnel engaged in administrative, enabling, or supporting activities that would be categorized generally as clerical overhead functions. Many clerical personnel are directly involved in production functions, as are most of the clerks in the sample UI division in Figure D–3, and the two claims clerks in the sample local office illustrated in Figure D–5.

The numerator of this variable comprises all clerical personnel, including clerical supervisors; the denominator is the total personnel in the unit of analysis under question. For the agency analysis the total number of clerks includes all clerical personnel in the headquarters and the local offices. The average state agency has 32 per cent clerical personnel. There are 157 clerical positions in the sample division illustrated in Figure D–3; thus, 56 per cent of the total divisional staff are clerical personnel. Eight out of 23 or 35 per cent of the local office staff shown in Figure D–5 are clerical personnel.

APPENDIX E

Service Measures

To measure how effectively various services were performed by the fifty-three employment security agencies, we first derived thirty-two indices from the 1966 statistical records of activities kept by these agencies. Next, a factor analysis was performed on these thirty-two variables in order to determine what meaningful underlying dimensions exist and which variables best represent these dimensions. The Data-Text Factor Rotation Program was used, which performs orthogonal rotations on factor loadings and factor scores. The rotations were the analytic type (as opposed to the fixed-position type) designed to be a mathematical approximation to the simple structure criteria proposed by Thurstone in *Multiple Factor Analysis*.[1] The analytic rotations utilized the varimax method proposed by Kaiser, which attempts to simplify the columns of the factor-loading matrix so that each factor can be readily identified by variables.[2] The thirty-two variables and their loadings in the six factors that emerged are given in Table E-1.

Four of the factors were conceptually interesting for our purposes. The three highest loadings of factor 1 are on per cent short-term placements (.84), placements per opening (.72), and per cent higher skills placements (−.62). This first dimension reflects placement quantity; it points to a type of employment service that emphasizes high production in basically rou-

---

1. Louis L. Thurstone, *Multiple Factor Analysis* (Chicago: University of Chicago Press, 1947).
2. See Arthur S. Couch, *Data-Text System* (Chicago: University of Chicago, Computation Center, October 25, 1966), p. 218 ff. for a more complete description of procedures.

TABLE E-1. Loadings of Thirty-Two Service Measures in Six Orthogonal Factors

		Factors						Communality
		1	2	3	4	5	6	
E-1.	Applications per Man-day	-.138	.029	.247	-.496	-.660	-.180	.795
E-2.	Applications per Initial Claim	-.059	-.364	-.057	.142	-.452	-.627	.757
E-3.	Number in Active File per Man-day	.012	.019	.736	-.402	.081	-.130	.727
E-4.	Initial Counseling Interviews/Man-day	-.399	-.615	-.029	.013	-.140	-.148	.580
E-5.	Initial Counseling Interviews/Application	-.280	-.675	-.119	.259	.281	-.039	.696
E-6.	Openings Received per Man-day	.014	-.241	-.369	-.042	-.662	-.437	.825
E-7.	Openings Unfilled per Opening Received	-.543	.074	-.357	-.030	.601	-.152	.812
E-8.	Nonag Referrals per Man-day	.445	.028	-.248	-.393	-.267	-.516	.752
E-9.	Nonag Referrals per Opening Received	.299	.217	.387	-.410	.458	-.146	.685
E-10.	Nonag Placements per Man-day	.581	.008	-.165	-.215	-.603	-.333	.886
E-11.	Nonag Placements per Opening Received	.721	.209	.492	-.165	-.185	.091	.875
E-12.	Nonag Placements per Nonag Referral	.464	-.037	.096	.211	-.685	.142	.759
E-13.	% Short-term Placements	.843	.050	-.181	.081	.192	-.064	.793
E-14.	Long-term Placements per Man-day	.207	.015	-.132	-.262	-.788	-.279	.828
E-15.	Long-term Placements per Opening Received	.057	.228	.700	-.238	-.262	.158	.696
E-16.	Nonag Employer Visits per Man-day	.515	-.392	-.041	.169	-.017	.141	.469
E-17.	GATB's per Application	-.087	-.939	-.096	.116	.017	.004	.918
E-18.	GATB's per Initial Counseling Interview	.141	-.598	-.004	-.208	-.234	.062	.479
E-19.	Total All Tests per Application	.256	-.732	-.182	-.195	-.031	-.144	.694
E-20.	Initial Claims per Man-day	-.163	.414	.014	-.264	.150	.720	.809
E-21.	New Claims per Man-day	-.127	.481	.076	-.333	.009	.568	.686
E-22.	Continued Claims per Man-day	-.135	.210	-.144	-.391	.478	.581	.802
E-23.	Tax Positions/1,000 Covered Employers	-.193	.357	.748	.071	-.003	-.090	.738
E-24.	Benefit Positions/1,000 Insured Unemp.	-.079	.055	-.037	.881	.144	.002	.808
E-25.	Overhead Positions/1,000 Insured Unemp.	-.038	.003	.027	.843	.113	-.083	.732
E-26.	% Claims with Monetary Determinations	.048	.078	-.691	-.162	-.114	.107	.536
E-27.	% Appeals Decided in 30 Days	-.075	.003	.046	.006	-.332	-.099	.128
E-28.	% Appeals Decided for Claimant	.088	-.124	.195	.011	.348	-.252	.246
E-29.	% First Payment in 14 Days	-.117	.029	.127	-.287	.154	.024	.137
E-30.	% Status Determinations after 12 mos.	-.138	.090	.369	-.116	.069	-.746	.738
E-31.	UI Laws Cover More Employers	.041	.269	.028	-.157	-.114	-.732	.649
E-32.	% Higher Skills Placements	-.622	-.010	.064	.041	.056	.183	.430
	Sums of Squares	3.572	3.788	3.222	3.167	4.056	3.661	21.466

tine or easy services since the loadings are high on per cent short-term and low on per cent higher skills placements. Relatively high loadings on other variables such as placements per opening, placements per man-day, and employer visits per man-day all indicate that the underlying dimension of this factor is placement quantity. Although per cent short-term placements has the highest loading, the variable with the second highest, placements per opening, is used as the single indicator of placement activities because of the nature of short-term placements. Short-term in this context means a job lasting three days or less. Such a placement usually results from referral of an applicant who happens to be in the office at the time of selection so that many of the activities that are necessary to make other placements are thereby circumvented. The measure of placements per opening is still an indication of placement quantity, and the numerator includes the number of short-term placements as well as all others. Both variables were tested for reliability.

The second factor has its highest loadings on the following three variables: General Aptitude Test Batteries (GATB's) per application ($-.94$), tests of all types per application ($-.73$), and initial counseling interviews per application ($-.68$). This factor provides a measure of the most professionally oriented activities that are performed as part of the employment service function, because the loadings are highest on testing and counseling measures. The index with the highest loading, GATB's per application, will serve as the single indicator of employment services requiring more advanced professional skills.

Tax positions per 1,000 covered employers, with a loading of .75, number in the active file per man-day, with one of .74, and long-term placements per opening, with a loading of .70, are the variables with the three highest loadings in factor 3. The combination of loadings in this factor makes it conceptually uninteresting, and none of these variables were further tested.

The three variables with the highest loadings in the fourth factor are benefit positions per 1,000 insured unemployed (.88), overhead positions per 1,000 insured unemployed (.84), and applications per man-day ($-.50$). A high score on this factor would indicate that an agency needs disproportionately many employees to handle the claims load and that it also utilizes much manpower for its applications service. The number of benefit positions per 1,000 insured unemployed, the variable with the highest loading, is chosen as the index for measuring man-hour economy of benefit operations.

The fifth factor is a measure of quality of employment services; it indicates how many job orders are coming in, how many referrals are resulting in placements, and how many of the more difficult, long-term placements are being made. The three highest loadings are on variables that tap such a dimension: long-term placements per man-day ($-.79$), placements per referral ($-.68$), and openings received per man-day ($-.66$). Although long-term placements per man-day has the highest loading in this factor, placements per referral was chosen as the single indicator of quality of employment service activities because the latter variable fared better in the tests of reliability, but it too was eventually dropped from the analysis.

The sixth and final factor also has a combination of loadings that makes it conceptually uninteresting. The three variables with the highest loadings are per cent status determinations made after twelve months ($-.75$), unemployment compensation laws covering more employers ($-.73$), and initial claims per man-day (.72). None of these measures was tested further.

Five of the thirty-two variables included in the factor analysis were selected, three with the highest loading in a factor and two with the second-highest loading. They were chosen as the most promising indicators of effectiveness and were subjected to reliability tests. A serious question of reliability is raised if one considers that employment service and unemployment insurance activities fluctuate from month to month depending on economic conditions, seasonal employment, and other changes affecting the labor market. Almost all the service measures that we computed for the factor analysis (and four of the five that we selected) were based on data for one month only, March 1966. Can any one month's activities be an accurate indicator of an agency's effectiveness? To answer this question averages were computed from data covering the final month of each quarter in 1966. March is a month when most activities are relatively stable; June is filled with hectic employment service activities because of students looking for summer jobs; September brings another increase in activities; and in December claims loads are high, because in winter unemployment is high and Christmas jars the labor market. Averages based on these particular four months might prove to be a more satisfactory measure of what an agency accomplishes than figures for just one month. At first, the raw values of the activities that constitute the numerators and denominators of the ratios were correlated. Table E–2 indicates that there is a high degree of intercorrelation between months. All the coefficients are above .97 except those for the number of GATB's, which range from .68 to .89.

These high correlations between activities in different months are misleading, however. They give the false impression that activities are quite stable from month to month and that the index based on any one month is a reliable indicator of the agency's activities in other months. But the last column in Table E–2 shows clearly that there is very much fluctuation in

TABLE E-2. *Correlation Matrix of Six Activities for March, June, September, and December 1966 and the Average of the Four Months*

	Mean	March	June	September	December	Mean Number
Short-term Placements						
Mean	1.000					3,129
March	.996	1.000				3,159
June	.995	.990	1.000			3,453
September	.994	.986	.987	1.000		3,320
December	.990	.984	.979	.979	1.000	2,584
Total Placements						
Mean	1.000					10,414
March	.997	1.000				10,326
June	.998	.993	1.000			11,726
September	.997	.991	.995	1.000		11,677
December	.997	.994	.994	.992	1.000	7,925
Applications						
Mean	1.000					17,382
March	.995	1.000				16,039
June	.995	.984	1.000			24,772
September	.996	.987	.991	1.000		15,115
December	.995	.993	.984	.991	1.000	13,601
GATB's						
Mean	1.000					1,094
March	.967	1.000				1,470
June	.924	.886	1.000			777
September	.837	.710	.766	1.000		975
December	.920	.880	.760	.677	1.000	1,153
Openings Received						
Mean	1.000					14,466
March	.997	1.000				15,145
June	.998	.994	1.000			15,679
September	.997	.992	.994	1.000		16,810
December	.997	.995	.994	.992	1.000	10,230
Referrals						
Mean	1.000					21,988
March	.995	1.000				22,340
June	.998	.995	1.000			25,588
September	.995	.984	.989	1.000		23,651
December	.996	.987	.992	.993	1.000	16,374

TABLE E-3. *Correlation Matrix of Four Measures of Services for March, June, September, and December 1966 and the Average of the Four Months*

	Mean	March	June	September	December
Per Cent Short-term Placements					
Mean	1.000				
March	.954	1.000			
June	.968	.915	1.000		
September	.966	.874	.910	1.000	
December	.962	.890	.896	.931	1.000
GATB's per Application					
Mean	1.000				
March	.821	1.000			
June	.587	.451	1.000		
September	.755	.398	.274	1.000	
December	.815	.577	.284	.514	1.000
Placements per Opening Received					
Mean	1.000				
March	.907	1.000			
June	.918	.741	1.000		
September	.953	.836	.818	1.000	
December	.932	.796	.867	.860	1.000
Placements per Referral					
Mean	1.000				
March	.867	1.000			
June	.907	.696	1.000		
September	.890	.637	.757	1.000	
December	.903	.789	.707	.824	1.000

these activities. The main reason that the correlations are nevertheless high is that all activities reflect to a large extent the over-all scope of operations of an agency. Large agencies make more placements, have more applicants, give more tests, and receive more openings than small ones, and this is the case in all seasons. It is precisely to control for the scope of operations when measuring the effectiveness of services that ratios are used rather than the sheer volume of activities. The crucial question is how highly correlated the ratios are from month to month. Despite the high correlations between numerators and between denominators, the ratios do not exhibit very high correlations for the four months, as Table E–3 reveals. These lower correlations of the ratios are due to the fact that the numerators and the denominators fluctuate independently over the various seasons, often in the opposite direction. In the ratio of GATB's to applications, for example, the number of GATB's is lowest and the number of applications is highest in June, whereas almost the opposite is the case in December, when the number of GATB's is second highest and the number of applications is lowest (see the means in Table E–2). Because some of the ratios fluctuate widely from month to month, it is more reliable to base the service measures on the means for the four months rather than on any one-month period. The correlation coefficients between the ratios based on the means and those based on data from each of the four months are all above .75 except in one instance: the correlation between average GATB's per application and the same ratio for June is .59 (see Table E–3).

One of the selected effectiveness measures, benefit positions per 1,000 insured unemployed, was not included in the reliability tests reported above because both the numerator and denominator of this ratio are means based on data for a full year, from July 1, 1964, to June 30, 1965. Hence, this measure is based on data from an entire year, and the four other measures used are based on data from four months distributed throughout a full year.

APPENDIX F

Zero-Order Correlations

This appendix contains two zero-order correlation matrices. Table F–1 includes forty-seven variables used in the analysis of the employment security agencies in the United States and is in three parts. The lower portion of Table F–1 gives the coefficients for the major, environmental, and supplementary variables based on all fifty-three cases. The upper portion of each part gives the coefficients for the variables based on data from fifty-one cases, excluding Puerto Rico and the Virgin Islands. These two jurisdictions had to be removed from the state environment analysis because comparable data on them were not available. Table F–2 reproduces the correlation coefficients for the thirty-six variables used in the analysis of the 1,201 local offices.

If the case base changes on any variable, the n's are given in Appendix C under "Definitions and Basic Statistics." The coefficients used here are the Pearsonian r computed according to the Mesa-85 statistical system (UCSL 510, 9/1/66) obtained from the program library of the University of Chicago's Computation Center.

TABLE F-1 (Part 1)

CORRELATION MATRIX FOR AGENCY ANALYSIS: VARIABLES 1-16 (Below Diagonal N = 53, Above Diagonal N = 51)

		1 SIZE	2 EXT REGS	3 CV SER APPTS	4 SALARY INTVWR	5 DIV OF LABOR	6 AUTO-MATION	7 ED REQ	8 ED QUAL	9 ED DIV HEADS	10 LEVELS	11 DIVSNS	12 DIR'S SPAN	13 SCTNS/ DIVS	14 SPAN DVHD	15 STAND RATNG	16 CLER RATIO
MAJOR VARIABLES	1 Size		0.578	-0.078	0.330	0.781	0.820	-0.193	0.020	0.238	0.600	0.378	0.239	0.137	0.194	-0.181	-0.100
	2 Extent of Regulations	0.570		-0.086	0.241	0.354	0.491	-0.107	0.034	-0.059	0.321	0.138	0.169	-0.024	-0.016	-0.032	-0.110
	3 Civil Serv Appointments	-0.077	0.251		0.092	-0.085	-0.013	0.216	0.257	-0.140	-0.050	-0.058	-0.060	-0.194	-0.101	0.130	-0.150
	4 Salary of Interviewers	-0.327	0.346	0.063		0.284	0.393	0.100	0.201	0.264	-0.141	-0.079	0.198	-0.028	0.091	-0.121	-0.073
	5 Division of Labor	0.778	0.488	-0.082	0.284		0.706	-0.118	-0.077	0.245	0.579	0.478	0.296	0.219	0.201	-0.369	0.275
	6 Automation	0.821	-0.091	-0.018	0.393	0.706		-0.138	-0.041	0.155	0.560	0.195	0.199	0.207	0.022	-0.052	-0.172
	7 Education Requirements	-0.169	0.027	0.201	0.100	-0.118	-0.138		0.313	0.025	-0.004	-0.220	0.081	0.023	0.026	-0.229	-0.177
	8 Education Qualifications	0.234	0.059	0.264	0.201	-0.077	-0.041	0.313		-0.002	-0.014	0.108	0.156	-0.035	-0.093	-0.186	-0.199
	9 Ed of Division Heads	0.602	0.308	-0.141	0.264	0.245	0.155	0.025	-0.002		0.132	0.074	-0.029	-0.336	0.166	0.067	-0.103
	10 Levels	0.380	0.122	-0.050	-0.141	0.579	0.560	-0.004	-0.014	0.132		0.191	0.100	0.274	0.007	-0.186	-0.009
	11 Divisions	0.245	-0.142	-0.037	-0.050	0.478	0.195	-0.220	0.108	0.074	0.191		0.667	0.184	-0.047	0.068	0.350
	12 Director's Span Control	0.163	-0.013	-0.028	0.042	0.323	0.232	0.091	0.167	-0.036	0.165	0.690		-0.207	0.029	-0.215	0.065
	13 Sections per Division	0.209	0.002	-0.180	-0.028	0.286	0.226	0.086	-0.036	-0.308	0.333	-0.109	0.184		0.117	-0.158	-0.090
	14 Division Heads' Span	0.184	0.037	0.084	0.091	0.298	-0.257	0.077	0.011	-0.093	0.200	-0.019	0.039	0.184		0.068	0.009
	15 Standardized Ratings	0.093	-0.104	0.120	-0.121	-0.365	-0.128	0.052	-0.057	-0.226	-0.195	-0.241	-0.106	-0.162	0.067		0.058
	16 Clerical Ratio	-0.425	-0.214	-0.157	-0.073	-0.249	-0.128	-0.177	0.191	-0.100	0.314	-0.076	0.039	-0.105	0.007	0.067	
	17 Supervisory Ratio: HQ	-0.437	-0.337	0.039	0.120	-0.436	-0.353	0.231	-0.177	-0.158	-0.180	-0.203	-0.233	-0.035	-0.281	0.245	-0.031
	18 Staff Ratio	0.219	0.179	-0.001	-0.003	-0.422	-0.346	0.235	0.056	-0.381	-0.329	-0.310	-0.025	-0.177	-0.282	0.245	0.134
	19 Delegation: Personnel	0.236	0.335	0.020	-0.157	0.187	0.340	-0.060	-0.155	-0.003	0.355	0.099	-0.174	0.037	0.207	-0.272	-0.178
	20 Delegation: Budget	0.327	0.104	-0.046	-0.221	0.231	0.286	-0.123	-0.114	-0.100	0.069	0.171	0.019	0.066	0.102	-0.071	-0.073
	21 Decentralizatn: Influence	0.064	0.192	0.180	0.251	0.257	0.220	-0.147	0.001	0.239	0.245	0.160	0.057	0.238	0.035	0.092	-0.168
	22 Delegation to Manager	-0.124	-0.038	0.328	0.180	-0.089	0.117	0.199	0.018	-0.176	0.071	-0.076	0.064	0.005	0.120	0.276	-0.168
	23 Applications/Employee	-0.351	-0.251	0.057	0.167	-0.044	0.028	0.022	-0.018	-0.032	0.121	-0.054	0.127	0.324	0.223	-0.177	-0.283
	24 GATB's per Application	-0.002	-0.160	-0.017	0.244	-0.419	-0.362	0.225	0.177	0.032	-0.453	-0.225	-0.221	-0.258	0.048	0.193	-0.035
	25 Placements per Opening	-0.135	-0.306	-0.202	-0.068	-0.011	0.069	0.213	-0.065	-0.026	-0.265	0.070	0.317	0.477	0.255	-0.317	-0.232
	26 Employee-Client Ratio	-0.144	-0.132	-0.151	0.057	-0.020	-0.127	0.036	-0.078	-0.049	-0.175	-0.130	-0.151	-0.070	0.007	0.125	0.181
STATE ENVIRONMENT VARIABLES	27 Midwestern Region	-0.033	0.021	0.046	-0.275	-0.142	-0.096	0.232	0.014	-0.120	0.078	-0.054	-0.147	0.068	0.238	-0.057	-0.108
	28 Southern Region	-0.030	0.150	-0.159	-0.018	0.773	0.815	-0.221	0.090	0.047	-0.232	-0.037	-0.191	-0.010	0.007	-0.109	-0.084
	29 Western Region	0.927	0.470	0.259	-0.068	0.815	0.385	-0.199	-0.093	0.280	0.603	0.439	-0.240	0.193	-0.211	-0.067	-0.183
	30 Population	0.469	0.193	-0.071	0.135	0.492	0.291	-0.114	0.109	0.114	0.444	0.391	0.263	0.149	-0.093	-0.237	-0.060
	31 Per cent Urban	0.319	0.135	-0.364	-0.040	0.307	0.163	-0.295	-0.145	-0.084	0.258	0.217	0.186	0.022	-0.095	-0.315	0.277
	32 Median Family Income	0.094	0.062	0.059	-0.332	0.309	0.106	-0.092	0.144	0.329	0.246	0.344	0.154	0.073	0.124	0.043	0.274
	33 % Manufacturing Employees	0.312	0.044	-0.173	0.433	-0.001	0.001	0.241	0.200	-0.067	0.131	-0.117	-0.078	-0.040	-0.158	0.017	0.207
	34 Median Education	-0.417	0.080	0.081	0.227	0.258	0.164	-0.092	0.214	-0.058	0.242	0.131	-0.043	-0.045	-0.048	0.112	0.037
	35 Per cent Foreign Stock	0.032	-0.047	0.030	0.196	-0.492	-0.309	0.241	0.093	-0.458	-0.349	-0.313	-0.154	-0.346	-0.299	0.296	0.357
	36 % Government Employees	0.271	-0.104	0.176	0.500	-0.056	0.106	0.051	0.076	-0.321	-0.026	-0.144	-0.024	-0.152	-0.339	0.148	-0.058
	37 Expenditures per Capita	0.319	-0.033	0.046	0.246	0.115	0.115	-0.089	-0.055	0.011	0.305	0.104	-0.024	0.203	0.263	-0.106	0.029
	38 Governor's Appoint Power	0.130	0.257	0.111	0.637	0.224	0.169	-0.126	-0.179	-0.165	-0.108	-0.044	-0.094	0.022	-0.297	0.090	0.139
	39 % Insured Unemployed	-0.204	-0.033	-0.043	0.112	0.169	-0.036	0.114	0.103	-0.104	0.073	0.081	-0.074	-0.066	-0.025	0.013	0.201
	40 Benefit Duration	0.814	-0.176	-0.024	0.469	-0.103	-0.115	0.246	0.103	-0.400	-0.280	-0.275	-0.147	-0.148	-0.264	0.075	0.350
	41 Funds/Taxes	0.296	-0.158	0.030	0.241	-0.252	-0.148	-0.189	-0.029	0.299	0.445	0.546	0.393	0.426	0.302	-0.302	0.003
SUPPLEMENTARY VARIABLES	42 Size (Log)	-0.343	0.408	-0.110	0.126	0.822	0.683	-0.189	-0.001	0.007	0.733	0.167	0.172	0.433	0.171	-0.260	0.099
	43 Automation (Dummy)	0.904	0.100	-0.189	0.293	0.440	0.581	-0.065	-0.001	0.007	0.445	0.167	0.172	0.433	0.171	-0.260	0.036
	44 Supervisory Ratio:Agency	0.266	-0.192	-0.103	-0.162	-0.263	-0.240	0.032	-0.161	-0.154	-0.105	-0.121	-0.303	0.262	-0.064	0.080	-0.004
	45 Size of Government	0.096	0.525	-0.010	0.246	0.733	0.807	-0.188	0.011	0.253	0.604	0.414	0.238	0.161	0.226	-0.260	0.027
	46 Merit System Coverage	0.266	0.310	-0.030	0.191	0.230	0.198	-0.034	0.070	-0.047	0.411	0.189	0.131	0.076	-0.172	0.136	0.226
	47 Population Expansion	0.096	0.119	-0.028	0.390	0.129	0.218	0.057	-0.112	-0.092	0.115	0.051	-0.091	0.061	-0.246	-0.092	-0.072

TABLE F-1 (Part 2)

CORRELATION MATRIX FOR AGENCY ANALYSIS: VARIABLES 17-32 (Below Diagonal N = 53, Above Diagonal N = 51)

		17 SUP RATIO	18 STAFF RATIO	19 DELCGTN PRSNNL	20 DELGTN BUDGET	21 DECENT INFLNC	22 DELGCTN LO MGR	23 APPLTN /EMP	24 GATB'S /APPL	25 PLCMTS /OPNG	26 EMP-CL RATIO	27 MIDWST REGION	28 SOUTHN REGION	29 WESTERN REGION	30 POPU-LATION	31 % URBAN	32 MEDIAN INCOME
MAJOR VARIABLES	1 Size	-0.440	-0.444	0.222	0.236	0.320	0.048	-0.163	-0.349	-0.091	-0.146	-0.034	-0.148	-0.031	0.950	0.481	0.327
	2 Extent of Regulations	-0.226	-0.347	0.173	0.346	0.115	0.194	-0.163	-0.286	-0.214	-0.334	-0.136	-0.022	0.155	0.485	0.200	0.140
	3 Civil Serv Appointments	0.046	0.001	0.032	-0.057	0.171	0.332	0.036	0.009	-0.085	-0.138	0.047	-0.163	0.265	-0.073	-0.066	0.061
	4 Salary of Interviewers	-0.263	0.258	0.158	-0.200	-0.274	-0.106	-0.279	-0.051	-0.077	0.090	-0.043	-0.352	0.460	0.241	0.211	0.533
	5 Division of Labor	-0.479	-0.442	0.134	0.237	0.219	-0.137	-0.122	-0.389	0.034	-0.028	-0.022	-0.038	-0.150	0.814	0.521	0.324
	6 Automation	-0.374	-0.355	0.339	0.294	0.216	0.102	0.011	-0.373	0.027	-0.149	0.075	-0.099	0.075	0.838	0.396	0.299
	7 Education Requirements	0.212	0.239	-0.072	-0.120	0.125	0.176	-0.009	0.284	0.187	0.006	-0.309	0.007	0.242	-0.231	-0.207	-0.119
	8 Education Qualifications	-0.172	0.058	0.167	-0.123	-0.007	0.018	-0.037	0.211	-0.125	-0.064	0.015	-0.104	0.092	-0.004	0.074	-0.111
	9 Ed of Division Heads	-0.158	-0.384	0.001	-0.098	-0.255	-0.174	-0.024	0.024	0.063	-0.052	0.123	-0.048	-0.238	0.286	0.116	-0.085
	10 Levels	-0.207	-0.344	0.381	0.060	-0.197	-0.030	-0.041	-0.407	-0.129	-0.188	0.082	-0.244	-0.001	0.637	0.468	0.272
	11 Divisions	-0.211	-0.319	-0.126	0.155	0.111	-0.110	-0.148	-0.153	-0.122	-0.112	0.056	0.039	-0.252	0.461	0.411	0.228
	12 Director's Span Control	-0.298	-0.183	0.055	0.028	0.088	0.025	0.009	-0.106	-0.133	-0.129	-0.160	-0.208	-0.160	0.286	0.205	0.020
	13 Sections per Division	-0.073	-0.194	0.042	0.065	0.181	-0.056	0.263	-0.181	0.398	-0.100	-0.073	-0.010	-0.005	0.210	0.161	0.024
	14 Division Heads' Span	-0.327	-0.301	0.201	0.118	0.007	0.090	0.213	0.089	0.240	-0.034	0.252	0.008	-0.223	0.293	-0.098	-0.101
	15 Standardized Ratings	0.246	0.247	-0.285	-0.063	0.115	0.289	-0.157	0.174	-0.371	0.117	-0.058	-0.112	0.069	-0.242	-0.323	0.044
	16 Clerical Ratio	0.031	-0.135	-0.191	-0.064	-0.150	-0.159	-0.267	-0.003	-0.236	0.175	-0.111	-0.188	-0.188	0.062	0.284	0.281
	17 Supervisory Ratio: HQ		0.349	-0.222	-0.154	-0.092	-0.277	-0.414	0.221	-0.156	0.012	-0.143	-0.371	0.317	-0.500	-0.203	-0.100
	18 Staff Ratio	0.352		-0.292	-0.132	-0.088	-0.138	-0.412	0.232	-0.160	0.397	-0.143	-0.371	0.317	-0.567	-0.229	-0.223
	19 Delegation: Personnel	-0.285	-0.292		0.179	-0.013	0.081	0.265	-0.163	0.120	-0.245	-0.127	-0.028	0.078	0.276	0.144	-0.075
	20 Delegation: Budget	-0.068	-0.084	-0.032		-0.098	0.115	-0.121	-0.246	0.043	-0.141	-0.124	0.021	0.215	0.222	0.055	-0.049
	21 Decentralizatn:Influence	0.165	-0.133	0.077	-0.077		0.115	0.236	0.046	-0.120	-0.296	0.157	-0.227	0.054	0.310	0.030	0.211
	22 Delegation LO Manager	0.291	-0.134	0.219	0.060	0.150		0.236	-0.086	-0.032	0.131	-0.067	0.448	0.130	0.037	-0.177	-0.167
	23 Applications/Employee	0.053	-0.385	-0.120	-0.101	-0.315	-0.210		-0.282	0.559	-0.429	-0.037	0.249	0.073	-0.027	-0.331	-0.667
	24 GATB's per Application	0.182	0.216	0.219	-0.003	0.057	0.054	-0.207		-0.282	0.476	-0.067	-0.013	0.092	-0.405	-0.137	-0.082
	25 Placements per Opening	-0.060	-0.104	-0.040	-0.010	-0.193	-0.026	0.559	-0.282		-0.192	-0.013	0.249	0.073	-0.016	-0.130	-0.351
	26 Employee-Client Ratio	0.030	-0.119	0.040	-0.010	-0.092	0.023	-0.414	0.086	-0.282		-0.122	-0.201	0.092	-0.178	0.188	0.340
STATE ENVIRONMENT VARIABLES	27 Midwestern Region	0.030	-0.138	-0.124	-0.154	-0.092	0.127	0.112	-0.061	0.005	-0.026		-0.380	-0.329	-0.100	-0.091	0.037
	28 Southern Region	-0.105	-0.360	-0.028	-0.122	-0.215	-0.064	0.412	-0.034	0.174	-0.192	-0.380		-0.380	-0.054	-0.216	-0.607
	29 Western Region	0.040	0.308	0.076	0.021	0.052	0.087	-0.182	0.118	0.051	0.087	-0.329	-0.380		-0.189	0.093	0.394
	30 Population	-0.487	-0.551	0.269	0.209	0.290	0.036	-0.025	-0.368	-0.011	-0.170	0.096	-0.052	-0.182		0.434	0.240
	31 Per cent Urban	-0.098	-0.222	0.140	0.053	0.026	-0.171	-0.305	-0.124	-0.011	0.179	-0.087	-0.208	0.090	0.434		0.652
	32 Median Family Income	-0.189	-0.135	0.346	0.309	0.128	-0.058	0.294	-0.342	-0.112	-0.186	0.034	-0.208?	0.090	0.240	0.451	
	33 % Manufacturng Employees	-0.267	-0.239	-0.065	-0.085	0.198	-0.213	-0.186	-0.183	-0.244	0.062	0.066	-0.082	-0.459	0.373	0.267	0.216
	34 Median Education	0.237	0.290	-0.075	-0.151	0.189	0.100	-0.375	-0.058	-0.112	0.243	0.032	-0.625	0.574	-0.048	0.482	0.680
	35 Per cent Foreign Stock	-0.035	0.280	0.017	0.022	0.057	-0.061	-0.543	-0.098	-0.322	0.172	-0.161	-0.204	0.536	-0.529	0.189	0.622
	36 % Government Employees	0.213	0.632	-0.104	-0.003	-0.193	0.054	-0.269	0.248	-0.182	-0.150	-0.161	-0.204	0.536	-0.529	-0.195	0.207
	37 Expenditures per Capita	0.052	0.530	0.040	-0.092	0.026	-0.026	-0.429	0.029	0.118	0.243	-0.110	-0.411	0.614	-0.529	0.095	0.598
	38 Governor's Appoint Power	-0.341	-0.162	0.153	-0.054	0.271	-0.018	-0.178	-0.184	0.005	-0.026	0.113	-0.214	-0.036	0.290	0.224	0.229
	39 % Insured Unemployed	-0.056	-0.333	-0.160	0.141	0.127	-0.210	-0.420	-0.192	-0.123	0.064	-0.371	-0.276	0.061	0.135	0.237	0.528
	40 Benefit Duration	-0.047	0.107	-0.239	0.088	-0.112	-0.148	-0.348	0.152	-0.218	0.123	-0.179	-0.028	0.044	0.044	0.196	0.248
	41 Funds/Taxes	0.158	0.713	0.268	0.212	-0.059	-0.170	0.215	0.149	0.106	0.185	-0.294	-0.218	0.569	-0.346	-0.245	0.152
SUPPLEMENTARY VARIABLES	42 Size (Log)	-0.448	0.713	0.268	0.212	0.354	0.021	0.167	-0.552	0.330	0.186	0.059	-0.004	0.053	0.833	0.492	0.197
	43 Automation (Dummy)	-0.189	-0.135	0.346	0.309	0.128	-0.058	0.294	-0.342	0.020	-0.186	-0.034	0.074	-0.202	0.340	0.205	0.107
	44 Supervisory Ratio: Agency	0.669	0.100	-0.094	-0.042	-0.178	0.202	0.181	0.160	0.020	0.062	0.074	0.001	-0.027	-0.322	-0.079	0.042
	45 Size of Government	-0.449	-0.568	0.308	0.201	0.303	0.080	0.009	-0.359	-0.014	-0.209	0.107	-0.033	-0.140	0.926	0.456	0.230
	46 Merit System Coverage	-0.022	0.129	-0.064	0.020	0.114	-0.032	-0.367	-0.160	-0.210	0.027	-0.099	-0.310	0.075	0.234	0.355	0.481
	47 Population Expansion	0.150	0.120	-0.011	0.256	0.057	0.015	-0.190	-0.147	-0.036	0.135	-0.187	-0.153	0.484	0.062	0.280	0.464

CORRELATION MATRIX FOR AGENCY ANALYSIS: VARIABLES 33-47 (Below Diagonal N = 53, Above Diagonal N = 51)

	33 % MANF EMPLY	34 MED ED	35 % FGN STOCK	36 % GOVT EMPLY	37 EXP/ CAPITA	38 GOV's APP PR	39 % INS UNEMP	40 BENFT DURATN	41 FUNDS/ TAXES	42 SIZE (LOG)	43 AUTO DUMMY	44 SUP RT AGENCY	45 SIZE GOVT	46 MER SY COV	47 POPLTN EXPNSN
MAJOR VARIABLES															
1 Size	0.324	0.096	0.319	-0.428	0.033	0.278	0.327	0.134	-0.205	0.927	0.284	-0.374	0.206	0.288	0.798
2 Extent of Regulations	0.064	0.046	0.083	-0.049	0.108	-0.034	0.255	0.162	-0.153	0.445	0.090	-0.214	0.542	0.329	0.123
3 Civil Serv Appointments	-0.177	0.083	0.031	0.180	0.048	0.114	-0.044	0.028	0.019	-0.135	-0.185	-0.095	-0.010	-0.037	-0.029
4 Salary of Interviewers	-0.118	-0.420	0.343	0.261	0.678	0.119	0.499	0.113	0.493	0.134	-0.260	-0.231	-0.231	0.242	0.413
5 Division of Labor	0.324	-0.000	0.271	-0.518	-0.059	0.375	0.236	0.071	-0.253	0.819	0.413	-0.330	0.773	0.282	0.242
6 Automation	0.167	-0.109	0.169	-0.318	0.109	0.119	0.173	-0.099	-0.141	0.707	0.572	-0.277	0.830	0.225	0.134
7 Education Requirements	-0.308	0.188	-0.096	0.251	0.054	-0.093	-0.056	0.044	-0.275	-0.265	-0.116	-0.016	-0.196	0.002	0.225
8 Education Qualifications	-0.148	0.147	-0.205	0.219	0.095	0.078	0.264	0.264	0.095	-0.040	-0.010	-0.153	0.012	0.063	0.060
9 Ed of Division Heads	0.335	-0.068	-0.059	-0.467	-0.328	0.011	-0.168	-0.128	-0.406	0.331	0.010	-0.156	0.258	0.046	-0.115
10 Levels	0.260	-0.139	-0.255	-0.368	-0.027	0.322	0.114	0.083	-0.294	0.711	0.429	-0.151	0.637	0.466	-0.093
11 Divisions	0.361	-0.123	-0.138	-0.329	-0.151	0.109	0.046	0.181	-0.305	0.522	0.165	-0.132	0.434	0.206	-0.122
12 Director's Span Control	0.167	-0.085	-0.047	-0.167	-0.139	0.027	0.024	0.024	-0.183	0.323	0.169	-0.342	0.258	0.157	0.054
13 Sections per Division	0.079	0.044	-0.049	-0.376	-0.165	0.221	-0.157	-0.157	-0.146	0.352	0.399	0.215	0.175	0.140	-0.099
14 Division Heads' Span	0.132	-0.168	-0.051	-0.317	-0.359	0.278	-0.314	-0.101	-0.253	0.271	-0.120	-0.133	0.240	-0.133	0.066
15 Standardized Ratings	0.018	0.056	0.115	0.303	0.151	-0.108	0.092	-0.024	0.084	-0.345	-0.267	0.081	-0.266	0.139	-0.260
16 Clerical Ratio	0.213	0.038	-0.366	-0.060	0.029	0.143	0.206	0.381	0.011	0.142	0.041	-0.003	-0.028	-0.227	-0.094
17 Supervisory Ratio: HQ	-0.274	0.243	0.036	0.219	0.053	-0.350	-0.058	-0.114	-0.174	-0.510	-0.221	0.664	-0.462	-0.002	-0.074
18 Staff Ratio	-0.246	0.307	0.288	0.651	0.546	-0.167	0.343	0.114	0.735	-0.663	-0.143	0.100	-0.585	0.136	0.154
19 Delegation: Personnel	0.067	-0.077	0.018	-0.107	-0.161	0.158	0.114	-0.037	-0.232	0.310	-0.347	-0.111	-0.317	-0.057	0.123
20 Delegation: Budget	-0.087	-0.154	0.024	-0.002	0.095	-0.056	0.145	-0.020	0.079	0.209	0.325	-0.032	0.205	0.014	-0.011
21 Decentralizatn:Influenc	0.211	0.199	0.061	-0.206	0.027	0.287	0.134	-0.097	-0.071	0.294	0.106	-0.216	0.324	0.146	0.262
22 Delegation LO Manager	-0.220	-0.103	-0.064	0.056	-0.027	-0.018	-0.217	-0.201	-0.171	-0.087	-0.092	0.180	0.082	-0.009	0.059
23 Applications/Employee	-0.702	-0.408	-0.591	-0.293	-0.467	-0.194	-0.457	-0.361	-0.249	-0.510	0.287	0.173	0.010	-0.370	-0.016
24 GATB's per Application	-0.201	-0.177	-0.177	-0.064	0.031	-0.203	-0.211	0.104	0.182	-0.489	-0.342	0.205	-0.396	-0.204	-0.206
25 Placements Per Opening	-0.351	-0.161	-0.462	0.273	-0.169	0.031	-0.179	-0.254	0.130	0.310	0.218	-0.077	-0.020	-0.203	-0.162
26 Employee-Client Ratio	0.065	0.254	0.181	0.158	0.254	-0.028	0.068	0.031	0.217	0.113	-0.226	0.030	-0.219	0.053	-0.052
STATE ENVIRONMENT VARIABLES															
27 Midwestern Region	0.069	-0.017	0.033	-0.167	-0.114	-0.118	-0.386	-0.216	-0.305	-0.262	-0.036	0.078	0.111	-0.103	-0.194
28 Southern Region	-0.286	-0.629	-0.650	-0.212	-0.427	-0.222	-0.287	-0.054	-0.226	-0.065	0.077	0.002	-0.034	-0.321	-0.159
29 Western Region	-0.477	-0.050	-0.212						0.004	-0.004			-0.321		0.503
30 Population	0.388	0.597	0.197	-0.550	-0.117	0.302	0.141	0.052	-0.591	0.171	0.055	-0.028	0.963	0.078	0.064
31 Per cent Urban	0.278	0.418	0.502	0.215	0.099	0.233	0.246	0.237	-0.359	0.539	0.356	-0.083	0.474	0.243	0.292
32 Median Family Income	0.224	0.707	0.647	-0.203	0.622	0.238	0.549	0.303	-0.254	0.476	0.214	-0.044	0.239	0.367	0.482
33 % Manufacturing Employees		-0.137	0.310	-0.482	-0.375	0.280	0.004	0.090	-0.539	-0.080	0.112	-0.106	-0.014	0.498	-0.203
34 Median Education	-0.132		0.441	0.321	0.592	0.045	0.398	0.090	0.303	0.171	0.111	-0.105	-0.473	0.299	0.394
35 Per cent Foreign Stock	0.298	0.569		0.306	0.321	0.112	0.419	0.198	0.089	-0.670	0.003	-0.137	-0.094	0.211	0.103
36 % Government Employees	-0.463	0.309	0.306		0.600	-0.236	0.661	0.214	0.596	-0.257	-0.233	0.111	0.273	0.446	0.204
37 Expenditures per Capita	-0.360	0.043	0.108	0.600		-0.126	0.131	0.105	0.689	0.361	-0.018	-0.029	0.121	0.048	0.560
38 Governor's Appoint Power	0.269	0.383	0.403	-0.227	-0.121		0.126	0.319	-0.257	0.110	0.098	-0.045	0.110	0.266	-0.062
39 % Insured Unemployed	0.004	0.075	0.164	0.244	0.636	0.126		0.036	-0.152	0.099	-0.004	-0.109	0.121	0.096	-0.405
40 Benefit Duration	0.064	0.292	0.075	0.177	0.177	0.087	0.036		0.324	0.070	-0.327	0.027	0.421	0.382	-0.108
41 Funds/Taxes	-0.520	0.424	0.086	0.196	0.538	-0.257	-0.152	0.324		-0.469	-0.090	-0.025	-0.315	-0.037	0.269
SUPPLEMENTARY VARIABLES															
42 Size (Log)	0.434	-0.073	0.156	-0.611	-0.234	0.329	0.101	0.070	-0.427		0.430	0.083	0.889	-0.053	0.279
43 Automation (Dummy)	-0.106	0.101	-0.003	-0.223	-0.018	0.098	-0.004	-0.327	-0.090	0.444		0.313	0.327	0.295	0.024
44 Supervisory Ratio:Agency	-0.101	-0.014	0.148	0.111	-0.029	-0.045	-0.109	0.027	-0.025	0.083	0.313		-0.301	0.236	0.253
45 Size of Government	-0.307	0.204	0.430	0.273	0.121	0.110	0.121	0.421	-0.315	0.889	0.327	-0.301		0.228	0.207
46 Merit System Coverage	0.289	0.379	0.099	0.446	0.048	0.266	0.096	0.382	-0.037	-0.053	0.295	0.236	0.228		0.155
47 Population Expansion	0.193		0.196	0.196	0.177	0.087	0.264	-0.108	0.269	0.279	0.024	0.253	0.047	0.150	

TABLE F-2. CORRELATION MATRIX FOR LO ANALYSIS: VARIABLES 51-86

Panel A — Variables 51–66

Group	Variable	51 ES FUNC	52 SPEC	53 LO SIZE	54 DIV OF LABOR	55 MECH-ANZTN	56 LEVELS	57 SECTNS	58 LO MGR SPAN	59 CLER RATIO	60 SUP RATIO	61 FLS SPAN	62 LO SIZE (LOG)	63 LO SZE X LVLS	64 LVLS X SCTNS	65 DoL X CLR RT	66 LVLS X CLR RT
MAJOR LO VARIABLES	51 ES Function	1.000															
	52 Specialization	0.488	1.000														
	53 LO Size	0.126	0.249	1.000													
	54 Division of Labor	0.148	0.058	0.507	1.000												
	55 Mechanization	0.064	0.110	0.246	0.369	1.000											
	56 Levels	0.043	0.204	0.683	0.422	0.205	1.000										
	57 Sections	0.204	0.308	0.606	0.455	0.242	0.333	1.000									
	58 LO Mgr's Span of Control	0.241	0.196	0.310	0.305	0.231	0.088	0.274	1.000								
	59 Clerical Ratio	-0.271	0.042	0.064	0.204	-0.022	-0.015	-0.015	-0.003	1.000							
	60 Supervisory Ratio	-0.081	-0.066	-0.455	-0.374	-0.147	-0.192	-0.160	-0.423	0.188	1.000						
	61 FLS Span of Control	-0.081	-0.089	-0.554	-0.317	-0.106	-0.250	-0.253	-0.100	-0.635	-0.725	1.000					
SUPPLEMENTARY VARIABLES	62 LO Size (Log)	0.130	0.276	0.892	0.615	0.301	0.686	0.667	0.255	0.041	-0.389	-0.651	1.000				
	63 LO Size x Levels	0.113	0.216	0.987	0.487	0.240	0.747	0.544	0.255	0.091	-0.389	-0.635	0.848	1.000			
	64 Levels x Sections	0.186	0.289	0.745	0.501	0.267	0.584	0.952	0.266	-0.017	-0.188	-0.286	0.769	0.715	1.000		
	65 Div of Lbr x Clrcl Ratio	-0.180	-0.025	0.275	0.592	0.125	0.156	0.191	0.114	0.863	-0.291	-0.314	0.344	0.250	0.205	1.000	
	66 Levels x Clerical Ratio	-0.237	-0.062	0.213	0.286	-0.020	0.210	0.060	0.013	0.963	-0.179	0.226	0.239	0.218	0.218	0.879	1.000
AGENCY CONTEXT	67 Size	-0.049	0.011	0.144	0.121	-0.014	0.163	0.102	0.016	-0.144	-0.277	-0.368	0.338	0.242	0.192	0.091	0.096
	68 Extent of Regulations	-0.011	0.077	0.285	0.153	-0.078	0.099	0.227	0.006	-0.034	-0.356	-0.277	0.242	0.262	0.141	-0.166	-0.107
	69 Division of Labor	-0.044	0.144	0.280	0.168	-0.159	0.135	0.218	0.012	0.323	-0.356	-0.298	0.335	0.221	0.229	0.373	-0.339
	70 Automation	-0.006	0.169	0.308	-0.017	-0.087	0.021	0.043	0.026	-0.034	-0.296	-0.118	0.334	0.229	0.103	0.093	-0.014
	71 Education Qualifications	-0.016	0.086	0.297	0.046	-0.083	0.021	0.121	0.071	0.296	-0.119	-0.091	0.118	0.108	0.108	0.223	0.301
	72 Clerical Ratio	-0.069	0.018	0.027	0.207	-0.079	-0.032	0.043	0.026	0.394	-0.124	-0.074	0.058	0.013	0.024	0.552	0.583
	73 Supervisory Ratio: Hq	0.049	-0.077	-0.131	-0.051	0.223	-0.007	0.121	-0.103	-0.171	0.218	-0.246	-0.147	-0.109	-0.088	-0.204	-0.167
	74 Delegation LO Manager	-0.019	-0.066	-0.134	-0.096	0.117	0.122	0.016	-0.033	-0.299	-0.105	-0.246	0.134	0.133	-0.054	-0.273	-0.272
	75 Placements per Opening	-0.016	-0.120	-0.156	0.112	0.222	-0.090	-0.053	0.076	-0.213	-0.119	-0.248	-0.133	-0.146	-0.077	-0.017	-0.136
	76 Employee-Client Ratio	0.023	-0.060	-0.125	0.176	-0.082	-0.066	-0.108	-0.057	0.194	0.147	-0.136	-0.113	-0.118	-0.054	-0.236	-0.182
COMMUNITY ENVIRONMENT	77 Town under 25,000	-0.105	-0.122	-0.438	-0.312	-0.305	-0.268	-0.346	-0.242	-0.123	-0.225	-0.178	-0.428	-0.287	-0.360	-0.206	-0.174
	78 Population	0.053	0.283	0.309	0.077	-0.087	0.136	0.200	0.049	0.227	-0.222	-0.225	0.325	0.316	0.384	0.273	0.316
	79 Population Density	-0.122	0.444	0.428	-0.029	0.062	0.146	0.167	0.025	-0.172	-0.190	-0.015	0.421	0.273	0.252	0.237	0.237
	80 Median Family Income	0.041	0.230	0.220	0.135	0.062	0.173	0.187	0.128	-0.024	-0.007	-0.007	0.164	0.157	0.252	0.249	0.237
	81 Per cent Negro	0.059	0.231	0.156	0.137	0.149	0.157	0.233	0.100	0.395	-0.282	0.164	0.252	0.157	0.207	0.104	0.073
	82 Per cent Foreign Stock	-0.607	0.323	0.292	0.137	0.157	0.127	0.255	0.156	0.017	-0.065	0.055	0.164	0.237	0.235	0.376	0.415
	83 % Negro x Family Income	0.079	0.333	0.242	0.195	-0.111	0.244	0.097	0.044	0.042	0.156	-0.065	0.271	0.237	0.286	0.286	0.073
STATE ENVIRONMENT	84 Western Region	0.014	0.017	0.167	0.163	0.056	0.094	0.097	0.024	-0.044	0.017	0.056	0.271	0.157	0.077	0.104	-0.205
	85 Per cent Urban	0.044	0.260	0.283	-0.167	-0.083	0.042	0.042	0.204	-0.212	-0.284	-0.193	0.193	0.249	0.208	0.323	-0.242
	86 % Government Employees	0.032	-0.040	-0.092	-0.103	-0.133	-0.078	-0.047	-0.047	-0.150	0.092	-0.146	-0.102	-0.085	-0.062	-0.180	-0.168

Panel B — Variables 67–86

Group	Variable	67 SIZE	68 EXT REGS	69 DIV OF LABOR	70 AUTO-MATION	71 ED QUAL	72 CLER RATIO	73 SUP RT AGENCY	74 DELGTN LO MGR	75 PLCMTS /OPNG	76 EMP-CL RATIO	77 TWN < 25,000	78 POPU-LATION	79 POP DENSTY	80 MEDIAN INCOME	81 % NEGRO	82 % FGN STOCK	83 % NGRO X INCM	84 WESTRN REGION	85 % URBAN	86 % GOV EMP
AGENCY CONTEXT	67 Size	1.000																			
	68 Extent of Regulations	0.751	1.000																		
	69 Division of Labor	0.839	0.711	1.000																	
	70 Automation	0.031	0.130	0.691	1.000																
	71 Education Qualifications	0.130	0.101	0.321	0.135	1.000															
	72 Clerical Ratio	-0.303	-0.200	-0.270	-0.428	0.298	1.000														
	73 Supervisory Ratio: Hq	0.610	0.321	0.315	0.367	-0.173	-0.288	1.000													
	74 Delegation LO Manager	0.297	0.610	0.000	0.173	-0.115	0.195	-0.175	1.000												
	75 Placements per Opening	-0.534	-0.200	-0.428	-0.367	-0.162	0.393	-0.118	-0.583	1.000											
	76 Employee-Client Ratio	-0.476	-0.521	-0.309	-0.359	-0.274	-0.115	0.099	-0.032	-0.175	1.000										
COMMUNITY ENVIRONMENT	77 Town under 25,000	-0.188	-0.047	0.047	-0.000	-0.162	0.070	0.020	-0.265	-0.160	-0.186	1.000									
	78 Population	0.407	0.068	0.389	-0.085	-0.083	0.185	-0.032	-0.061	0.034	0.089	-0.074	1.000								
	79 Population Density	0.236	0.037	0.315	0.213	0.119	0.243	-0.341	-0.008	-0.186	-0.077	-0.046	0.484	1.000							
	80 Median Family Income	0.270	0.289	0.388	0.388	0.231	0.392	-0.157	0.034	0.123	0.064	-0.448	0.211	0.168	1.000						
	81 Per cent Negro	-0.182	-0.107	-0.073	-0.097	-0.000	-0.060	-0.341	-0.061	-0.378	-0.077	0.154	-0.309	0.197	0.529	1.000					
	82 Per cent Foreign Stock	0.437	0.172	0.475	0.315	0.231	0.392	-0.294	-0.186	-0.098	0.064	-0.073	-0.255	0.207	0.443	-0.224	1.000				
	83 % Negro x Family Income	-0.103	-0.072	0.027	-0.010	0.007	-0.019	-0.051	-0.077	-0.128	-0.077	0.024	0.415	0.252	0.325	-0.075	-0.100	1.000			
STATE ENVIRONMENT	84 Western Region	0.336	0.456	0.040	0.383	-0.009	-0.368	-0.240	-0.128	-0.378	-0.274	0.089	0.191	0.237	0.267	-0.273	0.050	-0.252	1.000		
	85 Per cent Urban	0.653	0.390	0.666	0.386	0.184	-0.240	-0.581	-0.581	0.114	0.114	-0.419	0.052	0.157	-0.148	0.443	-0.204	0.618	0.201	1.000	
	86 % Government Employees	-0.387	0.005	-0.527	-0.290	0.044	0.421	-0.202	0.233	0.034	-0.202	0.114	0.291	0.249	0.311	0.026	-0.130	-0.173	0.477	-0.378	1.000

State Environment block — Variables 84–86

Variable	84 WESTRN REGION	85 % URBAN	86 % GOV EMP
84 Western Region	1.000		
85 Per cent Urban	0.201	1.000	
86 % Government Employees	0.477	-0.378	1.000

APPENDIX G

Bibliography of Sources on Employment Security

Haber, William, and Daniel H. Kruger. *The Role of the U.S. Employment Service in a Changing Economy*. Kalamazoo: Upjohn Institute for Employment Research, 1964.

Haber, William, and Merrill G. Murray. *Unemployment Insurance in the American Economy*. Homewood, Ill.: Irwin, 1966.

International Labor Office. *National Employment Services—United States*. Geneva: Imprimeries Populaires, 1955.

State of California, Department of Employment. "Functional Statements," *Administrative Manual*, April 23, 1958.

State of Louisiana, Division of Employment Security. "Functional Statements," *U.S. Employment Security Manual*, Part I, March 15, 1959.

State of Montana, Unemployment Compensation Commission. *Montana Operations Manual*, Part A, October 1, 1961.

U.S. Department of Labor, Bureau of Employment Security. "The Public Employment Service System, 1933–1953." *Employment Security Review*, 20, no. 6 (June 1953).

———. "Twenty Years of Unemployment Insurance in the USA, 1935–1955," *Employment Security Review*, 22, no. 8 (August 1955).

———. "Unemployment Insurance in the USA, 1956–1960," *Employment Security Review*, 27, no. 8 (August 1960).

———. "Public Employment Service in the Nation's Job Market, 1933–1963," *Employment Security Review*, 30, no. 6 (June 1963).

———. *Employment Security Manual*.

———. "Historical Statistics of Employment Security Activities, 1938–1966," January 1968.

———. "Thirtieth Anniversary, 1935–1965, Unemployment Insurance in the United States," No. 0-783-514, 1965.

U.S. Department of Labor, Manpower Administration. "Employment Service Task Force Report," *Employment Service Review*, 3, no. 2 (February 1966).

———. *Unemployment Insurance Review*, 2, no. 8 (August 1965).

APPENDIX H

Data for Divisions

Variables and Basic Statistics

TABLE H-1. *Major Divisional Characteristics*

	Type of Division	*n*	Mean	Standard Deviation	Skew
H-1 Size: number of full-time personnel in the division as of a given date in the first quarter of 1966.	All	387	51.8	83.76	4.06
	ES	68	32.4	32.00	3.80
	UI	71	128.2	146.08	2.07
	AS	67	47.4	67.10	3.08
	P&T	77	24.2	27.59	3.18
	DP	51	49.4	57.60	3.61
	LS	53	22.3	38.96	4.47
H-2 Division of labor (occupational positions): number of official job titles used in the division, not counting different grades within one job title.	All	387	9.6	5.91	1.56
	ES	68	10.1	4.49	0.16
	UI	71	14.1	6.60	0.56
	AS	67	12.1	7.28	1.79
	P&T	77	6.9	3.41	2.24
	DP	51	8.0	3.80	1.42
	LS	53	5.3	2.86	1.48
H-3 Levels: number of supervisory strata in the section with the most supervisory strata. Assistant supervisors are not counted as distinct levels.	All	387	3.5	1.19	0.77
	ES	68	3.3	0.95	0.82
	UI	71	4.5	1.31	0.04
	AS	67	3.6	1.24	0.61
	P&T	77	3.1	0.86	0.86
	DP	51	3.5	0.99	0.42
	LS	53	2.8	0.94	1.20
H-4 Sections: number of major subunits in the division whose head reports to the division director or his deputy.	All	387	2.5	1.88	0.48
	ES	68	2.8	1.90	0.25
	UI	71	3.4	1.67	0.13
	AS	67	2.7	2.01	0.35
	P&T	77	2.2	1.82	0.57
	DP	51	2.5	1.71	0.80
	LS	53	0.9	1.01	1.24
H-5 Division head's span of control: sum of all supervisory and nonsupervisory personnel who report directly to the division head.	All	387	6.2	3.04	1.53
	ES	68	7.5	3.88	1.91
	UI	71	6.2	2.45	0.82
	AS	67	5.9	2.47	0.77
	P&T	77	5.8	2.50	1.41
	DP	51	5.9	3.51	0.95
	LS	53	6.0	3.10	1.20
H-6 Middle managers' span of control: sum of all supervisory and nonsupervisory personnel who report directly to the section heads divided by the number of sections, in those divisions with four or more hierarchical levels.	All	169	5.6	2.65	1.90
	ES	27	5.2	2.08	1.29
	UI	54	6.3	2.42	1.28
	AS	35	4.7	1.46	0.73
	P&T	18	5.1	3.09	2.33
	DP	25	5.6	3.43	1.44
	LS	10	6.4	4.33	2.16
H-7 First-line supervisors' span of control: total number of people on the lowest organizational level of the division divided by the number of supervisors to whom they report, in those divisions with three or more hierarchical levels.	All	308	5.5	3.37	1.39
	ES	55	4.5	2.76	1.85
	UI	67	6.3	3.64	1.20
	AS	54	4.5	2.37	1.32
	P&T	58	4.4	2.12	0.87
	DP	44	8.3	4.04	0.74
	LS	30	6.0	3.58	0.93

Continued on following page

TABLE H-1 (continued)

	Type of Division	n	Mean	Standard Deviation	Skew
H-8 Clerical ratio: sum of all clerical personnel divided by total personnel in the division.	All	387	53.0	22.38	0.12
	ES	68	29.0	10.42	−0.06
	UI	71	54.0	18.16	0.05
	AS	67	64.0	20.75	−0.87
	P&T	77	44.7	14.84	−0.05
	DP	51	83.7	10.39	−0.62
	LS	53	51.5	15.08	−0.07
H-9 Supervisory ratio: sum of all supervisory personnel divided by total personnel in the division.	All	387	22.6	10.81	2.21
	ES	68	37.7	15.67	1.93
	UI	71	19.8	7.29	1.32
	AS	67	24.0	7.78	0.88
	P&T	77	21.9	8.19	0.71
	DP	51	16.0	5.91	0.69
	LS	53	19.0	7.94	0.85

TABLE H-2.   *Divisional Supplementary Variables*

	Type of Division	n	Mean	Standard Deviation	Skew
H-10 Size (log): logarithm to the base 10 of division size (variable H-1).	All	387	1.42	0.47	0.54
	ES	68	1.38	0.33	−0.02
	UI	71	1.84	0.52	−0.29
	AS	67	1.42	0.45	0.54
	P&T	77	1.22	0.36	0.48
	DP	51	1.52	0.37	0.32
	LS	53	1.12	0.38	1.29
H-11 Residual of division of labor on size (log): residual from the regression line of division of labor (variable H-2) on the logarithm of size (variable H-10).	All	387	−0.00	3.74	1.17
	ES	68	0.92	3.24	0.10
	UI	71	0.39	4.33	0.28
	AS	67	2.58	4.25	3.04
	P&T	77	−0.74	2.82	−0.38
	DP	51	−2.62	2.86	−0.11
	LS	53	−1.37	1.87	−0.45
H-12 Residual of levels on size (log): residual from the regression line of levels (variable H-3) on the logarithm of size (variable H-10).	All	387	0.00	0.60	0.21
	ES	68	−0.10	0.57	0.41
	UI	71	0.09	0.71	−0.09
	AS	67	0.15	0.60	0.21
	P&T	77	0.01	0.52	0.27
	DP	51	−0.19	0.61	0.60
	LS	53	−0.00	0.54	0.07
H-13 Residual of sections on size (log): residual from the regression line of sections (variable H-4) on the logarithm of size (variable H-10).	All	387	0.00	1.30	0.46
	ES	68	0.44	1.41	0.47
	UI	71	−0.28	1.44	−0.29
	AS	67	0.27	1.15	0.89
	P&T	77	0.30	1.19	1.01
	DP	51	−0.29	1.38	0.80
	LS	53	−0.69	0.74	−1.03
H-14 Residual of supervisory ratio on size: residual from the regression line of supervisory ratio (variable H-9) on size (variable H-1).	All	387	−0.00	10.58	2.16
	ES	68	9.60	15.46	1.94
	UI	71	−0.81	6.97	0.89
	AS	67	1.32	7.86	0.67
	P&T	77	−1.48	8.13	0.68
	DP	51	−6.67	5.89	0.55
	LS	53	−4.35	7.69	0.93

Continued on following page

TABLE H-2 (continued)

	Type of Division	n	Mean	Standard Deviation	Skew
H-15 Regularity of staff meetings: dichotomous variable with divisons that hold staff meetings "only when problems arise" coded zero, and those that do so regularly or both regularly and whenever problems arise coded one.	All	272	0.45	0.50	0.21
	ES	61	0.77	0.42	−1.29
	UI	61	0.41	0.50	0.37
	AS	57	0.35	0.48	0.63
	P&T	61	0.31	0.47	0.81
	DP	7	0.29	0.49	0.95
	LS	25	0.36	0.49	0.58
H-16 Division head's seniority: number of years the head of the division has worked in the agency.	All	292	22.8	7.87	−1.21
	ES	62	22.8	7.54	−1.25
	UI	65	25.6	4.47	−1.18
	AS	59	22.3	8.34	−1.17
	P&T	66	21.3	8.03	−0.78
	DP	6	18.3	10.07	−0.40
	LS	34	18.9	10.05	−0.74
H-17 Division head's stability: number of years the head of the division has held the top position as division director.	All	292	8.07	7.03	0.96
	ES	62	5.60	4.93	1.22
	UI	65	10.11	6.79	0.54
	AS	59	7.42	7.94	1.24
	P&T	66	9.00	7.25	0.82
	DP	6	8.67	6.44	0.47
	LS	34	7.91	7.67	0.86
H-18 Division head's college education: number of years of college and postgraduate education of division heads.	All	292	3.46	2.07	−0.34
	ES	62	2.87	1.88	−0.29
	UI	65	3.08	2.16	−0.22
	AS	59	3.22	1.93	−0.11
	P&T	66	3.73	2.05	−0.40
	DP	6	2.17	2.04	−0.09
	LS	34	5.41	1.21	−1.67

TABLE H-3. *Agency Context of Divisions*

	Type of Division	n	Mean	Standard Deviation	Skew
H-19 Size: see variable 1, Appendix C.	All	387	1,412.3	1,806.96	2.85
	ES	68	1,374.5	1,749.21	2.76
	UI	71	1,348.1	1,811.21	2.93
	AS	67	1,318.1	1,755.40	2.86
	P&T	77	1,485.0	1,759.20	2.77
	DP	51	1,156.6	1,643.87	3.52
	LS	53	1,505.9	2,144.16	2.26
H-20 Clerical ratio: see variable 16, Appendix C.	All	387	32.7	6.93	0.77
	ES	68	32.6	6.87	0.85
	UI	71	32.6	6.58	0.66
	AS	67	32.7	6.90	0.63
	P&T	77	44.7	14.84	−0.05
	DP	51	31.9	6.49	0.85
	LS	53	33.3	7.41	0.65
H-21 Supervisory ratio: see variable 17, Appendix C.	All	387	20.7	4.46	0.25
	ES	68	20.6	4.19	0.30
	UI	71	21.0	4.25	0.24
	AS	67	20.8	4.68	0.05
	P&T	77	20.7	4.55	0.57
	DP	51	21.2	4.57	0.08
	LS	53	20.0	4.67	0.23

Sources and Comments

MAJOR DIVISIONAL CHARACTERISTICS

The sources and comments for these variables are the same as those for the corresponding variables used in the analysis of the agencies and local offices. The numbers of the corresponding variables given below are from Appendix C. A full description of the coding procedures used in creating these measures of the major characteristics of divisions is contained in Appendix D.

H-1 Size: see variable 1.

H-2 Division of labor: see variable 5.

H-3 Levels: see variable 10.

H-4 Sections: see variable 13.

H-5 Division head's span of control: see variable 14.

H-6 Middle managers' span of control: see variable 14.

H-7 First-line supervisors' span of control: see variable 61.

H-8 Clerical ratio: see variable 16.

H-9 Supervisory ratio: see variable 17.

DIVISIONAL SUPPLEMENTARY VARIABLES

H-10, 11, 12, 13, 14 Derived variables: see the underlying variables identified under *Major Divisional Characteristics* above.

H-15 Regularity of staff meetings: CORP 7 self-administered questionnaire, "Are staff meetings for supervisors regularly scheduled or are they held irregularly whenever problems arise?" Respondents: all division heads.

H-16 Division head's seniority: CORP 7 interview, "How long has this Division Head been with the Agency?" The information was usually taken from the personnel files.

H-17 Division head's stability: CORP 7 interview, "How long has this Division Head been in his present position?" The information was usually taken from the personnel files.

H-18 Division head's college education: see variable 9, Appendix C.

AGENCY CONTEXT OF DIVISIONS

H-19 Size: see variable 1, Appendix C.

H-20 Clerical ratio: see variable 16, Appendix C.

H-21 Supervisory ratio: see variable 17, Appendix C.

TABLE H-4. Correlation Matrix[a] for All Divisions

	H-1 Size	H-2 Div of Labor	H-3 Levels	H-4 Sectns	H-5 DvHd's Span	H-6 Md Mgr Span	H-7 FLS Span	H-8 Clrcl Ratio	H-9 Sup Ratio	H-10 Size (Log)	H-19 Agency Size	H-20 Agency Cl Rto
H-1 Size	1.00											
H-2 Division of Labor	.65	1.00										
H-3 Levels	.71	.71	1.00									
H-4 Sections	.40	.60	.60	1.00								
H-5 Division Head's Span	.07	.18	-.01	.23	1.00							
H-6 Middle Managers' Span	.22	.13	.11	-.02	-.02	1.00						
H-7 First-Line Supervisors' Span	.40	.20	.22	-.02	-.03	.22	1.00					
H-8 Clerical Ratio	.19	.08	.17	.07	-.07	.05	.34	1.00				
H-9 Supervisory Ratio	-.21	-.10	-.07	-.00	-.02	-.49	-.64	-.33	1.00			
H-10 Size (Log)	.80	.77	.86	.72	.22	.32	.45	.23	-.23	1.00		
H-19 Agency Size	.46	.21	.31	.10	.08	.21	.34	.08	-.13	.35	1.00	
H-20 Agency Clerical Ratio	.09	.03	.05	.03	-.00	.00	.06	.13	-.04	.09	.09	1.00
H-21 Agency Supervisory Ratio	-.25	-.15	-.08	-.07	-.11	-.29	-.36	-.06	.28	-.21	-.46	-.03

[a]The coefficients used in Tables H-3 through H-9 are the Pearsonian r computed according to the Mesa-85 statistical system (UCSL 510, 9/1/66) obtained from the program library of the University of Chicago's Computation Center. The n's are given above in the first section; the coefficients are based on the actual n's in all of the matrices.

TABLE H-5. Correlation Matrix for Employment Service Divisions

	H-1 Size	H-2 Div of Labor	H-3 Levels	H-4 Sectns	H-5 DvHd's Span	H-6 Md Mgr Span	H-7 FLS Span	H-8 Clrcl Ratio	H-9 Sup Ratio	H-10 Size (Log)	H-19 Agency Size	H-20 Agency Cl Rto
H-1 Size	1.00											
H-2 Division of Labor	.49	1.00										
H-3 Levels	.75	.51	1.00									
H-4 Sections	.44	.59	.54	1.00								
H-5 Division Head's Span	.12	.20	-.15	.12	1.00							
H-6 Middle Managers' Span	.29	.21	-.03	-.03	.09	1.00						
H-7 First-Line Supervisors' Span	.60	.21	.40	-.17	.01	.34	1.00					
H-8 Clerical Ratio	-.02	.06	.18	-.01	-.10	-.06	.17	1.00				
H-9 Supervisory Ratio	-.28	-.41	-.36	-.27	.19	-.45	-.54	-.34	1.00			
H-10 Size (Log)	.82	.69	.80	.69	.28	.43	.54	.09	-.38	1.00		
H-19 Agency Size	.62	.11	.36	.05	.08	.43	.72	.18	-.24	.43	1.00	
H-20 Agency Clerical Ratio	-.10	-.06	.00	-.10	-.11	-.02	.07	.13	-.08	-.02	.20	1.00
H-21 Agency Supervisory Ratio	-.25	-.08	-.05	-.04	-.08	-.33	-.41	-.09	.22	-.21	-.48	-.13

TABLE H-6. Correlation Matrix for Unemployment Insurance Divisions

	H-1 Size	H-2 Div of Labor	H-3 Levels	H-4 Sectns	H-5 DvHd's Span	H-6 Md Mgr Span	H-7 FLS Span	H-8 Clrcl Ratio	H-9 Sup Ratio	H-10 Size (Log)	H-19 Agency Size	H-20 Agency Cl Rto
H-1 Size	1.00											
H-2 Division of Labor	.64	1.00										
H-3 Levels	.70	.67	1.00									
H-4 Sections	.31	.45	.41	1.00								
H-5 Division Head's Span	.10	.20	.15	.43	1.00							
H-6 Middle Managers' Span	.02	.15	-.08	.06	-.03	1.00						
H-7 First-Line Supervisors' Span	.47	.31	.15	.01	-.04	-.08	1.00					
H-8 Clerical Ratio	.34	.16	.21	.21	.01	-.13	.24	1.00				
H-9 Supervisory Ratio	-.35	-.29	-.11	-.16	-.13	-.31	-.59	-.24	1.00			
H-10 Size (Log)	.82	.76	.84	.59	.24	.05	.39	.38	-.39	1.00		
H-19 Agency Size	.64	.21	.28	.03	-.13	-.08	.31	.33	-.07	.34	1.00	
H-20 Agency Clerical Ratio	.19	.05	.03	-.02	.05	.03	.22	.36	-.17	.16	.01	1.00
H-21 Agency Supervisory Ratio	-.46	-.35	-.13	-.16	-.05	-.21	-.49	-.21	.57	-.34	-.45	-.03

TABLE H-7. Correlation Matrix for Administrative Services Divisions

	H-1 Size	H-2 Div of Labor	H-3 Levels	H-4 Sectns	H-5 DvHd's Span	H-6 Md Mgr Span	H-7 FLS Span	H-8 Clrcl Ratio	H-9 Sup Ratio	H-10 Size (Log)	H-19 Agency Size	H-20 Agency Cl Rto
H-1 Size	1.00											
H-2 Division of Labor	.74	1.00										
H-3 Levels	.76	.74	1.00									
H-4 Sections	.60	.71	.73	1.00								
H-5 Division Head's Span	.22	.27	.10	.28	1.00							
H-6 Middle Managers' Span	.20	-.03	.10	-.15	-.41	1.00						
H-7 First-Line Supervisors' Span	.50	.32	.19	.18	.14	.22	1.00					
H-8 Clerical Ratio	.16	.12	.08	.21	.23	-.18	.32	1.00				
H-9 Supervisory Ratio	-.16	-.05	.04	.07	-.32	-.31	-.66	.02	1.00			
H-10 Size (Log)	.84	.85	.88	.85	.30	.17	.48	.24	-.12	1.00		
H-19 Agency Size	.67	.34	.38	.25	.10	.27	.55	.10	-.04	.42	1.00	
H-20 Agency Clerical Ratio	.13	.11	-.03	.17	-.07	-.00	.07	.26	.13	.10	.16	1.00
H-21 Agency Supervisory Ratio	-.28	-.15	-.06	-.05	-.09	-.26	-.31	-.17	.37	-.16	-.47	.02

TABLE H-8. Correlation Matrix for Personnel and Technical Divisions

	H-1 Size	H-2 Div of Labor	H-3 Levels	H-4 Sectns	H-5 DvHd's Span	H-6 Md Mgr Span	H-7 FLS Span	H-8 Clrcl Ratio	H-9 Sup Ratio	H-10 Size (Log)	H-19 Agency Size	H-20 Agency Cl Rto
H-1 Size	1.00											
H-2 Division of Labor	.75	1.00										
H-3 Levels	.70	.61	1.00									
H-4 Sections	.55	.39	.61	1.00								
H-5 Division Head's Span	.18	.13	-.01	.20	1.00							
H-6 Middle Managers' Span	.70	.40	.28	.26	.07	1.00						
H-7 First-Line Supervisors' Span	.29	.43	-.03	.05	.27	.45	1.00					
H-8 Clerical Ratio	-.17	.07	.14	.15	-.02	.24	.01	1.00				
H-9 Supervisory Ratio	-.12	-.11	.29	-.06	-.48	-.52	-.73	.06	1.00			
H-10 Size (Log)	.85	.67	.81	.79	.37	.66	.42	.04	-.14	1.00		
H-19 Agency Size	.36	.08	.18	.08	.04	.40	.12	.18	-.15	.24	1.00	
H-20 Agency Clerical Ratio	.13	.01	.10	-.05	.05	-.06	-.13	.18	-.06	.05	.04	1.00
H-21 Agency Supervisory Ratio	-.19	-.11	-.04	-.03	-.18	-.12	-.31	-.08	.41	-.19	-.45	-.05

TABLE H-9. Correlation Matrix for Data-Processing Divisions

	H-1 Size	H-2 Div of Labor	H-3 Levels	H-4 Sectns	H-5 DvHd's Span	H-6 Md Mgr Span	H-7 FLS Span	H-8 Clrcl Ratio	H-9 Sup Ratio	H-10 Size (Log)	H-19 Agency Size	H-20 Agency Cl Rto
H-1 Size	1.00											
H-2 Division of Labor	.72	1.00										
H-3 Levels	.67	.61	1.00									
H-4 Sections	.29	.41	.35	1.00								
H-5 Division Head's Span	-.10	-.05	-.26	.16	1.00							
H-6 Middle Managers' Span	.13	-.05	-.08	-.09	-.01	1.00						
H-7 First-Line Supervisors' Span	.29	-.20	-.25	-.07	-.22	.15	1.00					
H-8 Clerical Ratio	-.02	-.35	-.19	-.02	-.13	.52	.14	1.00				
H-9 Supervisory Ratio	-.14	-.02	-.19	.09	-.22	-.64	-.67	-.29	1.00			
H-10 Size (Log)	.83	.70	.78	.60	-.08	.22	.46	-.03	-.18	1.00		
H-19 Agency Size	.91	.66	.62	.18	-.07	.18	.34	-.16	-.14	.73	1.00	
H-20 Agency Clerical Ratio	.08	-.04	.10	.25	.12	-.14	-.18	.02	.19	.16	.07	1.00
H-21 Agency Supervisory Ratio	-.40	-.39	-.32	-.26	-.11	-.41	-.33	-.02	.33	-.49	-.42	-.01

TABLE H-10. *Correlation Matrix for Legal Services Divisions*

	H-1 Size	H-2 Div of Labor	H-3 Levels	H-4 Sectns	H-5 DvHd's Span	H-6 Md Mgr Span	H-7 FLS Span	H-8 Clrcl Ratio	H-9 Sup Ratio	H-10 Size (Log)	H-19 Agency Size	H-20 Agency Cl Rto
H-1 Size	1.00											
H-2 Division of Labor	.74	1.00										
H-3 Levels	.73	.76	1.00									
H-4 Sections	.47	.73	.71	1.00								
H-5 Division Head's Span	.23	.50	.14	.39	1.00							
H-6 Middle Managers' Span	.92	.56	.84	.02	-.02	1.00						
H-7 First-Line Supervisors' Span	.53	.47	.39	.30	.18	.61	1.00					
H-8 Clerical Ratio	.22	.34	.28	.37	.09	.22	.38	1.00				
H-9 Supervisory Ratio	-.31	-.21	.06	-.02	-.42	-.76	-.64	.02	1.00			
H-10 Size (Log)	.82	.87	.82	.75	.49	.78	.69	.33	-.36	1.00		
H-19 Agency Size	.65	.67	.63	.50	.43	.47	.34	.18	-.17	.71	1.00	
H-20 Agency Clerical Ratio	.28	.34	.31	.18	-.05	.20	.32	.22	-.17	.35	.06	1.00
H-21 Agency Supervisory Ratio	-.38	-.27	-.18	-.18	-.15	-.61	-.54	-.12	.38	-.37	-.46	.03

APPENDIX I

Data for Finance Departments

Study Population

This is a study of the government finance departments in American states, cities with a population of 50,000 or more, and counties with a population of 100,000 or more in 1960 (according to the 1962 edition of the *County and City Data Book*). To ascertain the title of the major department responsible for keeping the financial records of the government, its size, the number of its main subunits, and a few other items of information, a short preliminary questionnaire was sent in 1965 to a government official in the 656 jurisdictions that met one of the three criteria. No questionnaire was returned by sixty-nine governments, and sixty of the 587 questionnaires that were returned were eliminated because the major government finance department had fewer than five members.

The 527 agencies remaining for further study were divided into two categories. The 264 departments with twenty or more employees and two or more major divisions were selected for personal interviews with key informants, and the directors of the 263 others were sent a questionnaire to be returned by mail, which elicited essentially the same information as the interview schedule. Actually, a few agencies that met the requirements of size and complexity for interviewing were nevertheless mailed the self-administered questionnaire, particularly, for reasons of distance and cost, those located in Alaska and Hawaii. On the other hand, some agencies that received an interviewer turned out to be smaller or less complex than had been assumed on the basis of the answers to the preliminary questionnaire.

431

Refusals, no returns, or inadequate answers from 111 of these 527 finance departments reduce the number of cases for analysis to 416. The over-all rate of usable returns is therefore 79 per cent, but this rate is much higher for those departments in which personal interviews were conducted (97 per cent) than for those to which self-administered questionnaires were sent (61 per cent). Hence, very small and simple finance departments are underrepresented in the study population. The number of cases that are not included and that are included in the analysis, by government jurisdiction and procedure of data collection, are shown in Table I–1.

TABLE I-1. *Finance Departments by Jurisdiction and Data-Collection Method*

	States		Counties		Cities		
	Inter-views	Question-naires	Inter-views	Question-naires	Inter-views	Question-naires	Totals
Not included in study	2	4	3	61	3	38	111
Included in study	37	5	64	64	155	91	416
Totals	39	9	67	125	158	129	527

Variables and Basic Statistics

TABLE I-2.   *Finance Department Characteristics*

	n	Mean	Standard Deviation	Skew
I-1. Size: number of full-time person-nel in the department as of the date of interview, April to September 1966.	416	70.4	137.4	6.27
I-2. Size (log): logarithm to the base 10 of size (variable I-1).	416	1.5	0.50	0.47
I-3. Division of labor: number of differ-ent job titles in the department, counting each grade separately.	404	24.5	26.34	2.82
I-4. Levels (mean): sum of the number of levels in all functional divisions in the department divided by the number of divisions.	415	3.6	0.92	0.80
I-5. Divisions: number of major operat-ing subunits in the department whose head reports to the administrator or his deputy. One person can constitute a division.	416	4.3	3.07	1.55
I-6. First-line supervisors' span of control: total number of people on the lowest organizational level of each operat-ing division divided by the number of people on the level immediately above them; this span then averaged for all the divisions in the department.	415	6.2	4.74	2.89
I-7. Scope of automation: proportion of four selected financial activities (pay-roll, billing, budget accounting, cost accounting) for which the department uses a computer.	408	34.2	42.90	0.66
I-8. Number of procedure manuals: total number of distinct procedure manuals used regardless of their size or content.	400	1.9	1.74	1.38
I-9. Per cent employees with B.A.'s: number of employees with a bachelor degree divided by the number of full-time personnel in the department.	378	11.6	11.55	1.38
I-10. Size X division of labor: product term of size (variable I-1) times division of labor (variable I-3).	404	4,763.4	19,411.80	10.86

Differences in Operational Definitions

Though the actual structural attributes we attempted to measure in the employment agency study are very similar to those measured in the finance department study, the operational definitions of variables differ somewhat in the two research projects. The differences do not destroy the comparability of the two sets of data. The following comments explain the differences between the measures used in the analysis of finance departments and the corresponding variables defined in Appendix C.

I–1,2 Size, size (log): same as variables 1 and 42.

I–3 Division of labor: each grade within a job title is counted separately for this measure, whereas the grades are not counted for variable 5.

I–4 Levels (mean): This measure is based on the average number of levels in the longest section of all divisions in the department, whereas variable 10 is based on the one longest section in the entire employment agency headquarters.

I–5 Divisions: no minimum size criterion was used to define finance department divisions, whereas for variable 11 a division must comprise at least five or more persons.

I–6 First-line supervisors' span of control: all the employees on the level immediately above the lowest level in the finance departments may not be bona fide line supervisors; they may include some functional supervisors or a few non-supervisory employees. For variable 61, the data were sufficiently detailed to guarantee that only line supervisors were counted as first-line supervisors. Also, there are by definition no first-line supervisors in offices with only two levels in employment agencies, whereas in finance departments with two levels the director is considered a first-line supervisor.

I–7 Scope of automation: this measure is the proportion of four activities for which a computer is used; variable 6 is the weighted number of computers and input/output units in use in the agency.

I–8 Number of procedure manuals: no comparable variable in the employment agency study.

I–9 Per cent employees with B.A.'s: this percentage is based on all employees in the department, whereas variable 8 is based on only one group of employees, namely, interviewers.

I–10 Size × division of labor: computed according to the same procedure used in the employment agency study.

TABLE I-3. Correlation[a] Matrix for Finance Departments

	I-1 Size	I-2 Size (Log)	I-3 Div of Labor	I-4 Levels (Means)	I-5 Divsns	I-6 FLS Span	I-7 Scope Autmtn	I-8 Procdr Manual	I-9 % B.A.'s	I-10 Size X Dv Lbr
I-1 Size	1.00									
I-2 Size (Log)	.713	1.00								
I-3 Division of Labor	.809	.804	1.00							
I-4 Levels (Mean)	.548	.660	.605	1.00						
I-5 Divisions	.496	.726	.521	.262	1.00					
I-6 First-Line Supervisors' Span of Control	.490	.726	.521	.316	.167	1.00				
I-7 Scope of Automation	.324	.488	.374	.425	.281	.173	1.00			
I-8 Number of Procedure Manuals	.255	.385	.284	.284	.348	.095	.302	1.00		
I-9 % Employees with B.A.'s	.094	−.036	.029	.068	−.058	−.057	.090	.101	1.00	
I-10 Size × Division of Labor	.914	.502	.718	.434	.288	.380	.221	.144	.096	1.00

[a]The coefficients used here are the Pearsonian r computed according to the Mesa-85 statistical system (UCSL 510, 9/1/66) obtained from the program library of the University of Chicago's Computation Center. The n's are given above in the second section.

NAME INDEX

SUBJECT INDEX

439

DATE DUE